Tax, Law and Development

Miranda Stewart dedicates this book to her brother, Thomas Alexander Stewart, who always strived for creative solutions.

Yariv Brauner dedicates this book to his parents, Judith and Isaac Brauner, who always seek fairness.

Tax, Law and Development

Edited by

Yariv Brauner

University of Florida, Levin College of Law, USA

Miranda Stewart

University of Melbourne Law School, Australia

Edward Elgar

Cheltenham, UK • Northampton, MA, USA

Published by
Edward Elgar Publishing Limited
The Lypiatts
15 Lansdown Road
Cheltenham
Glos GL50 2JA
UK

Edward Elgar Publishing, Inc.
William Pratt House
9 Dewey Court
Northampton
Massachusetts 01060
USA

A catalogue record for this book
is available from the British Library

Library of Congress Control Number: 2012946671

This book is available electronically in the ElgarOnline.com Law Subject Collection, E-ISBN 978 0 85793 002 6

FSC
www.fsc.org
MIX
Paper from
responsible sources
FSC® C018575

ISBN 978 0 85793 001 9

Typeset by Columns Design XML Ltd, Reading
Printed and bound by MPG Books Group, UK

Contents

Contributors

Yariv Brauner, Professor of Law, University of Florida, Levin College of Law

Allison Christians, H. Heward Stikeman Chair in Tax Law, McGill University Faculty of Law

Tsilly Dagan, Professor of Law, Bar Ilan University School of Law

Ana Paula Dourado, Professor of Tax Law, Faculty of Law, University of Lisbon

Tracy Gutuza, Senior Lecturer, University of Cape Town

Anthony C. Infanti, Professor of Law and Associate Dean for Academic Affairs, University of Pittsburgh, School of Law

Charlene D. Luke, Associate Professor of Law, University of Florida, Levin College of Law

Lisa Philipps, Professor, Osgoode Hall Law School and Associate Vice-President Research, York University

Pasquale Pistone, Ad Personam Jean-Monnet Chair in European Tax Law and Policy, Vienna University of Economics and Business, and Associate Professor, University of Salerno

Luís Eduardo Schoueri, Professor of Tax Law, University of São Paulo

Miranda Stewart, Professor of Law, University of Melbourne Law School

Wei Cui, Professor of Law, China University of Political Science and Law

Foreword

Stephen E. Shay*

The chapters in this volume examine a series of topics relating to the intersection of tax, law and development. The topics examine, among other matters, the relation of tax incentives in developing countries to tax competition, international tax relations, regional integration and traditional tax policy paradigms; tax expenditure reporting and fiscal federalism in emerging economy contexts; a broader and people-focused conception of tax equity; the expanding institutional role of NGOs in tax policy discussions; and how expanding international tax cooperation can benefit developing countries. The issues considered expand the limited scope of legal academy discussions of tax, law and development[1] and challenge us to adopt a more inclusive approach to thinking about how tax systems can be made more effective to improve the lives of global citizens who live in developing countries.[2]

The timeliness of this work is evidenced by the increasing recognition of 'revenue mobilization' as an important factor in sustainable development. At the turn of this century, the nations of the world adopted Millennium Development Goals (MDGs), including trying to eradicate

* Professor of Practice, Harvard Law School

1 Prior contributions are cited in the chapters in this volume.

2 The 2012 World Bank update on poverty in the developing world reports that in 2008 1.29 billion people lived on less than US$1.25 a day and 2.47 billion people lived on less than US$2.00 a day (in 2005 prices). World Bank Development Research Group Briefing Note, 'An update to the World Bank's estimates of consumption poverty in the developing world', at http://siteresources.worldbank.org/INTPOVCALNET/Resources/Global_Poverty_Update_2012_02-29-12.pdf (last accessed 9 July 2012). Anthony Infanti's Chapter 9 reminds us that per capita income is not the only measure of human wellbeing, and points us to other measures that achieve a more people-centered policy focus. Anthony Infanti, *Internation Equity and Human Development*, at p 209 in this volume.

poverty and achieve sustainable and inclusive growth and development.[3] In 2002 representatives from 109 countries assembled under UN auspices in Monterrey, Mexico, to address the challenges of financing achievement of the MDGs adopted just two years before. Acknowledging that there would be a dramatic shortfall in resources required to achieve MDGs, the resulting Monterrey Consensus set out a multi-part plan to address the resource needs, including mobilizing domestic financial resources for development.[4]

Not incidentally, in the face of post-9/11 market declines, Monterrey had the effect of placing a greater burden of meeting MDGs on developing countries. In general terms, it was anticipated that developing countries would have to increase their revenue performance (measured by tax–GDP ratio) by as much as 4 percent of GDP to be able to achieve MDGs.[5] More recently, the United Nations has set an objective that countries mobilize 20 percent of their GDP in tax revenues in order to achieve the MDGs.[6]

The 2008 global financial crisis and associated recession significantly reduced donor country resources for development aid. In its 2010 Seoul, South Korea meeting, the G-20 leaders added a revenue mobilization work stream to the agenda of the G-20 Development Working Group and tasked the International Monetary Fund (IMF), the Organisation for Economic Co-operation and Development (OECD), the United Nations and the World Bank with collaborating on a project plan that would identify actions supporting more effective tax systems in developing countries.

The resulting joint report included recommendations on: key capacity constraints faced by developing countries in their tax systems; helping tax multinational enterprises (MNEs) through effective transfer pricing rules; establishing measures to track progress in tax administrations'

---

3 Millennium Declaration, General Assembly Resolution 55/2 (18 September 2000). The Monterrey Consensus formulation in 2002 states: 'Our goal is to eradicate poverty, achieve sustained economic growth and promote sustainable development as we advance to a fully inclusive and equitable global economic system.' United Nations, *Report of the International Conference on Financing for Development*, A/CONF.198/11, para.1.

4 *Ibid.* paras 4, 15.

5 United Nations, *Investing in Development* (New York: United Nations, 2005) 245. The IMF has pared back expectations to a more realistic objective of increasing revenue mobilization by a range of 2 to 4 percent of GDP. IMF Fiscal Affairs Dept, *Revenue Mobilization in Developing Countries* (8 March 2011).

6 United Nations, *What Will It Take to Achieve the Millennium Development Goals? An International Assessment* (UNDP, June 2010) 26.

capacity improvements; and developing a knowledge management platform to support tax capacity of developing countries.[7] The topics and recommendations in the joint report to the G-20 Development Working Group did not address the impact of developed country tax policies on developing countries' revenue mobilization, such as fostering internation tax competition, continuing residence country revenue bias in international tax treaties and tolerating tax avoidance by MNEs.[8] The developed economies have remained steadfast in supporting national tax sovereignty and maintaining residence country treaty benefits for foreign direct investment (FDI).

The contribution of tax competition between developed countries to developed countries' fiscal shortfalls through erosion of business income taxes has not been fully acknowledged.[9] The pattern in recent years has been for developed countries to support their local champion MNEs by matching other countries' tax incentive mechanisms and shifting the cost to domestic taxpayers. Prime examples are the recent actions of the United Kingdom and Japan to finance lower corporate tax rates in material part with increases in consumption taxes.

Internation corporate tax competition reduces fiscal flexibility to an even greater extent in developing than in developed countries as the corporate tax remains an important component of developing country tax

---

[7] *Supporting the Development of More Effective Tax Systems: A Report by the IMF, OECD, UN and World Bank to the G-20 Development Working Group* (2011), available at www.imf.org/external/np/g20/pdf/110311.pdf (last accessed 9 July 2012).

[8] One sentence in the Report hinted tantalizingly at the issues that plague developed and developing countries alike: 'Perhaps most fundamentally, one theme is that pressures on revenue from trade liberalisation, regional integration and tax competition mean that, *absent greater international policy coordination*, the search for additional revenue will likely focus on relatively immobile bases – most obviously labour, consumption, and real estate' (emphasis in original). *Supporting the Development of More Effective Tax Systems: A Report by the IMF, OECD, UN and World Bank to the G-20 Development Working Group*, *supra* note 7, at 18.

[9] The US Treasury, however, has reported evidence of substantial income shifting to lower tax countries, including evidence from company tax data of operating margin increases correlated inversely with effective tax rates. Testimony of Stephen E. Shay, Deputy Assistant Secretary International Tax Affairs, US Department of Treasury, House Ways and Means Committee, Hearing on Transfer Pricing Issues (22 July 2010), http://democrats.waysandmeans.house.gov/media/pdf/111/2010Jul22_Shay_Testimony.pdf (last accessed 9 July 2012).

revenue. In this volume, Yariv Brauner addresses the pressure on developing countries to provide tax incentives to attract FDI, questioning the benefit of tax incentives for development and growth. He tellingly identifies the linkage of incentives to tax competition.[10] Lisa Phillips examines the use of tax expenditure analysis by India to examine the efficiency of incentives.[11] The chapters in this volume do not prescribe one answer for developing countries, but encourage examination of individual context and circumstances. Developed economies do not provide an unblemished model and their prescriptions require scrutiny.

Notwithstanding the new emphasis on revenue mobilization, there has been little change in the longstanding approach of bilateral income tax treaties, including the United Nations model convention, to require sacrifice of source country taxation in favor of the residence country. There is an important need for rethinking as to whether these treaties make sense for lower- and lower-middle income developing countries.[12] Evidence on whether bilateral tax treaties increase FDI in developing countries is mixed, but an important question for future research is whether treaties in their current form justify the revenue loss.[13] The argument that a double tax treaty provides an important signal to investors that the rule of law and tax system stability will be observed may be addressed by alternative measures that do not sacrifice tax revenue to the same extent. It might be possible, for example, to fashion

---

10 See Yariv Brauner, Chapter 2.

11 See Lisa Philipps, Chapter 8.

12 The World Bank divides countries into low income, US$995 or less; lower middle income, US$996–3,945; upper middle income, US$3,946–12,195; and high income, $12,196 or more (using 2009 gross national income (GNI) per capita). See *Supporting the Development of More Effective Tax Systems: A Report by the IMF, OECD, UN and World Bank to the G-20 Development Working Group* (2011) 52, available at www.imf.org/external/np/g20/pdf/110311.pdf (last accessed 9 July 2012).

13 See literature summary in Fabian Barthel, Matthias Busse and Eric Neumayer, 'The Impact of Double Taxation Treaties on Foreign Direct Investment: Evidence from Large Dyadic Panel Data' (2010) 28 *Contemporary Economic Policy* 366. From a revenue perspective, it does not make sense for a capital importing developing country to enter into a treaty with a low-tax country that is a mere conduit for investment by a treaty shopping intermediary. As a more subtle example, Tracey Gutuza's Chapter 4 on the South African adoption of a headquarters regime, which is principally a vehicle for treaty shopping using the South African treaty network, poses similar issues. It is questionable whether a headquarters company described in the chapter should be allowed treaty benefits by South Africa's treaty partners.

treaties limited to arm's length transfer pricing, mutual agreement and information exchange provisions.

Developed countries also have turned a blind eye to the publicly reported activities of their own MNEs that use tax havens and low tax treaty countries to strip income from the home country and other taxing countries and thereby earn 'homeless income' (or 'stateless income').[14] The difficulties developed countries have protecting their tax bases are multiplied for developing countries with limited tax administration resources. Revenue mobilization should include work on anti-abuse approaches that can be implemented by developing countries as well as ideas for coordinating tax policies among developed and developing countries to combat homeless income. Transfer pricing is an important cross-border tax issue, but a corporate income tax system should be structured to limit its reliance on transfer pricing to protect its revenue base. The current approaches to transfer pricing are not sufficiently robust to protect a revenue base against the incentives of material rate differentials.

An effective tax system is critical for development. The developed countries, and increasingly the emerging economies as well, are conflicted in assisting developing countries because addressing many of the issues in developing countries' revenue mobilization will result in taxation of local champion MNEs or state-owned enterprises. Not surprisingly, in light of its membership, the G-20 does not probe the linkage between developed countries' tax policies allowing tax competition and their impact on developing countries' ability to mobilize revenue.

There is an important need for independent academic scholarship like that in this volume that takes into account the differing perspectives of developing countries and does not look for 'one size fits all' theories or prescriptions. As Richard Bird has observed:

> What this complex and changing world needs is not some non-existent 'universal fix' but rather a sort of fiscal medicine kit containing a variety of remedies and treatments that may help us cope with the wide variety of fiscal problems and needs that arise at different times and often in different ways in different developing countries.[15]

---

[14] See, e.g., Bret Wells and Cym Lowell, 'Tax Base Erosion and Homeless Income: Collection at Source is the Lynchpin' (forthcoming in *Tax Law Review*); Edward D. Kleinbard, 'Stateless Income' (2011) 11 *Fla. Law Rev.* 699.

[15] Richard M. Bird, *Taxation and Development: What Have We Learned from Fifty Years of Research?*, International Center for Public Policy Working Paper 12-02 (January 2012), available at http://ideas.repec.org/p/ays/ispwps/paper1202.html (last accessed 16 July 2012).

The diverse group of legal scholars from six continents who have contributed to this volume critically address issues from perspectives not restricted to traditional tax policy conceptions and paradigms. As a result, this volume is rich with insights on new and old issues at the intersection of tax, law and development.

Acknowledgements

We acknowledge the support and financial contribution of the Law School, University of Melbourne, and the Graduate Tax Program at the Levin College of Law, University of Florida. We thank the Faculty of Law at the University of Lisbon, and particularly Prof. Ana Paula Dourado for hosting the Lisbon Workshop in 2011 and Alan Sturmer and the staff at Edward Elgar for their assistance and support. Finally, we thank the late Paul McDaniel for his enthusiasm for this project from the beginning. This has been a project that we have wanted to achieve for some time and Paul's support and active mentorship of each of the editors enabled this to happen. We would like to thank Ruth Ron for her original design featured on the cover. Finally, we would like to thank research assistant Livia Gonzaga for her contribution and preparation of the bibliography.

Abbreviations

BRICS	Brazil, Russia, India, China and South Africa
CBCR	country-by-country reporting
CFC	controlled foreign company
DTA	Double Taxation Agreement
ECJ	European Court of Justice
EITI	Extractive Industries Transparency Initiative
FDI	foreign direct investment
FRBM	Fiscal Responsibility and Budget Management Act (India)
FTA	Free Trade Agreement
GDP	gross domestic product
GII	Gender Inequality Index
HDI	Human Development Index
IBP	International Budget Project
LATC	Law on the Administration of Tax Collection (China)
LOB	limitation on benefits
MCRS	management contract responsibility system
MDG	Millennium Development Goal
MNE	multinational enterprise
NEPAD	New Partnership for Africa's Development
NGO	non-governmental organization

OECD	Organisation for Economic Co-operation and Development
OHADA	Organization for the Harmonization of Business Law in Africa
PRC	People's Republic of China
PWYP	Publish What You Pay
SADC	South African Development Community
SOE	state-owned enterprise
TIEA	Tax Information Exchange Agreement

PART I

Introduction: tax reform and financing for development

1. Introduction: tax, law and development

Yariv Brauner and Miranda Stewart

This book is the first collection of independent academic scholarship exploring the relationship between tax, law and development. The innovative legal scholars who contribute to this book examine the role of law in national and international tax regimes and the uses of tax law in the universal quest for human development, across a range of topical tax issues. The book includes discussion of tax issues from the perspective of China, Brazil, South Africa, India and other developing countries. Contributors engage critically with economic, political, social and institutional approaches to tax, law and development. They discuss substantive tax laws that are central to economic globalization, such as tax incentives for foreign direct investment, and overarching themes, including tax equity in a global context and the processes of transnational tax law and administration. The editors have chosen to emphasize independence and a critical and pluralistic approach in the choice of essays. Nevertheless, the chapters are organized around four themes, each of which is discussed below.

First, the chapters in this book require us to acknowledge fully the unavoidable challenge of tax competition in a global economy. We must confront the tragic choices faced, in particular by developing countries, but in general by all countries, as a result of this challenge. It is the authors' view that we cannot avoid the challenge of tax competition by calls to end taxation of mobile capital even if this may be perceived to be a theoretical economic inevitability due to the difficulty of collection in an uncooperative environment. What is needed are new solutions, and perhaps solutions that can alter the environment itself as suggested by many of the essays in this book. At the same time, the arm's length rules for assessing tax on global business which are the prevailing norms are inadequate to the task. It is also foolish to assume that it will be possible to eliminate all tax havens, as if these were static or finite in number, or the only cause of global tax dilemmas.

Second, these chapters call for us to abandon – or at least significantly downplay – the dominant normative approaches to tax policy for economic development. Instead, these chapters call for contextualized, diverse, partial and incremental tax law reform approaches. In this, the chapters are consistent with the 'new agenda for development' proposed by some development economists, notably Dani Rodrik and William Easterly, who take a more critical and nuanced approach to economic development.[1] Rodrik and Easterly, with many others, have concluded that the dominant approach to economic reform of the international financial institutions, including the International Monetary Fund (IMF) and the World Bank, has not led to economic growth and, indeed, may have contributed to lower growth in some regions over the last 30 years. This approach has tended to involve the adoption of apparently complete, overarching, unitary and easily articulated solutions, or plans, based on global norms and limited local data (sometimes termed the 'Washington Consensus'). In the broad field of economic development and aid policy, they have called for an acknowledgement of diversity, and of 'many recipes' to produce successful results in particular countries.

Third, these chapters highlight the constantly disappearing goals of equity and redistribution in tax policy. The issue of equity both within and between nations is raised in several chapters. Equity is fundamentally linked to political legitimacy of tax law, especially to democratic accountability and hence to the sustained success of tax reform.

Finally, these chapters emphasize that international tax cooperation – achieved through a range of informal and formal, incremental and top-down approaches – must be the way forward in reforming tax law for development. They raise questions about who participates in such international cooperation and how it is to be legitimated, and acknowledge the many difficulties and tensions in achieving such cooperation.

---

[1] See, e.g., Dani Rodrik, *One Economics, Many Recipes: Globalization, Institutions, and Economic Growth* (Princeton, NJ: Princeton University Press, 2008); William Easterly (ed.), *Reinventing Foreign Aid* (Cambridge, MA: Massachusetts Institute of Technology Press, 2008); William Easterly, *The White Man's Burden: Why the West's Efforts to Aid the Rest Have Done So Much Ill and So Little Good* (Oxford: Oxford University Press, 2006); Joseph E. Stiglitz, *Globalization and Its Discontents* (New York: W.W. Norton & Co., 2002); William Easterly, 'Can the West Save Africa?' (2009) 47 *Journal of Economic Literature* 373.

I. TAX REFORM AND FINANCING FOR DEVELOPMENT

To date, scholars and practitioners who are engaged in the study and practice of human development have interacted with taxation via two different types of mission. The first mission has been the implementation of tax reforms to encourage economic development, in particular in so-called developing countries. One focus of tax reforms to generate economic development has been to devise tax laws that will encourage foreign direct investment into and exports from a market economy, while maintaining tax revenues, partly through shifting the tax burden to domestic consumption. The second mission has been to increase tax revenues so as to fund development expenditures and poverty relief.[2] Tax reform with these goals has been a significant part of economic development projects since the Second World War.

There is now a substantial body of literature about tax reform projects, written by and for the reformers, including documentation produced by institutions such as the IMF, World Bank and the Organisation for Economic Co-operation and Development (OECD); expert reports for national governments; and academic commentary discussing the experiences, recommendations, and 'lessons' of tax reform projects.[3] While

---

[2] UN High-Level Panel on Financing for Development, *Report of the High-Level Panel on Financing for Development: Recommendations*, delivered to the General Assembly, UN Doc. A/55/1000 (2001) 3, 13, 15, available at http://www.un.org/reports/financing/report_full.htm ('the Zedillo Panel').

[3] Among the many books on this topic are Richard Gordon (ed.), *Taxation in Developing Countries: Six Case Studies and Policy Implications* (New York: Columbia University Press, 2010). The first major collection on the subject was the Harvard Law School International Program in Taxation, Bibliography on Taxation in Underdeveloped Countries (1962) and see Richard Bird and Oliver Oldman (eds), *Readings on Taxation in Developing Countries* (Baltimore, MD: Johns Hopkins Press, 1964), since reissued on numerous occasions, see, e.g., Richard M. Bird and Oliver Oldman (eds), *Taxation in Developing Countries* (Baltimore, MD: Johns Hopkins Press, 1990). Other collections include Ehtisham Ahmad and Nicholas Stern (eds), *The Theory and Practice of Tax Reform in Developing Countries* (New York: Cambridge University Press, 1991); Richard M. Bird and Milka Casanegra de Jantscher (eds), *Improving Tax Administration in Developing Countries* (Washington, DC: International Monetary Fund, 1992); Malcolm Gillis (ed.), *Tax Reform in Developing Countries* (Durham: Duke University Press, 1989); Wayne Thirsk (ed.), *Tax Reform in Developing Countries* (Washigton, DC: World Bank, 1997); and Michael J. Boskin and Charles E. McLure, Jr (eds), *World Tax Reform: Case Studies of Developed and Developing Countries* (San Francisco, CA: ICS Press, 1990).

global or cross-country influences are inevitable, national governments must play a central role in tax policy for development because tax reform requires enactment of laws, implementation by local bureaucracies and a level of acceptance by taxpayers. Tax reform projects may provoke a significant domestic political response, involving citizens either through the actions of representative government or through the actions of powerful domestic lobby groups.

Since the establishment of the Millennium Development Goals by the United Nations (UN) in 2000 and the Monterey Conference on Financing for Development held in 2002, the role of taxation in financing development has been widely emphasized. In 2002, the importance of tax reform was stated rather bluntly by the UN Panel on Financing for Development:[4]

> Financing an adequate level of social public expenditure while limiting budget deficits calls for substantial tax revenues. Most countries of the developing world must undertake significant tax reforms if they are to raise the additional revenue that they need. These reforms should generally aim to broaden the tax base and to encourage domestic savings.

The dominant model of tax policy for economic development of the last two decades, implicit in the above quote, has envisaged a broad based tax system that reduces the tax on capital (thereby in theory encouraging savings) with low, flat corporate and personal income tax rates; the elimination of tariffs; and the establishment of a general Value Added Tax on domestic consumption, as well as some more specific resource or excise taxes. The state envisaged in global development discourse since the 1980s is a small, open-market oriented entity operating in the context of economic globalization, in contrast to the interventionist and often protectionist state of earlier decades. The most obvious example is the recommendation to reduce or eliminate trade tariffs, but other tax reform recommendations posited as inevitable in the face of economic globalization – e.g., the reduction or elimination of taxes on mobile capital (as opposed to less mobile capital such as labour, or fixed capital such as land) as a result of globalization of capital markets – also seem to reduce the power of the state.

The 2002 UN Panel was cognizant of the potential impact of raising taxation and constrained public spending on the poor, but emphasized the reducing fiscal deficits because, following the debt crisis of the 1980s, developing countries were forced to try to pay down their debts to

---

[4] Zedillo Panel, *supra* note 2, at 15.

international lenders. In practice, for most developing countries, the goal of increasing tax revenues was in conflict with their other main goal of tax reform for economic development. Many countries sought to achieve their goal of economic development by reducing tariffs and corporate tax rates and by enacting tax incentives, thereby reducing their ability to collect tax revenues.[5] At the same time, there was an increasing need for government spending on poverty relief and in furtherance of development goals – such as education, health and infrastructure – as well as to ensure political acceptability of economic reforms. The resulting 'fiscal squeeze' has been widely recognized. Even the wealthiest developing countries, including China and India, face the challenge of this fiscal squeeze in a global context, as illustrated in a recent collection of country case studies.[6]

In 2011, the UN General Assembly, recalling the Monterey Conference, included the issue of financing for development in the provisional agenda for its 67th session.[7] The member states resolved:

> to enhance and strengthen domestic resource mobilization and fiscal space, including, where appropriate, through modernized tax systems, more efficient tax collection, the broadening of the tax base and the effective combating of tax evasion and capital flight … while each country is responsible for its tax system, it is important to support national efforts in these areas by strengthening technical assistance and enhancing international cooperation and participation in addressing international tax matters.[8]

The terms of the 2011 UN Resolution reveal a more subtle understanding of the complexities of the role of tax in the context of development. The member states placed the discussion of tax reform in the context of a 'global partnership' for development, and acknowledged the need for 'fiscal space'. The concept of 'fiscal space' refers to the combined role of tax *and* other sources of finance for the state, including borrowing. It implicitly acknowledges the need for countries to carry out development

---

[5] This common pattern is demonstrated in Michael Keen and Alejandro Simone, 'Tax Policy in Developing Countries: Some Lessons from the 1990s and Some Challenges Ahead' in Sanjeev Gupta *et al.* (eds), *Helping Countries Develop: The Role of Fiscal Policy* (Washington, DC: IMF, 2004) 302–52.

[6] See the case studies in Gordon, *supra* note 3.

[7] UN General Assembly, *Follow-up and Implementation of the Outcome of the 2002 International Conference on Financing for Development and the 2008 Review Conference*, Report of the Second Committee (13 December 2011). See www.un.org/esa/ffd/ for more on the UN Financing for Development project.

[8] *Ibid.* 3.

spending in spite of fiscal constraints. The Resolution acknowledges that tax reform should be adopted 'where appropriate', the implication being that tax reform is not always the right – or only – solution. It emphasizes that national tax systems operate in a global context, thus focusing on cross-border tax evasion, international cooperation and participation in the international tax system. However, the 2011 Resolution still does not engage – in its brief terms – with the varied and contradictory reality of reforming tax laws for development.

A clear theme of all the chapters in this book concerns these common difficulties and practical challenges that developing countries face in enacting and implementing effective tax laws in their quest for development, in each country's own unique context. These challenges include technical challenges related to the general legal framework of domestic legal systems, administrative challenges associated with collecting tax, and the challenge of enacting laws that interact with an international tax regime that is highly influential yet does not have a superior status to domestic laws. This raises further systemic questions. Has the international tax regime already risen to the level of customary international law,[9] and if so, what are the implications of this for developing country tax reform? Is it possible to coordinate tax policies in a world that is currently dominated by tax competition rather than cooperation between countries regarding their tax policies and enforcement? Finally, it must be noted that a similarity of challenges does not necessarily mean similarity of appropriate solutions. To what extent should differences between countries play a role in the design of solutions and methods for development? This theoretical critique and the potential for alternative solutions is clear in many of the essays in this book. The legal perspective that is essential for the implementation of economic theories for people and societies strongly illuminates the necessity of change in our approach to development approaches in general, and economic development viewed through a tax law prism in particular.

II. TAX COMPETITION AND TRAGIC CHOICES

The mission of reforming tax systems to encourage economic development has emphasized the use of incentives for investment based on

---

[9] Reuven Avi-Yonah, *International Tax as International Law* (New York: Cambridge University Press, 2007); but see Brian D. Lepard, *Customary International Law: A New Theory with Practical Applications* (New York: Cambridge University Press, 2010).

simplistic market theories, resulting in an impressive variety of tax incentives for investment in developing country tax systems. The widespread use of tax incentives to encourage foreign direct investment is premised on a series of weak assumptions.[10] These assumptions about the role of investment in economic growth; the importance and value of foreign direct investment in such growth; and the responsiveness of such investment to tax incentives, are shown by Yariv Brauner in Chapter 2, 'The future of tax incentives for developing countries' to be false, or else to be weak at best. Brauner explains that tax incentives are prevalent in both the developing and developed world, yet their story is more about tax competition than about growth and development as may be implied from the standard rhetoric in support of their use. This chapter explores what we know and do not know about tax incentives, and emphasizes the striking lack and weakness of available relevant data, which leads us to much doubt about their efficacy. It further examines how tax incentives may be reformulated to assist countries in their quest for development, highlighting the potential benefits to productive countries of coordination and the important role of developed countries in assisting such a process. Finally, the chapter advocates a reform of the way we approach development, supporting the new development agenda, referred to above, in contrast to current practice of the largest international and some aid based organizations.

The reliance on tax incentives in a globalized world, ironically, perpetuates for many developing countries the form of economic development strategy of an earlier era, but now focusing on foreign investment. After the Second World War, many developing countries adopted a strategy in which the state had the role of managing the process of economic growth, through giving high priority to the goals of industrialization, diversification and modernization.[11] For tax policy, this meant tariff protection for domestic industry, input subsidies, and favourable domestic tax regimes (containing tax concessions or incentives) for industry. Such favourable regimes were limited to domestic investment, as cross-border capital investment was relatively limited in the context of capital controls and an immature global financial system. Between the 1950s and the 1970s, tax policy was promoted as a legitimate means of

[10] An illustration of the continued importance of tax incentives in developing countries in the Asian region is provided by the Asian Development Bank database of regional country tax incentives, searchable on its website: www.aric.adb.org/tax incentives.php.

[11] Dharam Ghai, 'Introduction' to *The IMF and the South: The Social Impact of Crisis and Adjustment* (London: Zed Books, 1991).

intervention in the development process and taxes (and tax incentives) designed to direct firms and individuals into particular investments and activities were a key part of development policy.[12]

Developing countries persist in the use of tax incentives because of the trap of tax competition. This runs counter to the policy prescriptions of the IMF and other international organizations and experts, who repeatedly point out the problems inherent in such a tax incentive strategy. Yet, it is a rational response to the current global environment. In Chapter 3, 'The tragic choices of tax policy in a globalized economy', Tsilly Dagan explains that classic goals of income tax policy are affected by global tax competition among states for capital and residents. Global tax competition 'renders tentative and conditional everything from efficiency to redistribution and even the very concepts of community, national identity and democratic participation ... The state no longer only makes compulsory demands on its subjects in order to promote the collective goals of a given group. Instead, the state increasingly acts as a *recruiter*, to solicit investments as well as residents from the global arena.'[13] Tax legislatures are pushed to limit states' redistribution functions; they are required to choose between their current or historical group of citizens and others – possibly more attractive ones; they abandon democratic participation traditions of voice for exit-based practices; and they undermine classic ability to pay considerations, stressing mobility in their stead. Dagan raises the fundamental challenge that we must rethink both democratic accountability and distribution if we are to succeed in national tax reform to support development in a global context.

The enactment and goals of a specific tax incentive, a regional headquarter company regime, is examined by Tracy Gutuza in Chapter 4, 'Economic development and the role of tax in Southern Africa: the South African headquarter company structure'. Gutuza demonstrates that what seems to be a recent development has longstanding historical roots within South Africa since before the 1994 democratic regime. This tax reform is connected to the country's perceived role as leading and facilitating economic development in the region, while also competing with other tax incentive regimes, such as that in Mauritius. Tax reforms since 1994 have sought, among other things, to place South Africa in a strong position within the world economy, broaden the South African tax base and incentivize certain types of investment, in particular foreign direct

[12] Malcolm Gillis (ed), *Tax Reform in Developing Countries* (Durham: Duke University Press, 1989) 19–20.

[13] See Tsilly Dagan, Chapter 3.

investment. These reforms are clearly designed to support South Africa's economic development. Further recent changes include the introduction of withholding taxes on dividends and interest. The recently enacted non-resident headquarter company regime was introduced so that South Africa can be the gateway into Africa for foreign investors. It is intended that these changes will assist in attracting foreign direct investment into South Africa and also into Africa. In addition to these tax reforms, South Africa is also a party to NEPAD (the new partnership for African Development), under the auspices of the African Union. Gutuza's essay critically analyses these tax reforms undertaken by South Africa in the light of the development goals of both South Africa and regional initiatives such as NEPAD. In so doing, the chapter also considers normative proposals for tax law reform in a developing country regional context.

A common issue that arises when tax incentives are considered as a matter of national tax policy of developing countries is how these incentives interact with the international tax regime. In particular, an issue arises as to approaches to tax relief for cross-border investment in national law or bilateral tax treaties. Luís Eduardo Schoueri in Chapter 5, 'Tax sparing: a reconsideration of the reconsideration', analyses the role of tax sparing clauses in treaties. This direct measure that developed countries adopt on a fairly regular basis in the context of development and assistance to developing countries is generally perceived to be an exercise of foreign aid to support development – perhaps, to ease the global tax system with the injection of some equity. Such tax sparing clauses have been criticized by the OECD, and by several developed countries (most notably the United States) which tend to oppose their inclusion in tax treaties. Schoueri's chapter discusses the main arguments presented by the OECD against the use of tax sparing and proposes a new approach to tax sparing clauses that will validate their use, on the basis, not of international aid, but of sovereignty of taxing rights in developing countries. He argues that a decision by a developing country to enact a tax incentive is an exercise of its own right to tax on a source basis the activity or investment in the host jurisdiction. Such a decision by the host government does not entitle the residence, or investor home country, to levy tax on the profits from that investment, in the place of the host country government. Schoueri thereby challenges some of the current international tax norms as structurally embedding a hierarchy in which capital-exporting, developed countries will always benefit more, from a tax perspective, from the policy responses of developing countries seeking to encourage mobile foreign direct investment.

III. IN SEARCH OF 'SEARCHERS' TO FIND UNIQUE SOLUTIONS TO COMMON TAX CHALLENGES

Tax reform may be considered a 'speciality' of public finance or economic policy.[14] Tax reform is also law reform that almost always involves 'transplanting' legal notions or models across borders and hence may be theorized as a comparative law project.[15] Finally, tax reform can be thought of as an element of 'governance' reform with its focus on institutions, administration and (re)construction of modes of interaction of citizens and the state.[16] All of these aspects have been the focus of tax reform attention in the last few decades, in line with generalized tax policy, legal and governance prescriptions. Yet, in spite of this substantial effort, the difficulties – many argue widespread failure – to achieve successful tax reform has been acknowledged and discussed by many. While there have been successes, a closer look frequently indicates a more uneven performance and continuing challenges faced by governments.[17]

The failure of many tax reforms to achieve sustainable revenues and support economic development can be understood in the context of wider failures in economic reform for development, or in planning for poverty relief. Such failures have been until recently explained by international institutions and development experts as the result of governmental weaknesses and macroeconomic mismanagement in developing countries. However, it has become increasingly clear that the factors that affect the process of development are genuinely complex and diverse. The 'new' approach to development discussed in Part I above requires a different approach to finding solutions, including tax reform solutions.

In the context of poverty relief and international aid, Bill Easterly has argued that poverty can only be ended by 'searchers', both economic and

---

[14] Richard Bird, *Tax Policy and Economic Development* (Baltimore, MD: Johns Hopkins University Press, 2002) 183.

[15] See Alan Watson, *Legal Transplants: An Approach to Comparative Law* (Athens, GA: University of Georgia Press, 1993) 19–20.

[16] Global Governance Reform Project, *Reimagining the Future: Towards Democratic Governance* (Saint Kilda/VIC: Vista Publications, 2000) 14; Michael J. Trebilcock and Ronald J. Daniel, ch. 6 'Tax Administration' in *Rule of Law Reform and Development: Charting the Fragile Path of Progress* (Cheltenham, UK and Northampton, MA, USA: Edward Elgar, 2008).

[17] See, e.g., Gordon, *supra* note 3.

political. Searchers have the following characteristics, which are worth setting out in detail:[18]

> 'Searchers' ... explore solutions by trial and error, have a way to get feedback on the ones that work, and then expand the ones that work, all of this in an unplanned, spontaneous way. Examples of searchers are firms in private markets and democratically accountable politicians ... Searchers do not set predetermined problems and do not have big plans; they are just on the lookout for favorable opportunities to solve problems – any problem no matter how big or small, whose solution will benefit themselves or others. Searchers must learn enough about each little problem to solve it, which means they must get feedback from the people affected by the problem and what they need to fix it.

Easterly contrasts the 'searcher' approach to the 'planner' approach which assumes that the problem is known, and can be planned for, and that technical solutions exist for all contexts. Dani Rodrik would retain the insights of economics but calls for an end to 'advice based on simple rules of thumb, regardless of context'; for 'a careful reading of the empirical evidence' of economic development in particular countries; for an acceptance of a significant role for government in development; and for 'modesty' in recommendations for change in constrained contexts.[19] He also emphasizes the importance of institutions and most importantly of 'participatory government' – like Easterly, highlighting the role of democratically accountable politicians in sustainable economic growth.[20] Rodrik is more likely to support planning than Easterly, and is cautious about experimentation, but he would also always acknowledge the need for context-specific, locally accountable reforms evaluated according to local evidence.

In tax policy for development, as in other development policy arenas, a 'one size fits all' approach has dominated. In particular, the IMF has pushed forward 'one size fits all' type tax reforms.[21] The OECD and IMF have, more recently, promoted uniform approaches to budget laws and

---

[18] Easterly, *Reinventing Foreign Aid*, *supra* note 1, at 6–7.

[19] Rodrik, *supra* note 1, at 3–5.

[20] *Ibid.* at 169.

[21] Miranda Stewart and Sunita Jogarajan, 'The IMF and Tax Reform' (2004) 2 *British Tax Review* 146; Miranda Stewart, 'Tax Policy Transfer to Developing Countries: Politics, Institutions and Experts' in Holger Nehring and Florian Schui (eds), *Global Debates about Taxation* (Basingtoke: Palgrave Macmillan, 2007) 182–200. A recent acknowledgement of the 'checkered history of big ideas' in tax reform is made by Michael Keen of the IMF, in 'Taxation and Development – Again', IMF Working Paper WP/12/220 (September 2012).

fiscal transparency, including tax expenditures.[22] As in the general development context, historically at least, the failure of tax reform projects has been attributed to internal causes and not to the tax reform process itself. For example, the World Bank has observed that a number of problems of domestic country governments (including the perception that resistance to tax reform is insurmountable, the inability to understand the technical nature of the expert advice, the lack of familiarity with the issues, and changing economic conditions) impede the implementation of the Bank's technical tax advice.[23] Yet there are several more significant and interesting explanations of failure in reform.

First, as indicated in Part II above, and in the chapters of Brauner and Dagan, the failure of tax reform is a consequence of the 'tragic choices' which countries face in reforming their tax systems in unsustainable ways and impossible time frames, given global economic pressures and tax competition. Failure of countries to mobilize adequate tax revenue is not solely explainable by poor domestic governance, but is a consequence of the contradictions of development in a globalized world. In the face of such difficulties, a country may not be able to 'develop' in spite of attempts to carry out reforms and a global hierarchy of developed and developing countries will be perpetuated. Countries will continue to enact tax incentives in apparent defiance of institutional recommendations, if those recommendations continue to be made in isolation of wider global economic pressures. Enterprises and governments of the developed world continue to pressure developing countries to open markets, to provide concessions, and generally to become attractive targets for Western-based corporate investment. Tax reformers need to promote a new vision of the state that encourages cooperation between states, not merely in bilateral tax treaties (which may not provide much economic benefit), but in decision-making about domestic tax regimes that will benefit countries in the long term.

Second, failure of tax policy or law reform may indicate unwarranted haste or, more seriously, a mismatch or misunderstanding by tax reformers of the fit between particular tax reform proposals and the law, legal culture and broader social and economic context in which they are

---

22 IMF, *Manual of Fiscal Transparency* (Washington, DC: International Monetary Fund, 2007); OECD, 'Best Practices for Budget Transparency' (2002) 1(3) *OECD Journal on Budgeting* 7; Lisa Philipps and Miranda Stewart, 'Defining Fiscal Transparency: Transnational Norms, Domestic Laws, and the Politics of Budget Accountability' (2009) 34(3) *Brooklyn Journal of International Law* 798.

23 World Bank, *Lessons of Tax Reform* (1991) 74–5.

applied. In particular, problems in ongoing enforcement may be the result of importation of inappropriate tax laws or mass-produced policy prescriptions. Empirical research on the effectiveness of transplanted laws, including 'the massive importation of legal code' into the transition countries commencing in the late 1980s (of which tax code formed a part), supports this criticism of the wholesale 'model' approach to tax reform.[24] The evidence suggests that subsequent enforcement of transplanted law is weak and problematic, in particular where the transplanted legal code does not fit the history of development of legal structures in the recipient country.[25] Several chapters in this volume consider tax law and governance institutions, and the role of law itself in tax reform, from different perspectives. The essays emphasize the local context and inquiring as to what would be the actual effect of particular reforms.

There has been little self-reflexive analysis by tax law experts of their own position and approach to legal drafting and transplantation in developing countries. In Chapter 6, 'Is this a pipe? Validity of a tax reform for a developing country', Ana Paula Dourado presents a deep theoretical examination of the work and role of an external tax law drafter, who must operate between global norms of tax policy and plural domestic legal and tax regimes. She engages directly with the existential challenge: how to be a 'good' tax legal expert, acting at the intersection of the global and the local and seeking to ensure ownership, legitimacy and effectiveness of a tax reform. Her reflection carries particular weight in light of the author's hands-on experience with local country tax reform in the context of an international financial institution. To highlight the problems of mass solutions or 'model' codes is not to reject learning from experience, or the value of applying a tried and tested model instead of outright experimentation. Dourado's experience demonstrates that a diversity of approaches can be accommodated within more general tax reform principles, but, as she explains, general principles must always be tailored to fit the specific legal and tax cultures of each country.

A careful examination of a particular context may also reveal an unexpected role for law in general, or tax law in particular, in a particular country, with implications for approaches to tax reform. In Chapter 7, 'The place of law in the evolution of Chinese fiscal federalism', Wei Cui examines the role of law itself in one of the most important tax reform

---

[24] Daniel Berkowitz *et al.*, *Economic Development, Legality and the Transplant Effect*, Centre for Law and Economic Studies, Columbia Law School Working Paper No. 195 (2001) 7–10, available at www.law.columbia.edu/law-economicstudies/papers/wp195.pdf.

[25] *Ibid.*

contexts in China, that of the allocation of taxing powers among national and sub-national governments. He asks what role is played by tax *law*, as distinguished from the tax *policies* that it embodies more or less perfectly, in either enhancing or hindering fiscal federalism in China? Cui observes that many developing countries in search of appropriate tax policies also have fledgling legal systems and in these countries, a legal – including constitutional – framework for developing and implementing tax legislation cannot be taken for granted. While the law is often rhetorically treated as barely deserving of attention by China's tax policy-makers and their academic advisors, Cui suggests that legal institutions and mechanisms were important tools for the government in building tax administration where almost none had existed before and the law was used rhetorically by the central government to advocate and promote central government control in an era of decentralization. The analysis highlighting the role of the law itself is particularly interesting in the context of China, where the 'Western' conception of the rule of law is still only in its early stages. At the same time, China's acknowledged role as a leader among developing countries appears to be generating pressure for reform of the international tax law regime. Together with similar empowerment of the other emerging economies (in particular, the 'BRICS' – Brazil, Russia, India, China and South Africa), this opens a window of opportunity for genuine reform of the international tax regime in a manner that would consider fairness and development together for the first time.

Moving away from the role of tax law itself in a country's path to development, Lisa Philipps in Chapter 8, 'The globalization of tax expenditure reporting: transplanting transparency in India and the Global South', considers an aspect of fiscal or budgetary governance. Her chapter examines the challenges for low and middle income countries of undertaking tax expenditure analysis, which has been practised in OECD countries since the 1970s. A range of scholars and organizations have advocated for countries of the Global South to emulate these reporting practices in order to increase fiscal transparency and improve policy-making. The chapter reviews available evidence about current practices among developing countries and finds there is a trend toward more tax expenditure reporting. Somewhat ironically, however, the literature in OECD countries is rife with concerns and disappointments about whether tax expenditure reporting has achieved its alleged benefits. Philipps considers the potential benefits but also the challenges and problems that may arise in transplanting tax expenditure budgeting practices crafted in OECD countries to other economic, political and legal contexts. She then takes a closer look at the recent experience of India, which has developed a tax expenditure report within its Union Budget.

IV. TAX EQUITY, REDISTRIBUTION AND AID

In this global tax competitive world, how are we to understand tax policy principles of equity and redistribution? There is a link between the failure of tax reform and concerns about the equity, legitimacy or 'ownership' of tax reform. Some of our authors seek to draw closer together the discourse on substantive international tax law and norms, with development goals of freedom, human rights and alleviation of inequality.

Tax reform projects are frequently constructed in such a way as to remove them from the domain of domestic politics. Subtly, but pervasively, tax reform may be cast by external agencies as an essentially technical project which does not raise issues of politics at all. A tax reform may be required or recommended as a result of international negotiations conducted by the executive of the country, or it may be part of the conditions of a structural adjustment package that is not approved up front through the political mechanisms of the state. Consequently, failure of legal and administrative tax reform may be a result of the lack of ownership of the law, policies or processes by government executives, bureaucracies and political agencies in developing countries. Failure of tax reform may also be evidence of serious dissent among the population with respect to the specific reform or economic reforms more generally.[26] Yet taxation is inherently political; fiscal policy reform is 'central to the nation itself', as it 'shifts resources from one segment of society to another, directly or indirectly, intentionally or unintentionally … such decisions are political at their core'.[27] Ultimately, sustainable tax reform requires the continual (re)negotiation of 'fiscal compacts' about the fairness of tax law and distribution of the tax burden.[28]

---

[26] See, e.g., the reform of the VAT in Ghana, discussed in Stewart, *supra* note 21.

[27] UN World Economic and Social Survey 1997, at 65.

[28] Margaret Levi, *Of Rule and Revenue* (Berkeley, CA: University of California Press, 1988); Mick Moore and Lise Rakner, 'The New Politics of Taxation and Accountability' (2002) 33(3) *International Development Studies Bulletin* 1; OECD, *Governance, Taxation and Accountability: Issues and Practices*, DAC Guidelines and Reference Series (Paris: OECD, 2008), available at www.oecd.org/dataoecd/52/35/40210055.pdf.

Tax reform is concerned with strengthening the position of the state so that it can both further the goal of economic development and provide a buffer for its people against globalization, paying attention to so-called 'core activities' of infrastructure and poverty relief supported by an increase in its taxing capacity.[29] Developing countries are particularly vulnerable to the harms of economic globalization, in part because they do not begin with strong tax systems.[30] Yet they face the biggest hurdles in constructing effective tax systems in the face of economic globalization.[31] Collective action challenges are particularly severe in respect of attempts to generate international cooperation in tax matters, in particular on fairness-related issues.

Anthony Infanti's Chapter 9, 'Internation equity and human development', is directed to the problem of global fairness in taxation. Infanti takes on the challenge of developing the path-breaking work of Richard and Peggy Musgrave first proposed in 1969.[32] Since then, as Infanti observes, although some have engaged with the concept of internation equity, it has remained rather thin and has not been particularly tractable to substantive analysis.[33] Discussions of internation equity are typically framed in terms of allocation of the tax base or redistribution of tax revenues between richer (i.e., 'developed') and poorer (i.e., 'developing') countries. In respect of the tax base, a debate around definition of the jurisdictional allocation, primarily, defending the right of a source state to tax income which results from activities within its borders, is in any

---

[29] Vito Tanzi, 'Changing Role of the State in the Economy' in *Policies, Institutions and the Dark Side of Economics* (Cheltenham, UK and Northampton, MA, USA: Edward Elgar, 2000) 20–22.

[30] Vito Tanzi, 'The Impact of Economic Globalization on Taxation' (1998) *International Bureau of Fiscal Documentation Bulletin* 338.

[31] See, e.g., Vito Tanzi and Howell H. Zee, *Tax Policy for Emerging Markets: Developing Countries*, IMF Working Paper No. 35 (2000) 29–30, available at www.imf.org/external/pubs/ ft/wp/2000/wp0035.pdf; Sven-Olef Lodin, 'Outline of the Symposium' in *Visions of the Tax Systems of the 21st Century*, International Fiscal Association Jubilee Symposium (IBFD, 1996) 4.

[32] Richard A. Musgrave and Peggy B. Musgrave, 'Inter-nation Equity' in *Modern Fiscal Issues: Essays in Honor of Carl S. Shoup* (Toronto: University of Toronto Press, 1972) 63.

[33] An exception is Kim Brooks, 'Inter-nation Equity: The Development of an Important but Underappreciated International Tax Policy Objective' in John G. Head and Richard Krever (eds), *Tax Reform in the 21st Century: A Volume in Memory of Richard Musgrave* (Alphen aan den Rijn: Wolters Kluwer Law & Business, 2009) 471, 472.

event a central question of international taxation. This does not significantly advance the internation equity debate in the context of global development goals, although it must be acknowledged that source (capital-importing) states must constantly fight to maintain their source taxation base. The Musgraves also raise the possibility that internation equity might enable international redistribution, acknowledging the highly unequal distribution of resource endowments and per capita GDP among countries. To achieve this, they propose a corporate tax rate tied to the per capita income of both the capital-importing and capital-exporting states. As is seen in the chapters of this book that discuss tax incentives for foreign direct investment, this proposal has never been achieved and indeed, the opposite seems to be the result.

Infanti explains that even the Musgraves' 'redistributive' approach to internation equity focuses solely on the economic dimension of states, just as discussions of inter-individual equity tend to focus solely on the economic dimension of individuals and ignore other lines of difference (e.g., race, ethnicity, gender, and sexual orientation). But, as is true of individuals, the relative economic status of a nation is but one aspect of its development. Infanti points out that elsewhere in the development context, a broader notion of wellbeing or equity that is 'people-centred' rather than income-centred has been recognized since Amartya Sen worked on the first Human Development Index in 1990.[34] Infanti proposes that a developed country's tax credit, exemption or corporate tax rate rules for international investment could be linked, in various ways, to the HDI or aspects of it. Infanti's analysis widens the debate in two important ways. First, it situates the international tax rules of a country (such as the United States) in the wider context of its foreign policy and international aid and development programme. Second, it situates the internation tax equity debate in the wider context of international development equity, and seeks to link tax rules to country performance on a wider measure of human development. The difficulty remains, how to carry out the proposal in the context of the current international tax norms of reciprocity and bilateralism and of other policy goals of countries in setting their investment tax settings.

In Chapter 10, 'The role of developed world tax incentives in microfinance', Charlene D. Luke also turns her lens on developed country tax laws, in particular the United States. Luke focuses on microfinance as an element of aid policy and how this intersects with domestic US tax law.

---

[34] The approach elaborated by Amartya Sen, *Development as Freedom* (New York: Anchor Books, 2000).

In response to calls for developed countries to assist with development or poverty relief, developed country tax law reforms may be proposed that could support international aid. Luke examines one of the most unique, innovative and specific devices for economic development, microfinance, and discusses whether and how the US tax system could be reformed to strengthen the microfinance sector in developing countries. She points to the links between tax subsidies for international charitable giving and aid, and for international investment, and discusses the ways in which current US tax law may support or impede microfinance. Luke is cautious, however, as to whether further US tax subsidies for microfinance are warranted, in particular given the complexities and contradictory views concerning the different forms of microfinance programmes themselves within developing countries. Luke's article serves as a topical example for an implementation of the new development agenda and an example for the type of detailed examination of evidence it requires, in the tax context.

V. TAX COOPERATION

The theme of tax competition, however one defines it, and the need for some form of international cooperation and coordination of tax policies distinctly emerge from many of the essays in this book. The painfully slow process of such international tax coordination has been well documented by others. This Part includes chapters that take a visionary approach to the allocation of taxing powers in the international tax system, and more specifically related to the current 'hottest' issue on the international tax agenda – the coordination of policies regarding the critical issues of exchange of information and good tax governance in general.

In Chapter 11, 'Geographical boundaries of tax jurisdiction, exclusive allocation of taxing powers in tax treaties and good tax governance in relations with developing countries', Pasquale Pistone discusses whether the geographical boundaries of tax jurisdiction can be reconsidered in the treaty relations of developed countries with developing countries, in such a way that developing countries would remain masters of their own international tax policy decisions. This chapter queries whether the generally perceived 'best practice' of international tax principles established in the OECD Model Convention is really appropriate for developing countries, focusing in particular on the foreign tax credit method for relieving double tax (where applied especially to active business profits). Instead, Pistone considers a possible shift to an exclusive allocation of taxing powers over business and other forms of income to developing countries, or, at least for some types of income, a shared allocation of tax jurisdiction combined with non-compensatory methods for relieving double taxation in tax treaties. The chapter considers these specific issues in the broader context of good tax governance that is a dominant theme in EU and OECD documents on developing country tax relations. The concrete substance and standards for 'good tax governance' have not yet been clearly defined, although most work has been done to date on international tax information exchange procedures. The author reminds us that, again, it is important to consider what is good tax governance in terms of principles and practicalities, from a developing country tax perspective.

Allison Christians in Chapter 12, 'Tax activists and the global movement for development through transparency', identifies and explores the rise of a 'civil society' or non-governmental organization (NGO) movement for tax transparency in a global context. The chapter builds on Christians' substantial previous work analysing processes, players and institutions in tax policy at a global level. Christians has previously argued that poor countries are effectively absent from key intergovernmental organizations that create and disseminate global 'soft' tax models, norms and guidance, making them 'takers' rather than 'shapers' of global tax policy. In this volume, Christians traces the development of the tax transparency movement over the last decade. The movement grew out of anti-corruption activism, which led initially to some success in the resources industry sector with 'Publish What You Pay' advocacy and the establishment of the Extractive Industries Transparency Initiative.

The transparency tax movement has a number of striking features that may indicate the gradual development of a global tax politics engaging citizens of diverse states, but Christians' analysis also reveals that many obstacles remain to establishing such a global politics. First, the movement brings together NGOs and activist groups in developed countries with some citizen movements in developing countries, to engage with global institutions and multinational enterprises. Tax has long been a black box to development and aid activists; this movement begins to open that up to citizen scrutiny. Second, the movement differs from the resource sector initiative in that it directly engages with the concept of a 'fair share' of taxation for a particular country, or its citizens. The movement is not only about extracting an appropriate price for a non-renewable resource (which is, of course, a crucial matter for citizens in resource-rich countries). Although its focus is on transparency, it has potential to impact upon the fundamental questions of the substantive tax base including transfer pricing, tax incentives and the allocation of taxing jurisdiction between states.

Finally, Miranda Stewart in Chapter 13, 'Global tax information networks: legitimacy in a global administrative state' evaluates transnational cooperation in tax information exchange, and the enforcement and collection of taxes. She identifies the increasingly tight and legalized networks of transnational tax administration, in light of significant recent developments primarily between developed countries and institutions such as the OECD and EU. She then asks whether and how these networks can be extended to benefit developing countries and to bring to account multinational corporate actors and banks. It is postulated that transnational tax networks are slowly concentrating or agglomerating into a global tax bureaucracy 'from the ground up'. If this is true, how can we ensure accountability and legitimacy of this new bureaucracy? To answer this crucial question, this chapter examines forms of legal and political accountability that originate in classic hierarchical modes of governance, to see if they can be adapted to fit the new transnational tax networks.

The variety of chapters presented in this book forcefully demonstrate the deep need and the wealth of opportunities for progress in this avenue of study of tax, law and development. The primarily economic and 'one size fits all' focus of tax policy to date has not been sufficiently matched by detailed legal, historical and contextual policy analysis that can fortify and enrich it, supporting the implementation of tax reforms within real world social and legal structures. A range of alternative approaches to development arise out of the critique presented by the authors in this book and surveyed in this Introduction. The chapters call for a direct acknowledgement of the challenges and contradictions of tax law reform for development, and emphasize patience, diversity, a trial-and-error approach, transparency, legitimacy or 'ownership' and constant feedback and evaluation in tax reform approaches. Although less apparently streamlined and 'correct', these alternative approaches to tax, law and development do not imply a loss of focus,[35] even if they are slow, difficult to implement, and lack the appeal of promised panacea. Moreover, they often require careful coordination within and between countries that does not exist in the current international tax regime. This new approach does, however, promise some actual success. The goal of this book is unashamedly idealistic, to serve as the foundation that would jump-start further scholarship, and support real change in the global and national tax laws for economic development.

---

[35] *Ibid.*

PART II

Tax competition and tragic choices

2. The future of tax incentives for developing countries

Yariv Brauner*

I. INTRODUCTION

Governments of all kinds routinely use their tax systems to implement policies beyond the mere collection of general revenue. These uses, coined as 'tax expenditures', have advantages and disadvantages that are by now well-known and widely discussed in academic discourse.[1] In many developing countries, governments use tax expenditures specifically in their quest for economic development.

These tax expenditures targeted at economic development, often called 'tax incentives' in this context, almost universally stem from the desire of developing countries to attract investment – particularly foreign direct investment. Underpinning this desire is the theory that such tax incentives increase foreign direct investment, and foreign direct investment in turn generates economic growth that is essential for development. These tax

* I thank Ana Paula Dourado, Daniel Dominguez, James M. Maynor, Jr, Paul R. McDaniel, Martin M. McMahon, Pasquale Pistone, Luís Eduardo Schoueri, Miranda Stewart, and my co-contributors to this book for their insight and assistance in developing this chapter. All mistakes or inaccuracies are, naturally, mine.

[1] The legal analysis of tax expenditures evolved out of the work of Stanley S. Surrey, notably in *Pathways to Tax Reform: The Concept of Tax Expenditures* (Harvard University Press, 1973), and in Stanley S. Surrey and Paul R. McDaniel, *Tax Expenditures* (Harvard University Press, 1985), although there was an earlier discussion of some of the issues in Germany. See Harry A. Shannon, 'The Tax Expenditure Concept in the United States and Germany: A Comparison' (1986) 33 *Tax Notes* 201. See also, e.g., Victor Thuronyi, 'Tax Expenditures: A Reassessment' 1988 (6) *Duke Law Journal* 1155; Daniel N. Shaviro, 'Rethinking Tax Expenditures and Fiscal Language' (2004) 57 *Tax Law Review* 187; and Robert Peroni and J. Clifford Fleming, Jr, 'Can Tax Expenditure Analysis Be Divorced from a Normative Tax Base?: A Critique of the "New Paradigm" and its Denouement' (2010) 30 *Virginia Tax Review* 135.

incentives, like all tax expenditures, result in lost revenue. Yet the traditional theory suggests that such loss is minor in comparison to the benefits because tax incentives result in investment that would not otherwise be made, and hence there is no significant net loss of revenue.

This chapter challenges the traditional theory and claims that none of the components of the theory can be strongly supported in reality, i.e., that tax incentives do not necessarily result in more foreign direct investment; that foreign direct investment does not always generate economic growth; and that the relationship between economic growth and development is more complex than the general theory of tax incentives implies.[2] Consequently, this chapter questions the logic behind the widespread use of tax incentives in the search for development.

A second, related claim of this chapter is that the driving force behind the prevalent use of tax incentives is not a quest for development, but rather the phenomenon of tax competition. This implies that developing countries use tax incentives in a defensive, reactive manner rather than in a positive, proactive manner. As a result of this beggar-thy-neighbor approach, developing countries are unlikely to be able to use tax incentives effectively as a development policy.

Due to the obvious collective action difficulties that this reality presents, solutions are not easy or simple, and politics plays a major role in their design. Nonetheless, the chapter illustrates some action that countries could take, separately and collectively, to improve the efficacy of development in developing countries.

The chapter proceeds, next, in section II, with a review of the ubiquity and types of tax incentives used by developing countries. A critique of the theory supporting their use follows in section III. Then, section IV proposes an alternative explanation: that tax competition is truly behind the use of tax incentives. In section V, the chapter concludes with some suggestions about action that developed countries can take that would enhance the effectiveness of tax incentives and reduce the impetus towards destructive tax competition.

---

[2] The chapter focuses more on the relationship between tax incentives and foreign direct investment, and between foreign direct investment and economic growth, and less on the relationship between economic growth and development. A discussion of the latter would involve important philosophical, political and typological, as well as other, aspects that are beyond the scope of this chapter.

II. TAX INCENTIVES ARE PERVASIVE

Developing countries extensively use tax incentives. This section concisely reviews the main types of tax incentives used by developing countries, highlighting the features of these incentives that supposedly lead to growth and development via the encouragement of foreign direct investment.[3]

One can identify three basic categories of tax incentives: rate reducing, tax base eroding and special zones. The first and most straightforward type of rate reducing incentive simply reduces the nominal (and eventually the effective) tax rates that investors bear in the country that provides the tax incentive. The simplest form of such an incentive is a general rate reduction. This method is often associated with what are sometimes called 'tax havens'. These jurisdictions may eliminate (or fail to enact) a corporate income tax, or reduce the corporate tax rate to a level far below the global average. Ireland's 12.5 percent corporate income tax is a well-known example. One may argue that this is not a true tax incentive because it applies universally and equally within a jurisdiction. However, the diversion of the applicable tax rate from the normal or average level of corporate income tax rates internationally may be viewed as aimed at encouraging or luring investment from competitor jurisdictions. This seems particularly likely to be the motivation when domestic investment is small in magnitude. Corporate income taxes are often the focus of this method, yet various other taxes and administrative burdens may also be eliminated or reduced in a similar fashion.

Tax holidays exempt or significantly reduce the tax rates that investors are subject to, for particular kinds of investments and for a defined period of time. There is little debate on the categorization of tax holidays as tax incentives; indeed, these are probably the most common form of traditional tax incentives.[4] Tax holidays directly reduce the costs of investment in a country and consequently may, at least in theory, attract investors that would not otherwise have considered investing in the

---

[3] For a good survey of tax incentives in practice, see, e.g., Alex Easson, *Tax Incentives for Foreign Direct Investment* (2004); UNCTAD, *Incentives and Foreign Direct Investment: A Global Survey*, ASIT Advisory Studies No. 16 (United Nations, 2000); and David Holland and Richard J. Vann, 'Income Tax Incentives for Investment' in Victor Thuronyi, *Tax Law Design and Drafting* (IMF, 1998) vol. II, 986.

[4] See Easson, *supra* note 3, at 111.

country.[5] In addition to relieving investors from the direct costs of taxation, tax holidays also effectively save investors the compliance burden that can be particularly onerous for new market entrants. In theory, therefore, tax holidays are appropriately tailored towards 'new' investment or investors in a country. This narrative supposes that countries use tax holidays to entice new investors to enter, invest and establish their business within their jurisdictions, overcoming the difficulty and cost of entry. Thereafter, once the initial costly acclimation period passes, those newcomers start to pay taxes and participate in the economy.[6]

In reality, however, and in contrast to the narrative's assumptions, tax holidays are routinely extended for long periods, even when initially limited in length.[7] Moreover, the duration of tax incentives became standard, and, again, is quite regularly and almost automatically extended.[8] Long tax holidays are often granted to essentially all foreign investors, new and old, with little or no inquiry into their actual market penetration costs. Design difficulties also interfere with the efficacy of tax holidays. Most foreign direct investment faces losses in the initial investment period. If these losses cannot be carried forward and used in later fiscal years, then they may increase the effective tax rate that investors face. Depreciation deductions are also often available to such investors, which further delays the onset of positive tax liability. The solution to this problem appears to be straightforward: simply start the holiday period when profits are first generated. Yet this may postpone a developing country's actual receipt of tax payments by four or five years, a scenario in conflict with the theoretical argument that tax holidays exist to attract 'new' investment. Longer holidays also have higher costs (in the form of revenue forgone) and face increased susceptibility to tax planning.[9] Further, while different investors and industries face different 'start-up' periods, the duration of tax holidays is typically uniform, reducing their effectiveness. Even flexible, tailor-made holidays have their own shortcomings – they can bias investment decisions towards favored industries, and they present a more fertile environment for corruption to operate. In short, the theory underlying the use of tax

---

[5] *Ibid.* This approach is not dissimilar from the offshore regime model used by tax havens, only it is limited temporally and perhaps also limited in scope.

[6] *Ibid.*

[7] See, e.g., Holland and Vann, *supra* note 3, at 990.

[8] See, e.g., Howell H. Zee, Janet G. Stotsky and Eduardo Ley, 'Tax Incentives for Business Investment: A Primer for Policy Makers in Developing Countries' (2002) 30 *World Development* 1497, 1504.

[9] See, e.g., Holland and Vann, *supra* note 3, 991.

holidays is not supported by the reality of what happens when they are put into practice. A different explanation is thus needed for their pervasiveness. This chapter suggests that tax competition is a more likely culprit, as explored below.

Other tax incentives seek to limit the tax base rather than nominal rates, resulting in similarly reduced effective tax rates. Since they target the base, these incentives are less transparent than rate reducing incentives, and this opacity raises various concerns such as lack of accountability, inefficiency and inaccuracy. Yet base reducing incentives may be viewed as more directly targeted. Accelerated depreciation allowances are probably the most common of such measures.[10] In reality, tax depreciation in most countries is already accelerated vis-à-vis economic depreciation, so the acceleration is an added benefit further divorced from economic reality. These allowances and other 'acceleration' incentives focus on the timing, effectively deferring taxation. Theoretically, these tax incentives require clear identification of the investment sought, and they should be restricted to defined amounts to limit their effects to the extent desirable.

Application of this ideal in practice is very challenging. Taxpayers, and somtetimes officials, tend to try to maximize easily measurable indicators – such as total investment – rather than optimize the level of the relevant investment. Because this style of tax incentive is overbroad, one obvious negative consequence is a revenue loss that is larger than needed, perhaps to an extent that negates any positive effect of the incentive. Base reducing incentives also do not benefit investors who have no taxable income within the jurisdiction. This may be desirable, since it does not support unprofitable endeavors. Yet taxable income in the short term may not be the best proxy for the desirability of an investment, and the attendant uncertainty reduces the benefits from the incentives and hinders their efficacy.[11]

The third type of tax incentives, 'zones', is different from the above two in form. Custom-free trade or export-processing zones are used by many developing countries to attract export-oriented investment to operate within their jurisdictions. The investment is then treated as if it were extraterritorial[12] and, as a result, is untaxed in the incentive-granting country. If a product of the investment is sold in that country then it is treated as if it were produced outside the country's boundaries. The

---

10 See Easson, *supra* note 3, at 147–8.

11 This feature makes such incentives particularly vulnerable to tax planning. See, e.g., Holland and Vann, *supra* note 3, at 993.

12 *Ibid.* 1006–8.

alleged benefits of zones to target countries include: job creation, skill training, technology spillovers and general regional development. Additionally, developing countries often implement these schemes to improve their foreign exchange position, since the investments result almost exclusively in exports.[13]

Investors who choose zones are typically cost and tax conscious. However, they also tend to be mobile and therefore may not offer future tax receipts for the host country. The track record of zones ranges from mild success to notorious failure.[14] When meaningful foreign exchange (currency) was generated for the host country, zones were more useful than when not.[15] Zones are generally disfavored by experts also due to practical and non-tax issues.[16] Note too that all of the concerns raised above about rate and base reducing tax incentives apply to zones as well, since they use similar mechanisms – typically a complete tax holiday.

To conclude, this section briefly reviewed some of the most commonly used tax incentives and their traditional justifications. A preliminary practical assessment of these justifications indicates that their validity is questionable. Next, the chapter evaluates the more general theoretical case for tax incentives as a development-promoting mechanism.

III. TAX INCENTIVES FOR DEVELOPMENT: AN EVALUATION OF THE THEORY

The nearly universal use of tax incentives is founded upon a nearly universal supporting narrative.[17] Tax incentives are justified as essential for – and hence used by – all countries that wish to attract foreign investment.[18] The narrative proceeds as follows: at a rudimentary level, tax incentives should reduce the costs of cross-border investment and

---

[13] *Ibid.* 1007.

[14] See, e.g., Dorsati Madani, *A Review of the Role and Impact of Export Processing Zones* (1999), available at http://siteresources.worldbank.org/INTRANETTRADE/Resources/MadaniEPZ.pdf. See also World Bank, *Export Processing Zones* (1992).

[15] See Holland and Vann, *supra* note 3, at 1007.

[16] *Ibid.* 1006–8.

[17] This section further develops ideas presented first in Yariv Brauner, 'A Framework for an Informed Study of the Realistic Role of Tax in a Development Agenda' (2010) 42 *University of British Columbia Law Review* 275.

[18] See, e.g., Easson, *supra* note 3; UNCTAD/DTCI, *Incentives and Foreign Direct Investment*, Current Studies, Series A, No. 30 (United Nations, 1996); and Holland and Vann, *supra* note 3.

facilitate shifting such investment to the country providing the incentive. Then, shifted investment should benefit the country providing the incentive in an amount beyond the potential loss of revenue, if any, resulting from the incentive.

The main target of tax incentives, pursuant to the narrative, is foreign direct investment, considered desirable because it is alleged to presage economic growth. Economic growth, in turn, is essential for economic development – a primary goal of most countries.[19] This section argues that the validity of this universal narrative, and hence the justification for the use of tax incentives in search of development, is dubious.

A. Growth-based (Economic) Development

It is important to note first the relationship between development and growth. While the definition of economic growth is relatively straightforward (with widely acceptable methodologies for its measurement),[20] development is a more elusive concept.

This chapter focuses on economic growth that is a critical element of any development effort. Economic development clearly cannot be the only goal in a country's quest for improvement, as development encompasses improvements in various facets of individual and societal well-being. This includes diverse goals, ranging from improvements in education, to reductions in poverty and infant mortality, to gender equality.[21] A comprehensive study of the interaction between economic growth and overall development cannot be limited to mere causal analysis. Individual scholars differ in their emphasis on one or more of the components of development, so it is probably impossible to reach a consensus about its definition. Political, philosophical and social differences may result in significant typological divergences that, although interesting and worthy of independent study, do not contribute to the purpose of this chapter.

It is sufficient that one agrees with the contention that economic growth is an essential component of development to warrant the inspection of the theory behind tax incentives analysed here. This chapter

---

19 See Paul Collier, *The Bottom Billion* (2007) 190.

20 See, e.g., Paul M. Romer, 'Economic Growth' in the *Concise Encyclopedia of Economics*, available at www.econlib.org/library/Enc/EconomicGrowth.html.

21 See, e.g., United Nations Development Programme website, available at www.beta.undp.org/undp/en/home.html; and Amartya Sen, *Development as Freedom* (1999).

assumes that the role of economic growth in development is uncontroversial for purposes of this analysis. It notes, however, that a singular focus on economic growth and tax (or similar) incentives while neglecting other aspects of development is problematic.

B. Relationship between Foreign Direct Investment and Growth

One pillar of the theoretical argument in support of tax incentives by developing countries is the presupposition of a causal relationship between foreign direct investment and economic growth. For tax incentives to promote development in the way the theory predicts, foreign direct investment must generate economic growth.[22] However, manifold studies of the reality of this relationship have produced, at best, mixed results that cast doubt on the validity of conventional wisdom in support of tax incentives.

1. What do we know about economic growth?

The study of economic growth surged in the second half of the last century after the Second World War, yet it is still very much an evolving area of research, both theoretically and empirically.

The fundamental inquiry of this study is why some countries are poor while others are rich.[23] Post-Second World War economic growth rates were unprecedentedly high, yet they differed significantly among countries, resulting in a consistent widening of the gap between rich and poor nations.[24] Exacerbating this inequality was the fact that rich countries proved more resilient to economic downturns – they did not suffer long, significant economic declines following crises as poor countries did.[25] Concern about this phenomenon triggered much of the interest in the economics of growth. Economists developed standards, including a

---

[22] See Maria Carkovic and Ross Levine, 'Does Foreign Direct Investment Accelerate Economic Growth?' in Theodore H. Moran, Edward M. Graham and Magnus Blomström (eds), *Does Foreign Direct Investment Promote Development?* (2005) 195.

[23] This question, of course, has been subject to varying degrees of interest by economists ever since Adam Smith's 1776 *Inquiry into the Nature and Causes of the Wealth of Nations.*

[24] See, e.g., Elhanan Helpman, *The Mystery of Economic Growth* (2004) 2. See, more generally, Nathan Rosenberg and Luther Earle Birdzell, *How the West Grew Rich: The Economic Transformation of the Industrial World* (1986).

[25] For example, poor countries were more harshly affected by the oil crisis of 1973. See, e.g., Helpman, *supra* note 24, ch. 1.

measure of the change in gross domestic product (GDP) per capita, as a measure of economic growth rates.[26]

Early research in this area emphasized the role of accumulation of capital, both physical and human, owing to the belief that capital responded to economic incentives and therefore could be affected by economic policy. The most notable contribution to this research was that of Robert Solow,[27] who observed that in the long run, a country's growth depends on (and converges with) technological change. Since technological change was assumed to be unresponsive to economic incentives – and therefore not affected by economic policy – Solow predicted that economic policy and incentives cannot affect long-term growth. Empirical research generally supported Solow's observations with respect to rich countries, yet it could not explain the existence and growth of the gap between poor and rich countries that was supposed to vanish in the long term.[28]

Later research explored an alternative explanation: that productivity of inputs is an important factor for growth, perhaps even a more important factor than its raw accumulation.[29] Empirical research on this subject found that quality (or productivity) of individual inputs (labor, capital or land) does not alone explain overall productivity levels. It followed that a portion or even a significant amount of productivity should be attributed to total factor productivity, which measures the joint effectiveness of all inputs combined in producing output.[30] Investment in research and development explains much of the differing total factor productivity levels among countries.[31] Technological change, therefore, became an important focus of this research. Rising technological change could also reconcile the Solow model with the fact that the universal growth rate

---

26 *Ibid.* 1. The United Nations attempted, with its Human Development Index, to develop a more holistic measurement mechanism, including health and education in addition to income. See http://hdr.undp.org/en/reports/publications/title,4182,en.html.

27 See Robert M. Solow, 'A Contribution to the Theory of Economic Growth' (1965) 70 *Quarterly Journal of Economics* 65; and Robert M. Solow, 'Technical Change and the Aggregate Production Function' (1957) 39 *Review of Economics and Statistics* 312.

28 Some economists attempted to explain these differences through the relationship between physical and human capital. See N. Gregory Mankiw, 'The Growth of Nations' (1995) 1 *Brookings Papers on Econ. Activity* 275. Yet it is debatable that this explanation is sufficient. Helpman, *supra* note 24, at 17–18.

29 Helpman, *supra* note 24, ch. 3.

30 *Ibid.* 33.

31 *Ibid.* chs 4–5.

accelerates over time; Solow held technological change constant and predicted a decline in growth rates.

A critical contribution at this juncture was Paul Romer's model that based output not only on private factors of production, but also on a vast array (economy-wide stock) of knowledge that increases over time.[32] His key insight was to dispose of the assumption that technological change, the most important driver of growth, cannot be affected by economic incentives. Under such a model, investment in knowledge may yield economy-wide positive externalities, and governments are therefore empowered to contribute to the growth of their countries' economies. Further research expanded and developed this approach, proving that the effect of technology and innovation is indeed very important. Nonetheless, due to the multiplicity of 'moving parts', the design of growth policies remained complicated.

A further complication in the process of understanding economic growth was that growth in one country was dependent on growth in other countries. Cross-border flows of technology, knowledge, trade and investment affect all participating countries. The interdependence of countries' income levels is, sometimes directly and sometimes indirectly, correlated with their effect on productivity. This interdependence is a result of country specialization, a phenomenon possible only via participation in international trade. A critical aspect in this context is the effect of research and development. It is well known that almost all research and development is performed in a few rich countries.[33] The question, then, is whether this concentration of research and development benefits the rest of the world or simply fortifies the economic ramparts of rich countries, further distancing them from the rest of the world. Recent research indicates that research and development performed by rich countries significantly benefits developing countries that trade with them through the research's effect on the developing countries' total factor productivity. However, rich countries benefit from research and development more than developing countries do, and hence investment in research and development on balance widens the wealth gap between the rich and poor countries.

---

[32] See Paul M. Romer, 'Increasing Returns and Long-Run Growth' (1986) 94 *Journal of Political Economy* 1002, and Paul M. Romer, 'Endogenous Technological Change' (1990) 98 *Journal of Political Economy* 71.

[33] UNCTAD, *World Investment Report 2005: Transnational Corporations and the Internationalization of R&D* (United Nations, 2005) ch. 3, available at www.unctad.org/en/docs/wir2005ch3_en.pdf.

The effect of institutions (such as a country's substantive legal system, respect for the rule of law and form of government) is another critical factor in the realization of economic growth.[34] These institutions are practically managing the relevant policies that lead to innovation and knowledge accumulation. Limited progress has been achieved in measuring institutional effects, yet some things seem obvious: for example, that corruption, disregard for the rule of law and political instability limit the ability for growth promotion. Geography has also been blamed,[35] yet there is little support for this contention.

Another relevant aspect regarding economic growth has proven to be inequalities within and among developing countries themselves. It appears that inequality slows growth, yet research has neither convincingly demonstrated how this result occurs nor identified what we can learn about it in the context of development. For example, it cannot be said that a democratic decision to redistribute wealth within a country is necessarily detrimental to growth.[36] A more extreme contention regarding inequality is that growth is bad for the poor, a claim based on the decreasing share of the poor in world wealth and the increasing equality gap. Research, however, demonstrates that the average income of the poor has risen around the world.[37]

In sum, while the topic of economic growth will continue to engender much research (with a particular focus on the role of institutions), there is much that we know already. At least, we can be sure that the effect of institutions on growth is important. We understand the vital role of innovation as a driver of technological change, its effect on productivity, and the significance of productivity for growth. Additionally, we can appreciate the relationship between productivity and accumulation of capital, both physical and human. We also know that we need to take into account the interdependence of countries, especially when the least developed countries are involved. Unfortunately, it is readily observable that typical tax incentives, reviewed in the former section, are not regularly designed with this knowledge in mind. The challenge is how to design tax measures to best fuel these engines of growth.

---

[34] See, e.g., Helpman, *supra* note 24, ch. 7.
[35] Jeffrey Sachs, *The End of Poverty* (2006) 57–9.
[36] Helpman, *supra* note 24, at 93–4.
[37] *Ibid.* 109.

2. Foreign direct investment as a determinant of growth

At the same time as economic research explored the determinants of economic growth, foreign direct investment was simultaneously promoted by the 'Washington Consensus' as a critical generator of development; the more of it, the better.[38] This assertion was adopted and then promulgated by business groups and multinational enterprises as an argument for investment-promoting incentives. Some academic research, though, expressed skepticism about the uniqueness and utility of foreign direct investment for development.[39]

Generally, the main benefit attributed to foreign direct investment is efficiency. The simplified narrative is that, if investment flows freely, it will end up where it maximizes its owner's wealth and consequently global wealth (i.e., such allocation increases the global pie). Any restrictions or barriers result in less than maximum global wealth gain. Global efficiency is not, however, a consensus goal, and indeed it is typically an afterthought to the most important participants in this game. The capital-exporting country, which is the residence of the investor (sometimes called the 'home country'), naturally wishes to maximize its own wealth. Maximization of global wealth may not mean maximization of every country's wealth at the same time, and therefore such country may choose not to leave foreign direct investment free of its regulation. The target or 'host' country faces similar incentives. Note that interference and regulation from one country alone is sufficient to potentially force all countries to follow suit even if some are content with the free flow of investment.

Developing countries have generally subscribed to the notion of the importance of foreign direct investment, yet the strongest of them have emphasized selectiveness by seeking 'quality' investment that would ensure desirable positive externalities through technology transfers, domestic production, domestic ownership, and the like. This latter strategy signaled that some countries did not believe that foreign direct

---

[38] The term 'Washington Consensus' was coined by John Williamson in a 1989 summary of ten key development advice items commonly shared by the Washington, DC institutions, the IMF and World Bank, and the US Treasury Department. The original context was advice to Latin American countries following the 1980s crisis. See John Williamson, 'What Washington Means by Policy Reform' in John Williamson (ed.), *Latin American Readjustment: How Much Has Happened* (1989). This advice later became emblematic of what is often called market fundamentalism. For a reflection on the evolution of the term and its symbolism, see Pedro-Pablo Kuczynski and John Williamson (eds), *After the Washington Consensus* (2003).

[39] See, e.g., Dani Rodrik, *The New Global Economy and Developing Countries* (1999) 37.

investment was universally positive and worth incentivizing indiscriminately. If one conclusion may be drawn from the divergent relevant economic research, it is that the impact of foreign direct investment on growth is not one dimensional: it has some positive as well as potentially negative consequences, leading a recent study to conclude that 'the search for a universal relationship is futile'.[40]

The effectiveness of foreign direct investment is frequently strongly associated with certain existing attributes of the target economy. An economy that is open to trade and investment may benefit immensely from foreign direct investment that would carry with it positive spillovers such as (developed) world-class research and development, management techniques and quality control. Multinational enterprises (hierarchically organized) which trade internally between parents and subsidiaries may be instrumental to such growth effects, when they are allowed to perform such internal trading and freely invest. They are more likely to move more production, technology and capital to the target (developing) countries and generate more positive spillovers for such economies.[41] Foreign direct investment can make domestic firms perform better because it pushes the domestic economy to be more efficient, expand and diversify. This may happen directly through competition with domestic firms, collaboratively via joint ventures, implicitly by example, or through the creation of new opportunities through introduction to foreign or global networks or agglomeration.[42] In these cases, it has been argued that foreign direct investment can contribute beyond the mere capital it contributes to such economy.[43]

When foreign direct investment is accompanied by increases in trade, it has the potential to contribute to growth.[44] Particularly, research has established that foreign direct investment is positively associated with growth when the target economy has accumulated a minimal stock of

---

[40] Robert E. Lipsey and Fredrik Sjöholm, 'The Impact of Inward FDI on Host Countries: Why Such Different Answers?' in Moran *et al.*, *supra* note 22, at 23.

[41] *Ibid.* 14–15.

[42] Edward L. Glaeser defines 'agglomeration economies' as 'the benefits that come when firms and people locate near one another together in cities and industrial clusters', 'Introduction' in Edward L. Glaeser (ed.), *The Economics of Agglomeration*, NBER Conference held 30 November–1 December 2007 (unpublished drafts), available at www.nber.org/books/glae08-1/.

[43] But see Dani Rodrik, Appel Inaugural Lecture, Columbia University, 27 March 2003 ('One dollar of FDI is worth no more (and no less) than a dollar of any other kind of investment').

[44] Moran *et al.*, *supra* note 22, at 376.

human capital.[45] Conversely, when the target economy is protectionist – with significant restrictions on trade and investment – foreign direct investment may simply compete with domestic firms over domestic resources and so it may fail to provide an incentive either to use cutting-edge technology or to maximize cooperation, therefore leading to inefficiencies. In these cases, domestic welfare may effectively be 'exported' rather than augmented.[46] Such investment results in either utilization of inferior technology by a foreign firm with the narrow goal of domestic rent extraction, or involvement of inferior foreign investors that cannot positively contribute to the target economy. Therefore, when accompanied with restrictions on trade and investment, foreign direct investment may hurt rather than assist economic growth.[47]

A related distinction can be made between export-oriented foreign direct investment and domestic market-seeking investment. The former is typically associated with more liberal trade and investment policies and with foreign majority owned businesses (and accordingly with positive spillovers), while the latter is typically characterized by domestic majority ownership, restrictive trade and investment policies, and a lack of positive spillovers.[48] These observations, however, are not nuanced enough to be useful in guiding detailed policy towards foreign direct investment.

Finally, even if positive spillovers are produced and a causal link is demonstrated with foreign direct investment, it is still not clear that the foreign direct investment that generated them is desirable because its attraction involves costs. The challenge, then, is to measure the existence and magnitude of these externalities. Because this is difficult to prove and calculate, this link in the logical (causality) chain remains tenuous.

---

45 *Ibid.*, 'Introduction', at 10.

46 In these circumstances, foreign direct investment is usually targeting the domestic markets rather than focusing on exports. These investments are often required to be conducted through joint ventures with domestic ownership or even to relinquish control to domestic ownership. The use of domestic material is commonly mandated, as well as sharing of technology with domestic entities involved.

47 Moran *et al.*, *supra* note 22, at 376; Marc J. Melitz, 'Comment' in *ibid.* 12–13, and 273–7.

48 *Ibid.* ch. 11. China is a good example for the former (see *ibid.* ch. 12), and Africa generally evinces the latter type (see *ibid.* ch. 13). Most non-extractive industry in Africa was import-substituting. There is a suspicion that most activity is motivated by rent extracting from Africa.

C. Tax Incentives and Foreign Direct Investment

Tax is just one of many factors that multinational enterprises take into consideration when they make decisions regarding locations of their direct investment.[49] This section discusses the findings of the relevant research and their implications for the inquiry conducted by this chapter.

Foreign direct investment has grown steadily in the last three decades, consistent with increasing globalization. Most of this growth took place in developed countries; however, investment in developing countries has grown as well. Typical foreign direct investment in a developing country takes the form of what is commonly called 'greenfield investment', i.e., opening a business and penetrating the market rather than acquiring an already up-and-running domestic business. This may explain some of the difference between growth in developed and developing countries. Tax incentives, as already mentioned, are designed specifically to attract such greenfield investment by first-time foreign investors in a country.

Investors (i.e., multinational enterprises) may maximize their own profits by taking a course that is not necessarily wealth-maximizing, either for a particular country in which they invest, or from a global efficiency perspective. This is especially true – perhaps inevitable – once the relevant countries regulate investment and hinder its free deployment. Since we are without either a world government or strong cooperation among the countries of the world, seeking the goal of global efficiency is probably unattainable.

One may assume, however, that a multinational enterprise will not make an investment from which it expects to derive no benefit. One such benefit for the multinational enterprise could be low effective taxation. The literature attempting to isolate the effect of taxation on foreign direct investment, however, offers mixed results. The differences are large at times, so reaching general conclusions is difficult. In sum, one may say that taxation plays a relatively small role in the original decision to engage in foreign direct investment and that in many cases, political systems and market climate are more important. However, taxation is a factor relevant at the margin.[50]

For example, consider a multinational enterprise in the business of manufacturing sporting goods that wishes to increase production to respond to demand. It concludes that it needs another plant. It is manifest that the labor costs are critical in the decision to place the plant outside the United States. Labor costs, skills and general stability lead it to

---

[49] See, e.g., Easson, *supra* note 3, at 19–34.
[50] See UNCTAD, *supra* note 18, ch. IV.

choose Southeast Asia. Now, let us hypothesize that Thailand, Malaysia and Vietnam are all appropriate in terms of infrastructure, transportation costs and other institutional factors. It is only at this stage where one can see tax entering the equation. If one of these countries can secure a better financial package (with taxes considered) for the investor, it may be at an advantage. It is worth noting that, in recent years as globalization has thrived, it has become more likely that other conditions equalize, potentially leaving a more important role for taxation in such decisions.[51] This may be true only with respect to the final location decision, in contrast to the choice of region, etc. for investment.

The effects of taxation on foreign direct investment may also vary significantly for different types of investments. Studies have found that export-oriented investment is more sensitive to taxation than, for instance, investment that attempts to penetrate certain markets (import-substituting investment). For example, the choice to locate a computer chip manufacturing facility in China, Vietnam or the Philippines may be more sensitive to domestic taxation than the choice among the same countries for the purposes of locating a television assembly facility for distribution in the respective domestic markets. Recall that this distinction arose in the context of the efficacy of foreign direct investment, discussed above. Research supports the view that export-oriented foreign direct investment is more likely to contribute to growth than import-substituting foreign direct investment. This lends support to the case for tax incentives for export-oriented investment, since at least they have the potential to attract certain desirable types of investment. A less understood issue is the difference in impact of tax incentives across industries. Existing research suggests that there are significant differences among industries in their sensitivity to tax. Most obviously, more portable industries are more sensitive to taxation than less portable ones.[52] Much legal research into the design of tax incentives ignores differences between industries. In order to competently craft tax incentives, this kind of research seems particularly desirable.

---

[51] Some US studies support this contention. See, e.g., Harry Grubert and John Mutti, 'Do Taxes Influence Where U.S. Corporations Invest?' (2000) 53 *National Tax Journal* 825.

[52] See G. Peter Wilson, 'The Role of Taxes in Location and Sourcing Decisions' in Alberto Giovannini, R. Glenn Hubbard and Joel Slemrod, *Studies in International Taxation* (1996) 195. See also, although limited to a particular European context, Michael P. Devereaux, 'The Impact of Taxation on International Business: Evidence from the Ruding Committee Survey' (1992/2) *EC Tax Review* 105.

Finally, one must be careful when attributing weight to overall taxation, or the corporate tax rate, as an indicator of the impact of tax on foreign direct investment. The important roles of tax administration and other bureaucratic functions of tax authorities in respect of such investment have rarely been studied. Also neglected are other considerations such as customs duties and import taxes. The roles of individual tax rates, social contributions and consumption taxes are limited, and there is no evidence that they are material.

While the picture portrayed by current research is not entirely clear, we may accept for purposes of this analysis that foreign direct investment is sensitive, at least to some degree, to taxation on the margin. The next issue is whether tax incentives are capable of increasing desirable foreign direct investment. Most academics and tax experts answer this in the negative, claiming that tax incentives are undesirable on balance. The primary case against them is based on efficiency considerations: tax incentives distort behavior and thus must result in efficiency losses in the relevant markets. But this is less a criticism of tax incentives than a simple description of the essence of the policy behind tax incentives themselves – they aim to create an incentive for people to invest in a place where they otherwise would not. Global efficiency losses are not a primary concern of developing countries implementing tax incentives; rather, they seek to enhance their own economy. The second argument runs counter to our assumption above, as it states that tax incentives are simply not effective since tax is not an important determinant of foreign direct investment. If this contention is true then the entire practice of offering tax incentives is ill-conceived. Third, critics argue that even if tax incentives can encourage foreign direct investment, the price of tax incentives often exceeds their benefits – they are costly and difficult to administer and police. They are particularly exposed to corruption in countries where corruption is already a major *inter alia* economic concern, and they are almost by definition inequitable as a result of promoting certain investments and investors over others.

Against this consensus, a few have argued that tax incentives might be desirable from a developing country's perspective. The most serious argument, as explained above, is that they promote foreign direct investment that brings technology to these countries and correlative positive spillover effects that assist them in their quest for growth.[53]

---

[53] See Yoram Margalioth, 'Tax Competition, Foreign Direct Investment and Growth: Using the Tax System to Promote Developing Countries' (2003) 23 *Virginia Tax Review* 161.

1. Efficiency argument against tax incentives

The efficiency argument against tax incentives is based on concerns related to behavioral distortion. Investors are encouraged to do something that they would not otherwise do: invest in country A rather than country B, in zone A rather than zone B, (in the extreme case) in industry A rather than industry B, or hire X more workers than one optimally would. The achievement of the distortion is, of course, the goal of the tax incentive. If the distortion is not realized (e.g., because the investor intended to invest in country A or in zone A even in the absence of the incentive) then the incentive is a pure waste – it will not carry out its intended effect. Not only is such an incentive wasteful, but it is also inefficient because it provides an unintended advantage to the incentive recipient (over its competitors).[54] The competition distortion is exacerbated by the fact that developing countries' governments may be in a weak bargaining position vis-à-vis the multinational enterprises seeking tax incentives. As a result, tax incentives may be granted that benefit only certain investments, possibly in an inefficient manner as described above. This theme is the touchstone of the aforementioned tax competition problem.[55]

Distortion, however, is not necessarily efficiency reducing; it may be desirable if, for instance, it 'corrects' a market failure.[56] One such situation is when there is no functioning market to speak of, such as in ex-communist countries. Another potential market failure is a sub-optimal level of research and development in a country, however this is a questionable rationale for tax incentives of most developing countries.

Even if a market failure was evident, two more criteria would have to be met to justify an ameliorative approach based on tax incentives. First, the failure would have to be capable of correction by way of tax incentives. Second, governments would have to be able to use tax incentives for these purposes measurably and correctly. Governments are notoriously convinced that they can do so but, importantly, they seldom take into account the side-effects of such policies, such as decreased development of other industries or regions and diversion of skilled workers from a non-incentivized industry to one that receives incentives.

It is difficult to find evidence as to whether tax incentives do change behavior of investors. If they do not change behavior, then tax incentives

---

[54] This latter distortion may result even if the tax incentive is effective if competitors (direct or indirect) of the tax incentive recipient do not get an exactly equivalent tax incentive – a very likely scenario.

[55] See *supra* section II.A.3.

[56] See Easson, *supra* note 3, at 64, note 4.

are clearly wasteful. Evidence of general investment patterns may not be helpful since it averages many different situations and types of rules. However, the evidence available gives a general indication about the efficacy of this policy device, and suggests that only a small minority of tax incentives actually work.[57] Familiarity with the specifics of the available data is important for comprehension of the literature, as most of the data comes from survey studies, and little or no evidence comes from the relevant countries adopting the tax incentives. The lack of evidence from particular countries is a significant problem. It signals a lack of 'accountability' – the utilization of the incentives is not transparent and there is no control post-enactment. Note, however, that even if there was evidence of the need for changes to the design of a particular tax incentive, this would create a dilemma for policy-makers, since stability of the tax system is also important for effectiveness.

2. Costs and benefits of tax incentives

Even an effective tax incentive is not desirable if it does not generate enough of a benefit to cover its costs. The costs of tax incentives include both forgone revenue and indirect costs, such as the distortions that they create in the target market. The revenue loss may seem the more obvious cost; yet, upon reflection one should understand that there is no cost at all if the incentives are indeed effective. If a tax incentive indeed attracts a desirable investment that would not otherwise land in the target country – or more specifically, would not result in taxable income in the target country – then little to no revenue is forgone. Unfortunately, it is very difficult to determine which investment is in fact of the sort that would not otherwise be made in the target country. And if the investment is of the kind that was incrementally increased in response to the incentive or allocated at least partially in a different manner, it becomes still more difficult to delineate the part of the investment or allocation that is incremental.[58]

One direct response to this difficulty may be that better administration and enforcement can improve the desirability of investments that flow from deployment of tax incentives. Yet there is a catch: the less general an incentives regime is, the more it is exposed to indirect costs and distortions such as substitution, corruption or discrimination.[59]

---

57 *Ibid.* 66–7.

58 *Ibid.* 75 note 47, citing Bloch (also see at 76).

59 Substitution, for example, may occur when tax incentives particularly attract short-term, highly profitable investment that may not be of the type that involves beneficial spillovers. See, e.g., Holland and Vann, *supra* note 3, at 989.

Finally, there are some costs that are more technical. Tax incentives complicate the target countries' tax systems and often facilitate tax avoidance as well.[60] This not only increases the costs of compliance, administration and enforcement, but also potentially undermines the public perception of the tax system's clarity and fairness, which may lead to reduced efficacy.

On the benefit side, direct revenue benefits may include revenue from taxation, which may be raised as a result of the investment, beyond the particular type of tax, or capital invested, that enjoys the incentive. A possible example is that increased paid employment generated by an investment could increase personal income tax revenues, or a corporate investor may pay indirect taxes. Another potential direct benefit is the possibility of revenue collected in the future from the investment, for example when a tax holiday expires. Both types of benefit seem unlikely to eventuate, in particular the latter, since in practice it is observed that investors are strong enough to effectively avoid actual taxation for long periods of time. The more important benefits are the spillover effects such as skill training and technology transfers. It is easy to see how difficult it is to calculate such benefits, especially for shorter investment periods.

A cost–benefit analysis is therefore immensely difficult to accurately conduct, and most available studies took place in limited industries within developed countries where the availability and sophistication of data are materially different from that present in the developing world. An improved mechanism for such analysis is clearly required.

D. Conclusion

The evaluation conducted in this section of the theoretical argument in support of the use of tax incentives for development demonstrates the weakness of the theory. Tax incentives cannot be said to generally encourage new foreign direct investment and, in any event, governments seem either unwilling or unable to design them in a way that would. Tax is a minor consideration in locational decisions for foreign direct investment and, even when it may be relevant on the margin, tax incentives do not clearly serve to decisively generate new investment. Moreover, tax incentives are not effective in distinguishing between desirable and undesirable investment even when they are potentially effective. Finally, even assuming, *arguendo*, that tax incentives do

---

60 *Ibid.*

generate new and beneficial foreign direct investment, the benefits of such investment and its positive externalities are difficult to identify and measure. Similarly, the costs of tax incentives are difficult to measure; a difficulty that is compounded by the lack of political will or ability to collect, analyse and expose the relevant data to academic and other research. The argument that tax incentives generate desirable foreign direct investment is therefore weak.

The theoretical arguments discussed in this section cannot explain the practice of enacting tax incentives by developing countries, which are well aware of this research. Next, the chapter offers an alternative explanation, based on tax competition, for the pervasive use of tax incentives by developing countries despite the knowledge (or lack thereof) that we have about their effect on development.

IV. TAX COMPETITION AS AN ALTERNATIVE NARRATIVE

Few countries can claim their tax incentive programs are successful. The only countries worthy of serious consideration in this regard are Singapore, Taiwan and Ireland, which are transition economies rather than developing ones. Yet, tax incentives may not be the only or the optimal route toward development. Chile and Estonia, for instance, have achieved comparable development to that of the aforementioned countries despite their avoidance of tax incentives.[61] Still, it is apparent that the majority of developing countries regularly employ tax incentives in accord with the conventional wisdom promoted by the Washington Consensus, a wisdom that has been proven weak, at best, as demonstrated in the former section.

This section analyses the role played by international organizations, developed countries and developing countries in reaching the current state of affairs and claims that tax competition better explains the use of tax incentives. Developing countries are forced into granting tax incentives, not in a carefully measured attempt to draw foreign investment that they predict will be favorable, but rather in an attempt not to be disadvantaged vis-à-vis their neighbors.

---

[61] *Ibid.* 988 note 3.

A. What is Tax Competition?

Tax competition is not an easily defined concept, and it takes place at several distinct levels. Most simply, countries compete for foreign direct investment with other countries and in the process wish to present themselves as more attractive locations, *inter alia*, in terms of the tax burden that investors will face upon entry. A snowball effect would result in no taxation of foreign investment that is subject to tax competition, and indeed some argue that this is what has happened.[62]

Now consider a more intricate example, in which investors, primarily multinational enterprises, wish to establish a single factory in the Southeast Asian region. These investors are aware of the advantages of certain countries in that region, and the neighboring countries do not differ in terms of the relevant parameters – availability of skilled and unskilled workers, cost of labor, political and economic stability, etc. It is at this point, when input costs and institutional factors are similar across a region, that research counsels that investors are probably the most sensitive to tax rates.[63] They are primarily interested in cutting their costs, and it is predictable that they will request tax incentive packages. In turn, these solicitations intensify the tax competition in certain settings (Southeast Asia in our illustration).[64] Such intensification does not even require active lobbying on the side of multinational corporations – the governments' belief that tax is a crucial factor in investors' decisions may be sufficient to force all of the countries to offer essentially the same incentives. This is exactly what happens in reality.

Tax competition therefore changes the power balance between countries and multinational enterprises in the world economy *and* prevents countries in the above circumstances from tailoring tax incentives to their needs and wishes. Tax holidays become the baseline rather than extraordinary preferences that would have the power to incentivize investment.

---

62 Reuven S. Avi-Yonah, 'Globalization, Tax Competition, and the Fiscal Crisis of the Welfare State' (2000) 113 *Harvard Law Review* 1573.

63 See, e.g., Rosanne Altshuler and Harry Grubert, *The Three Parties in the Race to the Bottom: Host Governments, Home Governments and Multinational Companies*, CESifo Working Paper Series No. 1613 (December 2005), available at SSRN http://ssrn.com/abstract=875308; and Rosanne Altshuler, Harry Grubert and T. Scott Newlon, *Has U.S. Investment Abroad Become More Sensitive to Tax Rates?*, NBER Working Paper No. W6383 (January 1998), available at SSRN http://ssrn.com/abstract=226131.

64 See, e.g., Reed E. Hundt, *In China's Shadow: The Crisis of American Entrepreneurship* (2006) 21–2. See also www.pc.gov.au/__data/assets/pdf_file/0017/37340/sub008.pdf (Australian example).

Lack of a tax holiday in a given country is now effectively viewed as a disincentive to invest. Countries who need (or believe that they need) foreign investment cede control of their fiscal powers to foreign investors. The alternative, as they see it, is receiving undesirable investment or no investment at all.[65]

Another level of competition occurs within countries, among regions or states. In the context of the developing world, the decision to promote one region over another is still largely a decision of central or federal governments, so it is not materially different from international competition. However, it presents a different set of choices to investors who have already selected a country in which to invest.

A somewhat different level of competition occurs among regions of the world. Countries, both developed and developing, may explore opportunities to organize and improve their mutual goals. Alas, in most cases these are unsuccessful, at least in the context of tax incentives in the developing world.[66] The European Union presents a different model, yet it is a model that seems unlikely to be implemented in the developing world at the present juncture.[67]

Finally, there is internal competition among various sectors or industries. This is important since we have seen the importance of technology and technology spillovers to the success of incentives; they are a possible true determinant of growth. As noted above, this area warrants further research to assist the design of tax incentives.

---

65 Interesting evidence of this behavior may be found in OECD, *Tax Policy Assessment and Design in Support of Direct Investment: A Study of Countries in South East Europe* (2003) 88 (regarding the Czech and Polish response to Hungarian tax incentives) and 89 (describing the most well-known example of tax competition, in Southeast Asia), available at www.oecd.org/dataoecd/46/14/34466352.pdf. See also, Avi Nov, 'The "Bidding War" to Attract Foreign Direct Investment: The Need for a Global Solution' (2006) 25 *Virginia Tax Review* 835.

66 But there have been recent positive developments in the East African community. See, e.g., IMF, *Kenya, Uganda, and United Republic of Tanzania: Selected Issues*, IMF Country Report No. 08/353 (October 2008), available at www.imf.org/external/pubs/ft/scr/2008/cr08353.pdf.

67 Even in the EU, there is a serious ongoing struggle over what course of action to take in relation to corporate tax harmonization and the approach to tax incentives. The 'state aid' regime in the EU, which prohibits tax incentives except in limited situations, has gained strength only recently. See the relevant European Commission website, http://ec.europa.eu/competition/state_aid/reform/reform.html.

It is argued here that tax competition better explains the prevalent use of standard tax incentives by developing countries then does the traditional theoretical framework. As already mentioned, tax systems in general, and tax incentives in particular, affect locational investment decisions most significantly only when all basic business decisions have been made and the general region or type of country has been chosen (based on, for example, low labor costs, infrastructure and political stability). Naturally, a multinational enterprise that has several options would be in a position to negotiate benefits from the relevant governments. Tax incentives are likely to be one of the easier benefits to negotiate. Politicians can demonstrate evident success (attraction of new investment) without spending cash or other existing resources. They can do this in a non-transparent manner because while cost–benefit analysis is difficult to conduct, populist rhetoric touting job creation and tangible evidence of new investment are viscerally appealing to the populace.

B. Role of International Organizations

As discussed above in section III, the 'Washington Consensus' is that foreign direct investment is a critical factor in economic development. At the same time, it is striking that there is almost universal opposition by the international economic organizations to tax incentives aimed at encouraging such foreign direct investment.[68] These organizations regularly argue that tax incentives are inefficient and ineffective, using arguments similar to those explored already above. It is argued that tax incentives are inefficient because they distort investment decisions by encouraging investment in countries or activities other than those that would have been invested in absent the incentives, and that they are ineffective on the basis that tax is not an important determinant of investment. These two arguments against tax incentives contradict each other. Tax incentives either change behavior and lead to distortion, or are ineffective and fail to do so, but certainly not both simultaneously.

The most recent OECD publication on the relationship between tax and development does not refer directly to tax incentives, but focuses on better governance and international cooperation between developing and developed countries.[69] The OECD's position against tax competition

---

[68] See also Miranda Stewart, 'Global Trajectories of Tax Reform: The Discourse of Tax Reform in Developing and Transition Countries' (2003) 44 Harvard International Law Journal 139, 151.

[69] OECD, *Governance, Taxation and Accountability: Issues and Practices* (2008).

further illustrates a general resistance to tax incentives in both developed and developing countries.[70]

The International Monetary Fund (IMF) is probably the most active among international institutions in the field of taxation. Its policies, notably its infamous 'conditionalities' (i.e., conditions that it dictates to its borrowers) have historically been secret, although since the 1990s, IMF policies and conditions are more likely to be made public.[71] The IMF is the strongest opponent of the use of tax incentives by developing countries, although it has been willing to say that in some circumstances tax incentives may be used to correct for market failures, while still qualifying this statement by adding that this is a limited and essentially academic argument and in practice '[t]he cost-effectiveness of providing tax incentives to promote investment is generally questionable'.[72] While the IMF has not been successful in convincing even the poorest, most aid-dependent of countries to refrain from using tax incentives,[73] its influence has nonetheless created some imbalances between competitors who are bound by its arrangements and those who are not. Further research into the impact of IMF policies in this area is overdue.[74] The World Bank, while less active in this area, also generally follows a similar path.[75]

---

70 See the initiative's main website www.oecd.org/department/0,3355,en_2649_33745_1_1_1_1_1,00.html. The status and importance of this effort are still uncertain at the time of writing, yet one should note that its relevance here is limited. It is interesting that even this universal and powerful initiative chose not to address initially tax incentives related to manufacturing, but rather specially taxed regimes (centers). See Easson, *supra* note 3, at 208.

71 Miranda Stewart and Sunita Jogarajan, 'The International Monetary Fund and Tax Reform' (2004) *British Tax Review* 146.

72 See Vito Tanzi and Howell Zee, *Tax Policy for Developing Countries*, Economic Issues No. 27 (IMF, 2001), available at www.imf.org/external/pubs/ft/issues/issues27/. A more recent article by Sanjeev Gupta and Shamsuddin Tareq, 'Mobilizing Revenue' (2008) 45 *Fin. and Dev.* (September) (available at www.imf.org/external/pubs/ft/fandd/2008/09/gupta.htm) on reforms in sub-Saharan Africa says about tax incentives: 'Such incentives not only shrink the tax base but also complicate tax administration and are a major source of revenue loss and leakage from the taxed economy. Because investment decisions depend on a host of factors that often carry more weight than tax incentives, these countries need to improve the business climate while keeping the tax considerations as neutral as possible for investors.'

73 See, e.g., Gupta and Tareq, *supra* note 72.

74 Exceptional in this context is Stewart and Jogarajan, *supra* note 71.

75 See, e.g., Wayne Thirsk (ed.), *Tax Reform in Developing Countries* (World Bank, 1997); Joel Bergsman, *Advice on Taxation and Tax Incentives for Foreign*

It was explained above that there is significant academic opposition to tax incentives. Similarly, the various, international economic organizations all oppose the use of tax incentives as a general matter. However, the contradictions inherent in the arguments against tax incentives, coupled with a universal insistence on using tax incentives by developing countries, has resulted in a gradual shift in focus of the academic and policy discourse from the desirability of tax incentives in general towards their acceptance as something of a necessary evil. This has led to a shift in the focus of debate to the need to carefully use and design tax incentives.[76]

In conclusion, in practice, the policies of the international economic organizations generally involve a tacit permission for the use of such incentives. It is clear that the usual, market-based advice promoted by these institutions has been less influential in this context, since the large majority of developing countries do not believe that scrapping such incentives would result in an economic gain. It seems that despite the central role of the international institutions in the practice of development and their general opposition to tax incentives – opposition shared by this author – they are unlikely to be successful in contributing to progress in the use of tax measures as development promoting devices as called for by this chapter.

C. Role of Developed Countries

A different preliminary conclusion must be drawn regarding another set of important actors in the context of tax incentives – the developed countries. It is not difficult to understand the important role they play in the process of developing countries' development. They regulate and often tax the investors in developing countries, who overwhelmingly reside or headquarter in developed countries. They also set the tone on the world stage and inside international organizations where international trade and investment regimes are designed. Finally, developed countries are heavily involved in activities in support of development and devote

---

Direct Investment (1999); and Louis T. Wells, Jr, Nancy J. Allen, Jacques Morisset and Neda Pirnia, *Using Tax Incentives to Compete for Foreign Investment: Are They Worth the Costs?* (International Finance Corporation and World Bank, 2001).

[76] See, e.g., OECD, *Corporate Tax Incentives for Foreign Direct Investment* (2001). For a similar, yet consistently cautious approach to tax incentives, see OECD, *Checklist for Foreign Direct Investment Incentive Policies* (2003), available at www.oecd.org/dataoecd/45/21/2506900.pdf.

significant resources to this goal.[77] This section focuses on the most relevant aspects of developed country involvement. It analyses the efficacy of such involvement and its effect on the chances of developing countries to grow using tax incentives.

1. Tax sparing and matching credits

The most direct and controversial[78] measure taken by developed countries in support of tax incentive programs of developing countries to date is their agreement to include tax sparing provisions in tax treaties that they conclude with developing countries.[79] It is also an increasingly popular measure[80] despite the controversy over its effectiveness and its disfavor by international organizations.[81]

Tax sparing applies for countries that operate a foreign tax credit system, rather than an exemption system, for corporate profits. It amends the normal foreign tax credit rules[82] to make certain that tax incentives granted by developing countries benefit the foreign investors that they target rather than others, allowing these incentive programs a chance of

---

77 This is true regardless of one's opinion about the sufficiency of aid in general.

78 For a comprehensive review of the debate and the literature, see Kim Brooks, 'Denying Tax Sparing Provisions: Another Way for High-Income Countries to Dictate the Tax Policy of Low-Income Countries?', paper presented at the annual meeting of the Law and Society Association, Berlin, Germany, 25 July 2007 (unpublished manuscript, 2008-12-11), available at www.allacademic.com/meta/p177927_index.html.

79 For the origins of the practice, see, e.g., Stanley S. Surrey, 'The Pakistan Tax Treaty and "Tax Sparing"' (1958) 11 *National Tax Journal* 156.

80 However, some international organizations and some countries have expressed doubts about, or opposition to, tax sparing. See OECD, *Tax Sparing: A Reconsideration* (1998). The United States has consistently opposed the use of tax sparing. See, e.g., Paul R. McDaniel, 'The U.S. Tax Treatment of Foreign Source Income Earned in Developing Countries: A Policy Analysis' (2003) 35 *George Washington International Law Review* 265, 291–2. For the history of the position, see Richard D. Kuhn, 'United States Tax Policy with Respect to Less Developed Countries' (1963) 32 *George Washington Law Review* 262. See also Damian Laurey, 'Reexamining U.S. Tax Sparing Policy with Developing Countries: The Merits of Falling in Line with International Norms' (2000) 20 *Virginia Tax Review* 467, 480.

81 See Victor Thuronyi, 'Recent Treaty Practice on Tax Sparing' (2003) 29 *Tax Notes International* 301.

82 For a more detailed explanation, see Brauner, *supra* note 17.

success.[83] If the investor resides in a country that employs an exemption double taxation relief system rather than foreign tax credits, then there is no residual taxation by the residence country and the value of tax incentives is preserved. Some foreign investors may not suffer residual residence country taxation because of their particular tax position.[84] Others choose not to repatriate the earnings generated in the developing countries and hence defer – sometimes indefinitely – the residual taxation by the residence countries.[85]

Tax sparing is typically granted by developed countries in tax treaties with developing countries.[86] However, if one believes in the desirability of tax sparing then there is no reason to limit its use to tax treaties. A country may simply provide for tax sparing in its domestic (unilateral) foreign tax credit rules. This would require a country to create a list of target countries, or perhaps even particular tax incentives that may benefit from the sparing. Yet this is not extraordinary; countries often use black and white lists in their domestic tax laws. Such an approach would better reflect a commitment to tax sparing as a desirable policy device and allow a country to use it in cases of countries with which the conclusion of a tax treaty may not be probable for reasons unrelated to development. Research into the practice of tax sparing does not reveal any give-and-take involved in the inclusion of tax sparing in treaties between developed and developing countries.[87] As a result, the treaty context is not an

---

83 A similar mechanism that is often mentioned is the matching credit, i.e., the allowance of a fixed rate of a foreign tax credit regardless of actual taxation or tax rates in the source countries. This less popular mechanism is typically used in tax treaties and effectively embodies a taxing rights division or tax sharing that is formula-based. See, e.g., Convention between the Kingdom of the Netherlands and the Government of the Federative Republic of Brazil for the avoidance of double taxation and the prevention of fiscal evasion with respect to taxes on income (effective 1 January 1992) Art. 23.

84 One such tax position would be that of chronic excess credit. This, however, cannot serve as an argument against the use of tax sparing since a chronic excess credit position does not indicate strength, as is evident by the fact that most US multinational enterprises have excess limitation positions. Development policy may not want to encourage foreign direct investment by corporations with excess credit rather than excess limitation positions.

85 This is based on the dogmatic adherence to the legal fiction of the corporation as a separate legal personality. Most or all countries employ some anti-abuse or anti-deferral rules, such as the United States subpart F rules (see ss. 951–965), yet these rules never apply to genuine bona fide income generated through business activities in the subsidiaries' countries of residence.

86 See Brooks, *supra* note 78.

87 This may not be true for treaties between developing countries.

appropriate vehicle for instituting tax sparing measures. Furthermore, no country has conducted serious follow-up studies to assess the efficacy of tax sparing, bolstering the conclusion that it is probably considered mainly an altruistic mechanism rather than a true treaty measure.[88]

The design of tax sparing provisions may be important. Similarly to tax incentives themselves, tax sparing provisions are quite standard even though they do not follow a 'model'. One design issue relates to the type of income protected by the provision – passive or active. There is no reason to distinguish between the two unless one wishes to promote only foreign direct investment. In practice, the distinction is relevant for countries that use an exemption for one type of income (often, active income) and a credit for the other, a non-substantive distinction.[89] Another formal distinction is between individual and corporate taxpayers, excluding the former, possibly for anti-abuse reasons.[90] Similarly, abuse concerns lead countries to sometimes refer to specific tax incentives when they grant tax sparing.[91] A more serious distinction is the time limitation on tax sparing: some articles are general, and some sunset, yet in reality these often are extended.[92] The OECD survey reviews these design issues and suggests 'best practices', which focus on abuse concerns.[93]

Finally, the debate over tax sparing is confused. The opposition to it is based on immutable aspects of our current international tax regime – self-interest begets a lack of cooperation among countries (though admittedly there are very loose, decentralized coordination conventions). What the proponents of tax sparing really argue is that the current regime is unfair. Interestingly, their view corresponds to one recently popular alternative to our current regime: a formula-based system that would potentially result in a tax base sharing mechanism that would be more receptive to mechanisms such as tax sparing.[94] It could grant countries exclusive rights to tax certain incomes. A critical point is that only

---

88 See also the OECD report, *Tax Sparing: A Reconsideration* (1998).

89 Brooks, *supra* note 78.

90 *Ibid.* 20–21.

91 *Ibid.* 21–2.

92 *Ibid.* 22–3.

93 For an analysis of design issues and the OECD suggestions, see OECD report, *supra* note 88, at 24–8.

94 See, e.g., Reuven S. Avi-Yonah and Kimberly A. Clausing, *Reforming Corporate Taxation in a Global Economy: A Proposal to Adopt Formulary Apportionment*, Hamilton Project Discussion Paper 2007-08 (Brookings Institution, 2007).

through enhanced international cooperation and coordination of tax policies could these forms of mechanisms be advanced in a non-altruistic manner. This is one demonstration of the desirability of enhanced cooperation for developing countries.

2. Double tax relief

A distinct but related question relates to the choice of a double tax relief mechanism by developed countries and its effect on development. Karen Brown has suggested that moving to an exemption system would be beneficial to United States' investment in developing countries, particularly in Africa, since it would lead to enhanced effectiveness of developing countries' tax incentive programs.[95] Paul McDaniel responded that a similar result may be achieved through corrections made to our foreign tax credit rules, and that it is not clear that a complete or partial switch would in fact enhance investment in developing countries in general or in African countries in particular.[96] Beyond this particular debate, the choice between an exemption and a credit system involves weighing a multitude of factors, relative cost being an oft-debated consideration. In any event, there seems to be little evidence that a complete switch to an exemption system would benefit developing countries or United States' investment in such countries. A deeper analysis of this point may be a worthy future project.

V. CONCLUSION AND SOME MODEST PROPOSALS

This chapter has considered the logic underlying tax incentives, which are almost universally used by developing countries, with the goal of generating economic growth by encouraging foreign direct investment. It concludes that the primary narrative in support of this action is false and misguided. Tax incentives in their usual format cannot generally assist developing countries in their quest for development. Moreover, they are

---

[95] Karen B. Brown, 'Transforming the Unilateralist into the Internationalist: New Tax Treaty Policy Towards Developing Countries' in Karen B. Brown and Mary Louise Fallows (eds), *Taxing America* (1996); Karen B. Brown, 'Missing Africa, Should U.S. International Tax Rules Accommodate Investment in Developing Countries?' (2002) 23 *University Pennsylvania Journal International Economic Law* 45. See also Karen B. Brown, 'Harmful Tax Competition: The OECD View' (1999) 32 *George Washington Journal of International Law and Economics* 311.

[96] McDaniel, *supra* note 80.

not truly used by developing countries with development in mind, but rather as a shield to alleviate the harm of tax competition. An obvious consequence of this observation is that developing countries should, if possible, refrain from using such tax incentives, unless they are in a position to specifically identify their goals and tailor them for their needs, based on rigid and independent research, and are able to fine-tune them and monitor their effect (and success or failure) over time.

It is further concluded in this chapter that developed countries play a central role in the success of developing countries in their employment of tax incentives. However, the focus to date on tax sparing as the primary step taken by developed countries to support this endeavor is misguided, particularly when it is applied haphazardly with little research and understanding of its effects.

One overall solution that would directly deal with the controversy would be an international (formulary) reform of business taxation that would likely have other merits as well. However, this may seem an extreme solution that requires a massive effort in global political organization. It also would require more research, particularly because the details of such reform will dictate the losers and winners that result.

Developed countries interested in supporting development could also create tax incentives of their own rather than support tax incentives employed by developing countries. Investors residing in developed countries are naturally more sensitive to their residence country taxation than to source taxation, yet direct reduction of residence country taxation to investors in developing countries may be very problematic. Tax planning, corruption and the lack of integrity of the domestic tax systems may make this second proposal difficult to implement. Yet, it may be useful to use this possibility on a very limited, targeted basis.

Third, a less extreme example of a measure that developed countries may adopt may be to implement tax incentives for business or investment in their own tax system, for the benefit of developing country residents. In particular, the opening of developed countries' markets for trade and relief of the tax burden there may be useful.

Finally, developed countries that seek to support development may be most influential in the support of international cooperation and coordination of tax policy initiatives. If the argument made in this chapter – that much of the difficulty of the current state of tax incentives is a result of tax competition – is correct, then breaking the competition trap may be the most important challenge, beyond unilateral and smaller scale reform. The creation of a forum for the discussion of cooperation and coordination of tax matters may be a crucial first step. This step should also be in the interest of developed countries, since they suffer some of the consequences of tax competition themselves. Indeed, if support for such a forum is not forthcoming, developed countries may otherwise find themselves excluded from an inevitable organization of developing countries, aiming to curb crippling tax competition.

3. The tragic choices of tax policy in a globalized economy

Tsilly Dagan

I. INTRODUCTION

Tax is considered one of the main vehicles for debating the sometimes conflicting normative considerations underlying our collective lives in the state. Tax decisions are known for affecting the size and distribution of the national welfare pie, but they are also highly significant for taxpayers' identities and the types of communities we live in.

Ordinarily, when we discuss normative questions of tax policy we envision a country ruled by a sovereign that is entrusted with exclusive legislative powers. The sovereign, we would like to believe, designs tax rules that are compatible with the underlying normative values shared by its constituents. Ideally, the sovereign would aim to maximize the welfare pie (efficiency) and justly (re)distribute it, while reinforcing citizens' identity, supporting their communities and representing their democratically pronounced collective will.

Globalization in general, and international taxation in particular, change this setting dramatically. Zooming out to the international level, we realize that the powerful sovereign we envisioned is but one of 200 or so sovereigns that compete with each other. They compete for investments, for residents and for tax revenues. Such set-changing requires rethinking of existing norms.

The competition for residents and investments undermines the very basis for countries' vision about tax policy. It renders tentative and conditional everything from efficiency to redistribution and even the very concepts of community, national identity and democratic participation. In classic tax policy discussions, tax is a compulsory tool to be used by the state to overcome collective action problems in financing public goods. Absent international tax competition, policy-makers could design their tax policy with at least one clear thing in mind: the group of people (their residents or in some cases their citizens) whose interests they are supposed to serve, and to whom they are accountable.

Once the relevant group is clear, tax policy-makers need to set their goals (e.g., maximizing welfare, promoting distributive justice and supporting desirable social institutions and communities) and determine the optimal strategies to obtain them. These goals often conflict and require sophisticated balancing. This makes policy-making anything but trivial, but at least it is relatively clear who we would like the policy to touch upon and what are the means available for the task.

Tax competition[1] adds another rather dramatic dimension of complexity to the mix. Competition provides taxpayers with an alternative: to shift either their capital, their residency, or even their citizenship, to another country. In the extreme case, tax competition changes taxation from the mandatory regime it used to be, to a regime that is basically elective, or more precisely, elective for some. Tax competition is, of course, by no means perfect competition. There are some barriers to shifting capital and higher barriers to shifting residency from country to country, and tax issues are certainly not the only consideration affecting residency, investment and citizenship choices. Yet it seems plausible to assume that, at least for some individuals and even more so for some enterprises, altering the taxing jurisdiction is viable enough an option that it may actually affect their investment, residency or even their citizenship decisions.

By providing such taxpayers with a viable alternative, tax competition gradually turns the tax policy decision-making process on its head. The state no longer only makes compulsory demands on its subjects in order to promote the collective goals of a given group. Instead, the state increasingly acts as a *recruiter*, to solicit investments as well as residents from the global arena. Thinking strategically, the government needs to provide incentives that both maximize the benefits to the current constituency, and also attract 'the right kind' of residents, investors and investments. And since the tax strategy being adopted affects (among other things) the incentives of individuals as well as multinational enterprises to be (or to become) residents and/or investors in the country, the policy adopted should be competitive with the policies of other, competing, countries.

Different groups of potential taxpayers can offer and provide different benefits to the state in terms of efficiency, distribution, political power

---

1 Where countries compete for capital, residents and investors by providing tax incentives.

and even the group's collective identity. Policy-makers thus shape not only the size of the welfare pie and the way it is distributed but also the size and make of the very group they are supposed to represent. In fact, designing the size and composition of the group is not optional for policy-makers in a competitive world, as – whether they like it or not – their decisions will affect both factors. Tax policy goals are no longer tailored to fit a set group of constituents. Instead, the group of taxpayers and the regime[2] designed for it are being shaped and molded simultaneously. Surprisingly, perhaps, these seemingly additional powers of policy-makers to shape the group of their constituents undermine their ability to set policy goals to match some of the classic goals of tax policy.

The bottom line is that classic goals of tax policy are seriously affected by tax competition. The incentive to cater to the preferences of the more attractive and mobile among the potential residents and investors pushes policy-makers to curtail states' redistribution functions. It requires them to choose between their original constituents and others – possibly more attractive ones (in terms of their own political interests as well as in terms of the collective welfare pie); it induces them to trade democratic participation traditions of voice for exit-based practices and to highlight the importance of mobility as a relevant factor (though by no means the only factor) in gaining economic rights and benefits.

In what follows I will commence by briefly presenting what I consider to be the key normative underpinnings of tax policy. I will then discuss tax competition and focus on its effect on these normative considerations.

II. GOALS OF INCOME TAX POLICY IN A CLOSED ECONOMY

Income tax is traditionally viewed as a vehicle for allocating the costs of government in an equitable and efficient manner.[3] Under this canonical description, income tax aspires to achieve the sometimes conflicting goals of maximizing social welfare while promoting distributive justice.

---

[2] Of course, tax policy is not the only policy that affects investors and residents' decisions. This chapter, however, focuses on tax policy.

[3] See, e.g., Adam Smith, *An Inquiry into the Nature and Causes of the Wealth of Nations* (4th edn, 1925) 310–11; Liam Murphy and Thomas Nagel, *The Myth of Ownership* (2002) 12; see also Michael J. Graetz and Deborah H. Schenk, *Federal Income Taxation: Principles and Policies* (4th edn, 2002) 25–7.

In modern times it is widely believed that tax should be delinked from the benefits one obtains from the state and should instead be determined according to an individual taxpayer's ability to pay – a concept broadly based on her material wellbeing.[4] The idea underlying ability to pay taxation seems to be that the state has grown so distinct and meaningful that it is no longer feasible, and more significantly, it is no longer important, to measure the level of services provided by the state to each individual. Thus, taxpayers should pay their part ('equal sacrifice' being the established standard) in financing the public fisc, simply because they are part of the group. Their taxes, as well as the public goods to which they are entitled, should be based on some function of *distributive justice* focused on taxpayers' material wellbeing rather than on the benefit they receive from being members. Indeed, income taxation is considered a key tool (some even argue that it is *the* optimal tool)[5] for income redistribution. Progressive taxation is thus widely accepted as the key mechanism for financing the welfare state, irrespective of the benefits one reaps from the state.

A good tax policy will also promote *efficiency* in order to maximize the social welfare pie given (distributively just) taxation. The challenge is to promote tax policies that maximize social welfare (by minimizing the distortion created by tax) and justly distribute the (increased) welfare pie to achieve more desirable distribution.[6] While public finance experts agree that lump-sum taxation is the least distortive (and thus most efficient) tax, they view it as unfeasible and recommend optimal taxation

---

[4] See, e.g., Richard A. Musgrave, 'Ability to Pay' in *Encyclopedia of Taxation and Tax Policy* (2005) 1. Distribution does not and should not focus on material wellbeing alone. Attributes such as health, physical state, marital status, gender, prestige, quality of living, and level of education do not necessarily translate into material differences, yet they certainly affect people's wellbeing. See Amartya Sen, *Inequality Reexamined* (1992) 150; Edward J. McCaffery, 'Tax's Empire' (1996) 85 *Georgetown Law Journal* 71, 106. Taxation, which is the main vehicle for redistribution, simply cannot ignore such other attributes of taxpayers, especially when it is often advocated as the only appropriate tool for redistribution. See, e.g., Louis Kaplow and Steven Shavell, 'Why the Legal System is Less Efficient than the Income Tax in Redistributing Income' (1994) 23 *J Legal Studies* 667. But the discussion of these non-material attributes is beyond the scope of this chapter.

[5] See, e.g., Kaplow and Shavell, *supra* note 4.

[6] In traditional thinking, efficiency was understood as requiring 'neutrality' – keeping taxation from interfering with the free market. See, e.g., Joel Slemrod and Jon Bakija, *Taxing Ourselves* (1996) 103.

in lieu.[7] Optimal taxation focuses on minimizing the deadweight loss caused by taxation. Hence it recommends that we impose higher taxes on inelastic activities (i.e., activities in which taxpayers are likely to engage at approximately the same level with or without taxation) than on elastic ones, as the effect of tax on the latter would be greater, and with it the deadweight loss.

Beyond these classic normative considerations, tax is a powerful social instrument that also participates in the construction of people's identities.[8] It affects the way in which people perceive themselves and influences the way in which they interact with others. Income tax law reflects – and simultaneously shapes – a certain vision of the self, as well as taxpayers' functions in various contexts. When, for example, income taxation acknowledges some differences (e.g., ability to pay, marital status, costs of personal assistance) while ignoring others (e.g., disability, the taxpayer living with a partner or her childcare expenses), it reinforces a certain conception of a taxpayer and undermines alternatives. In doing so, it draws on some image of an archetypical individual taxpayer and at the same time shapes it.[9] If we assume an archetypical taxpayer to be healthy, married, childless, or living near his workplace, we exclude those who are disabled, single, have children, or live farther away from their workplaces. These assumptions are not merely expressive. They obviously entail real-life consequences. Thus, for instance, in many countries the expenses of a taxpayer on childcare, health, and her commute to work are considered personal expenses and thus non-deductible, while her expenses on work-related travel, personal assistance, etc. are allowed.

Tax may thus affect not only taxpayers' perception of themselves and others but also their choices (to live away from work, to go out to work or stay at home). Assuming enough taxpayers change their choices, social meanings may change and social norms may be altered. As a result, tax may affect the ways in which taxpayers function within their families, communities and workplaces. Moreover, the make-up, size and nature of the communities that taxpayers form and the social institutions that they

---

[7] See McCaffery, *supra* note 4, at 170–77; David A. Weisbach, 'Line Drawing, Doctrine, and Efficiency in the Tax Law' (1999) 84 *Cornell L Rev.* 1627, 1655–6).

[8] See, e.g., McCaffery, *supra* note 4, at 106; Edward J. McCaffery, *Fair Not Flat: How to Make the Tax System Better and Simpler* (2002) 114; Miranda Stewart, 'Domesticating Tax Reform: The Family in Australian Tax and Transfer Law' (1999) 21 *Sydney Law Review* 453.

[9] See Tsilly Dagan, 'Commuting' (2006) 26 *Virginia Tax Review* 185.

construct may change.[10] Accordingly, a comprehensive analysis of income taxation must consider, alongside the traditional goals of efficiency and distributive justice, the less traditional notions of identity and community.

Finally, as the key source of finance for government, as well as one of the key issues of concern for voters everywhere, tax is also one of the most prominent manifestations of participation in democratic societies. Having a say on tax policy issues, and the accompanying idea of accountability of policy-makers to taxpayers are seen as a prerequisite for taxation. As the famous 'no taxation without representation' phrase implies, there are (at least perceived) strong links between the duty to pay taxes and having a voice in the democratic process. If one is to be subject to taxation imposed by the state, they should be able to have a say in the process of designing such taxation.[11]

All in all, the sound basis for a normatively justified income tax is a nuanced equilibrium reflecting society's considered judgment of all of the above: efficiency, distributive justice, identity, community and democratic participation considerations. Globalization, and in particular global competition, challenges each of these considerations as well as their 'proper' mix.

---

[10] Hence, for example, tax may support and encourage certain family-related arrangements (e.g., stay at home mothers) and prefer them over others (two-earner families); it supports non-profit organizations, living nearby one's workplace, and gift-giving. See, e.g., Stewart, *supra* note 8; Lisa Philips, 'Taxing the Market Citizen: Fiscal Policy and Inequality in an Age of Privatization' (2000) 63 *Law and Contemporary Problems* 111; Tsilly Dagan, 'Ordinary People, Necessary Choices: A Comparative Study of Childcare Deductions' (2010) 11(2) *Theoretical Inquiries in Law* 588; Dagan, *supra* note 9; Tsilly Dagan, 'Itemizing Personhood' (2009) 29 *Virginia Tax Review* 93.

[11] For a comprehensive analysis of tax policy, democracy, accountability and legitimacy in the international tax context see Diane M. Ring, 'What's at Stake in the Sovereignty Debate?: International Tax and the Nation-state' (2008) 49(1) *Virginia Journal of International Law* (Fall) 155. For some examples of the intricate links between taxes and democratic participation, see, e.g., Saul Levmore, 'Taxes as Ballots' (1998) 65 *University of Chicago Law Review* 387; Nancy Staudt, 'Taxation Without Representation' (2002) 55 *Tax Law Review* 555; Lisa Philipps and Mary Condon, 'Connecting Economy, Gender, and Citizenship' in Law Commission of Canada (ed.), *Law and Citizenship* (Vancouver: UBC Press, 2006).

III. IMPACT OF GLOBALIZATION

In the international tax arena, each state independently decides whether and how to tax its own residents and foreign investors. In spite of views supporting multilateral arrangements of various sorts, there is no multilateral organization, let alone a universal government, with the authority to make or even coordinate tax policy decisions. Although some have argued for the emergence of a soft international tax regime[12] there is no doubt that such a regime – even if it does exist – lacks any legislative or enforcement capabilities. Hence, instead of the lone, powerful sovereign we imagined in discussions of tax policy on the national level, the international level presents us with 200 sovereigns competing with one another for investments, residents and tax revenues. Since tax is one of the factors that people weigh in making investment and residence decisions,[13] it emerges as a competitive tool in the game governments play in the global arena. Subsequently, governments must think of tax in the international setting in a way that is quite different from the way they think about it in a closed economy. Instead of (to take the ideal case) setting taxes optimally to promote a government's normative goals, tax competition turns countries (depending of course on the mobility of their residents and capital and on various political and infrastructure constraints) into competitive players.

In this competition, countries do not only offer packages of public services for a price. They must also be aware of their role as recruiters of both investors and residents into the country. In other words, in order to be competitive, governments must aim to provide both incentives that maximize the benefits for their current constituency from the level and the mix of activities and investments, and, crucially, the kind of policies that would attract 'the right kind' of residents.

This double-layered competition for residents and investments alters the very basis for governments' thinking about tax policy, making everything from efficiency to redistribution and even the very concepts of community, national identity and democratic participation tentative. In what follows I discuss the implications of such competitive position for tax policy in a global economy.

---

[12] See, e.g., Yariv Brauner, 'An International Tax Regime in Crystallisation' (2003) 56 *Tax Law Review* 259; Reuven Avi-Yonah, *International Tax as International Law: An Analysis of the International Tax Regime* (Cambridge: Cambridge University Press, 2007).

[13] See James R. Hines, Jr, 'Will Social Welfare Expenditures Survive Tax Competition?' (2006) 22(3) *Oxford Review of Economic Policy* 330, 332.

A. Efficiency

Competition provides mobile taxpayers with an alternative – to shift their capital, their residency, their labor (if possible) and even their citizenship to another jurisdiction. In the extreme case, the result is that competition among governments changes each state's tax regime from an obligatory one, where taxpayers can only choose between alternative behaviors (e.g., work more or less, save more or less, invest time and energy in certain activities or not, etc.), to a regime where the most mobile taxpayers can choose the very jurisdiction they would like to be subject to. This modified perspective alters the role of the government from a central regime seeking to impose the most efficient rules (which usually means: the least distortive rules) on an existing group of individuals, to a market player, facing competition by alternative jurisdictions and seeking to recruit (and keep)[14] the 'best' residents, the most profitable investments and the most beneficial corporations by designing the most attractive regime. Such a market player is interested, perhaps even eager to tilt things in its direction.

First, competition provides an incentive for host countries to reduce their taxes in order to attract more capital. Although it might seem, at first glance, that a country's interest would be to collect as much tax revenue as possible from foreigners, economic analysis explains that the optimal policy for a small host country would actually be to eliminate all taxes other than benefit taxes imposed on foreign investors.[15] The rationale is that, if the international capital market is competitive, a small country (whose market power can have no effect on the worldwide rate of return) seeking to attract foreign investment must compete with investment opportunities offered elsewhere.[16] In order to maximize benefits from foreign investments, the host country has a genuine interest in attracting foreign investors by imposing as little tax as possible. The

[14] Note, however, that while countries are increasingly competing for desirable residents, they are less likely to be able to push away unwanted (individual) residents. This is due to various reasons, ranging from a sense of commitment of governments to their original constituents, to the disturbing fact that such residents are often unwanted by other countries, and thus are unable to immigrate away from the country.

[15] See, e.g., Joel Slemrod, 'Tax Principles in an International Economy' in Michael J. Boskin and Charles E. McLure, Jr (eds), *World Tax Reform: Case Studies of Developed and Developing Countries* (1990) 11, 13.

[16] See A. Lans Bovenberg *et al.*, 'Tax Incentives and International Capital Flows: The Case of the United States and Japan' in Assaf Razin and Joel Slemrod (eds), *Taxation in the Global Economy* (1990) 283, 291–2.

taxes it would lose by doing so will, in theory, be outweighed by the profit to local factors of production.[17]

Second, competition encourages countries to offer tax and spending packages that cater to the needs of the more mobile and more valuable potential residents. Under the classic Tiebout model,[18] in the local government context, competition among a sufficiently large number of jurisdictions, each of which is offering its own mix of tax and expenditure combined with free migration of residents, can provide efficiency gains. Each local government provides a 'package' of public services for a price – the tax the residents pay. Assuming that residents are completely mobile, they can choose a package they prefer for the price they can afford. This, in turn, will provide governments with an incentive to provide the packages which taxpayers desire most, hence the increased efficiency.[19]

Yet, in the international arena (as is probably true for the local government context as well) not all residents are equally mobile and not all of them are equal in their costs and benefits potential. Some residents (e.g., multinational enterprises (MNEs), and certain highly skilled individuals, or those who reside near borders) are more mobile than others (and thus might be easier to lure into the country). Even more importantly, some residents are more highly sought-after by certain countries than other residents. Desirable residents may include MNEs who provide jobs or funds, wealthy individuals who will invest or spend considerable amounts of money, talented individuals who will contribute to the development of local knowledge, or young individuals who will contribute to currently weakening social security systems. Less desirable individuals may unfortunately include the sick, elderly and poor. In a competition, countries have an interest in designing tax and spending packages that cater specifically to the needs of the more sought after and most mobile residents. Assuming a government is interested in maximizing national welfare, this would mean designing a policy that would attract the most profitable taxpayers (i.e., the ones with the smallest

---

[17] Obviously, the country's optimal strategy should be modified when special features that can provide the state with excessive (or inferior) market power, are available.

[18] Charles M. Tiebout, 'A Pure Theory of Local Expenditures' (1956) 64 *Journal of Political Economy* 5.

[19] For a discussion of the Tiebout model in the international arena, see Julie Roin, 'Competition and Evasion: Another Perspective on International Tax Competition' (2001) 89 *Georgetown Law Journal* 543.

demands on the public fisc, and the ones providing the most economic benefits for the national economy).

A third effect of turning the government into a competitive player in a global market for capital, residents and tax revenues, is the motivation it provides for governments to practice 'price discrimination' techniques.[20] Price discrimination allows governments to optimize their tax collection according to taxpayers' susceptibility to tax planning. In a competitive world, taxpayers (especially those who are mobile or those whose sources of income are mobile) have the opportunity to alter their behavior in a range of ways beyond those available in a closed economy. In a competitive global market, taxpayers can use a variety of tax-sheltering techniques in order to reduce their tax liability or, possibly, pay no tax (or even negative taxes).[21] Not only resident's mobility nor the elasticity of their investments' location but also the degree of responsiveness of taxpayers to such sheltering options vary among taxpayers.[22] Thus, in order to maximize the benefits of their economic activity and the level of taxes they pay, a country's best option might be to practice price discrimination: to offer lower effective tax rates for those with inclinations and abilities to tax plan or with opportunities to shift their tax base elsewhere. This may be done through offering wide categories of lower tax (e.g., tax capital at rates lower than labor);[23] alternatively, a country may offer a variety of loopholes (e.g., tax deferral for business income, or through the dispersed holdings of controlled foreign corporations), allowing residents with extensive investments overseas to more freely plan their taxes, and allowing foreigners to use the local tax jurisdiction to plan around their own countries' tax rules.

The bottom line for an individual state, is that the global competitive environment changes countries' national tax regimes from obligatory regimes in which taxpayers have to comply with tax rules (and thus can only choose between alternative behaviors within such regime, e.g., work more or less, save more or less, invest time and energy in highly encouraged activities or not, etc.) to regimes in which the most mobile taxpayers can choose the very jurisdiction in which they would like to be

---

20 Benjamin Alarie, *Price Discrimination in Income Taxation: Defending Half-Hearted Anti-Avoidance* (26 March 2011), available at SSRN http://ssrn.com/abstract=1796284.

21 See, e.g., H. David Rosenbloom, 'International Tax Arbitrage and the "International Tax System"' (2000) 53 *Tax Law Review* 137.

22 Alarie, *supra* note 20, at 24.

23 See Alarie, *ibid.*, described as '3rd degree price discrimination'.

subject to tax, or possibly pay no tax at all.[24] This transforms governments into market players whose taxing and spending decisions are affected, limited and, in extreme cases of highly mobile investments and people, even dictated by their position in the global market. This transformed perspective alters the considerations of governments, as they now have more balls in the air to try and keep an eye on: the elasticity of the various activities within the market; the elasticity of current and potential residents; *and* the elasticity of current as well as potential investments. The tragic choice for governments is thus between joining the game of global competition (and maximizing their national welfare under such competition) while renouncing their sovereign power to unilaterally set tax and expenditure policies, on the one hand, and barricading their borders so as to maintain their sovereign decision-making powers, yet encountering costs in terms of economic efficiency and in terms of their residents' freedom, on the other.

Some have suggested cooperation among countries as a way to bypass this dilemma. Under harmonization, it was argued, countries will be able to cooperate in order to maximize efficient allocation of resources and avoid the costs of what they describe as strategic behavior. Elsewhere I have discussed the costs and benefits of such harmonization, and argued that harmonization does not necessarily entail efficiency gains.[25] In any event, I suspect that collective action problems render cooperation in curtailing competition unlikely, hence, the tragic choice for governments remains a tough one: renouncing much of their sovereign power to the market forces of global competition or enduring the freedom and prosperity costs of closing their borders.

B. Distributive Justice

The competitive setting of globalization limits states in their pursuit of distributive justice as well as in their ability to set tax rates independently. The result of the struggle to attract investments (by lowering the tax rates) and to woo residents (individuals as well as multinational enterprises) by offering attractive taxing and spending deals is the infamous 'race to the bottom': residence and host countries keep reducing their tax rates, and according to the theoretical predictions even to

---

24 See Rosenbloom *supra* note 21.

25 See Tsilly Dagan, 'The Costs of Cooperation in International Taxation' in Eyal Benvenisti and Georg Nolte (eds), *The Welfare State, Globalization, and International Law* (2004) 49 and references there.

the point of zero taxes,[26] thereby undermining their ability to redistribute wealth. Although empirical evidence does not unequivocally support the zero tax prediction,[27] and even though there are certainly other plausible scenarios,[28] it is now widely agreed that tax competition curtails countries' ability to redistribute wealth within countries.[29]

The theory is straightforward: under competition, countries striving to draw (and keep) investors and residents offer attractive taxing and spending packages. This means, on the one hand, lowering taxes on the most mobile elements and, on the other hand, offering those public goods and services that will most interest them. Investors, for example, will seek services that the government can supply more efficiently than the free market (such as infrastructure, security and rule of law). Presumably, they will be less interested in governmental functions aimed at assisting the weaker segments of society, such as welfare, public health and education (in case of types of investors who seek low-skilled workers or

---

26 For comprehensive surveys of the research, see John Douglas Wilson, 'Theories of Tax Competition' (1999) 52(2) *National Tax Journal* 269; John D. Wilson and David E. Wildasin, 'Capital Tax Competition: Bane or Boon?' (2004) 88(6) *J Public Economics* 1065. See also Vito Tanzi, *Taxation in an Integrating World* (Washington: Brookings Institution, 1995) (arguing that rates of tax on capital should approach zero).

27 Empirical evidence does not clearly indicate that the race to the bottom is a serious problem; see, e.g., Sijbren Cnossen, *Tax Policy in the European Union*, CESifo Working Paper No. 758, Category 1: Public Finance (August 2002); Thomas Plümper, Vera E. Troeger and Hannes Winner, 'Why Is There No Race to the Bottom in Capital Taxation? Tax Competition among Countries of Unequal Size, Different Levels of Budget Rigidities and Heterogeneous Fairness Norms' (2009) 53(3) *International Studies Quarterly* 761. 'No doubt, the prediction of zero capital tax rates was not in line with reality when it was first formulated and it did not come true since.' See also Hines, *supra* note 13, at 331.

28 See, e.g., Hines, *supra* note 13, at 331, arguing that it is also possible that globalization will invigorate advanced economies, thereby making them more able to support significant social welfare spending.

29 For a detailed analysis of the phenomenon of tax competition, see Reuven S. Avi-Yonah, 'Globalization, Tax Competition, and the Fiscal Crisis of the Welfare State' (2000) 113(7) *Harvard Law Review* 1573, 1575–603. It has been argued that tax competition will drive tax rates down to a suboptimal level, where states are forced to under-provide public goods. For a formal model supporting this argument, see George R. Zodrow and Peter Mieszkowski, 'Pigou, Tiebout, Property Taxation, and the Underprovision of Local Public Goods' (1986) 19(3) *Journal of Public Economics* 356. Although it is unclear what exactly constitutes the 'optimal' level of public goods (see Roin, *supra* note 19), it is pretty clear that redistribution would be reduced.

no workers at all).[30] Hence, tax competition pushes states to lower taxes on capital and curb redistribution as well as services targeting non-investors.[31]

Competition between states to attract residents may have problematic distributive effects as well if (as seems plausible) residents who benefit from the welfare state have a stronger preference for it than those who do not derive any benefit therefrom (or are at lower risk of requiring its benefits). Indeed, rich taxpayers who are supposed to be on the contributing side of redistribution will conceivably prefer less distribution to more distribution (even if they are altruistic, they may prefer to fund charities of their own choice rather than governmental redistribution). By contrast, taxpayers on the receiving end of redistribution will presumably have a preference for greater redistribution.[32] But higher taxes, which are required to finance the welfare state, might push the wealthy away. If this presumption is true, it would force the government to choose between either keeping taxes high while risking the departure of the wealthy (if they were indeed to leave, it would mean, in practical terms, shifting taxes to mid-level taxpayers) or reducing taxes (and welfare) and keeping the wealthy.

In the extreme case, driving down tax rates on mobile residents and on the mobile factors of production will shift the tax burden to the less mobile (and often less well-off) factors,[33] which may lead to a reduction in tax revenues, thereby undermining the ability to sustain the welfare

---

30 Some differences may arise between features that are attractive to prospective residents (clean environment, public parks, etc.) and those that interest future investors (who might find lower environmental standards attractive, for example). But such discrepancies are immaterial to the discussion in this chapter, the point of which is that neither potential residents nor investors are interested in the redistributive functions of tax.

31 Other factors may have the opposite effect (which is why, some explain, tax rates don't actually race to the bottom). See Plümper *et al.*, *supra* note 27, arguing that while tax competition does, in fact, drive tax rates downwards, other factors – budget rigidity and fairness norms – have counter-influence.

32 Evidence is provided by the US federal system, with regard to welfare at the state level. Unlimited mobility of residents posed a risk of turning states with an extensive welfare system into 'welfare magnets'. This significantly decreased their ability to sustain their welfare systems. See, e.g., Roderick M. Hills, Jr, 'Poverty, Residency, and Federalism: States' Duty of Impartiality toward Newcomers' (1999) *Supreme Court Review* 277.

33 Avi-Yonah, *supra* note 29, at 1624, stating that 'a shift in the tax burden from capital to labor tends to render the tax system more regressive. Such a tax system is also less capable of redistributing resources from the rich to the poor.'

state and, in particular, redistribution. But even under the less extreme scenario, tax competition indisputably puts pressure on countries to reduce their taxes and limit redistribution or else to pay the (political and overall welfare) price.[34]

As mentioned earlier, some have argued in favor of cooperation among countries in order to solve this dilemma: let countries cooperate in order to collect higher taxes. But cooperation does not in fact solve this dilemma, as decreasing rates of taxation does not curtail redistribution for the residents of all countries alike. In fact, poor capital importing countries, where the potential for redistribution is trivial (call them 'poor countries') may improve the position of their least well-off residents by having more capital flow into the country. The reason is that higher taxes, which limit cross-border investments, affect groups within each country differently.

In capital-exporting countries, higher taxes (should the government be able to impose and collect them) may allow the government to collect taxes from capital owners and redistribute wealth. However, the case is different in poor countries. There, local factors of production (most importantly labor) may benefit most from foreign investment. Higher taxes imposed by such countries on the (mostly foreign) investors may reduce the level of foreign investment and thus prevent larger gains from reaching the host's labor. Even if some foreign investment continues and tax revenues can be collected by the government, the option to redistribute through income taxation could be significantly less attractive for those poor country workers. First, a large part (if not all) of the taxes imposed will probably simply decrease worker's net weight. Moreover, poor country tax systems are frequently ineffective and may be subject to a larger degree of tax evasion. Poor country decision-makers may be less inclined to redistribute tax revenues, due to political costs or corruption.[35] As a result, there might be lower profits for labor, without additional

---

[34] Plümper *et al.*, *supra* note 27, at 22: 'Holding everything else constant, countries in which governments are least restricted by fairness considerations implement the lowest tax rates on mobile capital and become capital importers. This result remains valid for the opposite case: governments which are most restricted by fairness norms implement the highest tax rates on mobile capital and become capital exporters. Accordingly, fairness norms come at a price; the price a country with an egalitarian electorate has to pay is the highest when fairness norms are weaker in other countries.'

[35] For an argument explaining why developing countries in particular should not rely on personal income taxation to redistribute income, see Eric M. Zolt and Richard M. Bird, 'Redistribution via Taxation: The Limited Role of the Personal Income Tax in Developing Countries' (2005) 52 *UCLA Law Review* 1627.

redistribution. Thus, in spite of competitive pressure to decrease tax rates curtailing the ability of countries to redistribute, in certain countries the alternative of higher tax rates will not improve redistribution, and might even increase the income gap.

This leads us to another tragic dilemma for policy-makers in a competitive global market. Governments may choose to be competitive or to redistribute. If governments choose to compete, they might lose their ability to redistribute income. If they choose to redistribute (by maintaining or increasing taxes), they risk losing their competitive edge and leveling down the entire national economy.

For poor countries, the choice is clearer and yet not necessarily less tragic. Poor countries are probably better off competing for foreign investment and having funds flow into the country. Yet, while this choice may be preferable to increasing taxation and losing foreign investment, it may mean that poor countries are unable to collect taxes that would provide for redistribution or other goals that are less desirable to foreign investors. Moreover, even if countries were able to cooperate in order to collect higher taxes that could allow for redistribution, a tragic choice would still exist, as redistribution in rich states would come at the expense of the poor in poor states.

C. Community and National Identity

The emphasis on recruiting taxpayers in this global competition requires decision-makers to look beyond their original constituents in an effort to search for other, possibly more attractive constituents, both in terms of their own political interests and in terms of the collective welfare pie. As explained above, the competitive context leads to an emphasis on two artifacts that are not usually part of taxpayers' identity under classic closed-economy tax policy: first, the taxpayer's attractiveness for the state, and second, the taxpayer's mobility. That is, the competitive context places emphasis on exit powers and the use-value of taxpayers. These market features color the relationships between individuals and their governments, as well as between individuals and their communities, with the traits of market relationships, thus reshaping individual as well as national identities, reshuffling community ties and commitments and restructuring political power and even the forms of democratic participation, by trading traditions of voice for exit-based practices.

Taking into account the use-value of potential residents in this way, governments perceive potential residents by their prospective contribution (mostly of economic value) for the country, or by their political impact on decision-makers. Decision-makers therefore ask: 'How beneficial are these potential residents and investors for us?' This criteria undermines the idea of what it means to be a viable part of the community, since potential residents are evaluated according to whether or not they are beneficial for the country. While this perception may be reasonable for business enterprises, it is not when individuals are at stake, because this use-value perception commodifies them and commodifies their interaction with the state. The reduction of the interaction between the state and its subjects to what is no more than a market transaction undermines the idea of what it means to be a viable part of the community, and a member of the state. Instead of being members of the group, residents are evaluated according to whether or not they are useful for the state. This may challenge other merits that one would imagine should be part of the focus of viable immigration policies, such as their cultural significance, national sentiment, shared traditions, or commitment to the community. This use-value perspective may alter the way we value the state as well as the way the state looks at us.

The commodification comes not only through their perception in terms of their use-value, which is commodifying in itself; but also in an even more specific way. It is not any use-value that tax policy encourages, but rather their economic value. The form of encouragement – tax incentives – highlights the economic value of the 'transaction': tax benefits are monetary payments. And tax policy confers larger monetary payments upon people with larger incomes. Thus, it would be the wealthiest potential residents that find it beneficial to immigrate to a country that offers them tax benefits. Paying according to one's economic worth can be viewed as either bluntly trading political power for monetary consideration (in cases where the new recruits are best serving the political interests of decision-makers), or, if political power is not what decision-makers are after, tax benefits simply put higher emphasis on the economic worth (rather than other qualities) of new recruits.

Even more disturbing is that, in this context, the very question of who is 'us' becomes debatable. Are 'we' in any meaningful sense a cohesive group with a shared sense of community – one that reinforces commitment and belongingness? Or is 'us' merely a group made up of our shared interest to increase our collective net worth? The emphasis on recruiting the most beneficial new residents highlights the latter, more commodified version of 'us'.

Taxpayers' mobility raises a slightly different set of concerns regarding the state and the community within it. Mobility stresses taxpayers' provisional status and rewards it. The more impermanent taxpayers are, the better deal they can expect. Foreign investors, repatriates, owners of MNEs and capital owners are all taxed more lightly than those with no available exit option. A policy that lowers tax on such investors may indeed attract mobile residents. As explained below, rewarding mobility entails a risk that communities may become tenuous – dependent on the quality and extent of the services they provide and lacking a sense of belongingness based on some shared commitment of their residents. Mobility may also affect distributive justice if mobility and the focus on market contribution reduce people's sense of belongingness and their commitment to their peer-citizens. It may undermine the willingness and ability of communities to provide significant support to their members.

A relatively short-term, service-focused commitment of taxpayers to their communities limits their emotional and material investment in these communities, as well as their ability (and incentive) to broaden and deepen their interpersonal and other ties to the place where they live. Tax-motivated communities can be expected to consist of a larger number of mobile residents. Mobile residents might be less committed to the local community and more tenuous. Some people and businesses (perhaps those least attached to their communities) will be tempted to trade them for a better tax–expenditure ratio and might be triggered to leave their communities. Their departure might have a snowball effect. If a significant enough number of significant enough members and investors choose to leave, those who stay behind might find the community less attractive or be inclined to relocate. In other words, even if at first only the investors and/or residents who are less committed or do not ascribe a significant value to the benefits of community choose to leave, their departure might gradually erode the community by reducing the benefits others assign to that same community.[36] For individuals, the negative effect of this lack of attachment is even more severe: people who were tempted to relocate because of tax benefits may also be less attached to their new communities, treating them more as economic opportunities than as a significant part of their personhood. Eventually the nature of communities might change and, with it, people's interest in living there. Communities may become tenuous – dependent on the quality and value of the services they provide and lacking a sense of belongingness based on some shared commitment of their residents.

On the other hand, unlimited exit options and viable alternative opportunities may be necessary to build a true commitment to one's

[36] See Gideon Parchomovsky and Peter Siegelman, 'Selling Mayberry: Communities and Individuals in Law and Economics' (2004) 92 *California Law Review* 75, 121.

community. As 'part of what makes our normative communities meaningful is that they are realized through voluntary choice, if not ex ante, then at least ex post … In order to assure that any given community is good *for* people … the participation of individuals in social groups [should be] voluntary by securing the ability of members to decide whether and for how long to participate.'[37] Absent exit options, if one is 'trapped' in a community with no real choice of leaving, it is hard to describe one's being part of the community as a commitment, rather than through various forms of coercion or simply inertia.

Thus, again, in the context of globalization, alongside the drawbacks of competition and the toll it takes on our communities, there is a positive effect of increased freedom and enhanced autonomy. Mobility may make governments realize that their constituents are not captive audiences, and may increase people's control over their lives. The choice between competition and non-competition is, again, difficult in this context, as mobility – and with it the freedom to choose – is not distributed equally. Some people are more mobile than others. Hence, a tragic choice must be made between an open community that enhances people's autonomy, but is less equal, and a community that is less open and thus, hopefully more cohesive and less tenuous but at the same time imposes a toll on its members' autonomy.

D. Democratic Participation

A last effect of mobility, and of the pursuit of attractive newcomers, is their potential bearing on the political processes that govern the state. In particular, it is argued that having the state function as a recruiter may alter traditions of democratic participation.

Accountability is one of the key sources of legitimacy for any tax system. Such accountability derives from the democratic process, in which both voice and exit are important components of adhering to taxpayers' preferences, and for the empowerment of individuals in the democratic process.[38] A government seeking to collect the most accurate citizens' preferences, should use both voice and exit as sources of data. The power to leave is not necessarily less democratic than voice since it provides yet another route for citizens to signal their preferences to the government. It does, however, entail certain disadvantages in democratic terms. Thus, for example, those with easily available exit options may be

---

[37] Hanoch Dagan, *Property: Values and Institutions* (2011) 69.

[38] Albert O. Hirschman, *Exit, Voice and Loyalty* (Cambridge, MA: Harvard University Press, 1970).

less inclined to facilitate change from within. Yet absent exit options, voice loses its impact.[39]

Now consider mobility in a global context and its unequal distribution among citizens. The existence of mobility leads to greater stress being placed on exit over voice, and thus enhances one form of democratic participation relative to the other. Beyond a certain level, exit might be even more destructive, since it would no longer be just another way of conveying one's discontent from current policies, but can rather be an independent contribution to the decline of the state. The departure of strong segments of society also means less public funds (alongside fewer public services) for the remaining residents.

The greater emphasis placed on exit also reshuffles political power. In terms of relative participation and influence in the democratic process, stronger emphasis on exit means that capital owners, as well as young or talented individuals, may exercise more influence over the national decision-making process pursuing a more competitive market, less distribution and lower commitment. Decision-makers may have an incentive to internalize the interests of such mobile individuals into policy-making. If the preferences of mobile individuals or investors are not met, and they exercise exit, the negative externalities on local factors of production may be substantial. Thus, in order to protect the interests of other segments of society (the ones with no exit option), the interests of mobile individuals should be protected. On the other hand, older, middle-income and thus less mobile voters may not appreciate the benefit in competing for capital and residents, and thus push decision-makers towards less competitive, less integrated and thus overall less prosperous countries that might, in the long term, hurt their own interests.

Further, because of the competitive pressure to recruit attractive residents and investors, non-citizens may also have significant political power to affect national policies of tax, expenditure and distribution of wealth. The very presumption that such benefits are required in order to attract some such non-residents into the country may have a significant effect on local policies. Hence, such foreigners may have an important role in local decision-making without having a formal voice in the process. In fact, it is not even actual foreign investors or potential

---

[39] See *ibid.* 34–5: 'the role of voice would increase as the opportunities for exit decline, up to the point where, with exit wholly unavailable, voice must carry the entire burden of altering management to its failings … Voice functions as a complement to exit, not as a substitute for it' and at 76: 'Exit was shown to drive out voice … and it began to look as though voice is likely to play an important role in organizations only on condition that exit is virtually ruled out.'

residents that have this role in the process but rather their imagined portrayals in the eyes of decision-makers. In other words, the best that decision-makers can do is try to assess what might be the preferences of foreign residents and investors to whom they are not even accountable.

Here, once more, decision-makers face a tragic choice under competition: they have to choose between recruiting new members and their old constituents; they have to determine whether they should use monetary incentives to lure new recruits or whether they can afford to avoid it. They have to choose between an open, yet commodified and somewhat tenuous community and one that is glued together by a sense of no viable alternative. They have to focus on the preferences of foreigners (to whom they are not even accountable) and grant them privileges beyond the ones available to their current constituency in the hope that the positive externalities from their prospective investments and residency will outweigh the costs of such benefits.

IV. CONCLUSION

The global competition for residents and investments inevitably transforms the very foundation of countries' tax policy. It alters the way we (should) think of the classic normative goals of income tax policy. Efficiency, redistribution and even the concepts of community, national identity and democratic participation all pose significant new dilemmas due to this new perspective. Under competition tax ceases to be the compulsory tool used by the state to overcome collective action problems and becomes an instrument in competing for residents and capital.

The incentive to attract mobile residents and investments pushes policy-makers to limit tax's redistribution functions; to choose between their original constituents and others – possibly more attractive ones; to depend less on voice-based and more on exit-based practices; and it renders mobility a particularly significant factor for gaining economic rights and benefits. Under these conditions, tax policy does not only determine the level and distribution of tax, nor does it restrict itself to determining the kinds and level of the services being provided. To an increasing degree tax policy determines who counts and who doesn't. By inevitably providing higher incentives for some and lower ones for others, tax policy in fact participates in determining who belongs to 'us'.

4. Economic development and the role of tax in Southern Africa: the South African headquarter company structure

Tracy Gutuza*

I. INTRODUCTION

In 2010, the concept of a headquarter company structure was introduced in the South African Income Tax.[1] The premise of this development was that South Africa, already the headquarter location for many regional operations of investors, is perfectly suited to be the investment gateway into Southern Africa and that this position could be enhanced with tax and regulatory reforms. This introduction of a headquarter regime, which is in fact a reintroduction, must be understood in the context of the role of South Africa within the African institutional structures and the development of the Southern African region. The Southern African Development Community (SADC)[2] Memorandum of Understanding on Co-operation in Taxation and Related Matters states that member countries will cooperate in tax matters and furthermore that member countries

* This material is based upon work supported financially by the South African National Research Fund.

[1] The definition of 'headquarter company' was inserted in s. 1 of the South African Income Tax Act, 58 of 1962, by s. 6(1)(o) of the Taxation Laws Amendment Act, 7 of 2010. The definition was amended by s. 7(1)(x) of Act 24 of 2011 to define the definition of 'headquarter company' by reference to s. 9I.

[2] The South African Development Community (SADC) was established in 1992 and currently comprises of the following countries: Angola, Botswana, Democratic Republic of Congo (DRC), Lesotho, Madagascar, Malawi, Mauritius, Mozambique, Namibia, Seychelles, South Africa, Swaziland, United Republic of Tanzania, Zambia and Zimbabwe. For more information, see the official SADC website at www.sadc.int.

will endeavour to avoid harmful tax competition.[3] In addition, the New Partnership for Africa's Development (NEPAD)[4] provides for the integration of Africa into the global economy and that regional cooperation with integration will be used to address poverty and underdevelopment in Africa.[5] In this regard, NEPAD has identified an African owned framework for development as the foundation for partnership at regional and international levels.[6] It envisages, *inter alia*, economic and investment harmonization and the promotion of intra-African trade and investment.[7] A further factor to consider in the development of the headquarter company structure is South Africa's recent membership in the alliance between Brazil, Russia, India, China and South Africa, known as the BRICS group.[8] The latter has to be taken into account despite the view of

---

3 See Southern African Development Community Memorandum of Understanding on Co-operation in Taxation and Related Matters. The Memorandum was signed by the SADC Committee of Ministers for Finance and Investment in August 2002. Available at the official SADC website at www.sadc.int/index/browse/page/167 and also at www.tralac.org/wp-content/blogs.dir/12/files/2011/uploads/20060629_memo_tax_coop.pdf.

4 The New Partnership for Africa's Development was adopted in 2001 as a programme of the African Union. For more information on NEPAD, see www.nepad.org.

5 Articles 90 and 91 of the NEPAD Framework provide for sub-regional and regional approaches to development. Article 67 also sets out the long-term objectives of NEPAD, one of which is 'to eradicate poverty in Africa and to place African countries, both individually and collectively, on a path of sustainable growth and development and thus halt the marginalisation of Africa in the globalisation process'. The NEPAD Framework document is available at www.nepad.org/nepad/knowledge/doc/1767/nepad-framework-document.

6 Article 47 of the NEPAD Framework states that '[t]he New Partnership for Africa's development centres on African ownership and management'.

7 Article 92 of the NEPAD Framework provides that '[t]he New Partnership for Africa's Development focuses on the provision of essential regional public goods … as well as the promotion of intra-Africa trade and investments. The focus will be on rationalising the institutional framework for economic integration by identifying common projects compatible with integrated country and regional development programmes, and on the harmonisation of economic and investment policies and practices. There needs to be coordination of national sector policies and effective monitoring of regional decisions.' See also Edwin Okey Ijeoma, 'Evaluating Development Projects and Programmes in Africa: The Case of the New Partnership for Africa's Development' (2008) 37(4) *African Insight* 61.

8 South Africa gained membership of this alliance in 2010. See announcement by the South African Department of Foreign Affairs, available at www.dfa.gov.za/docs/2010/brics1224.html.

commentators that South Africa's membership or joining of the BRICS group was for political rather than economic reasons.[9]

As indicated by the use of the word reintroduction, the idea or concept of the use of South Africa as a gateway into Africa through the use of either a regional headquarter structure or a holding company is not new. Historically, the source, or territorial basis of taxation adopted in South Africa until 2001 meant that South Africa was, in effect, a natural headquarter structure for companies wishing to trade or invest in the region. Under this regime, as explained below, foreign sourced income, except for limited taxation of dividend income, was exempt from tax in South Africa. However, South Africa's political situation during most of the twentieth century, that is, its practice of a policy of racial separation, largely prevented the use and exploitation of the headquarter structure to encourage investment into Africa. In 2001, when the residence basis of taxation was implemented, it was accompanied by the first formal headquarter structure regime adopted in South Africa. However, this structure was later repealed due to its not being utilized.[10]

A number of questions arise as a result of the South African authorities introducing a headquarter company structure. First, why is such a structure needed and what is its role? This is a particularly interesting question, given that the headquarter structure may fall foul of both the OECD's Harmful Tax Practices regime[11] and the regional agreement in

---

[9] Narnia Bohler-Muller, 'South African International Relations and the Emergence of China: Is Development at All Costs the Answer' (2011) *AfricaGrowth Agenda* (African Institute of South Africa, AISA) 6; Mildred Pheeha and Dirk Troskie, 'An Analysis of the Inclusion of South Africa to BRIC Countries: The Fit for South Africa's Agricultural Sector' (2011) 8(1) *Agriprobe* 28.

[10] National Treasury of South Africa, *Explanatory Memorandum on the Revenue Laws Amendment Bill* (2003) 38; see also Ernest Mazansky, 'New Headquarter Company Regime' (2011) 65(3) *Bulletin for International Taxation* 166, at 167–8.

[11] It may fall foul due to its possibly being viewed as being ring-fenced from the domestic economy and only being available for non-residents. See the following OECD Reports: *Harmful Tax Competition: An Emerging Global Issue* (1998); *Towards Global Tax Co-operation, Report to the 2000 Minister Council Meeting and Recommendations by the Committee on Fiscal Affairs: Progress in Identifying and Eliminating Harmful Tax Practices* (2000); *The OECD's Project on Harmful Tax Practices: The 2001 Progress Report* (2001); *The OECD's Project on Harmful Tax Practices: The 2004 Progress Report* (2004); *The OECD's Project on Harmful Tax Practices: The 2006 Progress Report* (2006).

the form of the Southern African Development Community.[12] Second, how is the headquarter structure to be implemented? Third, what is the potential effect of the headquarter structure on the development of South Africa and the Southern African region? This third question is particularly concerned with the impact on investment into the region. A fourth question raised is the 'inter-nation' equity considerations with respect to the division of the tax revenues between the various countries involved. In attempting to answer these questions, the chapter will consider the role of South Africa in the region and the different ways in which such a structure has been attempted in the past. The current structure will then be considered with respect to both the encouragement of investment and the allocation and division of tax revenue in the region.

II. WHY IS THERE A NEED FOR A HEADQUARTER COMPANY STRUCTURE?

In considering why there is a need to establish a headquarter company structure in South Africa, two issues can be separated. First, why would South Africa establish such a structure? Second, why would a foreign investor or trader locate its regional base in South Africa?

The answer to the second question is perhaps more easily established than the answer to the first question. According to the South African National Treasury, it is South Africa's location, sizable economy, political stability, and relatively sophisticated financial and commercial sector which make it an ideal headquarter company location for companies wanting to invest or trade or do business in the rest of Africa.[13] Other reasons include the view of South Africa as the economic power-house of Southern Africa, and by some of the whole African continent.[14] These

---

[12] Article 4(3), read together with Art. 1 of the SADC Memorandum of Understanding on Co-operation in Taxation and Related Matters.

[13] National Treasury of South Africa, *Explanatory Memorandum on the Taxation Laws Amendment Bill 2010* (2010) 77.

[14] 'History: South Africa Attend their First BRICS Leaders' Summit in China: Special News Report, (2011) 29(2) *Management Today* 24–5 (May); Tiyanjana Maluwa, 'The African Union, the Southern African Development Community, and the New Partnership for Africa's Development: Some Observations on South Africa's Contribution to International Law-making and Institution Building in Africa, 1994–2000: Symposium (2004) 29 *South African Yearbook of International Law* 5 at 12.

factors, it would seem, make South Africa a natural holding company gateway into the African continent, and in particular, Southern Africa.[15]

The answer to the first question assumes that the economic benefits of attracting foreign investment through the headquarter regime outweigh the potential loss of tax revenue to South Africa. The South African National Treasury has indicated the desire for South Africa to have a reputation as a host of headquarter companies in view of the potential positive effect that such a structure would have on 'creating additional skills and related intellectual infrastructure' in South Africa.[16] Another factor may be a response by South Africa seeking to usurp Mauritius's reputation as the headquarter company location within the region.[17]

Like South Africa, Mauritius is a member of SADC, and it is also a member of the Common Market for Eastern and Southern Africa (COMESA).[18] Also like South Africa, Mauritius has a relatively extensive treaty network which, together with the tax allowances granted to certain companies, allows it to be used as a gateway into Africa.[19] Mauritian companies holding Global Business Licences are commonly used as a conduit company for investing in Africa and to locate the African headquarters of such company in Mauritius. There are two types of Global Licence companies, with a category 1 company being classified as a tax resident in Mauritius and therefore being able to be used in treaty shopping.[20] A company holding a category 2 Global Business Licence is a non-resident for tax purposes[21] and therefore is not able to be used for treaty shopping. The use of treaties when using the Mauritian company structure is important in the context of Africa because Mauritian Double Taxation Treaties with African countries commonly contain a tax sparing provision.[22] The combination of the tax sparing provision,

---

15 *Management Today*, *supra* note 14.

16 National Treasury of South Africa, *Draft Explanatory Memorandum on the Draft Taxation Law Amendment Bill 2011* (2011) 110. See also 2011 Presentation by the South African National Treasury and South African Revenue Services 1 on the 2011 Draft Taxation Law Amendment Bill made to the Parliamentary Standing Committee on Finance, dated 15 June 2011.

17 Thabo Legwaila, 'The Tax Treatment of Holding Companies in Mauritius: Lessons for South Africa' (2011) 23 *South African Mercantile Law Journal* 1.

18 For membership of countries see www.sadc.int and also www.comesa.int.

19 Legwaila, *supra* note 17, at 5.

20 See http://mra.gov.mu; Legwaila, *supra* note 17, at 6.

21 See http://mra.gov.mu.

22 Legwaila, *supra* note 17, at 5; as of 24 January 2012, Mauritius had entered into 36 Double Taxation Treaties with other contracting states, 13 of

the overall low effective tax rate,[23] no tax being imposed on capital gains,[24] the relatively extensive treaty network,[25] the lack of exchange control regulations,[26] the lack of thin capitalization provisions,[27] and the lack of controlled foreign company provisions[28] makes the use of the Mauritian Global Business category 1 licence company a popular structure to use when investing or trading in Africa.

Another possible reason for introduction of the headquarter regime is political and trade relations of South Africa with particular trading partners, such as its BRICS counterparties and in particular with China.

Although one could speculate on the economic and political reasons for the establishment of the headquarter company structure, the one certainty of a headquarter company structure is the effect it has on the allocation or division of tax revenues between the countries involved, namely the investor (resident country), the headquarter country (South Africa), and the investee country (the neighbouring African or SADC member country). The headquarter company would primarily operate as a conduit for the income of the investor company. By acting as a conduit for the income of the investor company, the headquarter structure may qualify as one of the OECD's Harmful Tax Practices.

However, given South Africa's OECD observer status and the possible future membership of the OECD, it is unlikely that South Africa would enact a structure that would fall foul of the OECD's Harmful Tax Practices. It is more likely that the two aforementioned factors, namely the observer status and the future OECD membership, would drive South

---

which were with African countries. See http://mra.gov.mu/index.php/taxation/double-taxation-agreements.

23 The tax rate in Mauritius is 15 per cent. See www.mra.gov.mu.

24 For information, see www.mra.gov.mu.

25 The treaties Mauritius has entered into with other contracting states are listed at http://mra.gov.mu/index.php/taxation/double-taxation-agreements. The list as of 24 January 2012 includes treaties with Barbados, Belgium, Botswana, Croatia, Cyprus, Democratic Socialist Republic of Sri Lanka, France, Germany, India, Italy, Kuwait, Lesotho, Luxembourg, Madagascar, Malaysia, Mozambique, Namibia, Nepal, Oman, Pakistan, People's Republic of Bangladesh, People's Republic of China, Rwanda, Senegal, Seychelles, Singapore, South Africa, State of Qatar, Swaziland, Sweden, Thailand, Tunisia, Uganda, United Arab Emirates, United Kingdom, Zimbabwe.

26 Legwaila, *supra* note 17, at 4.

27 Ridha Hamzaoui, 'Mauritius: Corporate Taxation' in *Country Surveys International Bureau of Fiscal Documentation*, available at www.ibfd.org (last accessed 7 September 2011); Legwaila, *supra* note 17, at 4.

28 *Ibid.*

Africa's conformity to the standards set by the OECD.[29] In addition, the OECD Global Relations programme[30] and its call on non-OECD members to associate themselves with its recommendations to preserve the tax base would have affected South Africa's conformity to the OECD's standards.[31] It is furthermore well accepted that the OECD is influential in the tax policies adopted by South Africa.[32]

The OECD's 1998 Report on Harmful Tax Practices focused on four criteria which were also used in the 2006 Harmful Tax Report to determine whether a preferential tax regime was harmful. These criteria are listed as: (1) no or low taxation on the relevant income; (2) lack of transparency; (3) lack of effective exchange of information; and (4) the regime is ring-fenced from the domestic economy. The 2006 Harmful Tax Report indicates that the Committee had reviewed holding company and similar preferential regimes and determined that the regimes of Austria (as amended), Belgium, Denmark, France, Germany, Greece, Iceland, Ireland, Luxembourg (participation exemption), Netherlands, Portugal and Spain were not harmful. Thus, from the 2006 Report, it is clear that not all holding companies' structures are necessarily harmful. These structures would need to be considered against the four criteria indicated above. The South African headquarter company structure is likely not to qualify as a harmful tax practice because it is not ring-fenced from the domestic economy.[33]

In addition to considering whether the headquarter company structure would qualify as an OECD harmful tax practice, the structure may also fall foul of the regional agreements that South Africa has entered into with its neighbouring countries. Article 1 of the SADC Memorandum of Understanding on Co-operation in Taxation and Related Matters defines harmful tax competition as a situation where the tax systems of a jurisdiction are designed in such a way that they erode the tax bases of other jurisdictions and attract investments or savings originating elsewhere, facilitating the avoidance of taxes in other jurisdictions. Article

---

29 See Annet Wanyana Oguttu, 'A Critique on the OECD Campaign Against Tax Havens: Has It Been Successful? A South African Perspective' (2010) 21(1) *Stellenbosch Law Review* 172 at 187.

30 Oguttu, *supra* note 29, at 188.

31 *Ibid.*

32 For example, the format of Double Taxation Agreements entered into by South Africa follows OECD Model Taxation Convention format. South Africa's transfer pricing guidelines follow the OECD Transfer Pricing Guidelines.

33 Section 9I of the South African Income Tax Act does not limit the shareholders of the investor company to South African non-residents.

4(3) provides that Member States will, in the treatment and application of tax incentives, endeavour to avoid harmful tax competition. It furthermore provides that Member States will avoid harmful tax competition by introducing tax legislation that prejudices another Member State's economic policies, activities, or the regional mobility of goods, services, capital or labour.[34]

While it may be that the headquarter structure appears, *prima facie*, to fall foul of the above articles, perhaps the headquarter company must be seen as one aspect of regional integration and regional growth through the foreign investment that it seeks to attract for the region, particularly as regional integration has been noted as a 'corner stone of the post-apartheid government's foreign policy' since 1994.[35]

III. REGIONAL CONTEXT

The New Partnership for Africa's Development (NEPAD) is a programme that was formed in 2001 with the objective of addressing poverty and underdevelopment in Africa.[36] It identified the integration of Africa into the global economy and the use of regional cooperation and integration as methods to address these objectives,[37] with an African owned framework for development as the foundation for partnerships at both regional

[34] Articles 1 and 4 of the SADC Memorandum of Understanding on Co-operation in Taxation and Related Matters.

[35] Harry Stephan and Angus Fane Hervey, 'New Regionalism in Southern Africa: Functional Developmentalism and the Southern African Power Pool' (2008) 27(3) *Politeia* 54 at 55.

[36] See www.nepad.org/history where it states that 'NEPAD was adopted by African heads of State and Government of the Organisation of African Unity (OAU) in 2001 and ratified by the African Union (AU) in 2002'.

[37] J. Botha, 'Towards Africa's Global Integration: Trade, Investment and Development' (2003) 27(2) *Studies in Economics and Econometrics* 53 at 57, where it is stated that '[t]he main thrust of NEPAD is to create conditions within the continent that would see African countries becoming the preferred destination of both domestic and foreign investors', and at 64, where it is stated that 'NEPAD's objectives for the removal of constraints on business activity must be supported by independent and legislator institutions; the development of national policies relating to favourable tax regimes.' See also Ijeoma, *supra* note 7, at 62, where it is stated that '[c]entral to the NEPAD framework is … the need for African countries to pool their resources'.

and international levels. In this regard, NEPAD has identified regional integration and infrastructure as one of its themes.[38]

The main objectives of NEPAD have been listed as: '(1) the promotion of peace, security and political stability; (2) the entrenchment and protection of democracy; (3) establishing a human rights culture and good governance; (4) poverty eradication; (5) sustained high economic growth and development; (6) improving Africa's competitiveness; and (7) strengthening Africa's participation in global institutions, including working for a new global finance and trade architecture'.[39] Therefore, the headquarter company structure should perhaps be seen in this context given the alignment of the views of the South African government in the form of the National Treasury as indicated in section I above, and the main objectives of NEPAD.

NEPAD has identified SADC as one of the regional structures through which it aims to achieve its stated objectives. At a Southern African regional level, the SADC is comprised of 15 African countries,[40] of which South Africa is a member. As is the case for NEPAD, the Preamble to the SADC Treaty recognizes the regional goals of interdependence, the integration of the national economies, and economic integration.[41] In addition, the goal of regional economic development is linked to the attraction of foreign direct investment as is evidenced by Article 5(1) and (2) of the SADC Treaty, which indicates that economic integration and the creation of bigger regional markets are objectives of SADC.

Article 5(1)(a) of the SADC Treaty provides that the objectives of SADC are, *inter alia*, (1) to promote sustainable and equitable economic growth and socio-economic development that will ensure poverty alleviation with the ultimate objective of its eradication, and (2) to enhance the standard and quality of life of the people of Southern Africa and support the socially disadvantaged through regional integration. Article 5(2), in particular subsections (g) and (i), provides that in order for SADC to attain its objectives, it shall, *inter alia*, (1) improve economic management and performance through regional cooperation,[42] and (2) secure

---

[38] The other themes identified are climate change and natural resource management, human development, economics and corporate governance, and other cross-cutting issues. See www.nepad.org.

[39] See Ijeoma, *supra* note 7, at 64; NEPAD Framework.

[40] Angola, Botswana, Democratic Republic of Congo (DRC), Lesotho, Madagascar, Malawi, Mauritius, Mozambique, Namibia, Seychelles, South Africa, Swaziland, United Republic of Tanzania, Zambia and Zimbabwe.

[41] See the Preamble to the SADC Treaty, available at www.sadc.int.

[42] SADC Treaty, Art. 5(2)(g).

international understanding, cooperation and support, and mobilize the inflow of public and private resources into the region.[43] These SADC Treaty principles, objectives and undertakings should be kept in mind when any of the SADC countries embark on the introduction of tax incentives and similar initiatives, especially in the case of South Africa, given its more powerful economic position in the region. The ultimate objective of the SADC Treaty is the economic integration of the Member States, and it is perhaps within this context that tax reform initiatives, such as the headquarter company regime, must be considered.

The implementation of the SADC Free Trade Agreement (SADC FTA), which began in 2000[44] as an objective of the SADC Protocol on Trade,[45] is a further indication of the regional integration objective. The SADC FTA in particular deals with the removal or reduction of import tariffs on imports for other Member States. The SADC Protocol on Trade must also be taken into account, in particular the cross-border investment Article 22, which provides that 'Member States shall adopt policies and implement measures within the Community to promote an open cross-border investment regime, thereby enhancing economic development, diversification and industrialisation.'

The role of taxation in this objective of regional integration and investment is found in the SADC Protocol on Finance and Investment, approved by the SADC summit on 18 August 2006, which indicated, as one of its main areas, cooperation in taxation and related matters.[46] It is also dealt with in the SADC Memorandum of Understanding on Co-operation in Taxation and Related Matters. Article 5 of the SADC Protocol on Finance and Investment provides that 'states parties shall co-operate in taxation matters and co-ordinate their tax regimes within the Region as set out in Annex 3'.[47] Annex 3 deals with cooperation in taxation and related matters.

---

43 *Ibid.* Art. 5(2)(i).

44 Following the signing of the SADC Protocol in 1996. See www.sadc.int.

45 SADC Protocol on Trade, Art. 2(5).

46 SADC Protocol on Trade, Arts 2(2)(i) and 5.

47 Of interest for Double Taxation Agreements is Art. 17 of Annex 1 which deals with cooperation in investment, which provides that states parties undertake, in line with undertakings in Annex 3, to conclude agreements between themselves for the avoidance of double taxation. Article 17(2) of Annex 1 provides that, in line with the undertakings set out in Annex 3, states parties approach their negotiations for agreements for the avoidance of double taxation with countries outside the region on the basis of mutually agreed principles.

The SADC Memorandum of Understanding on Co-operation in Taxation and Related Matters recognizes, in its Preamble, 'the need to take such steps as are necessary to maximise the co-operation of Member States in taxation matters and to harmonise the tax regimes of the Member States in accordance with Articles 21 and 22 of the SADC Treaty'. Article 4.1 of this Memorandum provides that 'Member States will endeavour to achieve a common approach to the treatment and application of tax incentives and will, amongst other things, ensure that tax incentives are provided for only in tax legislation'. Article 4.2 provides a list of tax incentives which are allowed, while Article 4.3 provides a list of tax incentives which a Member State will endeavour to avoid. Permissible tax incentives include: (1) investment allowances in addition to full depreciation allowances; (2) an investment tax credit where a certain percentage of the acquisition cost is deducted in addition to normal depreciation deductions, from the tax liability; (3) the full cost of acquisition of the asset is allowed as a deduction from the taxable profits of the year in which the investment was made; (4) accelerated depreciation allowances; (5) declining balance depreciation allowances; (6) tax privileged export processing or enterprise zones; and (7) tax holidays. Discouraged tax incentives include harmful tax competition evidenced by zero or low effective tax rates, a lack of transparency, lack of effective exchange of information, restricting tax incentives to particular taxpayers (usually non-residents), promotion of tax incentives as vehicles for tax minimization or the absence of substantial activity in the jurisdiction to qualify for tax incentives, as well as the introduction of tax legislation that prejudices another Member State's economic policies, activities, or the regional mobility of goods, services, capital or labour. In terms of Article 4.3, a Member State will also endeavour to avoid introducing legislation that 'prejudices another Member State's economic policies, activities, or the regional mobility of goods, services, capital or labour'.

One interpretation of the headquarter company structure could be that it seems to contradict the SADC Memorandum of Understanding on Co-operation in Taxation and Related Matters. Given South Africa's role in the region and the recognition of South Africa that its development is closely linked or connected to the development of the region, it is unlikely that South Africa would have adopted a regime that goes against the tenets of its regional commitments. The headquarter structure therefore has to be viewed as a regional development structure which enables a multinational company to establish a regional headquarter base in South Africa with its operating structures being based in South Africa or elsewhere in Africa. An analysis of the way in which the structure has been implemented, in section IV below, is indicative of this.

IV. ROLE AND IMPLEMENTATION OF THE HEADQUARTER STRUCTURE IN SOUTH AFRICA

The use of South Africa as a gateway into Africa has arisen in the context of income tax law over a long period of time. It is, however, since the establishment of democracy in 1994, bringing with it South Africa's reintegration into the world economy and into an active role in African politics and economic development, that the role of income tax law in the African context has become more apparent.

The combination of the above non-tax reasons with the tax concessions allowed in the headquarter structure, together with South Africa's extensive treaty network, would potentially be the decisive factors for a multinational or company wanting to trade or invest in Africa in deciding to locate its holding company in South Africa. The requirements to be classified as a headquarter company in terms of the legislation and the required asset base and income streams expected for the multinational company would have the likely effect that such company would then be used to manage, control and finance operations within South Africa.

A. History of the Headquarter Company Structure

The reform of the South African income tax system commenced largely with democracy in 1994 and was part of the strategy of government to integrate the South African economy into the world economy. Most significant, as already noted, was the change from an almost pure source basis of income taxation to a residence basis of taxation. In tracing the headquarter company reforms, four periods can be identified, with the latest being from 2010 onwards. The four periods are the period prior to democracy (pre-1994), the transition period (from 1994 to 2001), the millennium period (from 2000 to 2009) and the post-millennium period (from 2010 onwards). The development of the headquarter structure must be contextualized within the four periods identified.

1. Prior to democracy

Prior to 1994 and up until 1998, South Africa imposed income tax on income which had its source located in South Africa. The source rules have been developed by the South African courts with the tax legislation providing a limited range of deeming source provisions.[48] The source rules as developed by the South African courts place emphasis on the activity of the taxpayer from which the income originates. In *CIR Lever Bros & Unilever Ltd*,[49] the leading South African case dealing with source, the court stated that in order to locate the source of income, the first step is to determine the originating cause of the income, namely the activity which gives rise to the income, and then to locate that originating cause. Thus, the source of business income would be the place where the activities of the taxpayer resulted in the income;[50] for interest income, the location of the services that the lender performs for the borrower;[51] and for income from intellectual property, the source of royalties was the location of the author's wits, labour and intellectual property.[52]

Under the source-based system, a multinational corporation could theoretically incorporate and establish a company in South Africa and use the South African financial and commercial sectors without attracting a tax liability in South Africa, provided it ensured that the source of its income was not located in South Africa. Because the South African source rules are closely linked to the activities and presence of the taxpayer being located in South Africa, if such a company ensured that most of its activities, including its business activities, took place in another African country, no tax would be imposed in South Africa. Except for specific provisions for certain neighbouring countries, the South African income tax legislation did not at the time have controlled foreign company rules or transfer pricing provisions.[53] The structural barriers for the establishment of a headquarter company therefore did not exist. This meant that under a source system, South Africa could have been an attractive headquarter company or a holding company location for investment and trade into the rest of Africa. However, this proposition was never truly tested because, prior to 1994, South Africa was largely a

---

48 Section 9 of the South African Income Tax Act provides the deeming source provisions.

49 1946 AD 441.

50 See *CIR* v. *Epstein*, (3) SA 689 (A) (1954).

51 *Commissioner for Inland Revenue* v. *Lever Bros*, 1946 AD 441; *First National Bank of Southern Africa Ltd* v. *Commissioner for South African Revenue Service*, 2002 (3) SA 375 (SCA).

52 *Millin* v. *Commissioner for Inland Revenue*, 1928 AD 207.

53 Section 9A of the South African Income Tax Act at the time deemed, *inter alia*, the untaxed profits of a foreign investment company to be from a South African source if, first, it was received from a company resident in Botswana, Lesotho and Swaziland and second, the company was controlled by a resident of South Africa. Section 9A was repealed by Act 59 of 2000.

closed economy as a result of its political regime. In addition, South Africa's strict foreign exchange system would have hampered the distribution of funds from the South African subsidiary to its non-resident parent.

2. Transition period

In 1994, a government commission, commonly known as the Katz Commission,[54] was established by the newly elected democratic government, to investigate and make recommendations on the tax reform of the South African tax system. The Katz Commission considered headquarter company structures and recommended that the current source system facilitates the development of South Africa as a major location for domestic or foreign business to base holding companies, headquarter companies and finance companies for investment and trade into Africa, and in particular, Southern Africa. Preserving and extending that state of affairs will benefit the South African economy directly and help the country to acquit itself of its regional development responsibilities.[55]

The Katz Commission recommended that then-current source rules that were favourable for corporate headquarter and holding companies should be further enhanced. It proposed, first, that the tax law exempt certain fee income of such headquarter companies[56] and, second, through a 'statutory commitment that headquarter companies and holding companies established at the time of any change in legislation that affects this favourable status would be protected by delayed implementation, or would be given a phase-in period in which to adjust'.[57]

The Katz Commission recognized both the use of the source basis of taxation as a way in which South Africa would be able to position itself as an attractive location for headquarter companies and the link between the headquarter company concept and the development of both South Africa and the region. The Katz Commission, however, also recommended that the passive income of South African residents be deemed to be from a South African source and in this manner recommended a limited residence basis of taxation,[58] commonly referred to as the 'source-plus' basis of taxation. This would have meant that South African

---

[54] The Commission of Enquiry into Certain Aspects of the Tax Structure of South Africa (Katz Commission), *Government Gazette* 15924, *Regulation Gazette* 5378 of 1994, available at www.treasury.gov.za.

[55] *Ibid.* 82. See also *ibid.* chapter 7.1.

[56] *Ibid.* 52, para. 7.1.7.

[57] *Ibid.* 52, para. 7.1.8.

[58] *Ibid.* 82.

resident companies would have been taxed on passive income, particularly interest and royalty income, irrespective of the source. Under source, this income was not necessarily taxed in South Africa. At one level this is a contradiction of the Katz Commission recognition of the utility of South Africa as a headquarter location. At another level, it is not, as the headquarter company structure is being balanced against the expansion of the South African tax base.

In 1998, following the recommendations of the Katz Commission with respect to retaining the source basis of taxation, a source-plus basis of taxation was introduced.[59] The source-plus basis deemed the source of certain types of passive income to be located in South Africa if such income was received by or accrued to a South African resident.[60] For a company, residence was determined by the use of 'place of effective management'.[61] This meant that a multinational enterprise would still be able to incorporate a company in South Africa and use South Africa as the base for its trade and investment into the region, subject to two provisos: first, that it ensured that the source of income was located outside of South Africa and, second, that the South African incorporated company was not effectively managed in South Africa. With the South African Revenue Services indication that their interpretation of 'place of effective management' is largely centred on the place where the company's day-to-day activities took place, and where decisions were implemented, and not necessarily where the company's high level decisions were made,[62] it allowed the headquarter company structure to continue to operate.[63] Thus at this time, in an indirect manner, the possibility of the

---

[59] By the introduction of section 9C into the South African Income Tax Act under which certain passive income received by South African residents was deemed to have the source located in South Africa.

[60] Section 9C of the South African Income Tax Act.

[61] Definition of 'residence' in section 9C of the South African Income Tax Act.

[62] South African Revenue Services Interpretation Note No. 6, issued on 26 March 2002, titled 'Resident: Place of Effective Management (Persons Other Than Natural Persons)'.

[63] Other interpretations given to 'place of effective management' within the South African context can be found in David Clegg and Rob Stretch, *Income Tax in South Africa* (Durban: Lexis Nexis, 2010) para. 8.3.2, where the view is expressed that the place of effective management is the place at which the central executive management is located. According to their view, it is typically the place where the managing director exercises his function and is distinct from the place where the Board meets and where the day-to-day operational management is located. Similarly, Lynette Olivier, Emile Brincker and Michael Honiball,

South African headquarter company as the gateway into Africa continued.

Perhaps pertinent in the change to residence in 2001 was the 1998 OECD Harmful Tax Practice Report and the statement that foreign source income being exempt from residence country tax amounts to a harmful tax practice because it 'reduces the effective income tax rate and encourages the location of activities for tax rather than business purposes. Since entities which take advantage of these regimes can be used as conduits or engage in treaty shopping, they may have harmful effects on other countries.'[64]

Support for the influence of international sentiment is provided by the view expressed by Olivier[65] that the change to a fully fledged residence basis of taxation was the result of the views expressed by 'international experts' at an international tax symposium hosted by the South African Department of Finance in 1999 that South Africa was 'out of line with the rest of the world as far as the principle on which tax is levied is concerned' and that changing to the residence basis of taxation would align the South African tax system with accepted international norms.[66]

The combination of being a newly established democracy, the desire to be part of the global arena, and the call by the OECD for non-member states to associate themselves with the fight against harmful tax practices, would, it is submitted, have influenced the decision to introduce a residence basis of taxation.

International Tax: A South African Perspective (3rd edn, Cape Town: Siberink CC, 2005) provide an interpretation which considers the substance of the operation, identifying the nature of the business of the taxpayer and the location of this place.

[64] OECD, *Harmful Tax Competition: An Emerging Global Issue* (Paris: OECD, 1998) 32, para. 73.

[65] Lynette Olivier, 'Residence Based Taxation' (2011) 14 *Tydskrif vir the Suid Afrikaanse Reg* 20 at 22.

[66] *Ibid.* 22; see also the South African Department of Finance, *Chapter Four Revenue Issues and Tax Proposals of the 2000 South African Budget Review*, at 66, where it is stated that '[i]n 1999, the Department of Finance hosted an international tax symposium to review the interim reports of the Katz Commission and assist government in responding to its recommendations. The rigorous debate at the tax symposium informed the proposals in this budget, as well as initiatives that will guide future tax reforms', available at www.treasury.gov.za/documents/national%20budget/2000/review/Chapter%204.pdf.

3. Millennium period

With effect from 1 January 2001, a worldwide residence basis of taxation was introduced in South Africa.[67] Initially, the foreign source active income of South African residents which was received by or accrued to companies, where the actual or deemed source was located in a designated country[68] and tax was imposed on that income in the designated country at a statutory rate of at least 27 per cent, was exempt from tax in South Africa.[69] This exemption of foreign source active income was repealed in 2003.[70] Between 2001 and 2003, for multinational companies wanting to use South Africa as the gateway into Africa, this meant that as long as the active income of their South African resident subsidiary was not located in South Africa, such active income was potentially exempt from tax in South Africa.

In addition to the change to a residence-based system, the definition of 'residence' in the South African Income Tax Act for companies was broadened to include companies which were incorporated in South Africa.[71] The combination of a fully fledged residence or worldwide income tax system and the broadening of the 'residence' definition meant that the role of South Africa as a headquarter company location was somewhat diminished.

The controlled foreign company rules introduced in 1997[72] also exempted active income of the controlled foreign company. In terms of the Controlled Foreign Company legislation, the income of a foreign company in which a South African resident holds more than 50 per cent participation rights was attributed to such resident(s). Certain categories of income were, however, not to be attributed to the resident. Although the rules are relatively complex, in general, income attributed to a 'business establishment' in the country of residence of the foreign company would not be attributed to the resident.[73]

---

67 By Act 50 of 2000.

68 A designated country at the time was a country which had concluded a treaty for the prevention of double tax with South Africa.

69 Section 9F of the South African Income Tax Act at that time.

70 Section 9F was repealed by the Revenue Laws Amendment Act 45 of 2003.

71 Definition of 'residence' in South African Income Tax Act, s. 1.

72 By Act 28 of 1997, as amended from time to time.

73 For details, see South African Income Tax Act, s. 9D.

The government introduced at the same time (presumably to relieve the problem of the diminished support for multinational headquarter companies) a formal international headquarter company structure.[74] The motivation for introducing this special type of headquarter company was to attract foreign investors or multinationals to set up regional headquarter companies in South Africa to monitor their regional subsidiaries.[75] This version of the headquarter company regime largely mimicked the source basis of the taxation. However, it was not very successful in attracting multinational corporations to use South Africa as their regional base.[76] The lack of success, it is alleged, can be attributed to the strict requirements needed to qualify as an international headquarter company, the non-residence status of such a company, and the effect of the South African exchange control regulations.[77]

In order to qualify as an international headquarter company, in terms of the definition in the South African Income Tax Act,[78] the company would have to be incorporated in South Africa with the entire share capital of the company held by non-residents. Where a South African resident had in indirect shareholding through, for example, holding shares in the non-resident company, the South African resident's indirect shareholding was not to exceed 5 per cent of the total equity share capital of the company. In addition to the shareholding of the company being restricted to non-residents, at least 90 per cent of the value of the company's assets had to represent interest in equity or loan capital of non-resident subsidiaries in which a beneficial interest of at least 50 per cent was held. Where the above criteria were met, such a company was treated as non-resident for tax purposes.

If these strict conditions were met, the South African incorporated company would not be taxed on its worldwide income, as compared to

---

[74] By Act 59 of 2000 in South African Income Tax Act, s. 1.

[75] See South African National Treasury, *Explanatory Memorandum on the 2003 Revenue Laws Amendment Bill*, at 38, available at www.sars.gov.za.

[76] *Ibid.* 38.

[77] *Ibid.* Mazansky, *supra* note 10, at 167–8.

[78] Section 1 of the South African Income Tax Act 58 of 1962 as at the time defined an 'international headquarter company' as a company: (a) the entire equity share capital of which is held by persons who are not residents or trusts; (b) where any indirect interest of residents and of any trust in such equity share capital does not exceed 5 per cent in aggregate of the total equity share capital of such company; and (c) where 90 per cent of the value of the assets of such company represents interests in the equity share capital and loan capital of subsidiaries (which are not residents) of such company in which such company holds a beneficial interest of at least 50 per cent.

other South African incorporated companies. In addition, as it was deemed to be a non-resident, such a company would bypass South African domestic legislation dealing with outward investment by a South African resident company, namely, the controlled foreign company, transfer pricing and thin capitalization rules. Such a company would also bypass the South African legislation which was specifically applicable to South African resident companies, such as the tax on companies which accompanied the distribution of dividends (secondary tax on companies) and capital gains tax which accompanied the disposal of any asset, whether local or foreign. The secondary tax on companies is a tax levied on a South African resident company when such a company distributes a dividend. This tax, although akin to a dividends tax, differs in that it is the company, not the shareholder, who is liable for the tax.[79]

Although it appears at first as if the legislature had met all the requirements for the establishment of an international headquarter company in the form of a passive holding company and retained the 'source' basis of taxation for such companies, there were some problems with this regime that led to its failure. In particular, the deemed non-resident status of a company in the regime meant that such a company would not be able to use Double Taxation Agreements (DTAs) entered into between South Africa and the relevant African or foreign investor countries.[80] Under the previous source basis of taxation, where South Africa had entered into treaties for the elimination of double taxation, companies which were incorporated in South Africa or managed and controlled in South Africa usually met the treaty residence criteria. The new headquarter company, by deeming an eligible company to be a non-resident for the purposes of the South African Income Tax Act, which would nonetheless meet the requirements of a residence for the treaty purposes, created a potential problem as the taxpayer would not be able to use the treaty.

In addition to the problems of the tax residence of such a company, the South African exchange control regulations meant that such a company would either not be able to remove its funds from South Africa or would do so with difficulty.[81] In other words, the interaction between this

---

[79] Section 64B of the South African Income Tax Act, 58 of 1962.

[80] Mazansky, *supra* note 10, at 167–8, where he states that the non-coordination of tax and exchange control, and the non-residence status of the international headquarter company were the reasons for its failure. He further states that he is not aware of a company that had used the millennium structure.

[81] The Exchange Control Regulations are issued under Currency and Exchange Act 9 of 1933.

international headquarter company structure and DTAs, and with other legislation, was not free of obstacles. The international headquarter company regime was accordingly repealed in 2004.[82]

The lesson to be learned from this experience is that a holistic approach is needed when introducing a new tax incentive for international trade and investment. This holistic approach requires that cognisance be taken of the interaction with other domestic legislation, international treaties entered into, and the views of international bodies. With respect to the latter, one of the reasons given for the removal of the international headquarter company structure was that 'special exemption from worldwide taxation and the foreign dividends tax' could be viewed as an OECD 'harmful preferential tax regime' because it was ring-fenced. The exemption only applied to foreign controlled taxpayers.[83]

At the same time that the headquarter company structure was removed, the exemption of foreign sourced active income of a South African resident was also removed,[84] and a foreign tax credit was introduced for all categories of income.[85] Thus, South Africa adopted a new overarching policy approach to cross-border trade and investment. However, the exemption of the active income of the controlled foreign companies remained in the law.

4. Post millennium

Six years later, in 2010, a new policy approach was introduced, once again with the idea that South Africa was to be the gateway into Africa. The second attempt at the headquarter company structure commenced on 1 January 2011.[86] As was the case for the first attempt, the motivation for the second version is to encourage foreign multinationals to establish regional holding companies in South Africa.[87] Also as was the case for the first attempt, three areas in the South African Income Tax Act were identified as being barriers to the use of South Africa as a headquarter

---

[82] Repealed by s. 12(1)(g) of Act 45 of 2003.

[83] South African National Treasury, *Explanatory Memorandum on the Revenue Laws Amendment Bill 2003*, at 38.

[84] Section 9F of the South African Income Tax Act was repealed by s. 24(1) of Act 45 of 2003.

[85] Section 6*quat* of the South African Income Tax Act as amended by s. 16(1) of Act 45 of 2003.

[86] Introduced by s. 6(1)(o) of Act 7 of 2010 and amended by s. 7(1)(x) of Act 24 of 2011.

[87] South African National Treasury, *Explanatory Memorandum Accompanying the 2010 Taxation Laws Amendment Bill*, at 77.

company regime: namely, the controlled foreign companies rules, the tax on outgoing dividends, and the thin capitalization rules.[88] The concerns with these three areas were set out by the South African National Treasury in their Explanatory Memorandum to the new regime.

First, the controlled foreign companies rules were seen as causing a double administrative burden on the foreign shareholders of the South African headquarter company. This was because the subsidiary of the headquarter company would qualify as a controlled foreign company in South Africa and, in addition, the headquarter company itself would most likely qualify as a controlled foreign company in the event that the country of residence of the multinational holding company had controlled foreign company rules.[89] The South African National Treasury also questioned whether 'the application of South Africa's CFC rules makes any sense if the bulk of the holding company's funds originate from abroad'.[90] Perhaps added to this should be 'and are used in a country outside South Africa'. In other words, South Africa was neither the country where the recipient of the income was resident nor the country where the income arose.

Second, the secondary tax on companies (STC), an additional tax payable by the company distributing the outgoing dividends, as explained earlier, would add an extra cost to the headquarter company because this tax was imposed on a company resident in South Africa at the time of distributing dividends to its parent company.[91] It is worthwhile mentioning that the STC is to be replaced by a dividends tax which will be imposed on the shareholder.[92]

Third, the application of South Africa's thin capitalization rules would affect the tax liability of the headquarter company when it made loans to its foreign subsidiaries and passed on the interest payment to its foreign holding company.[93]

Accordingly, similar to the first attempt, the 2010 version sought to ensure that the regional headquarter company would not be subject to the South African controlled foreign company rules, the South African thin capitalization rules, and legislation which levied tax on a resident company when it distributed dividends by deeming the company to be a non-resident for such limited purposes.

---

88 *Ibid.*
89 *Ibid.*
90 *Ibid.*
91 *Ibid.*
92 With effect from 1 April 2012.
93 *Ibid.* at 78.

In order to qualify as a regional headquarter company, the company must qualify as a South African resident for tax purposes.[94] This means that it must either be incorporated in South Africa or its place of effective management must be located in South Africa.[95] Each shareholder of the holding company must hold at least 10 per cent of the equity shares and voting rights in the headquarter company for the relevant year of assessment and 80 per cent or more of the cost of the total assets of the company must be attributed to equity, debt or intellectual property investments in foreign subsidiaries in which the headquarter company holds at least 10 per cent of the equity shares.[96] In other words, 80 per cent of the total receipts and accruals of the holding company must be derived from foreign companies in which the holding company holds at least 10 per cent of the equity shares. These qualifying receipts and accruals would at least include interest, royalties and dividends. The 20 per cent balance would likely include management fees for management services supplied by South African residents.

A key difference between this regime and the earlier one is that under the current regime, the company retains its status as a South African resident in general, while being 'released' from certain domestic legislation[97] by being deemed a non-resident for the purposes of the controlled foreign company[98] and thin capitalization rules.[99]

---

[94] Section 9I(1) of the South African Income Tax Act provides that 'any company that: (a) is a resident; and (b) complies with the requirements prescribed by subsection (2), may elect in the form and manner determined by the Commissioner to be a headquarter company for a year of assessment of that company'.

[95] Section 1 of the South African Income Tax Act defines residence of a company by incorporation in South Africa or if its place of effective management is located in South Africa.

[96] Section 9I(2)(b) of the South African Income Tax Act provides that 'at the end of the year of assessment and of all previous years of assessment of that company, 80 per cent or more of the cost of the total assets of the company was attributable to one or more of the following: (i) any interest in equity shares in; (ii) any amount loaned or advanced to; or (iii) any intellectual property as defined in section 23I(1) that is licensed by that company to, any foreign company in which that company … held at least 10 per cent of the equity shares and voting rights'.

[97] Section 1 of the South African Income Tax Act 58 of 1962 defines residence of a company by incorporation in South Africa or where its 'place of effective management' was located in South Africa.

[98] See s. 9D(2) which states '[t]here shall be included in the income for the year of assessment of any resident (other than a resident that is a headquarter company)'.

A second difference is that the shareholding in the South African headquarter company is not limited to non-residents. In this way, it can be considered that the provision is not a harmful tax practice in terms of the OECD Harmful Tax Competition Report because there is no ring-fencing of residents or non-residents, and the headquarter company structure would apply irrespective of whether the company is owned by residents or non-residents.[100] One of the OECD's criteria for a harmful tax practice is ring-fencing, in terms of which a preferential tax regime is denied to resident taxpayers or domestic activities. The OECD further indicates that ring-fencing can be identified by the explicit or implicit exclusion of resident taxpayers from taking advantage of the benefits of the preferential regime.[101] The South African headquarter structure, although indirectly, does appear to be geared towards non-resident shareholders, but it is not denied to resident taxpayers.

By comparison, the Mauritian Global Business Licence category 1 company can only conduct offshore business activities with non-residents and in a currency other than the Mauritian rupee.[102] The company is not allowed to own Mauritian immovable property and certain securities in Mauritian corporations and is furthermore not allowed to hold an account in a bank in Mauritian currency.[103] The Global Business Licence category

---

99 Section 9D(5) provides that '[w]here any transaction, operation, scheme, agreement or understanding has been entered into between a headquarter company and (a) any other person that is not a resident and that transaction, operation, scheme, agreement or understanding is in respect of the granting of financial assistance by that other person to that headquarter company, this section does not apply to so much of that financial assistance that is directly applied as financial assistance to any foreign company in which the headquarter company ... holds at least 10 per cent of the equity shares and voting rights; or (b) any foreign company in which the headquarter company ... holds at least 10 per cent of the equity shares and voting rights and that transaction, operation, scheme, agreement or understanding comprises the granting of financial assistance by that headquarter company to that foreign company, this section does not apply to that financial assistance'.

100 The 1998 OECD Harmful Tax Competition, *supra* note 11, at 26–7, focused on four criteria for harmful tax practices: (1) no or nominal tax rates in the case of tax havens and no or low effective tax rates on the relevant income in the case of preferential regimes; (2) lack of effective exchange of information; (3) lack of transparency; and (4) no substantial activities in the case of tax havens and, in the case of preferential regimes, ring-fencing – where the preferential regime is denied to its resident taxpayers or domestic activities.

101 *Ibid.*

102 See http://mra.gov.mu/; Hamzaoui, *supra* note 27.

103 See http://mra.gov.mu/; Hamzaoui, *supra* note 27.

1 company is also limited in its use in that it can only be used for certain qualified businesses, such as aircraft financing and leasing, asset management, consulting services and employment services.[104]

B. Headquarter Company Structure or Holding Company?

Although called a headquarter company in the South African income tax legislation, the structure of the company, in order to obtain the relevant allowances and beneficial treatment, indicates that the company envisaged has more in common with a holding company structure. The only assets that such a company would control are intellectual property assets and loans made to the subsidiary operating companies. It is a headquarter company insofar as it would be the holding company or management company for all the African operations of the multinational or relevant company.

Its role as a headquarter company, even as a regional one, is somewhat limited as it does not have specific rules relating to the tax exempt status of either such companies or the income of such companies, and it does not have low corporate and individual tax rates applicable to such companies. However, the tax allowances for such a company, which apply irrespective of whether shareholders are resident or non-resident, are more akin to a conduit type company, with South Africa being the conduit country for income flowing from a neighbouring country into other countries through the use of the South African treaty network.

While the purpose and motivation of the introduction of the regional headquarter company is stated as being linked to the development of Southern Africa through the company being a gateway into this region, the relevant legislation does not make any reference to the relief being granted only if such operating company is located in a Southern African country or if the income of the headquarter company arises from activities in Southern Africa or any other African country. The reason for not making reference to this may be that it could undermine other relevant legislation, but not making reference to it does undermine the use of the headquarter company regime as a regional development tool.

V. HOW IS TAX REVENUE DISTRIBUTED?

Given that the South African headquarter regime is in place, and that it is the goal to lead the economic development of both South Africa and

---

[104] See http://mra.gov.mu/; Hamzaoui, *supra* note 27.

Southern Africa more generally, the question of who gets the tax revenue still has to be answered. For example, consider a non-resident multinational enterprise (MNE) incorporating or establishing a subsidiary in South Africa (Holdco), with the 10 per cent required shareholding in the company. The South African subsidiary Holdco then establishes an operating subsidiary company in a neighbouring country (Opco) ensuring that it, Holdco, meets the requirements to be classified as a headquarter company.

A. In the Absence of Treaties

Where there is no treaty network, the inflow of interest, dividends, royalties and management fees from the neighbouring country Opco to Holdco will most likely be taxed both in South Africa and in the neighbouring country – in South Africa on the basis of residence, and in the neighbouring country on the basis of source. South Africa will, where the income is not exempt from tax in South Africa, provide a limited tax credit for the taxes paid by Holdco to the neighbouring country's fiscus for the first three categories of income in terms of the South African Income Tax Act.[105] However, South Africa will potentially allow only a deduction for the neighbouring country tax on the management fees income stream because it is likely that the application of the South African source rules will locate the source of the management fees, if provided from a South African location, in South Africa.[106] If the tax rates in the neighbouring countries are relatively high, then the result is that there is no tax advantage for the multinational enterprise with respect to Holdco's taxation in South Africa.

Where the dividend qualifies as a foreign dividend, it will be exempt from tax in South Africa.[107] The absence of the controlled foreign company rules and the thin capitalization rules would mean that funds could be repatriated to South Africa without considering the implications of these provisions with the potential reduced tax and administrative burden.

---

[105] In terms of s. 6*quat*(1) which provides, *inter alia*, that a South African resident can obtain a limited credit where the source of the income is located outside South Africa.

[106] In terms of s. 6*quat*(1) and s. 6*quat*(1C).

[107] Definition of foreign dividend in South African Income Tax Act, s. 1, read with s. 10B, which provides for the circumstances under which foreign dividends are exempt from tax in South Africa.

The absence of thin capitalization rules would also mean that the outflow of payments from the South African Holdco to the MNE would not have to conform to the arm's length principle. The only consideration would be the limitation of the deduction with respect to the interest expense incurred by Holdco. The amount of interest that is allowed as a deduction is limited to the amount of interest received by or accrued to Holdco, with the balance, if any, carried forward to the next successive tax year.[108] In addition, the MNE, as a non-resident, will not pay tax in South Africa on the interest it receives from Holdco as interest income received by or accrued to a non-resident from a South African source is exempt from tax in South Africa.[109] The dividends paid or declared by the headquarter company to the MNE are exempt from tax in South Africa.[110] No provision has been made for the exemption of royalty income paid by Holdco, and in fact such royalty income is likely to be subject to the withholding tax on royalties.[111] The withholding tax on royalties will apply where the deemed source of the royalty income is located in South Africa.[112] The deeming source provisions would apply where, *inter alia*, (1) the royalty income is incurred by a South African resident, unless that royalty income is attributable to a permanent establishment situated outside South Africa, in which case the deeming source rules would not apply;[113] or (2) the intellectual property is used in South Africa; or (3) the royalty income is incurred by a resident and is received for the imparting of, or assistance or services in imparting, scientific, technical, industrial or commercial knowledge or information, unless the royalty is attributable to a permanent establishment situated outside South Africa. If Holdco is a purely conduit company and the

---

[108] Section 20C of the South African Income Tax Act provides for the ring-fencing of interest incurred by headquarter companies.

[109] Section 10(1)(h) of the South African Income Tax Act exempts interest from tax if the interest is received by or accrued to a non-resident. The exemption does not apply if the non-resident is a natural person who is physically present in South Africa for a period exceeding 183 days in aggregate during that year of assessment or if that person carried on business in South Africa through a permanent establishment.

[110] Section 10B of the South African Income Tax Act provides for the exemption of dividends paid or declared by headquarter companies.

[111] Section 35 of the South African Income Tax Act provides for a withholding to be imposed on non-residents who derive royalty income from a source located in South Africa.

[112] South African Income Tax Act, s. 35(1).

[113] South African Income Tax Act, s. 9(2)(c).

royalty income is attributable to a permanent establishment located in the neighbouring country, then the withholding tax would not apply.

From the above analysis, it appears that South Africa would only receive a limited portion of the tax revenue. However, it must be noted that although the MNE would have limited taxation in South Africa, it may be taxed in its country of residence and the headquarter company, Holdco, may be subject to tax in the neighbouring African country. Thus, the overall tax liability of the group may not be substantially reduced.

B. Role of Treaties

In addition to South Africa's economic position being given as a reason for locating the regional headquarter company in South Africa, South Africa's treaty network has also been identified as a factor which would favour the location of the regional headquarter company in South Africa. A comparison with Mauritius, as the other headquarter company location in the region, indicates that Mauritius has entered into 37 DTAs with other contracting states, of which 13 are with African countries.[114] South Africa has entered into 70 DTAs with other contracting states, 19 of which are with other African countries.[115] In order for the treaty network to apply, the relevant headquarter company will have to be resident in South Africa, hence the change in the regime from the first version.

The treaties entered into between South Africa and other Southern African countries generally limit the taxation of the country of residence of the distributing company where the beneficial owner of the dividends, interest and royalties is resident in the state of the recipient company. In other words, the treaties generally conform to the approach used in the OECD Model Tax Convention. Thus, in accordance with Articles 10 and 11 of the OECD Model Tax Convention, the limitation of the neighbouring country's right to tax the dividends and interest income flowing from Opco to Holdco will depend on whether the South African headquarter company is the beneficial owner of the dividends and interest income. Recognizing that the dividends and interest income will eventually be paid to the non-resident (or, possibly, resident) shareholder, it could potentially be argued that the headquarter company is not the beneficial owner of the interest and dividend income in terms of the general treaty definition provisions but merely acts as a conduit company. This means that the use of the treaties allocates the right to tax to the neighbouring

---

114 See http://mra.gov.mu.

115 For DTAs entered into by South Africa, see www.sars.gov.za.

country (where Opco, the distributing company is resident), with South Africa having, potentially, to provide relief for any possible double taxation experienced by Holdco. This allocation of the rights to tax to the other Southern African country does mean that South Africa can be seen as fulfilling its role within SADC and NEPAD as set out in the objectives, discussed in sections II and III above. Where, however, Holdco is considered to be the beneficial owner, then the neighbouring country's right to tax is limited, ranging from 5 to 20 per cent in the treaties entered into between South Africa and its neighbouring African counterparts. This means that South Africa may have the ultimate taxing rights in terms of the treaty. Similarly, whether or not South Africa or the country of residence of Opco as the distributing company is allowed the right to tax the royalty income depends on the issue of beneficial ownership. In particular, as South Africa exempts, under certain circumstances, the interest payments made from Holdco to the MNE, the tax liability of Holdco is substantially reduced in the region. As interest income[116] and dividend income[117] paid by Holdco to the MNE are largely exempt from tax in South Africa, there is no issue of double taxation occurring. South Africa's tax revenue arising from the use of the headquarter structure is therefore limited to the tax revenue allocated to Opco in the neighbouring country, and even this allocation may be limited in the event that Holdco is viewed as the beneficial owner of the income flowing from Opco.

Based on the analysis above, it seems that the new South African headquarter company structure acts as a conduit or flow-through company between the actual country of trade and investment, that is between the neighbouring Southern African country and the non-resident shareholder holding or parent company of the investor or trader, in the event that there are treaties in place between South Africa and its neighbouring country, on the one hand, and South Africa and the country of residence of the MNE, on the other.

VI. CONCLUSION

The South African government has attempted over a period of time to establish South Africa as a base for companies who want to invest and trade in Africa, and in particular Southern Africa. South Africa's strengths within the region are its relatively sophisticated economy, its

[116] In terms of South African Income Tax Act, s. 20C.

[117] In terms of South African Income Tax Act, s. 10B.

financial institutions, and its educated and skilled labour force. It is hoped by the South African government that the combination of these non-tax factors with tax allowances would strengthen the South African economy and this in turn would strengthen the region, given the close links and regional commitments in the form of various regional and African institutions.

The structure of the headquarter company, through limiting the types of income flows, ensures that it is not an operating company but a company which mostly earns passive income, thus ensuring that it is a conduit company. The structure attempts to ensure that the tax liability of the investing company within the African context is limited through the use of the combination of income tax allowances and Double Taxation Treaties.

Only time will tell whether the establishment of the headquarter structure assists in attracting foreign direct investment into the Southern African region and thus assists with the development of the region, especially in the light of the region giving up some of its taxes in order to enhance its attractiveness.

5. Tax sparing: a reconsideration of the reconsideration

Luís Eduardo Schoueri

I. INTRODUCTION

Tax sparing has traditionally been included in the debate concerning tax and development. Such a traditional approach derives from ideas based on the existence of an 'international tax law of development' providing for the rules for the 'proper solidarity between developed and less developed states'.[1]

In such context, it is not surprising that when, on 23 October 1997, the OECD Council approved a report issued by the Committee on Fiscal Affairs on 'Tax Sparing: A Reconsideration'[2] ('OECD Report'), the aim was to reflect member countries' more reluctant position vis-à-vis the adoption of tax sparing.

The purpose of this chapter is to examine the main issues presented in the OECD Report, in order to investigate whether the arguments presented therein can be deemed to be strong enough to convince countries to reject negotiating tax treaties with tax sparing clauses.

After having defined 'tax sparing' and 'matching credit' (in section II), this chapter reviews the main arguments presented in the OECD Report and offers some reasons to show their lack of consistency (section III). Finally, the idea itself that tax sparing and matching credit are mechanisms appropriate only to tax treaties between developed and developing countries will be challenged, since the author argues that there are good reasons for applying these mechanisms in all tax treaties, under the assumption that each contracting state should respect the other contracting state's sovereign decision as to how to exercise their tax policy

---

1 See Manuel Pires, *Da dupla tributação jurídica internacional sobre o rendimento* (Lisbon: Centro de Estudos Fiscais, 1984) 517–18.

2 OECD, *Tax Sparing. A Reconsideration* (Paris: OECD, 1998).

(section IV). This chapter concludes that the OECD tax sparing (re)consideration has taken a paternalistic approach (assuming that tax sparing is only a subsidy from developed countries to developing countries), which leads to a misleading focus by the OECD on whether this mechanism is effective to assist developing countries. Rather, the author argues that tax sparing should be seen as an element of treaty negotiation that aims to respect each contracting state's tax policies and it is on this basis that its adoption should be encouraged.

II. TAX SPARING AND MATCHING CREDIT

The debate between the two basic international tax principles of territoriality and worldwide taxation is a never-ending debate. In tax matters, territoriality may be understood, in general terms, as the principle whereby a state is only allowed to tax facts that have a nexus with its territory, i.e., income arising from sources located within its territory ('pure territoriality'). To the contrary, by adopting the worldwide taxation principle, a state may tax the income derived from both internal and foreign sources. There are certainly several arguments on both sides.[3] Some authors suggest that there is a general consensus for the latter, at least in respect of passive income, in a so-called 'international tax regime'.[4] However, the mere fact that no country is prepared to exempt non-residents from source taxation shows that a complete consensus, and a definitive and uniform solution for double taxation, is not to be found in the near future. Unilateral and bilateral measures to avoid this phenomenon will continue to be the focus of international tax lawyers.

In respect of a territorial approach, although several countries are prepared to exempt some foreign business income (for example, adoption of a participation exemption seems to be a trend in developed countries, at least in Europe), this does not mean that territoriality has been recognized. On the contrary: even European countries will generally adopt a worldwide taxation system and provide unilateral exemptions for only some items of income. Several countries, including the United States, take the approach of taxing their residents on a worldwide basis

---

3 See Klaus Vogel, 'World-wide vs. Source Taxation of Income: A Review and Reevaluation of Arguments' in *Influence of Tax Differentials on International Competitiveness* (Amsterdam: Kluwer, 1989) 117–66.

4 See Reuven S. Avi-Yonah, *International Tax as International Law: An Analysis of the International Tax Regime* (Cambridge: Cambridge University Press, 2007).

and avoid double taxation by means of the foreign tax credit system, whereby taxation in the source country will be offset against taxes due to the resident country.

The main argument for worldwide taxation with a foreign tax credit system is capital export neutrality: tax systems should be neutral, i.e., economic efficiency would be achieved if taxpayers would decide where to invest globally, independent of tax concerns; moreover, the ability-to-pay principle would require residents and non-residents to have the same taxation. However, this argument is not definitive, since the competing principles of capital import neutrality and the (objective) ability-to-pay principle[5] also play a role in supporting the approach of taxation at source. As one may know, the concept of capital import neutrality is based in the source principle, i.e., local investors should have the same treatment that foreign investors are entitled to, and the latter should be equally taxed, no matter where they are resident.[6] This can only be achieved if the state of residence limits its taxation to the income derived from sources in its territory and if the source state grants equal treatment to all investors.

Moreover, the mere fact that countries limit foreign tax credit, e.g., to the amount of tax due in the country of residence, shows that taxpayers investing abroad will always be subject to the highest taxation, i.e., where the residence country's rate is higher, then the taxpayer is subject to paying the difference to his/her residence country; if the source country's rate is higher, than he/she will not be reimbursed for the over-taxation.

When countries enter into tax treaties, on the other hand, they may be prepared to agree on the exemption method,[7] whereby foreign source income is not taxed in the residence country. On the other hand, they will insist on the credit method, similar to their own domestic provisions.

The exemption method applied by the residence state leaves to the source state the decision whether or not to tax. In contrast, the credit method neutralizes any such decision of the source state (at least, where the residence state's tax rate is higher). Upon application of the credit

---

[5] See Klaus Vogel, 'Tributação da renda mundial' in *Cadernos de Direito Tributário e Finanças Públicas* (São Paulo: Revista dos Tribunais, 1994) vol. 7, 133–43.

[6] The ideas regarding 'capital export neutrality' and 'capital import neutrality' were first developed by Richard Musgrave. See Richard Musgrave, 'Criteria for Foreign Tax Credit' in *Taxation and Operations Abroad* (Tax Institute Symposium, 1960) 84.

[7] The United States rejects the exemption method based on the savings clause which they expect to include in all their treaties.

method, the residence state will tax its residents on the worldwide basis, but will grant a (limited) credit equivalent to the amount paid to the source state. This means that the residence state's tax has a residual effect, the extent of which depends on the source state's taxation. The more the latter taxes at source, the less will be the (residual) tax due to the residence state. Such a method implies a conflict of interest, since the residence state's taxation will increase if the source state reduces its own right to tax. On the other hand, the source state will be encouraged to tax non-residents at the highest level possible, since any decrease in its rate will not benefit the taxpayer, but will rather increase the residence state's (residual) taxation.

It is in this context that we come to the idea of tax sparing. This mechanism intends to ensure that the residence state's taxation will not increase even if a unilateral decision is made by the source state not to tax (or not to tax fully) non-residents, so that this benefit granted by the source state (reduced taxation) will directly benefit taxpayers and not the residence state.

Tax sparing can aim at assuring that treaty benefits will be maintained, or it may be intended to maintain unilateral tax exemptions. Although both phenomena are quite similar, it is common in literature[8] to refer to the first case as 'matching credit', reserving the expression 'tax sparing' to a more restricted case. Since this chapter examines both cases, mechanisms referring to unilateral measures will hereinafter be referred to as 'tax sparing *sensu stricto*'.

Matching credit is a mechanism whereby, if the source state determines not to tax non-residents at more than some level fixed upon between the two contracting states, the residence state agrees to grant a foreign tax credit which will correspond to a fixed amount, usually higher than the maximum taxation in the source state. In other words, the credit granted by the residence state does not depend upon the amount paid to the source state. On the contrary, although the source state is constrained by the treaty to tax up to a certain limit, the residence state's credit is determined by the same treaty on an independent (usually higher) level.

Several Brazilian treaties have included matching credit provisions, especially those signed in the 1970s; examples may be found in the

---

[8] See Klaus Vogel, in Klaus Vogel and Moris Lehner, *Doppelbesteuerungsabkommen der Bundesrepublik Deutschland auf dem Gebiet der Steuern vom Einkommen und Vermögen* (5th edn, München: Verlag C. H. Beck, 2008) Art. 23 Rz. 194–5.

treaties concluded with Austria, Denmark, France, Italy, Luxembourg and Sweden, all of them signed in the 1970s and still in force.

Brazil only commenced to enter upon negotiation of tax treaties in the 1960s. The reigning tax ideology at that time in Brazil (and in Latin America more generally) was that the source state should have the exclusive right to tax income derived from its economy. This can be seen from the fact that the Brazilian regular tax rate on non-residents was 25 percent of the gross amount remitted abroad (in some cases, remittances would be subject to additional taxation). From this point of view, double taxation would derive from some kind of intrusion of the residence state in the source state's resources. It was considered that the source state should not agree to reduce its taxation, since this could imply a recognition of the residence state's right to tax the same income.

In 1964, there was a change in the Brazilian international tax policy, which was not due to a different tax ideology, but rather to the economic policy of the military regime which entered into power. The new policy was that the development of the Brazilian economy would depend upon attracting foreign investment, and that international taxation could be used as a tool for such purpose. From this time onwards, Brazil would be prepared to reconsider its 25 percent taxation at source, in treaty negotiations, provided that any reduction would accrue to the benefit of the foreign investors and not the foreign country's fisc. So, Brazilian negotiators would not agree to reduce Brazilian taxation, if the only effect of such a reduction would be to increase the residence state's (marginal) taxation. Brazil would not be prepared to reduce its taxation from 25 percent to, say, 15 percent, if there would be no benefit to the taxpayer. If one keeps in mind that Brazil understood that it had the exclusive (or at least primary) right to tax income from its sources, there would be no reason to reduce its tax (and thus reduce the credit that the residence state should grant).

The matching credit mechanism was therefore designed to ensure that although the source state would limit its right to tax, the residence state would continue granting credits as if there were no such limitation. Generally speaking, in specific treaty provisions, Brazil would reduce its taxation at source to (e.g.) 15 percent, but the residence state would grant a credit of (e.g.) 25 percent. This would generate an immediate benefit for taxpayers derived from the treaty, since they would earn at least 10 percent free of taxation. The benefit could be even greater, since the source state could (unilaterally) decide not to tax at the full 15 percent rate: in any case, the residence state would grant a credit as if the source state had imposed a 25 percent tax.

This mechanism could be analysed as a benefit granted by the residence state to the source state (investment aid to developing economies). However, it is interesting to see that, from the source state's perspective, there is no such favor perceived. Accordingly, in the example above, Brazil would claim that before the tax treaty entered into force, Brazil would tax non-residents on a 25 percent level, and the residence state would only tax such income if its internal rate would be higher; in other words, the residence state's possibility to tax would have begun at the 25 percent rate. A matching credit mechanism, therefore, would not change the residence state's position. It would continue to tax the same amount (i.e., the amount above 25 percent). Brazil could argue, therefore, that the matching credit mechanism is neutral for residence states, and that it should not be considered a benefit granted to the source state. If one keeps in mind that the reigning ideology was that the source state would be the one entitled to tax, then such argument should be taken into account.

Tax sparing *sensu stricto,* on the other hand, aims at unilateral measures taken by the source state. While matching credit considers the case when the source state's ability to tax is limited by the treaty, i.e., when both countries agreed upon a limitation of taxation in the source state, tax sparing *sensu stricto* has a different approach: in principle, the source state would tax up to a determined level and by treaty (or unilaterally) the residence state would grant a foreign tax credit for said taxation. However, where the source state decides not to tax its non-resident up to the limit which was granted to it by the treaty, the residence state must respect such decision and grant a credit equivalent to the maximum amount the source state could have taxed.

As one can see, the matching credit mechanism derives directly from a decision of the contracting states upon signing a treaty: both states agree that the source state should limit its tax to a certain amount, but they also agree that the residence state's credit will (usually) be higher than said limit. In other words, taxpayers are granted a benefit which is independent from countries' later decisions. The matching credit is therefore independent from unilateral measures. Tax sparing *sensu stricto*, on the other hand, only benefits taxpayers if the source state unilaterally decides to reduce its taxes (reduction independent from any treaty provision), i.e., if the source state decides to grant a benefit to non-residents, which implies a taxation below the level allowed by the treaty.

One can also refer to matching credit in cases where there is no difference between the maximum taxation at source and the credit granted by the residence state, provided such credit is fixed by the treaty independent from any investigation about which was the real taxation at source. In other words, the matching credit mechanism contemplates a fixed credit by the residence state, which will always be granted upon remittances from the source state. So, the matching credit method is also pragmatic, since the contracting states (or taxpayers affected) do not need to provide any evidence concerning the level of taxation at source, which is irrelevant for purposes of determining the credit to be granted by the residence state.

III. OECD REPORT: REASONS FOR RECONSIDERATION

The OECD Report starts by addressing the changes in the global economic framework. As stated by the Report, the traditional assumption that all OECD members are major exporters of capital while the non-members are major importers of capital can now be questioned. Further, the globalization and liberalization of financial markets have 'blurred a number of traditional distinctions which underlie existing international tax arrangements'.[9]

Taking into account the differences between the current global context and the one of four decades before, when the first tax sparing provisions were negotiated (and especially the alleged considerable improvement in the economy of developing countries in this time), the OECD Report states that 'the new global environment has encouraged, and in some cases even compelled, countries to re-examine established tax structures and the policies upon which taxation arrangements are based'.[10] The Report then suggests that these new structures and policies would comprise tax sparing arrangements. To this effect, the OECD Report suggests a reconsideration of tax sparing provisions. The OECD proposes that tax sparing is no longer good policy, based on a number of arguments. In contrast, it is interesting to observe that the United Nations still observes that 'it is of primary importance to developing countries to ensure that the tax incentive measures shall not be made ineffective by taxation in the capital-exporting countries using the foreign tax credit system' by means of the adoption of tax sparing clauses in their tax treaties.[11]

---

9 See OECD Report, *supra* note 2, at 9–10.

10 *Ibid.* 12.

11 See United Nations Model Double Taxation Convention between Developed and Developing Countries, United Nations, New York, 2001, at 265.

The OECD Report states that a re-evaluation of the benefits of tax sparing is underway within both members and non-member countries of the Organisation. This statement, itself, must be put to the test. In an interesting analysis intended to verify the tax treaty practice since the publication of the OECD Report, Victor Thuronyi (himself an officer with the IMF) concluded that tax sparing provisions may be found in about one-third of tax treaties signed from 2000 until 2003.[12] Moreover, as Thuronyi verified in this research, half of the tax treaties with tax sparing provisions involved OECD member countries. Such a circumstance may be enough for one to debate to what extent the alleged 're-evaluation' regarding the granting of tax sparing would be underway both in and outside the OECD area.

The main argument of the OECD Report against tax sparing is the alleged view of most OECD member countries that tax sparing is not an effective way to promote foreign investments or to promote national economic growth. This view is reinforced, states the OECD, by a so-called 'overall disappointing experience of most Member countries and many economies in transition with the use of tax incentives', as well as the 'ample opportunities for tax planning and tax avoidance'.[13] From this point of view, therefore, negotiating tax sparing provisions is an 'illustration of good intentions leading to bad results', as their adverse consequences would outweigh their benefits.[14]

According to the OECD Report, the primary rationale for granting tax sparing has been the promotion of economic development in developing countries – the alleged development experienced by said countries in the last years would justify the reluctance of OECD Members in granting tax sparing in new or renegotiated tax treaties. Deeming tax sparing to be an instrument of foreign aid, the OECD Report also criticizes the mechanism on the basis that it lacks transparency when compared to direct aid, as the latter can establish, 'in relatively precise terms', the recipient, the amount and the anticipated use of the foreign aid.[15]

One should note at this point that there is no empirical evidence of 'bad results' from tax sparing. On the contrary, the continued use of tax

---

12 See Victor Thuronyi, 'Recent Treaty Practice on Tax Sparing' (2003) 29(3) *Tax Notes International* 301.

13 See OECD Report, *supra* note 2, at 12.

14 See Kim Brooks, 'Tax Sparing: A Needed Incentive for Foreign Investment in Low-Income Countries or an Unnecessary Revenue Sacrifice?'(2009) 34 *Queen's Law Journal* 508.

15 See OECD Report, *supra* note 2, 22.

sparing provisions in many countries' treaty policies suggests that negotiating parties consider that there may be good results from these provisions. It is, furthermore, not clear who should be entitled to evaluate whether results are good or bad. One might suggest that the contracting states involved in treaty negotiation should be deemed to be able to decide whether or not to provide for tax sparing.

A second reason for reconsidering tax sparing proposed by the OECD Report is based on the free-rider effect. The argument is that there is a misconception (presumably, by the contracting states) of the views of foreign investors, which would not depend or even be influenced by tax sparing provisions in taking investment decisions.[16] According to the OECD Report, multinational enterprises would base their investment decisions on a wide range of factors, linked to political, market and infrastructural conditions of the host country, with taxation being only one issue in a whole set of factors which are taken into account. If this is the case, any increase in foreign investment would be independent of the existence of tax sparing provisions, as they would be irrelevant to the multinational enterprises' investment decisions.[17] Thus, tax sparing provisions would not be justified in face of the supposed inappropriateness of the mechanism as a tool for economic development.[18]

If one were to take this argument seriously, however, one would need to know what is the overall effect of tax treaties on foreign investment decisions. There does not seem to be much research about this, and such research tends to be inconclusive, since one is comparing effective data (i.e., the amount of investments in a country) with prospective (wishful) information.

Showing the lack of a uniform conclusion on the matter, Barthel, Busse and Neumayer, after the analysis of several studies concerning the influence of tax treaties on foreign investments, concluded that while the researchers who use bilateral FDI data fail to find a positive effect of the treaties on FDI, the studies that use aggregate FDI data in a large and representative sample reach the opposite conclusion, i.e., tax treaties increasing the FDI.[19] Thus, it is not surprising that the said authors, in spite of concluding that tax treaties increase the bilateral FDI stock

---

16 *Ibid.* 12.

17 See Morvan Meirelles, 'Tax Sparing Credits in Tax Treaties: The Future and the Effect on EC Law' in *European Taxation* (IBFD, May 2009) 263.

18 See OECD Report, *supra* note 2, at 25.

19 See Fabian Barthel, Matthias Busse and Eric Neumayer, 'The Impact of Double Taxation Treaties on Foreign Direct Investments: Evidence from Large Dyadic Panel Data' in (2010) 28(3) *Contemporary Economic Policy* 366.

between 27 percent and 31 percent, allow that the debate is still open, 'as the empirical evidence of existing studies is anything but conclusive'.[20]

As an example of how this information cannot be considered reliable, one should take the Brazil-Germany Tax Treaty, revoked recently.[21] If one compares the level of German investment in Brazil five years before the said treaty revocation and five years thereafter, one would be surprised to see that the level of German investment has increased in this time.[22] This could lead one to a surprising (and wrong!) conclusion that the treaty was an obstacle to German investment in Brazil. Such a naïve understanding would ignore the fact that the worldwide economy increased in such period, and especially that the Brazilian economy has been attracting increased investments throughout the period. To obtain a full picture of German investment, one would also have to include German investments made through third countries. The author therefore argues that this is not an easy analysis and that the free-rider argument should not be considered for a reconsideration.

Third, the OECD Report refers to some developing countries' concerns as to 'whether the price of obtaining tax sparing is too high given the limited benefits of such provisions',[23] taking into account that residence countries require a lower taxation at source as a condition for agreeing with tax sparing. The argument is correct concerning the lower taxation at source. However, one should take into consideration that the OECD itself has always advocated that treaties should provide for lower taxation at source (except for cases where taxation on a residence basis would be very difficult and low taxation at source would increase harmful tax competition). Indeed, the level of taxation at source seems to be one of the most relevant differences between the OECD and UN approaches. An example may be found in the provision concerning royalties: while Article 12 of the OECD Model Convention provides for the exclusive right of the residence state to tax royalties, the UN Model Convention allows their taxation at source.

From such perspective, one may understand Tsilly Dagan's assertion that the tax treaties, especially those based on the OECD Model, were constructed by and for developed countries with mutual interests and

---

[20] *Ibid.* 366.

[21] The Tax Treaty signed with Germany in 1975 was revoked by the German authorities on 7 April 2005.

[22] See the reports on the FDI in Brazil published by Brazilian Central Bank, available at www.bcb.gov.br/?INVED.

[23] See OECD Report, *supra* note 2, at 13.

ideology.[24] To this effect, Dagan observes that the tax treaties, being based on a model primarily designed for developed countries, tend to allocate the revenues to the benefit of the residence state in such a way that the refusal of developing countries to enter into treaties which have no mechanisms to assure the improvement in the level of foreign investment would be justified.[25] Thus, before reconsidering tax sparing, the OECD should seriously reconsider its view concerning the limitation of taxation at source. Should the OECD agree that source countries should be granted a higher amount of taxation, then the OECD's argument about tax sparing may be more convincing.

The claim as to an increase in the standards of living in developing countries, pointed to by the OECD Report as a further reason for the reconsideration of tax sparing, may also be criticized. To this effect, one should follow Kim Brooks' argument, according to which the OECD's statements would not match the UN's conclusions in its 2000 Millennium Development Goals Report, which points to an 'ever-increasing inequality between countries'.[26] Something similar can be derived from an article written by Cristiane Coelho, who points out that the OECD Report does not rely on any specific data when listing countries like Russia, Singapore, China and India as countries which, due to a supposed economic development, would be able to implement their tax policies independently of external concessions.[27] Coelho's analysis of countries' GDP per capita evolution from 1985 to 2005 enables one to conclude that, due to the enormous gap between countries like the United States and the United Kingdom, and China and India, it is impossible to argue that the latter have the same economic condition as the former, which can implement their tax policies on their own.[28] In any event, the vulnerability of developing countries' economies would still justify the adoption of tax sparing provisions, since one could not say that the economic growth alleged by the OECD Report was shared by all developing countries.[29]

A fourth argument of the OECD against tax sparing concerns the allegedly burdensome concessions made by treaty negotiators in exchange for the obtaining of tax sparing provisions. With regard to this

---

[24] See Tsilly Dagan, 'The Tax Treaties Myth' (2000) 32(939) *Journal of International Law and Politics* 47.

[25] See Dagan, *supra* note 24, at 51.

[26] See Brooks, *supra* note 14, at 528.

[27] See Christiane Coelho, 'Tax Sparing and Brazil's Tax Treaties' (2008) 51(8) *Tax Notes International* 690.

[28] *Ibid.* 692.

[29] *Ibid.* 693.

argument, Brooks observes that it could be challenged by the mere fact the OECD Model Convention itself deprives the source state of 'much needed' revenue, e.g., by providing for no withholding tax on royalties at source.[30] As a matter of fact, it is not clear that treaty negotiators would grant fewer (or smaller) concessions if no tax sparing provision would be considered, or that such concessions would be smaller than the gains from such provision. The tax treaty Brazil has signed with Belgium in 1972, for instance, in spite of having a tax sparing clause, provides for withholding tax rates for dividends, interests and royalties which are similar to the ones in the treaty signed with South Africa in 2003, which does not contain such a clause. In summary, one should not generalize the idea that treaty negotiators would not be capable of deciding what to concede.

Fifth, the OECD suggests that there is now a greater awareness regarding the potential for abuse deriving from tax sparing provisions and the ineffectiveness of tax incentives in promoting economic development.[31] However, arguing that a review is necessary due to the potential for abuse of tax sparing provisions is not convincing. If one were to consider not including a provision in a treaty because it would be subject to abuse, sooner or later no single article of tax treaties would survive. A more consistent approach to this problem would be to discuss treaty shopping and treaty abuse in general, adopting clauses which could avoid both (e.g., limitation on benefits provisions in tax treaties). The mere fact that there can be abuse is not enough to reject a treaty provision which would otherwise be interesting to the parties.

Finally, the OECD Report suggests that a tax sparing provision would have a counterproductive effect as a tool to attract foreign direct investment, since it would encourage an excessive repatriation of profits to the residence state.[32] To this effect, when faced with the existence of a tax sparing credit on the distributed profits of their subsidiaries, the foreign investors would be encouraged to return the said profits to the residence state rather than re-investing them in the source state. This would only be a valid argument if tax sparing provisions would be time conditioned. Provided benefits are the same, investors' decisions to repatriate profits should not be dependent on those provisions.

In conclusion, given the above reasons addressed in its Report, the OECD recommends that the granting of tax sparing should be considered

---

30 See Brooks, *supra* note 14, at 528.

31 See OECD Report, *supra* note 2, at 21.

32 *Ibid.* 22–3.

by member countries only in regard to countries whose economic level is considerably below that of the countries within the OECD. Member countries should, then, employ objective economic criteria to define countries eligible for tax sparing.[33] At least in the case of the GDP per capita criterion, one could argue the absence of reasons for the denial of tax sparing, as the suggestion that developing countries have achieved a GDP per capita higher than many OECD member countries is misleading.[34]

IV. RECONSIDERING THE OECD'S RECONSIDERATION

As one can see from the previous section, the OECD's reconsideration of tax sparing is based fundamentally on the idea that tax sparing would be a mechanism for developed states to assist developing states. From an historical perspective, one should confirm that assumption. In the case of Brazil, its first tax treaties were signed with Sweden and Japan because both countries were prepared to grant tax sparing provisions as part of their policy to assist developing countries. This seems to be the view of treaty negotiators to date. However, matters now have changed for some countries, as suggested by the OECD Report. The Brazil–Germany treaty revocation is an example thereof: German authorities would require a revision of the treaty due to the fact that Brazil would allegedly no longer be a developing country and therefore tax sparing provisions would not be acceptable.[35]

In the previous section, the author has outlined the OECD Report's arguments for a reconsideration of tax sparing and has identified the problems or weaknesses in these arguments. Even so, the author accepts that if tax sparing provisions are considered only as a development mechanism, it is understandable that the OECD has suggested a reconsideration. From the residence state's perspective, tax treaties aim at avoiding double taxation. On the basis of capital export neutrality, the residence state is supposed to reduce its taxes in an amount equivalent to the taxes charged in the source state. If taxes are not collected by the

---

33 *Ibid.* 42–3.

34 See Coelho, *supra* note 27, at 693.

35 Besides the tax sparing clause, the qualification of income derived from technical services in Art. 21 ('other income') by the Brazilian authorities and issues derived from the Brazilian transfer pricing rules should also be pointed out as reasons for the revocation of the Tax Treaty with Germany.

source state, there would be no reason for a credit by the residence state. From this point of view, tax sparing appears to offend one of the main principles of the so-called international tax regime: tax neutrality. As tax neutrality is recognized as an important principle, this suggests that tax sparing clauses should be avoided. Developed states should instead choose direct mechanisms to promote state aid to developing states.

In this section, the author proposes a different way of viewing tax sparing that enables a reconsideration of the OECD's reconsideration. This different approach is based on several arguments: (1) capital export neutrality is not the only target for international taxation; (2) tax sparing clauses are not a favor (or aid) granted by the residence state; and (3) exemption by the residence state does not increase the source state's prerogative.

A. Capital Export Neutrality

The main argument against tax sparing mechanisms seems to be based on capital export neutrality. States adopting the credit method argue that investors should be subject to the same level of taxation in their inbound and outbound investments. This would avoid a distortion in their decisions and the most efficient allocation of resources would be achieved.

The author argues, however, that there is no international consensus regarding this perspective. On the contrary, it seems convincing that capital export neutrality does not bring efficiency. Should the tax credit mechanism work according to its stated aim – i.e., to neutralize the tax burden – then the effect of this is not to generate neutrality in investors' decisions. On the contrary, equalization of tax rates operates as a mechanism to convince investors not to invest in developing countries but, instead, to focus their investment on developed countries. To understand this, first one can make an assumption that there is, in general terms, some relationship between tax rates and services provided by states. Although some jurisdictions demand high taxes and do not offer their taxpayers a corresponding level of services, due to the states' own deficiencies, it is generally true that a state will not be able to offer good services if its taxation is too low. Therefore, one can generally say that if the jurisdiction charges lower taxes, taxpayers must be prepared to supplement some services which could otherwise be offered by the state.

Applying this perspective to developed and developing states, one can consider that developed states will usually impose higher taxes, but on the other hand, their taxpayers will have a stronger state. Developing states may have lower taxes, but one will easily note some deficiencies, including in infrastructure. In this scenario, neutralizing the tax burden would require taxpayers to pay the taxes on the same level, independent of whether they invest in their own residence state or abroad. This is not a neutral outcome. Under the same level of taxes, investors will prefer to invest in an environment where infrastructure corresponds to the level of tax the investor is paying. It does not make sense to invest in a jurisdiction which offers less infrastructure (unless there are other factors, such as non-renewable, immobile resources, at play), since investors will have to pay for services which would otherwise be offered by the state. In sum, when a developed state adopts capital export neutrality, it invites its taxpayers to invest locally (or in another developed state); investors will only dare to invest in developing states if their remuneration is high enough to make such investment attractive in spite of the gap between (developed state) tax level and (developing state) infrastructure. One should not be surprised, therefore, if one notes a divergence in the interest rates derived from investments made in developed states vis-à-vis those made in developing states.

At an international level,[36] capital export neutrality is even more unacceptable, since it implies keeping relevant resources in developed states, while developing states need such means for their development. Furthermore, residence states can tax the income of their resident taxpayers upon consumption but source states can only tax the income upon payment.

Finally, one should note that capital export neutrality is not an aim in itself. Accordingly, if residence states really consider that taxes should be neutral, then they would not only tax the (positive) difference between their taxes and source state taxes: where the latter would be higher, residence states should be prepared to reimburse their taxpayers on the (negative) difference. In reality, no state would reimburse taxes paid to foreign states. However, this analysis shows that the capital export neutrality argument of developed states is not applied equally across all contexts.

B. Tax Sparing is Not a Favor Granted by Developed Countries

As already explained, behind the OECD's reconsideration of tax sparing, there seems to be a view that tax sparing is a concession granted by residence countries to multinational investors, to provide a subsidy to developing states. This is why tax sparing, in the OECD analysis, should

---

[36] See Vogel, *supra* note 3.

only be applicable to tax treaties between developed and developing countries, and should be seen as an exceptional measure.

This argument has been made by David Rosenbloom and Daniel Hora do Paço, according to whom review of the 'Brazilian insistence' as regards tax sparing would be 'imperative', as it would have forbidden 'serious negotiations' within the last 40 years.[37] Under the said authors' understanding, the Brazilian policy regarding the adoption of tax sparing clauses would be 'contradictory' vis-à-vis the position currently occupied by the country in the international scenario, i.e., tax sparing should only be granted to developing countries, what would no longer be the Brazilian case.[38]

On the other hand, if one takes into account the fact that tax treaties share taxing power between two jurisdictions, then one would immediately recognize that tax sparing is not a favor granted by the residence state. Tax treaties are only negotiated (or applicable) when two jurisdictions are simultaneously entitled to levy tax on the same event due from the same taxpayer. Tax treaties apply where double taxation would otherwise occur. When a country agrees to sign a tax treaty and therefore agrees to limit its own jurisdiction, it recognizes that its treaty partner also has jurisdiction in respect of the same event. In other words, by means of a tax treaty, the two states limit their own taxing jurisdictions, recognizing their treaty partners' jurisdiction. Upon signing a tax treaty, a state accepts that it will not trespass upon some material limits, which are granted to its treaty partner.

Considering an item of income which may be taxed at source up to a certain limit, one can see that both countries have shared their jurisdiction, determining that the source state's jurisdiction reaches said limit and the residence state's jurisdiction begins from that point on. This is very important to update the discussion concerning tax sparing: one must keep in mind that the very same item of income would be subject to two jurisdictions, but they have shared their taxing powers; one jurisdiction is not supposed to tax beyond its own limits, or it would otherwise tax an item of income which was reserved by treaty to the other jurisdiction. Thus, if the source state taxes foreign residents up to the limit foreseen in the tax treaty, the residence state will grant a credit equivalent to such tax. In other words, the residence state's jurisdiction begins at the very same point where the source state's jurisdiction ceases to exist.

---

37 See H. David Rosenbloom and Daniel Hora do Paço, 'Considerações sobre a negociação de um tratado para evitar a dupla tributação da renda com os EUA' in 174 *Revista Dialética de Direito Tributário* (São Paulo: Dialética, 2010) 25.

38 *Ibid.* 18–19.

When, however, the source state decides not to tax said item of income, the residence state claims that no credit should be granted. One can understand that, as a matter of practice, the residence state would tax an amount originally under the jurisdiction of the source state.

In other words, the basic credit mechanism only works as a tool to share taxing jurisdictions if the source state exercises its taxing power in a positive way, i.e., if it fully taxes the item of income granted to it. If, however, the source state decides to exercise its taxing jurisdiction in a negative way, i.e., if it decides not to tax the item of income, then the residence state claims its right to tax the same item.

As the basic credit mechanism is currently structured, therefore, the residence state does not seem to be prepared to recognize that it has originally shared tax jurisdiction with its treaty partner. It does not recognize its treaty partner's right to fully exercise its jurisdiction on the amount reserved to it. The credit method does not work as a mechanism to share jurisdictions between two equally entitled jurisdictions. On the contrary, the residence state keeps a 'gun to the head' of the source state, forcing it to tax the amount which was granted to it. The source state's sovereign right to exercise its jurisdiction is therefore disregarded: the residence state believes that taxation by the source state would be a concession under the treaty, but where the source state decides not to tax, then the residence state would keep its tax jurisdiction on the full amount.

The author argues that, from this perspective, one can see that tax sparing (especially the matching credit approach) is a mechanism aimed at correcting the distortion in the basic credit mechanism. By means of a tax sparing clause, the residence state recognizes the source state's right to tax or not to tax an item of income which was granted to its jurisdiction.

Thus, a tax sparing clause (matching credit) is not a favor granted by the residence state. By means of its adoption, the residence state simply confirms that it has no taxing right on an item of income which was granted to the source state.

C. Exemption by Residence State

When the residence state claims that tax treaties aim to avoid double taxation and therefore no credit should be granted where the source state exempts an item of income, one should also ask whether the same principle should be applied in the opposite case, i.e., if the residence state exempts an item of income which would be taxable in the source state.

By means of tax treaties, source states usually limit their own taxing power to a level established therein, which tends to be less than the amount which would normally be due from non-residents under domestic source state tax law. A good explanation for this is that the source state's limits are necessary in order to grant a (residual) taxing power to the residence state.

If one were to apply the same arguments against tax sparing in this situation, then one would claim that where a residence state does not tax an item of income, then no limit should be applicable to the taxation of the source state, since there would be no risk of double taxation.

Thus, if a country rejects tax sparing provisions, it should also accept that the source state's limitations are only applicable if the residence state taxes the same item of income. In other words, since residence states usually argue that tax treaties' sole objective is to avoid double taxation, then tax treaties should not limit source states' taxation if residence states do not tax an item of income (or if they tax such item of income up to a level lower than the one which would be applied by the source state). This would imply a complicated reverse credit mechanism, whereby the source state would be entitled to tax the item of income (or to complete the taxation) if the residence state would not do so.

Of course, such a mechanism, besides being very complicated, has never been considered in any known tax treaty. It is only presented here as an argument to show that the residence state's claim to tax an amount reserved to the source state has another side, which should be taken into account. Although it seems absurd to consider a 'residual' tax power of the source state, the argument is not different from the one employed by residence states when they claim the prerogative to tax an item of income reserved by the treaty to the source state.

V. CONCLUSION: TAX SPARING, JURISDICTION AND TERRITORIALITY

This chapter shows that there has been a misunderstanding when countries discuss the adoption of tax sparing in their treaties. From a traditional (residence state) perspective, tax sparing is perceived to be a concession given by developed states to developing states. If this analysis is correct, then it makes sense to reconsider such a mechanism and its efficiency, as is proposed in the OECD Report.

However, the author has argued in this chapter that tax sparing (especially if a tax matching provision is adopted) may be seen, instead, as a mechanism of (partial) recognition of territoriality.[39] That is, by this mechanism, residence states would recognize source states' sole jurisdiction over (part of) the income. If source states decide to grant a tax incentive, this is to be considered a unilateral sacrifice made by the latter, which does not affect residence states, since the subject is beyond their jurisdiction.

It is therefore argued that it is time to reconsider tax sparing, but not in the sense of the OECD's reconsideration. Instead of simply rejecting tax sparing provisions, the author argues that they should be reinvigorated and expanded to treaties between developed countries as well. Not only developing, but also developed countries should be granted the prerogative of deciding their tax policy within the jurisdiction reserved to them by the treaty. Tax sparing would be a step forward in the direction of the recognition of each state's tax jurisdiction. The exercise of said jurisdiction may be equally done by means of taxing or not taxing an item of income.

From a practical perspective, it is further argued that matching credit provisions are more convenient than tax sparing *sensu stricto*, since the latter would depend on the analysis of internal legislation of the source state (usually states list the benefits to be observed). Matching credit provisions, on the other hand, simply respect the jurisdiction of the source state, establishing the point where the jurisdiction of the residence state begins.

[39] See Vogel, *supra* note 8, Art. 23, Rz 195, 1648.

PART III

In search of 'searchers' to find unique solutions to common tax challenges

6. Is this a pipe? Validity of a tax reform for a developing country

Ana Paula Dourado*

I. INTRODUCTION

René Magritte's painting illustrating a pipe and entitled 'this is not a pipe' highlights the difference between the object and its representation. A tax reform in a developing country where plural legalities coexist (the object, Magritte's pipe or pipes) will induce the tax legislator to represent a unitary solution that is to be enforced by officials who may initially identify themselves with diverse legalities. The challenge for the drafter of the tax reform will be to identify the legalities in force, to grant validity to some of them, and to represent the result in a unitary tax law that will be accepted as valid by tax officials and taxpayers. The result will then be another pipe with selected elements of the underlying pipes.

Assume that the technical assistance of an external legal drafter is requested to draft and discuss with local officials, parliamentary members and publicly with other players and taxpayers, a whole or partial tax reform in a developing country. The external legal drafter is expected to play the Hercules legislator[1] in a society in transition and rich in plural legalities. Assume further that she is an expert contracted by an international organization, and in her skin as Hercules legislator she will have an excellent knowledge of the topic, both from a theoretical and a practical perspective. Our external legal drafter is an academic, and therefore has a good acquaintance with the legal system and existing tax law that is to be reformed, with the family of law to which it belongs,

---

* Has been acting as expert at the legal department of the IMF, drafting and negotiating the tax reforms in Portuguese-speaking countries since 2003.

[1] In analogy to Dworkin's Hercules judge: G. Dworkin, *Taking Rights Seriously* (Cambridge, MA: Harvard University Press, 1978 (1977)) 105–7; G. Dworkin, *Law's Empire*, Fontana Masterguides (Glasgow: Frank Kermode (ed.), 1986) e.g., chs V and VI.

and with many other legal systems belonging or not to the same legal family. She is open to engaging with multiple legalities, including the traditional ones, and she is aware that some of the comparable tax legislation in force in other countries is considered to be a bad example while others may be seen as a model to be followed. Beyond her theoretical knowledge, our external legal drafter has experience participating in previous tax policy definition and legal drafting at the OECD, the EU and in developing countries, and has worked for a national Ministry of Finance.

Assume also, that she acts with considerable policy independence and is engaged in taking her work on tax reforms seriously, fulfilling the role of rational draft legislator envisaged by John Stuart Mill and Enlightenment thinking.[2] This rational draft legislator will not be an obstacle to the aspiration that legislation should emerge from communication and disagreement in democratic assemblies that will internalize dissenting opinions[3] and enact tax law according to the principle of separation of powers.[4] In fact, it is contended here that she will be acting with a national tax reform committee to which she will present her ideas and receive adequate input. In that process, a thorough discussion will occur in respect of tax policy and the concrete legal solutions proposed. It is then expected that the tax legislation will be enacted by a deliberative assembly debating different views and that this assembly is structured with procedural rules securing a democratic decision-making: rules about representation, hearings, debates, amendments and voting.[5] It is therefore assumed that the rule of law will be observed, at least in its formal and basic aspects, as may be observed by an external legal drafter.

This chapter aims to discuss the challenges that policy principles, legal choices and constraints pose to the perfect legislator, our Hercules legislator, in a developing country, in a globalized world, and in a market economy. This Hercules legislator will not only have to perfectly grasp

---

[2] Jeremy Waldron, *Law and Disagreement* (Oxford: Oxford University Press, 1999) 42–5, 51–5, 70–71, 97–9.

[3] *Ibid.* 21–4, 27, 39–41, 66, 69 *et seq.*

[4] Ana Paula Dourado, 'General Report, In Search of Validity in Tax Law: The Boundaries between Creation and Application in a Rule-of-Law State' in *Separation of Powers in Tax Law* (The Netherlands: EATLP, 2010) 29–33; 'The Delicate Balance: Revenue Authority Discretions and the Rule of Law – Some Thoughts in a Legal Theory and Comparative Perspective' in Chris Evans, Judith Freedman and Rick Krever (eds), *The Delicate Balance, Tax, Discretion and the Rule of Law* (IBFD, 2011) 16–19; Waldron, *supra* note 2, at 49 *et seq.*, 69 *et seq.*

[5] Waldron, *supra* note 2, at 40.

the best technical solutions, their complexity and consequences. She will have to deal with the plural legalities in force. She will face, for example, a market economy organized according to state law, involving different sectors of activity and local and foreign investors. She will learn that foreign investors related to certain sectors of activity require tax holidays as a condition to invest in the country. She will be aware that the informal sector has a strong participation in the economy and that there are high levels of corruption, possibly involving several hierarchical levels of the state. She will learn that different communities with a diverse economic organization, concepts of family, wealth and ability to pay coexist in that state.

II. LEGAL PLURALISM

A. Legal Pluralism in the Anthropological-Sociological Sense

Legal pluralism can be described as the coexistence of two or more legal systems in the same social field.[6] When first mentioned in the literature in the 1920s and 1930s, legal pluralism was linked to colonial societies. It was at the time realized, to a certain extent to the surprise of lawyers and anthropologists, that pre-colonial legal orders coexisted with colonial laws, and legal pluralism was understood as a result of the introduction of European colonial law.[7] The complexity of the pre-colonial orders themselves was not questioned until recently.[8]

In S.E. Merry's article, the strictest meaning of legal pluralism is related to the situation in countries that are European ex-colonies, even though it was known that world migrations have long since led to exporting legal concepts and systems, together with the exportation of culture. In a sociological sense, legal pluralism exists in every society since each group – universities, communities, etc. – has its own set of rules, which coexist with state rules.

---

[6] Alessandra Facchi, *I Diritti nell' Europa Multiculturale,Pluralismo Nomativo i Immigrazione* (4th edn, Rome/Bari: Editori Laterza, 2008) 38; Leopold Pospisil, *The Anthropology of Law: A Comparative Theory of Law* (New York: Harper and Row, 1971); John Griffiths, 'What is Legal Pluralism?' (1986) 24 *Journal of Legal Pluralism and Unofficial Law* 1; Sally Falk Moore, 'Law and Social Change: The Semi-Autonomous Social Field as an Appropriate Subject of Study' (1973) 7 *Law and Society Review* 719; Sally Engel Merry, 'Legal Pluralism' (1988) 22(5) *Law and Society Review* 870 at 869–901.

[7] Merry, *supra* note 6, at 869.

[8] *Ibid.* 869–70.

Even where legal theorists adopt a broad concept of law, the concept of legal pluralism used by sociologists and anthropologists tends to be broader, covering the rules adopted by every subgroup of a society, such as families, lineage, communities, factories, corporations, universities, as well as tribunals and security forces.[9] As Griffiths has put it, there is a social science view of legal pluralism as an empirical state of affairs in society (the coexistence within a social group of legal orders that do not belong to a single 'system') and a 'juristic' view. However, contrary to Griffiths' juristic view of legal pluralism, the latter does not confine itself to state law or, in his words, to situations where 'the sovereign commands different bodies of law for different groups of population varying by ethnicity, religion, nationality, or geography, and when the parallel legal regimes are all dependent on the state legal system'.[10]

B. Legal Pluralism in the Strict Legal Sense: Law is Not Exclusively State Law

The aforementioned misunderstanding lies in the fact that law does not have to correspond to the Kelsenian concept characterized by a pyramid or a rigid hierarchy of rules, where the state has the monopoly in enacting or validating and recognizing them.[11] Moreover, legal positivism is not necessarily or even essentially statist, since custom and customary law, in the sense it is understood by legal theorists, can also comply with positivistic parameters.[12]

For example, Hart's concept of law, packaging primary and secondary rules, accommodates sources of law that do not necessarily emanate from the state, since law exists and is valid if there are commonly accepted rules of recognition.[13] That is, law exists and is valid as long as there is a 'concordant practice by courts, officials and private persons' identifying

---

[9] Merry, *supra* note 6, at 870; David Nelken, '*Eugen Ehrlich*, Living Law, and Plural Legalities' (2008) 2 *Theoretical Inquiries in Law, Legal Pluralism, Privatization of Law and Multiculturalism* 446; Martha-Marie Kleinhaus and Roderick A. Macdonald, 'What is a Critical Legal Pluralism' (1997) 12 *Canadian Journal of Law and Society* 25.

[10] Griffiths, *supra* note 6, at 7; Merry, *supra* note 6, at 871.

[11] Hans Kelsen, *'Teoria Pura do Direito'* (4th edn, Coimbra: Arménio Amado (ed.), João Baptista Machado (trans.), 1976) *Reine Rechtslehre* (Vienna: Verlag Frank Deuticke, 1960) ch. 6; Waldron, *supra* note 2, at 138 *et seq.*

[12] Jeremy Waldron, 'Legal Pluralism and the Contrast between Hart's Jurisprudence and Fuller's' in Peter Cane (ed.), *The Hart–Fuller Debate in the Twenty-First Century* (Oxford/Portland, OR: Hart Publishing, 2010) 141 *et seq.*

[13] *Ibid.* 138–40.

the validity of law according to publicly known criteria and applying it (internal statement), those criteria (rules of recognition) exist and are valid (external assessment),[14] and the legal system as a whole is valid (due to the internal and the external assessment). Hart even mentions the case of pathological systems evolving from a colonial status to independency[15] and in that context he foresees the case of conflicts of validity due to conflicts among different officials applying conflicting rules of recognition and a break of unity among them.[16]

It seems indisputable, however, that outside pathological situations, legal pluralism, including coexistence of pre-colonial with colonial legal systems and the latter with post-colonial legal systems, were not on Hart's agenda. On the one hand, Hart distinguishes between pre-legal and legal societies, where in the former there are only primary rules shared by the community, but no officials imposing them, and in the latter primary and secondary rules, namely, rules of recognition; on the other hand, Hart essentially discusses scenarios of unity of law.

In *The Concept of Law*, Hart's primary rules impose duties and his secondary rules confer powers, public or private, leading to the creation or variation of duties or obligations.[17] Hart's secondary rules contain the criteria for identifying the law, and they 'specify the ways in which the primary rules may be conclusively ascertained, introduced, eliminated, varied, and the fact of their violation conclusively determined': secondary rules are classified by Hart in categories that include rules of recognition, specifying the criteria of legal validity; rules of change, empowering an individual or a body of persons to introduce new primary rules for the conduct of the life of the group, and to eliminate old rules; rules conferring private power (to conclude a contract or transfer property); and rules of adjudication (defining judges or courts, jurisdiction, and judgment), as well as rules centralizing the official sanctions of the system. A primary rule is valid if it passes all the tests by the rule of recognition, even if they conflict with other rules of the system and even if the latter are to prevail, namely, because the system contains an ultimate rule of recognition with a supreme criterion of validity.[18]

Such a concept of the legal system corresponds to a more complex legal system and does not describe pre-colonial societies and their

---

14 H.L.A. Hart, *The Concept of Law*, Clarendon Law Series (Oxford: Oxford University Press, 1961) 97–107.

15 *Ibid.* 116–20.

16 *Ibid.* 118–20.

17 *Ibid.* 79.

18 *Ibid.* 100–103.

traditional legal systems (with their own methods of enacting law and with their own rules to apply it, even if they are based on oral transmission and include ordalia). Hart refers to pre-legal societies consisting only of primary rules, where there are no officials; and, in that case, the rules must be widely accepted by the group, no distinction existing between obedience to rules (by the normal citizen) and acceptance of legal validity (by the official).[19] This is connected to the fact that in traditional communities there are no individual rights and duties as opposed to the community's rights and duties.[20]

Even if those systems, still to be found in substate communities belonging to states recently formed, acquire a status of legality by Hart's rules of recognition, the latter seem to imply that colonial and post-colonial legal systems will determine the validity of the former. In fact, these are recognized by officials (e.g., the tax administration or tax judges) whose competence is given approval in a constitutional legal system.

In other words, Hart's concept of law does not exclude non-state law, and in this sense is able to grant us some framework for the analysis of legal pluralism in developing countries undergoing a tax reform. However, since traditional legal systems are pre-legal for Hart they are not included in the concept of law, unless we see them in a dynamic perspective and conclude that in a colonial and post-colonial setting they are habitually accepted by the majority of a community, involving both private persons and officials provided with authoritative criteria.

In Hart's concept of law, obedience and validity will be congruent in non-pathological situations, but dynamic situations, such as colonized states becoming independent, will lead to changes in rules of recognition. Even if some of the previous colonial legislation is still in force, it will only be valid if the rule of recognition locally accepted grants it validity.[21] This is the case where post-colonial rules of recognition acknowledge traditional tax rules and solve any conflicting overlapping problems with the colonial tax law still in force (for example, a post-colonial constitutional rule accepts that traditional poll taxes coexist with state and municipal taxes, contrary to the colonial income tax code still in force). Hart's rules of recognition grant us by their nature the criteria to solve conflicts among plural legalities at the application level,

---

[19] *Ibid.* 114.

[20] See Jürgen Habermas, *Faktizität und Geltung, Beiträge zur Diskurstheorie des Rechts und des demokratischen Rechtsstaats* (2nd edn, Frankfurt-am-Main, 1992) 39–45.

[21] Hart, *The Concept of Law, supra* note 14, at 117.

where constitutional rules will normally prevail above others, and therefore any moral concept of law is unnecessary to solve such conflicts.

For the purposes of this chapter, the dynamic dimension of 'pre-legal' and 'legal' systems is taken into account. Moreover, the meaning of traditional rules adopted here, includes Hart's 'pre-legal' set of rules and the rules of the diverse communities coexisting in a certain state and originally belonging to different states, nations, cultures and languages. Furthermore, for the purposes of its relevance to the process of tax legal drafting, it is assumed that these communities reside in a developing country undergoing a tax reform.

III. ACKNOWLEDGING LEGAL PLURALISM AS THE BASIS FOR A SUCCESSFUL TAX REFORM

Legal pluralism is far from being exclusive to developing countries or ex colonies of European countries. Legal drafting in the current globalized world is characterized by a plural discourse, where legal players, although originally having different backgrounds, are used to critically sharing and spreading their legal knowledge and values, in global discussion forums, such as the OECD, the Global Forum, the International Monetary Fund, the World Bank, the European Union, the Inter-American Center of Tax Administrations (CIAT), the International Fiscal Association (IFA) or the European Association of Tax Law Professors (EATLP).[22] In this context, the global legal discourse travels fast in respect of every legal field, and is a product of global identity, solidarity, and a sense of global fairness and unfairness, global human and fundamental rights.[23] Examples of this in tax law are the awareness of phenomena such as tax evasion and avoidance by certain groups of taxpayers, the consequences of tax secrecy and tax havens for each and every country, the importance of exchange of information on tax matters,

---

22 Klaus Günther, 'Rechtspluralismus und Universaler Code der Legalität: Globalisierung als Rechtstheoretisches Problem' in Lutz Wingert and Klaus Günther (eds), *Die Öffentlichkeit der Vernunft und der Vernunft der Öffentlichkeit*, Festschrift für Jürgen Habermas (Frankfurt-am-Main: Suhrkamp, 2001) 541.

23 Amartya Sen, *Identity and Violence: The Illusion of Destiny* (New York/ London: W.W. Norton & Company, 2006) e.g. chs 2 and 7; Boaventura Sousa Santos, 'Por uma Concepção Multicultural de Direitos Humanos, Reconhecer para Libertar, Os Caminhos do Cosmopolitismo Multicultural' in B.S. Santos (ed.), *Civilização Brasileira* (Rio de Janeiro 2003) 427–551.

the right to a fair hearing in tax litigation, information duties and the *nemo tenetur se ipsum accusarem* principle, among other ones.

The aforementioned international legal players tend to favor best practices and seek to reduce diversity and this also explains the reciprocal influences that characterize tax legislation policies. In some domains, solutions are a theme with variations as in a classical composition, in respect of which the interpreters (tax administration, domestic courts and taxpayers) will make the difference. For example, VAT and transfer pricing rules are similar in many tax systems as a result of the aforementioned discourse. Yet, their correct application is far from satisfactory and tax administrations can seldom hire the best interpreters to bring the enacted tax rules, amendments and reforms into a fully successful application. The situation is even more critical in developing countries, where those interpreters will never be hired. The story is different in respect of legal drafters, since time spent and degree of difficulty are significantly less than time and difficulty required in correctly interpreting and applying the law and because legal drafters with comparative law backgrounds provide technical assistance, as is the case for our external legal drafter, in the framework of international assistance programs, such as those of the IMF or the World Bank.

IV. FACTICITIES AND VALIDITY: HABERMAS AND TAX REFORM

Hart's rules of recognition are relevant in this chapter in order to solve any conflicts among plural legalities. However, it is contended here that Hart's rules of recognition are insufficient to grant validity to legal systems, since validity requires that the rules are the product of genuine argumentative interaction among the representatives of different legalities (facticities in the Habermasian sense)[24] and that includes tax reforms. As a consequence, it is herein contended that the rules of recognition also have to be valid in the Habermasian sense.[25] Thus, our Hercules legislator will not only have to deal with the plural legalities in force and the rules of recognition, but also solve the challenges of facticity and validity and the tension resulting therefrom.

---

24 These concepts are therefore used here in the Habermasian sense and further discussed below: see Habermas, *supra* note 20, at 32–55.

25 *Ibid.*

In this context, facticity broadly corresponds to the individual legalities in force in a certain state, as stated by each participant in a communication discourse. Those individual legalities may include strict tax legalities, if there are any (for example, traditional poll taxes and taxes on transactions, language and currency used in tax accounting duties), and legalities with consequences in a tax regime (such as the concept of marriage and family, traditional contracts and inheritance rules).

First, consider the example of the family unit for tax purposes. Are polygamous marriages recognized by state tax law, for the purposes of aggregate taxation and allowances? In a state facing diverse meanings of marriage are all of them valid, in a communication process? In a dynamic and normative perspective, should all of them be recognized by state tax law?

Second, consider the example of how tax rules apply to diverse immigrant communities in a state. Assume that an immigrant community organizes itself according to its own economic rules, which differ from the rules of the mainstream population, and that its economic activity is subsidized by its state of origin. As a condition for investing in our developing country that community requires that its tax accounting is accounted for in its own language; it moreover requires that the value of the transactions carried on in the course of business is written down in its own or another foreign currency. Do the principles of equality and of the market economy require a free use of diverse languages for tax purposes? Do they require that transactions are to be accounted for in any currency? Does, in contrast, the ability to pay principle require that every immigrant community has to account for its economic transactions in the language of the host country, for tax purposes? Does the principle of a sovereign state require that transactions are exclusively written down, for tax purposes, in its national currency?

Facticities and legalities will hereinafter be used as synonyms. It is assumed here that each kind of legality will be directly or indirectly represented in the legislative commission. In turn, validity is the result achieved by the argumentative interaction among those participants and among the members of the parliament in a democratically elected assembly voting on the tax reform.[26] This implies that our external legal drafter will have the opportunity to be aware of the rules derived by traditional legalities, the rules derived by colonial inheritance, the rules that will attract foreign investment in general and some foreign industries in particular (e.g., oil companies) and the rules that will allow the country

---

26 *Ibid.*

to be part of the international tax legal community. She will have to acknowledge to an adequate extent each of these legalities and, like the Hercules judge, our Hercules legislator will have to find a coherent compromise among them. Through that coherence she will seek to ensure that her drafts become law reform proposals and ultimately legislation in force (becoming a fact and valid).

As mentioned above, a Hercules legislator has to draft her proposals in a foreign legislative commission hosting her, to which she presents her fundamental ideas on a certain tax code and corresponding essential tax elements (tax object, tax subject and the quantification elements) – hereinafter, the legal type of tax.[27] If she starts by presenting her model or the legal type of tax corresponding to what she believes to be a universally valid tax code, she will do it using her previous background.

In the context of drafting new legislation for a foreign legal system, the external legal expert's initial proposal is a 'fact', and not the 'real truth' in the Habermasian sense.[28] Facts are statements corresponding to mere individual truths that the external legal expert wants to communicate to the addressee (the national legislative commission, her clients) as an objective truth. This objective truth is a valid solution,[29] a best practice. However, it is only the starting point, and as such, facts and individual truths brought by the external legal drafter are not the 'final assessment'. To achieve validity in the host legal system implies acting by communicating, and this requires her to carefully consider her clients' facticities.[30] She is expected to act in this commission through genuine communication and critical reasoning aimed at reaching an agreement on the right tax solutions.

For the Hercules legislator, like the Hercules judge, coherence will result from a compromise among different legal principles coexisting hand-in-hand, and from correct interpretation of those principles. For example, the meaning of wealth and of ability to pay can be different for different religious and community groups, for inhabitants of the countryside and for those residing and working in the city, for the different cultural communities and nations. An external legal drafter facing plural legalities will have to interpret them and try to reach a compromise that should be a right answer – in order to represent it in the communicative discourse, a normative perspective will be adopted, as will be explained below.

---

27 Dourado, *supra* note 4, at 16.

28 Habermas, *supra* note 20, at 29 *et seq.*

29 *Ibid.*

30 *Ibid.* 30–31.

However, unlike the role of a judge, who arguably can grant the right answer,[31] a Hercules tax legislator can merely aim at a right answer, not only because it is imaginable that the combination of facticities can be achieved in more than one valid manner (for example, what is taxable wealth and what is the amount of tax to be imposed), but also because a legislative right answer is general and abstract (it has also been claimed by some of the literature that what Dworkin's Hercules judge can reach is merely *a right answer* instead of *the right answer*).[32] Whereas the Hercules judge interpreting conflicting principles in a concrete case will determine the validity of some of them in that case and leave others dormant, our Hercules legislator when excluding some legalities from her draft law will assess them as invalid as a result of a communication process and on the basis of critical reasoning. Detailed process rules regarding competence, political representation in parliament, frequency of parliamentary sessions, enacting procedures, constraints and others in the legislative procedure are all relevant to a law that aims to be valid, but they are not the focus of this chapter.

If the communication process with the legislative commission composed of national authorities is not carefully handled, and if the national authorities do not in turn represent the plural legalities in a certain state legal system, it is likely that the enacted tax law will not be valid, because it will not be recognized as such by all relevant players: tax administration, tax judges and the different communities of taxpayers. One of the major challenges for our Hercules legislator is to assess whether and to what extent traditional facticities are valid. In order to assess this, she and the legislative commission have to verify whether those traditional truths can be critically discussed in the communication process: for example, whether the enforcement of a traditional tax system is recognized by the addressees, whether it is enforced on the basis of a traditional authority or a religious one, or whether there are individual rights resulting from any taxes paid to traditional authorities. If traditional facticities cannot be critically discussed and are respected on the basis of mythical, ritual and cultural transmission of knowledge, if those truths are enforced by a traditional authority or a religious one, and if human penalties are secondary, they will not qualify for the communication process and will not be assessed as valid.[33]

---

[31] See *supra* note 1.

[32] Jules L. Coleman and Brian Leiter, 'Determinacy, Objectivity, and Authority' in *Law and Interpretation, Essays in Legal Philosophy* (Oxford/New York, Clarendon Press, 1997 (1995)) 214–15.

[33] Habermas, *supra* note 20, at 39–41.

The result achieved from this communication process aims to be valid over time, but our external legal drafter will be aware that the validity of some of the rules of the legal type of tax will be relative both in time and in space. More concretely, the timeframe of validity depends substantially on the type of tax code and tax elements that are handled in a tax reform. For example, a general tax code will tend to be valid for a long period, whereas the validity of a corporate income tax will very much depend on the underlying domestic, regional and international economy and on the domestic political regime and corresponding policies. Moreover, within a corporate income tax code, some rules corresponding to the legal type of tax are more stable (tax object, tax subject and some aspects of the tax base, such as the option between source and worldwide taxation or the meaning of profits and costs), and others less stable (the ones corresponding to the quantification of the tax, such as deductible costs).

Whereas approval of the more stable group of rules is normally subject to the parliament's competence, approval of the less stable group is often delegated to the Ministry of Finance or to the tax administration[34] and implying a faster approval procedure. The same distinction between groups of tax rules – more stable and less stable ones – applies in respect of their universal validity (validity beyond national frontiers of the legal tax solutions agreed upon).

In general, however, contrary to the validity of legal solutions considered by Habermas,[35] validity in tax law is often limited to relatively narrow time and space frames. This is because taxes are very much dependent on other legal and economic institutions and policies and the latter vary quickly in the current era of open and globalized economies. The only exceptions are the fundamental principles of tax law, which may be granted either constitutional ranking or are in general tax codes.

A. Plural Legalities Ignored by the Legislator and the Role of Tax Officials and Traditional Authorities

This chapter focuses on legal drafting, but difficulties and constraints regarding legal interpretation also have to be mentioned. Consider again the example of the married tax unit. Imagine that income tax law provides for a tax regime for married couples that is more favorable than the one applied to single individuals. Marriage, for the purpose of personal income tax, means monogamous heterosexual marriage,

---

34 Dourado, *supra* note 4, at 22.

35 Habermas, *supra* note 20, at 36–7.

although in that country, Muslims, Animists, Christians, Hindus and many other religious and atheist communities coexist. If it is accepted here that this example illustrates a case of underlying conflicting legalities that have not been solved in a satisfactory manner by the state law, the application of law by state officials – administration and courts – will imply an assessment of the multiple legalities in force, in order to reach the whole and the inner morality of law.[36] The latter will be reached by the official in the manner in which she manages to combine the diverse legalities, but its achievement will be better or worse depending on the state legal conditions to become an agent of the administration, a judge, or an arbiter and to exercise those functions.

If a state manages to grant some central guidance by a precedence rule to the courts, or by somehow imposing settled case law by supreme courts on lower courts, and by rulings by the central tax administration that bind the different tax departments and officials, then the aforementioned subjective combination of legalities by each official will turn out to be a combination achieved with some harmony by the state officials. The more the central state guidance is exercised and is binding, the faster the plurality of legalities will convert into a state legal order, accommodating the underlying legalities and contributing to the effectiveness of the separation of powers in tax law, generality of law and equality. Application of state law by officials can be combined with the nomination of a local authority or arbiter, to resolve disputes according to a traditional legality in a certain cultural community.[37] The local authority or arbiter can act either alone or by integrating a jury of state officials, who have discretion to combine state and non-state law according to the concrete circumstances of the case.

Later in this chapter we will refer to the dynamic perspective of legal pluralism in contemporary developing countries. At this point, it is enough to note that the requirements to be a public official or an arbiter applying a traditional legality are dictated by state law or regulations and the same is true in respect of procedural rules (competence, law

---

[36] On the inner morality of law, see Lon Fuller, 'Positivism and Fidelity to Law: A Reply to Professor Hart' (1958) 71 *Harvard Law Review Forum* 630 at 637, 645; and on that inner morality being applicable not only to the state legal system but also to 'subordinate legal systems', see Lon Fuller, *The Morality of Law* (revised edn, New Haven, CT: Yale University Press, 1969) 126; Waldron, *supra* note 12, at 150–54.

[37] On non-state justice systems and their relationship to state justice systems: see Miranda Forsyth, 'A Typology of Relationships between State and Non-State Justice Systems' (2007) 56 *Legal Pluralism and Unofficial Law* 67.

applicable, etc.). State law may well provide for or authorize a combined application of traditional and state law by those officials and arbiters.

However, if it is expected that the officials exclusively apply state law, the inner morality of the whole will depend on the recognition of the state law by the officials, and assuming Hart's rule of recognition[38] applies, the submission of those officials to the state law in detriment to other legalities, is a question of degree, and will depend on how much discretion state law will grant the officials. Depending on the field of regulation, there can be both positive conflicts and recognition between these officials and their respective functions, on the one hand, and the traditional authorities accepted as such by the pre-colonial society rules, on the other hand.

In any case, the dynamic of legalities within a particular country implies that conflicts among them will not always be solved at the level of the enacted tax reform, that is, at the level of the written law. On the one hand, not all conflicting legalities will be foreseeable, and on the other hand, the balance among them is to be found in a dynamic perspective. For this assessment, it is irrelevant whether an external legal drafter proposes a tax reform or whether the latter is exclusively carried out by national committees and by the national parliament. It can be assumed, as a general proposition, that there will be more conflicts if external legal drafters intervene, since they may not be familiar with the different legalities. However, our Hercules legislator knows that if she becomes acquainted with the plural legalities in force she will avoid some conflicts that may occur among them at the moment of application, even if it is not possible to solve all of them in the enacted state law.

If the rules of recognition still accommodate some non-state rules, namely, by granting discretion in some tax matters to the officials, validity of the tax reform will be more likely to be successful in space and time. The vaguer the norm, the more it will accommodate the complexity of society, different normative viewpoints and appropriateness to the concrete case will be a decision left to the application level.[39] However, in respect of tax base rules and tax offences rules, legal vagueness should be avoided if the level of corruption among officials is high (see section VIII B below).

In order to test whether our external legal drafter has managed to reach validity of a tax reform in a communication process, the application

---

38 In the sense of Hart, *supra* note 14, at 97–120.

39 See Klaus Günther, *The Sense of Appropriateness: Application Discourses in Morality and Law* (John Farrell (trans.), New York: State University of New York Press, 1989) e.g., 77–85, 113–35, 167–70.

moment is crucial: whether the instances applying the law recognize that state tax law as valid (Hart); whether they recognize it as the only valid law or valid at all if it is not inherently moral (Fuller); whether after a tax reform non-state legalities oppose state legality and to what extent the former are still recognized by the competent officials; and whether the competent officials are granted discretion by state law in order to weigh other legal rules enacted by non-state authorities.

V. COMPLEXITY OF LEGALITIES

A. Vertical and Horizontal Dimensions

The complexity of the legalities that can be found in our developing country can bring together the whole amount of combined possibilities an academic can imagine in a theoretical exercise and, with them, some constraints on a tax reform compliant with the rule of law. The multiple legalities can be divided in a vertical dimension (and by that is meant the state versus traditional legalities) and a horizontal dimension (meaning the relationship among the different traditional legalities).

In a vertical dimension, the multiple legalities may be separate and prohibited by state law, may be separate but ignored by the state (i.e., tolerated) or may be explicitly recognized by state law.[40] For example, a poll tax charged in a traditional community by the traditionally recognized authority may be incompatible with the constitutional ability to pay principle and in that case prohibited, it may be ignored by state law or it may be expressly foreseen by state law.

Non-recognition of different legalities by state law can be as damaging as their prohibition. In relation to our example of marriage above, if the state law only recognizes certain types of private contract, such as monogamous marriage between two persons of different sex, it does not prohibit other marriages concluded according to different rules and legalities, but it will not recognize any rights resulting thereof. State non-recognition will amount to state discriminatory treatment, in respect of taxes, if monogamous heterosexual couples and corresponding family aggregates are handled in a more favorable way than other couples or unmarried individuals.

Another example relates to the application of property tax exclusively to the onerous transfer of building sites ('urban immovable property'),

---

40 See Facchi, *supra* note 6, at e.g., 3–11, 37–45, 51–7.

where the transfer of land ('rural immovable property') is not taxable. This tax regime is justified by a constitutional prohibition (state legality) to the transfer of land (land belongs to the state and cannot be transferred).[41] Nonetheless, the right to use and exploitation of the soil for agricultural, industrial, commercial or building purposes, as well as sites built on it, can be transferred. The right to transfer the use and exploitation of the soil between private parties is granted by the municipalities and a fee is charged upon that transfer. Furthermore, a market price is being applied between those private parties to this transfer: the market price will vary according to market elements such as dimension and location and will be reflected both in the market and in the effectively applied price. These private contracts are tolerated but not recognized by the state (and municipalities), and state law does not grant them any tax value either. The result of this complex set of legalities is that the transfer of land will have a more beneficial tax treatment than the sale of a building site and this will lead to distortions.

Different vertical legalities in force can equally be recognized in the coexistence of state, regional and municipal rules, binding international law and law enacted by international organizations to which a state belongs. The latter meaning can be found in federal states and in regional integrations, such as the Member States of the European Union[42] and many others around the world, including developing countries and within these African sub-Saharan countries (e.g., OHADA[43] and SADEC).[44]

In a horizontal dimension, different legalities can coexist under the umbrella of the same state and of the same state law (e.g., Muslims and

---

[41] Mozambican Constitution, arts 109 and 110.

[42] Miguel Poiares Maduro, *We the Court: The European Court of Justice and the European Economic Constitution* (Oxford: Hart Publishing, 1998); Miguel Poiares Maduro, 'Contrapunctual Law: Europe's Constitutional Pluralism in Action' in Neil Walker (ed.), *Sovereignty in Transition* (Oxford: Hart Publishing, 2003: 501–37; Miguel Poiares Maduro, *A Constituição Plural, Constitucionalismo e União Europeia* (São João do Estoril: Principia, 2006) chs I, IV; Koen Lenaerts, 'Constitutionalism and the Many Faces of Federalism' (1992) 38(2) *American Journal of Comparative Law* 205.

[43] The Treaty of the Organization for the Harmonization of Business Law in Africa was signed on 17 October 1993, and the OHADA has 16 member states: Benin, Burkina Faso, Cameroon, Central African Republic, Comoros, Congo, Ivory Coast, Gabon, Guinea, Guinea-Bissau, Equatorial Guinea, Mali, Niger, Senegal, Chad and Togo. This number is likely to evolve to include new members, whether or not members of the Organization of African Unity (OAU). The signatories to the OHADA Treaty are also members of the CFA (common currency linked to the French franc).

Animists) in multiple adjacent communities without dialogue and interaction and that amounts to mutual tolerance of the adjacent communities without the recognition of their rules as binding outside each of the communities.[45]

It is here assumed that our developing country constitutionally recognizes fiscal and regulatory competence of municipal communities and that it is member of a regional integration the treaty of which is inspired by the Treaties of the European Union. The first assumption corresponds to the horizontal dimension of legal pluralism, and may facilitate coexistence of different local taxes based on traditional legalities. The second assumption corresponds to the vertical dimension of legal pluralism and will lead to an increase of transplanted categories. The dynamic dimension of legal pluralism and the assessment of transplanted categories in the context of tax reforms in developing countries will be discussed below.

B. Global Tax Legal Discourse and its Layers of Influence

It is contended here that the global legal discourse should have different layers of influence. In private legal relations or private law fields, such as family law, the global dialogue is restricted to areas of fundamental rights, or to a certain concept of the rule of law, at least where that discourse is essentially liberal and tends to acknowledge diversity.[46] In contrast, in respect of global business, the global discourse aims at handling multinationals, charities, and other non-governmental organizations, according to uniform principles and rules. The fact that developing countries are not able to influence the rules of the current global order leaves them the 'tragic choice'[47] between granting full tax incentives in order to attract investment by multinationals, and accepting sophisticated and controversial rules adopted by OECD member states,

---

44 South African Development Community Treaty, 17 August 1993, as amended. SADC has the following members: Angola, Botswana, Lesotho, Malawi, Mozambique, Namibia, Swaziland, Tanzania, Zambia, Zimbabwe.

45 See, e.g., Facchi, *supra* note 6, at 3 *et seq.*

46 For example, Ayelet Shachar, *Multicultural Jurisdiction, Cultural Differences and Women's Rights* (Cambridge: Cambridge University Press, 2001) 45–63; and also Werner Menskim, 'Indian Secular Pluralism and its Relevance for Europe' in Ralph Grillo *et al.* (eds), *Legal Practice and Cultural Diversity* (Farnham/Burlington: Ashgate, 2009) 31–47; Gordon R. Woodman, 'The Challenge of African Customary Laws to English Legal Culture' in *Legal Practice and Cultural Diversity', id.* 135–47.

47 See Tsilly Dagan, Chapter 3.

such as arm's length transfer pricing rules, and which are also unsatisfactory to the latter states. This very often means that developing countries have to be satisfied with only appearing on the map of international investment, even if by reducing corporate tax rates and granting tax holidays to international investment, in order to participate in the uncoordinated global tax competition.[48] Sometimes, they create offshore centers to become destinies of dematerialized financial services. It is disputed that offshore centers bring economic benefits from a worldwide point of view[49] and they seem to contribute very little to the GDP of inefficient host developing countries, except by creating an obscure area outside the state control, or a parallel state the rules of which are unclear, and by granting loans at interest rates generally not available to the local population and local investment.[50]

Global norms of taxation are not, however, restricted to taxation of multinational companies, or to non-governmental organizations operating worldwide, but also apply to other taxpayers. In fact, international legal players tend to export rules in respect of every taxpayer, including medium and small-sized companies and individuals. The reason for this seems to be the use of a basic legal language and technique, understood by a drafter as the only one that brings legal preciseness to a legal system and improves it. Tax concepts such as net income, resident taxpayer, source of income, permanent establishment, depreciation, proportional or progressive rates, and withholding taxes are in their broad terms common to every jurisdiction. Where some jurisdictions have identified tax planning activities, especially cross-border tax planning activities and have generated a legislative reaction to such tax planning, these may prove to be best practices that could be followed by other jurisdictions, whether they are OECD member states or developing countries.

Whereas pure exportation of legal solutions will lead to uniformity without the recommended critical analysis, such best practices should be critically reviewed taking into account their appropriateness for the

---

48 Clemens Fuest and Nadine Riedel, 'Tax Evasion, Tax Avoidance and Tax Expenditures in Developing Countries: A Review of the Literature', *Report Prepared for the UK Department for International Development*, I–VI, 1–69, spec. 39–46, available at http://94.126.106.9/R4D/PDF/Outputs/EcoDev/60670_TaxEvasionReportDFIDFINAL1906.pdf.

49 *Ibid.*

50 See, e.g., the offshore regime in São Tomé e Príncipe, Decree-Law No. 61/95, Diário da República de S. Tomé e Príncipe, 31 December 1995, 3.º Suplemento; Decree-Law No. 70/95, Diário da República de S. Tomé e Príncipe, 31 December 1995, 7.º Suplemento.

country undergoing a reform.[51] Full rejection of globalization would not only imply rejecting global business, but also exchange of ideas and knowledge.[52]

VI. A NORMATIVE AND DYNAMIC APPROACH TO LEGAL PLURALISM

If a tax reform does not comply with some of the existing plural legalities, and in its application, administrators are not granted discretion to apply non-state rules, the consequence will either be generalized tax evasion in respect of state taxes and corresponding complicity by the officials or pressure to impose state law if the authorities accept the rule of recognition. Nevertheless, the acknowledgement of plural legalities in force in a developing country does not imply that all of them will be accepted in a tax reform. Our Hercules legislator will handle plural legalities not only in a descriptive perspective, but also in a normative one.[53] Achieving validity of a tax reform in the Habermasian sense also implies a normative perspective of legal pluralism.

The rule of law is inherent to this normative perspective, since it contains criteria that should apply universally, and therefore, also to developing countries in the context of globalization. Our external legal drafter will also take into account the dynamic nature of legalities, that is, that pluralistic settings evolve. A resolution of tensions among and between legal pluralities ideally leads to (valid) rules of recognition that contain criteria that solve any emerging conflicts uniformly. Validity of the tax reform depends on the communication process, on the rule of recognition and also on its inherent morality – ultimately, on whether the rule of law is accomplished.[54]

This approach is required to modernize a tax system, and improve its justice and efficiency by taking into account comparative legal solutions.

---

[51] See a critical perspective on globalization of pseudo universal categories: David Schneiderman, 'Commentary, Pluralism, Disagreement, and Globalization: A Comment on Webber's Legal Pluralism and Human Agency' (2006) 44(1) *Osgood Hall Law Journal* 199 at 205–9.

[52] Sen, *supra* note 23, at 122–5; Santos, *supra* note 23.

[53] On the descriptive and normative levels of legal pluralism, see Waldron, *supra* note 12, at 136–7. See also, William Twinning, 'Normative and Legal Pluralism: A Global Perspective' (2009–2010) 20 *Duke Journal of Comparative and International Law* 473.

[54] See Fuller, *supra* note 36.

The absence of that perspective would mean ignorance and carelessness, and a barrier to the movement of values, knowledge and ideas that can contribute to mutual understanding and improvement of the situation of the most disadvantaged members of a society and of the world population.[55]

The normative dimension assesses legal pluralism as a dynamic process, justifies amendments to law and reforms based on local and universal principles inherent to the rule of law, as well as policies aimed at a certain result. It ultimately aims at reaching unity instead of pluralism, for the sake of the principles of generality and equality. Similarly to the Hercules judge, who is expected to fulfill the principles of certainty and legitimacy by a coherent reasoning, in order to reach a unitary answer, our Hercules legislator will use substantive arguments (reasoning) and seek an agreement rationally motivated.

Thus, in a normative and dynamic perspective, unity of law will result from the parliament's decision on the basis of a proposal drafted by experts that take into account plural legalities and as long as the community and officials accept the corresponding rules of recognition.[56] A parallel between the concept of law, its validity in the static perspective, and its validity in the normative and dynamic perspectives (the perspective of reforms) can be drawn with the public choice theories and welfare economics, respectively, where for the former, justice is assessed in light of the procedural criteria adopted (procedural aspects assessed in themselves, on their legitimacy and illegitimacy) whereas for the latter equity and efficiency are a result of a trade-off.[57] The validity in the normative and dynamic perspective – the perspective of a reform – fulfills the purpose of material justice in a more satisfactory manner. In other words, the normative approach to legal pluralism implies not only an assessment on legitimate procedures – whether legalities are valid or not – but also a material assessment of the legalities and their potential overlap.

If a Hercules legislator proposes what she considers to be the best legal solution, plural legalities also have to be assessed in light of the rule of

---

55 Sen, *supra* note 23, e.g. chs 2 and 7; Santos, *supra* note 23.

56 See this dynamic perspective in Waldron, *supra* note 12, at 150–55.

57 See, e.g., A.C. Pigou, *The Economics of Welfare* (3rd edn, London: Macmillan, 1929); Amartya Sen, 'The Impossibility of a Paretian Liberal' (1970) 1 *Journal of Political Economy* 152; versus James Buchanan, e.g., *The Demand and Supply of Public Goods* (Chicago, IL: McNally, 1968) and Gordon Tullock, 'Problems of Majority Voting' in K. J. Arrow and T. Scitovsky (eds), *Readings in Welfare Economics* (London: George Allen & Unwin, 1969) 169–78.

law parameters considered adequate to a certain state in the world. It is not important that legal solutions are exported in one or the other direction, the important aspect is that the best practices and solutions are adopted wherever they are adequate.[58]

Contrary to the situation assumed under section IV, above, if our Hercules legislator carefully steers the process, some conflicts among plural legalities at the application level will be avoided, and the competent officials will seldom have to solve conflicts among primary rules when applying rules of recognition. State law will incorporate the traditional legalities that were judged as valid during the communication process and the rules of recognition will assess state law as valid.

In the next sections it will be discussed how the normative and dynamic perspectives of legal pluralism apply to a tax reform.

VII. FROM PLURALISM TO UNITY IN TAXES

A. Common Colonial Tax Regimes, Common Constraints and Common Challenges

Let us now assume that our Hercules legislator will be in charge of reforming taxes not only in one developing country but in a group of them with a common political and legal (past) history, because they were colonies of the same colonial master. The first round of tax reforms in each of those countries is based on a common tax legal history, a colonial tax system, with schedular taxes and flat rates and no separation between the tax administration and the tax courts (no independent tax courts). It can moreover be assumed that tax reforms and corresponding introduction of global and progressive taxation of income and of a value added tax has been delayed in each of those developing countries, because they went through a socialist period immediately after independence, and during that period, the colonial tax system was kept in force.

Each of these developing countries is willing to apply a non-discriminatory tax regime independently of the nationality of the shareholders (in the sense that no major obstacles exist to constituting a company and to providing services to any of these developing economies). It is also assumed that they are, at least formally, rule-of-law states. Separation of powers is a provision included in their written

---

[58] See, in a broad context, Sen, *supra* note 23, at 122–4.

constitutions, although the extent to which that separation of powers is effectively applied is not totally known.

However, it can be concluded that in those countries where the constitutional court has already declared tax laws unconstitutional, namely, because the government has passed decree-laws without being authorized by parliamentary law, separation of powers is working in a satisfactory manner. Literacy of population and tax administration and corruption indexes are broadly taken into account for the purposes of the reform, since the former are presumed to be relatively low outside the main cities and the latter to be relatively high throughout the territory of those countries. Both the low literacy of the population and corruption are constraints to the tax reform, because they will be an impediment to equality (of 'subjective freedoms in action') and consequently to the communication discourse and to validity of laws.[59]

The purpose of introducing tax reforms coincides with the opening of those economies to the market. Our developing countries rely more on revenues from trade taxes and foreign assistance, have high levels of public debt, and lag behind in terms of public spending regarding basic goods. Legal drafting issues and administrative constraints in their implementation compromise adequate revenues in general, and especially in respect of taxes requiring high administrative skills on application and control.[60] The classic goals of tax systems and tax reforms corresponding to the most equitable and efficient taxes,[61] even if valid in the context of plural legalities, are not easy to apply to our developing countries, due to the aforementioned constraints.

B. Common Normative Solutions

Taking into account the above, it is necessary for the Hercules legislator to establish a tax reform that finds a balance among traditional legalities

[59] Habermas, *supra* note 20, at 153–65.

[60] William Crandall and Jean-Paul Bodin, *Revenue Administration Reform in Middle Eastern Countries, 1994–2004*, IMF Working Paper WP/05/203 (IMF, 2005); Richard M. Bird and Eric M. Zolt, 'Tax Policy in Emerging Countries' (2008) 26 *Environment and Planning C: Government and Policy* 73; Richard Bird, 'Administrative Dimension of Tax Reform' (2004) *Asia-Pacific Tax Bulletin* (March) 134, available at http://unpan1.un.org/intradoc/groups/public/documents/UNPAN/UNPAN015761.pdf.

[61] See James Banks and Peter Diamond, *The Base for Direct Taxation,* Prepared for the Report of a Commission on Reforming the Tax System for the 21st Century, Chaired by Sir James Mirrlees (Institute for Fiscal Studies, 2008), available at www.ifs.org.uk/mirrleesreview.

and state legalities. The reform will have to deal with the past colonial legality, the aforementioned economic, social and cultural constraints and the challenges the new state faces in light of globalization and the concomitant aim to attract foreign investment. It is contended here that, in a normative approach, tax principles based on the rule of law have to prevail over the traditional legalities, in the case of conflict (including the principle of ability to pay and the connected tax principles of net income, progressive or at least proportional taxation of individual income, proportional taxation of corporate income, broad tax bases).

As discussed above, there are many ways to design tax laws in line with those principles and the particular approach should depend on the specific economic and social circumstances of the country undergoing a tax reform and on the policies to be followed. Even so, modernization of the colonial tax system complying with the rule of law will require application of general recommendations. Assuming that the country is able to attract investment in diversified economic sectors (such as agriculture, tourism, minerals and oil, building sites, roads and rails, telecommunication, water and energy resources, commerce, research in science and technology), and the services sector is relatively well organized,[62] these general recommendations include replacing schedular proportional taxes by a single progressive personal income tax (or, more accurately, by a dual tax system) and a single corporate tax, and taxes on transactions by VAT. Whereas income tax will be aimed at a broad tax base, if tax incentives are simultaneously introduced in order to attract foreign direct investment, the tax system will become incoherent. In the current era of global tax competition and regional integration, the reduced ability of governments to tax mobile factors and to raise revenue under corporate income tax put pressure on productive government expenditure (infrastructure, education, health care) that are vital for the group of developing countries we are considering in this chapter.[63]

In contrast, if the economy and social organization are totally dependent on one industry (for example, the oil industry), and the other economic sectors are non-existent or much simpler, a special tax regime on petroleum operations, combined with simple proportional taxes, will be recommended: a simple tax on business income and services, a wage

---

62 Jean A.P. Clément and Shanaka Aianath Peiris, *Post-Stabilization Economics in Sub-Saharan Africa: Lessons from Mozambique* (IMF, 2008).

63 Liam Ebrill, Janet Stotsky and Reint Gropp, *Revenue Implications of Trade Liberalization* (Washington, DC: IMF, 1999).

tax, a simple excise tax, and an export/import duty tax, all of them with proportional and low rates.[64]

Even if the tax principles and the main aspects of the tax types in a rule-of-law state are identified worldwide and are not exclusive to one or another legal system, they are very much dependent on the recognition of state legality. If a small country with a poor economy lacks basic state organization and cohesion and if traditional legalities prevail, the concept of tax will be practically non-existent. If, moreover, there are no foreign economic operators interested in investing in that country, it is recommended that very simple taxes be adopted, observing the basic principle of ability to pay, that are easy to administer.[65] The basic effort should then be concentrated in organizing a rule-of-law state and bringing the informal sector into the formal economy.

Every tax system also has to reflect the country's economic structure, its capacity to administer taxes, its public service needs, its access to other sources of revenue such as aid or oil and, in a normative perspective of legal pluralism, the constitutional principles regarding taxes that are common to rule-of-law states and are often part of general tax codes. The tax morale and the tax culture in a certain country and system have likewise to be taken into account and possibly improved.[66] This requires joint work by the tax legal drafters, improvement of the atmosphere of trust between the taxpayer and the tax administration, and reduction of corruption level by granting morals to the function, through the good example of the top officials, training courses abroad, increase of salaries, reduction of legal indeterminacy in tax base rules and tax offences rules, and strong promotion of independent courts.

Moreover, tax policy has to be connected with the macroeconomic fiscal goals of reducing inflation, interest, budget deficits and public debt to one digit and measures taken to achieve them. Those goals follow the general consensus: broadening the tax base (both in income and consumption taxes), reducing tax rates (especially in income taxes, where corporate income tax and inflation have lead to higher rates than in OECD countries) and improving administration performance through

---

64 See the example of the tax legislation of Timor L'Este: Decree-Law 8/2008; available at www.pwc.com/en_ID/id/publications/assets/east-timor-tax-book-2005.pdf; www.mof.gov.tl/wp-content/uploads/2010/07/Taxes_and_Duties_Act_2008.pdf.

65 See Banks and Diamond, *supra* note 61.

66 Richard M. Bird, *Tax Challenges Facing Developing Countries*, University of Toronto, Institute for International Business Working Paper Series, IIB Paper No. 12 (2008) 1–33.

intensive investment in new technologies. Efficient organization of the tax administration, through avoidance of labor-intensive structures, and overlapping of functions by different departments, and simultaneously finding a structure that corresponds to the administrative culture of the country, is a challenge in order to avoid spillover of resources.

In this context, legal drafting solutions inspired by comparative law and global tax legal discourse will vary, taking into account the constraints, challenges and the purposes of tax policy in each legal system: for example, either the purpose regarding attraction of foreign investment or the purpose of taxation at source of such foreign investment, through withholding taxes; or a balance between both purposes; the purpose of simplifying the tax system or combating tax avoidance of certain groups of risk or an adequate balance between both of them.

C. Unity, Equality and Validity

It has been mentioned above that traditional tax legalities could be related to taxes imposed by traditional authorities (pre-colonial legalities), to compliance with duties in different languages and currencies and to different concepts of ability to pay that neither coincide with the structure of state taxes nor with the concept of ability to pay according to the state rule of recognition. In a normative perspective, as long as taxes imposed by traditional authorities result from the communication discourse and are considered to be valid by the members of a traditional community in the Habermasian sense, they may coexist with state taxes, since they will not be contrary to the rule of law and to the normative perspective of legal pluralism. Those traditional taxes can be an income tax, a sales tax, a property tax or a poll tax adopting a commonly accepted concept of ability to pay. In such a case, state taxes must take into account the total tax burden imposed on a taxpayer, in order to prevent double taxation resulting from traditional and state taxes leading to confiscatory taxation or generalized tax avoidance and/or evasion. In contrast, taxes imposed by traditional authorities that are not valid in the Habermasian sense described above are to be rejected.

Moreover, state taxes must take into account other legalities with influence on taxes, such as traditional contracts and traditional concepts of wealth, traditional concepts of the family aggregate, as well as contracts based on market rules, but not recognized by state law (such as the transfer of use and exploitation of land to which a market price is granted, beyond the payment of a fee). Otherwise, state taxes will not cover many contracts revealing ability to pay, on the one hand, and will not cover all meanings of the family aggregate, which will lead to inequities, inefficiencies and abuse. Major challenges to state taxes in a developing country are taxation of multinationals, taxation of the informal sector and taxation of immigrant communities unable to benefit from special tax regimes who seek a privileged treatment in respect of tax compliance.

State taxes must try to cover all valid meanings of ability to pay in the state, even if this leads to some overlapping with infra-state taxes: this is an issue to be solved by an assessment about the vertical tax legalities. Thus, in taxes, unity of law means accepting and discussing the fundamental principles regarding equality among taxpayers, on the one hand (of ability to pay, of direct versus indirect taxes, of worldwide versus source taxation of income, progressivity versus proportionality or the amount of progressivity, global taxation of income versus dual systems, of taxing the formal and the informal sector) and equality among different political communities in the sense of fiscal federalism, on the other hand, and efficiency. The meaning of equality in personal and corporate income taxes is not self-evident, since measuring the ability to pay of an individual is far from undisputed. In fact, equality will very much depend on the concept of income, on the assessment rules, and on whether there is an option between net and gross taxation of income.

In personal income taxes, a decision may have to be taken on whether ability to pay is the individual ability to pay or the ability to pay of a group, such as a family. In that respect, it may have to be discussed whether the ability to pay of a family aggregate is relevant, what is a family aggregate for income tax purposes, and ultimately whether ability to pay of an aggregate as determined by traditional legalities is to be accepted and to what extent. Before unity of law is reached, ability to pay of plural aggregates according to plural legalities could be taken into account and it could be concluded that infra-state taxes or even infra-state fees to tax them would be more adequate than state taxes.

Tax equality in income taxes is also dependent on the concept of income, as well as on what constitutes net income, which assessment methods are adequate, to whom and when they are applicable (direct versus indirect methods), how the informal sector, on the one hand, and groups of companies and multinationals, on the other hand, are to be assessed.

D. Role of Transplanted Categories

The smooth evolution of a tax system calls for the previous colonial system to be taken into account, in order to avoid discontinuities, and that the tax systems belonging to the same legal family are taken into closer consideration than other comparative solutions. The fact that taxes fall on private law relations and that tax law interacts with nearly all legal fields (constitutional, administrative, company, insolvency, family and inheritance, contracts, penal law and administrative offences law, as well as public international law) also implies that prior attention has to be granted to the domestic legal system, and to those legal systems belonging to the same family.

This is true not only in respect of the written law in force, but also in respect of the courts' case law, since courts often rely on the case law of the ex-colonial master courts, transplanting categories in a more or less accurate way.[67] Both national courts and tax administration very often quote tax law commentaries and tax books regarding the tax laws of the ex-colonial master. This is especially true for general tax codes and any procedural and judicial process laws.

Two categories of transplanted concepts and regimes have to be taken into account, when discussing tax reforms in developing countries belonging to a certain family of law: the transplanted legal categories imported by tax law from other legal areas, such as dependent workers, independent workers, private property, building sites, land, sale, usufruct, rental, inheritance, gift – where the private and public law domestically written concepts are transplanted from the ex-colonial master legislation in force at the time of the reform; and the transplanted tax concepts or regimes such as taxpayer, allowances, burden of proof. These concepts and regimes can either be transplanted by the legislator or by national courts and tax administration when interpreting domestic law.

Transplantation of legal categories is also a dynamic process involving diversified influences.[68] Many tax concepts and regimes reveal a universal language, overcoming the traditional division between civil law and common law systems (for example, transfer pricing regimes, beneficial ownership, neutral taxation of restructuring operations, thin capitalization rules). That is due to the lobbying of multinationals, exercising legitimate pressure to benefit from identical or similar regimes worldwide and

---

[67] See the discussion on the transplanted categories in the Anglo tax jurisprudence, in Richard Krever, 'Interpreting Income Tax Laws in the Common Law World' in Markus Achatz, Tina Ehrke-Rabel, Johannes Heinrich, Roman Leitner and Otto Taucher (eds), *Steuerrecht, Verfassungsrecht, Europarecht, Festschrift für Hans Georg Ruppe* (Vienna: Facultas wuv, 2007) 354–78.

[68] On the role of comparative tax law in respect of various tax principles, concepts and tax codes, see Victor Thuronyi, *Comparative Tax Law* (The Hague/London/New York: Kluwer Law International, 2003).

aimed at reducing compliance costs. In general, foreign investors operating in developing countries are willing to be handled in the same manner independently of where they are operating, and this implies that income tax codes, consumption tax codes and general tax laws, as well as tax litigation procedures, are expected to contain some sophisticated regimes that will be a challenge to the tax administration and local courts.

The role played by international organizations such as the OECD, Global Forum, IMF, World Bank, the EU (e.g., TIEAS), CIAT, IFA, EATLP in respect of recommending best practices, providing technical assistance to the concepts and drafting of tax legislation, or providing international fora of debate, has greatly contributed to this universal language both within the OECD and in developing countries and to transplantation of legal categories, beyond the corresponding legal families.

The fact that tax legislation in developing countries is being drafted by lawyers of different legal traditions who meet and discuss in global fora, and/or in the framework of international organizations, grants to comparative law a role that is especially important in this context. Legal pluralism, as a basis for legal drafting of taxes, is experimented with and practiced, on a permanent basis, in an attempt to answer the expectations of pluri-located investors.[69] Finally, autonomous interpretation of tax concepts and the corresponding rejection of interpretation according to the meaning in the exporting legal field also makes it easier to transplant tax concepts and regimes such as sale, rental, interest.

The phenomenon of regional integration will provoke a dynamic change in the transplantation of categories that cannot be ignored by the external legal drafter: for example, the aforementioned OHADA,[70] where Guinea Bissau, a Portuguese ex-colony, is a member state among French ex-colony member states, and where harmonization measures are being mainly drafted by French lawyers. Another example is SADC,[71] where Mozambique, also a Portuguese ex-colony, is a member state, among ex-colonies of the United Kingdom, and where many solutions thus are or will be of a common-law type. That change will be bigger if there are independent courts (as in OHADA) with recognized competence for uniform interpretation.

---

[69] See Günther, *supra* note 22. For a critical view on global categories: Nelken, *supra* note 9, at 443–71.

[70] Mozambican Constitution, arts 109 and 110.

[71] See *supra* note 44.

VIII. DRAFTING OPTIONS AND CHALLENGES: MODELS OF LEGISLATION AND FOLLOW-UP OF THE REFORMS

Let us now assume that as a result of the technical assistance program, the work of the external legal drafter and the corresponding communication process in search of validity, a draft on a general tax code is enacted. It can be asked whether the tax principles and rules of a particular tax code that are assessed as valid beyond any legal pluralities and circumstances can be later used as a model of tax legislation. That could be done either by the same drafter or by others. If the drafter of the tax reform is the same expert regarding a group of countries, she will have her own concept of an ideal tax law/system and will tend to adopt as much as possible those ideas.

If a scale is adopted, such subsequent use will certainly be more accurate in legal systems belonging to the same legal family and having comparable economies than in legal systems that, although belonging to the same legal family, have very distinct economies and levels of human development. The latter can occur because their dimension is very different, the economic sectors are very different, the rule of law is observed in a satisfactory manner in one state but not in the other, or in one case there is political stability and in the other there is not.

Thus, as long as the legal background and the political, economic and social environments are similar, there are groups of solutions that can be considered ideal in a rule-of-law state. In respect of the subject topics under a general tax code, it is easier to find a common proposal that will correspond to a current idea of relationship between the tax administration and the taxpayer in a rule-of-law state and to human rights: issues such as interpretation, non-retroactivity, obligations of withholding agents and tax responsibility, tax domicile, transfer of tax credits and debts, prescription, the right to be notified of administrative acts, the obligation to fundamental acts, the burden of proof as a risk of spheres, the right to a fair hearing, the right to be notified before the tax administration implements a new tax assessment, presumptions regarding abusive practices, indirect methods wherever the taxpayer does not comply with his/her legal duties, the principles of investigation of the relevant facts (*Untersuchungsprinzip*) and of the true facts (*materielle richtigkeit der Sachaufklärung, princípio da verdade material*), administrative rulings and their publicity, accounting obligations, voluntary payment and payment in instalments, guarantees of credits, interest for delayed delivery of tax assessment or for delayed payment of taxes, the principles of legality, proportionality, equity, confidentiality of data.

The same reasoning applies wherever the groups of taxpayers and tax objects can be identified and are similar worldwide: taxation of multinationals, taxation of charities and non-governmental organizations, taxation of the informal sector, taxation of small and medium-sized companies, taxation of interest, dividends and capital gains. Another issue is whether it makes sense to have one legal drafter for the whole tax system, or at least for all direct taxes or income taxes, or for all indirect taxes, and for procedural tax laws. Consistency of a tax system will call for one or a small committee of legal drafters to be responsible for related tax codes.

Enactment of tax drafts ideally involves not only national officials from the tax administration and ministry of finance, but also public discussion with all interested parties, namely, the private sector, practitioners, tax consultants, accountants, and also judges. If the process is public all their comments will be taken into consideration by the national government before submitting the draft to discussion in specialized committees in parliament and to final approval by the plenary. Parliamentary procedures are not, however, the best way to ensure coherence and consistency of the tax regimes: parliaments often introduce amendments in plenary sessions, including last-minute amendments, and this jeopardizes the aforementioned purpose of coherence and consistency of the regime: examples of last-minute amendments are the ad hoc amendments to deadlines granted to the taxpayer in respect of different procedural and judicial process steps, and the amendments to the amount of penalties, without considering the internal consistency of the different deadlines and penalties proposed.

It has also to be taken into account that in developing countries, the negotiation between governments and parliaments take place without the presence of foreign experts, for obvious reasons of sovereignty. Taking into account the lack of national expertise, the amendments in the specialized committee will also more often than not introduce incoherence and inconsistencies to the proposed law and jeopardize the expected results of the law.

Another aspect relates to the fact that where technical assistance in drafting is granted by international organizations, the follow-up of the reforms and their implementation may not be accomplished in an optimal manner. Two problems will often occur. On the one hand, there will be problems related to correct implementation, due to different interpretation of the legislation by the tax administration throughout the country. Rulings often do not exist and case law will not be publicly available. In the worst cases, either the legislation or the rulings or the case law or all of them will not be publicly available. On the other hand, when the tax legislation enacted faces lobbies and negative reactions from important groups of voters, amendment will often be drafted by the national officials at the tax administration, and even if the underlying purpose may be adequate, the lack of expertise may lead to a technically inconsistent result.

However, if both legislators and officials applying the law use technically deficient legal language, a domestic, neutral result may be achieved, as long as there is agreement on the meaning used.

IX. CONCLUDING REMARKS

This chapter aimed at discussing the role that an external legal drafter should play when invited to assist a tax reform in a developing country. She is an ideal tax law drafter – our Hercules legislator – who aims to acknowledge the plural legalities in force in the host country, the existing constraints and challenges. Plural legalities comprise pre-colonial traditional tax legalities, the colonial tax legality, tax legalities of the various communities originally belonging to different states, nations and cultures and that can overlap either in a vertical or horizontal manner. In order to be fully aware of those facts, she will act through genuine communication with the national tax officials in a legislative committee. She aims at having her tax legal drafts enter into force and be valid, not only by being compliant with Hart's rules of recognition, but also according to the concept of validity in Habermas.

In order to reach validity, she will have not only to identify the plural legalities in force (descriptive approach), but also to adopt a normative and dynamic approach. For this, she will have to select which traditional and colonial legality (or legalities) in force must be included in the tax reform; which ones are to be rejected; which transplanted categories of the ex-colonial master are to be adopted; which global tax concepts can be imported. This normative approach has to comply with the rule of law and inherent principles of taxation.

The fact that our external legal drafter is expected to carry on a very demanding task led us to call her a Hercules legislator by analogy to Dworkin's Hercules judge. It was, however, recognized that although the Hercules judge aims to reach the right answer, our Hercules legislator can merely aim to reach one right answer due to the vast number of combinations her tax law drafts may reveal. Moreover, where validity of law as imagined by Habermas aims at being valid over time, tax reforms have limited validity in time, due to the oscillation of economic and political conditions and constraints, which is increasing faster in the global order (although the timeframe will vary depending on the tax matters at stake).

Admitting that our Hercules legislator does not exist, this chapter contends that where an external legal drafter plays her role seriously, she will be able to contribute to the validity of a tax reform of a developing country, in compliance with rule of law parameters. Her tax reform will not be the arithmetic sum of the existing pipes, but she will try to represent a valid pipe.

7. The place of law in the evolution of Chinese fiscal federalism

Wei Cui*

I. INTRODUCTION

The importance of tax design for economic development is well understood and uncontroversial.[1] The drafting of tax legislation to implement tax policy in developing countries has also received attention from organizations such as the International Monetary Fund.[2] However, the role of tax law as a determinant of economic development has been less often explored. What part has tax law, as distinguished from the tax policies that it embodies more or less perfectly, played in either enhancing or hindering development? This is not a whimsical question. Many developing countries in search of appropriate tax policies also have fledgling legal systems. In these countries, a legal – including constitutional – framework for developing and implementing tax legislation cannot be taken for granted. As a result, the legal perspective is often missing or barely present in tax policy debates. By contrast, it is customary for scholars in developed countries to structure discussions about taxation by reference to a wide range of legal doctrines, norms and interpretations. Herein lies a gap between the respective tax policy discourses in developed and developing countries, and legal scholars have a particular stake in assessing the significance of the gap: even if the law cannot be easily dismissed as superfluous, its importance for tax policy in

---

* I am grateful for comments by audiences at the University of Melbourne, University of Minnesota and Peking University law schools on presentations on the material in this chapter.

[1] See, e.g., Richard M. Bird, *Tax Policy and Economic Development* (Baltimore: Johns Hopkins University Press, 1992).

[2] See Victor Thuronyi (ed.), *Tax Law Design and Drafting* (Washington, DC: International Monetary Fund, 1996).

developing countries may be sufficiently elusive that one is tempted to neglect it.

In this chapter, I hope to shed light on these issues by exploring the role of law in one of the most important areas of tax policy in China – the allocation of taxing powers among national and sub-national governments, or fiscal federalism in taxation. To this day, the law is often treated as no more than an after-thought, something barely deserving of attention, by many of China's tax policy-makers and their academic advisors. A recent example is a pronouncement by Mr Jia Kang, head of the Fiscal Science Academy of the Chinese Ministry of Finance (and probably the tax policy advisor most frequently cited by the Chinese media), in reply to a reporter's question about whether a recent local tax policy experiment breached the law: 'Reform and experiments do not need legislation. Once you understand the word "experiment", you will get over this problem.'[3] This is of course consistent with the generally underdeveloped state of the rule of law in China.[4]

Yet this chapter shows that the law has played salient roles in the development of Chinese fiscal federalism. Substantively, legal institutions and mechanisms were important tools for the government in building tax administration where almost none had existed before. Rhetorically, the law was used by the central government to advocate and promote central government control in an era of decentralization. These roles have been underdocumented in official Chinese sources that Western social scientific studies of Chinese public finance tend to rely on, and therefore are particularly likely to be hidden to outside observers. Identifying them helps to reveal some of the key political dimensions of Chinese tax policy-making.

I focus in particular on the role of law in Chinese taxation during the period between 1977 and 1993. The choice of this particular period for study is based on three reasons. First, central-local fiscal relations in China experienced dramatic changes during this time: the country

[3] See Shijie Ye, 'Member of the Political Consultative Conference strongly opposes the Property Tax, asks the government to "save face" for the Constitution', *21st Century Business Herald*, 27 January 2011.

[4] For the state of rule of law in China, see, e.g., Randall Peerenboom, *China's Long March toward Rule of Law* (Cambridge: Cambridge University Press, 2002); R. Peerenboom *et al.* (eds.), *Judicial Independence in China: Lessons for Global Rule of Law Promotion* (Cambridge: Cambridge University Press, 2010); Donald Clarke (ed.), *China's Legal System: New Developments, New Challenges* (Cambridge: Cambridge University Press, 2008).

experimented with many different fiscal arrangements in quick succession, with major policy consequences. Indeed, this era of China's transition from a planned economy to a market economy has been receiving intense international social scientific scrutiny for the last two decades, from which a very prominent debate, about whether fiscal decentralization played a major part in producing China's economic growth, has emerged.[5] Bringing the perspective of law to this period, therefore, could make a significant contribution to an important literature. Second, given that China began to revive its legal system only after the end of the Cultural Revolution in 1976, the rule of law was also at its weakest during this part of recent Chinese history. One's expectations for the place for law in fiscal politics and tax policy during these years would accordingly be rather low. Yet in taxation, the law played a salient and increasing role at this time. Third, the later boundary of this period, 1993, saw the launching of China's most important tax reform in the post-Mao period. Both Chinese tax law and tax policy after 1993 are better known to international readers.[6] The role of law in regulating central–local relations during this subsequent period requires more in-depth research.[7]

This chapter will be organized as follows. Section II demonstrates how the legal aspect of the allocation of taxing power among national and sub-national governments – in particular the allocation of tax legislative power – followed a line of evolution that is distinct and independent from other aspects of Chinese central–local fiscal arrangements between 1977 and 1993. Section III more closely analyses the substantive and rhetorical functions law played in tax policy and fiscal politics during this period. Section IV discusses the potential significance of this previously unnoticed role of law for current discussions of the rule of law in Chinese taxation, as well as for the evolving social scientific literature on federalism.

---

[5] See Hehui Jin, Yingyi Qian and Barry R. Weingast, 'Regional Decentralization and Fiscal Incentives: Federalism, Chinese Style' (2005) 89 *Journal of Public Economics* 1719; Hongbin Cai and Daniel Treisman, 'State Corroding Federalism' (2004) 88 *Journal of Public Economics* 819; Olivier Blanchard and Andrei Shleifer, *Federalism With and Without Political Centralization: China Versus Russia*, 48 IMF Staff Papers, Special Issue (2001) 171–9. Also see Chenggang Xu, 'The Fundamental Institutions of China's Reforms and Development' (2011) 49(4) *Journal of Economic Literature* 1076.

[6] See Jiwei Lou and Shulin Wang (eds), *Public Finance in China* (Washington, DC: World Bank, 2008).

[7] I have already offered a summary of it elsewhere: see Wei Cui, 'Fiscal Federalism in Chinese Taxation' (2011) 3 *World Tax Journal* 455.

II. EVOLUTION OF THE LAW ON CENTRAL–LOCAL FISCAL RELATIONS BETWEEN 1977 AND 1993

The evolution of the legal element in Chinese fiscal federalism between 1977 and 1993 is bounded by two seminal documents, the 1977 Measures on the System of Tax Administration,[8] and the 1993 Decision regarding the Implementation of the Tax Sharing System of Fiscal Management.[9] I will first explain the significance of these documents by comparing them to the practices that preceded the 1977 Measures and those that followed the 1993 State Council Decision. I then turn to the developments that transpired between the issuances of the two documents and explain what is distinctive about them.

The 1977 Measures were concerned exclusively with the questions of which government entities had the authority to make tax rules, and which entities were allowed to authorize deviations from these rules under certain circumstances. First, 'any change of national tax policies, the promulgation and implementation of tax laws, the initiation or termination of the collection of any tax, and the increase or decrease of taxable items and adjustment of tax rates insofar as they constitute changes of national tax policy' fell within the State Council's exclusive jurisdiction.[10] Second, important sub-national tax policies must be approved by the national Ministry of Finance (MOF), including 'the imposition or repeal of (or exemption from) a certain type of tax within a provincial jurisdiction; tax reduction or exemption for a taxable product or a certain industry within a provincial jurisdiction; any tax reduction or exemption under the industrial and commerce tax for cigarettes, alcohol, sugar, and watches ... and all issues involving foreign relations and the taxation of foreign merchants'.[11] Third, provincial-level governments received permission to grant tax reductions and exemptions to address the special needs of specific types of businesses, under a detailed set of guidelines about when such authority may be exercised. (These needs were mainly

[8] Issued by the Ministry of Finance and approved and released by the State Council, 13 November 1977 ('the 1977 Measures').

[9] State Council, 15 December 1993 ('the 1993 State Council Decision').

[10] The State Council is China's cabinet – the organization at the top of the national executive branch – and is headed by the Premier.

[11] While China operated under a planned economy in the 1970s, there was a complex set of turnover taxes on industrial products in addition to the expropriation of the profits of state-owned enterprises (SOEs). Christine P.W. Wong, 'Fiscal Reform and Local Industrialization: The Problematic Sequencing of Reform in Post-Mao China' (1992) 18 *Modern China* 200.

couched in terms of 'difficulties' businesses were having as a result of various government policies under the planned economy.) Moreover, such authority cannot be further delegated. In other words, a limited range of sub-national tax policies can be made by provincial authorities, but not by lower levels of government.

The 1977 Measures represented a significant recentralization of tax legislative power, compared not only to the immediately preceding years, but also to all previous arrangements for tax legislation since the founding of the People's Republic in 1949. Because of the central government paralysis in the aftermath of the height of the Cultural Revolution,[12] and because of the fear of a major war with the Soviet Union, fiscal management in China reached its most decentralized phase after 1969.[13] For the period between 1970 and 1973, most provincial governments only had to make lump sum transfers to the central government, and were otherwise able to control their own expenditures, retain surplus revenues, and divide revenues and expenditure responsibilities with lower levels of government in their jurisdictions. As a correlate of this, the power to make many items of tax policy had been delegated to the provinces.[14] While, between 1974 and 1976, the central government reclaimed greater revenue shares, significant sub-national fiscal autonomy remained. Indeed, a permanent legacy of this period was that provinces became exclusively responsible for determining the fiscal relations with subordinate administrative units.[15] What the 1977 Measures proclaimed, however, was that whatever bargains were struck among provincial and sub-provincial governments, the delegation of tax law-making power was not to be part of it. This position regarding the 'lower bound' of decentralization of tax legislative power has persisted to this day.

Moreover, even compared to the pre-1970 period, the 1977 Measures' posture towards centralization of tax legislative power was remarkable.

---

12 The height of the Cultural Revolution lasted from 1966 to 1968. The Chinese Communist Party declared an official end to the Cultural Revolution only in 1976, after Mao's death.

13 Michel Oksenberg and James Tong, 'The Evolution of Central–Provincial Fiscal Relations in China, 1971–1984: The Formal System' (1991) 125 *China Quarterly* 1, 7–13. 'The Cultural Revolution was the turning-point during which provinces acquired increased autonomy through greater budgetary authority.' *Ibid.* 7.

14 State Council, Notice Forwarding the Report of the Military Management Council of the Ministry of Finance, on Decentralizing the Authority to Manage Industrial and Commercial Taxes, adopted on 13 April 1970.

15 Oksenberg and Tong, *supra* note 13, at para. 4.3.

Both Chinese and Western scholars of the history of public finance in the People's Republic of China (PRC) tend to refer to the system adopted in 1950[16] as a paradigm of 'total centralization'.[17] However, under the core document for the 1950 system, county-level governments were able to adopt locally applicable tax rules.[18] In any case, given that national unity was newly established at the time, fiscal centralization was mostly an aspiration, a direction in which China would move. In fact, the central government quickly began to retreat from total centralization in order to give incentives to local governments to build government capacity.[19] And in 1958, the central government pronounced certain strong decentralizing principles.[20] Indeed, these principles were formulated in a way that almost resonates with modern day public finance recommendations: 'any tax that could be managed by [provincial-level jurisdictions] should be managed by them; for those taxes that remain managed by the central government, [provincial-level] governments should be given some scope for flexible adjustments; and [such governments] should be allowed to make tax regulations and introduce local taxes'.[21] Even though some attempts at recentralization were made in the early 1960s, none restricted the range of government authorities capable of tax law/rule-making to the degree that the 1977 Measures did.

---

16 This was the year when the national government under the Chinese Communist Party was just formed, when it had still to support a wartime army (including in preparation for the Korean War), and when it tried to coordinate administration across China for the first time. Having little revenue, the central government managed largely through printing money. To avoid inflation, however, it had to start raising taxes. See Chen Yun, 'Unifying fiscal and economic work', *People's Daily*, 4 March 1950.

17 See Oksenberg and Tong, *supra* note 13, at 5; Jun Huo, 'Sixty Years of Evolution of the System of Tax Administration in New China' (2010) 3 *Research on Contemporary Chinese History* 52; Hongwei Fu, 'The Understanding and Evaluation of the Framework Rules for Tax Legislative Power' (2004) 12 *Taxation Research* 33.

18 Subject to the approval of the relevant administrative/military district authority then lying between provinces and the central government. State Council (*zhengwuyuan*), Key Rules for Implementing National Taxation Policies, adopted on 30 January 1950.

19 See Deng Xiaoping, 'Six Doctrines of Fiscal Work', speech made on 13 January 1954.

20 Provisions for Improving the Tax Administration System, adopted by the 75th Plenary Meeting of the State Council on 11 April 1958, approved by the 97th Meeting of the Standing Committee of the National People's Congress on 5 June 1958, and publicly released as a State Council Decree on 5 June 1958.

21 *Ibid.*

We turn now to the 1993 State Council Decision, which marks the end of the period here examined. As noted above, this was one of the core documents that launched the 1994 tax reform in China and founded the structure of Chinese taxation that still stands today. It laid out a 'tax sharing' system that governs how revenues for different taxes were to be collected and shared amongst central and provincial governments.[22] Here we find even greater centralization of tax legislative power. The objectives of the 1994 tax reform included increasing the central government's share of total tax revenue, and allowing the central government to take control of certain broad-based taxes so as to use them as national economic policy tools. But going beyond what was necessary to achieve these objectives, the 1993 State Council Decision announced that the 'legislative authority for central, shared, and local taxes must all be vested in the Central Government, so as to ensure the uniform command of the Central Government, and to maintain a uniform national market and fair competition among enterprises'.[23] As a consequence of this position, all local tax exemptions and reductions had to be approved by the Ministry of Finance, in contrast to the 1977 Measures.

These pronouncements in 1993 did not strictly characterize the system of tax law-making that subsequently developed as there were some exceptions in which local or provincial governments had some tax law-making power. The power to decide whether or not to impose three very minor taxes was delegated to provincial governments. Provincial governments have also been allowed to vary tax rates and bases in connection with certain other taxes the revenues of which are entirely allocated to local governments, and to choose different administrative methods for such taxes.[24] These discretions are strictly speaking legislative in nature. However, they can be viewed as pursuant to specific delegations from the central government, and in that sense, they are consistent with the centralization of legislative power.

Aside from these limited delegations, however, the main tax 'policy' instrument left to local governments became tax administration rather than tax law-making. Some parts of the shared taxes (i.e., part of the enterprise income tax and all of the individual income tax) and all of the local taxes are locally administered. The operation of administrative discretion in the absence of clear rules, or of an effective rule of law, allowed local governments to alter tax policy during implementation.

---

22 For a discussion of this system, see Cui, *supra* note 7.

23 1993 State Council Decision, para. 2(3).

24 See Cui, *supra* note 7, Chart 1.

Further, the centralization of tax legislative power is a rule that itself had to be enforced, and both the diligence and success with which the central government did so since 1993 have varied.[25] Nonetheless, the centralization of tax legislative power has been the dominant fiscal doctrine since 1993.

So what transpired between 1977 and 1993? In a way, the answer is simple: the 1977 Measures were kept in place until they were superseded by the 1993 State Council Decision. The meaning of this pattern, however, is anything but simple. Both China's economy and its tax system went through paradigm changes during this period. A vibrant private market economy, including foreign-invested enterprises, was allowed to develop alongside the state-owned sector where prices were not completely liberalized. Multiple attempts at reforming the state-owned sector were made and privatization began.[26] A new system of taxation built upon the VAT and related indirect taxes, as well as an enterprise income tax with much lower rates, was experimented with and then widely adopted in 1994. Importantly, fiscal relations between the central and provincial governments, in addition to going through multiple changes and reversals, were also characterized by strong decentralizing features. Indeed, the decentralizing forces of the era were so strong that some of the central government's key tax reform efforts were aborted. Both the monotonic development in the allocation of tax legislative power and the fact that such allocation maintained a high degree of centralization from beginning to end thus bucked the trend of the period. The question is how to interpret this seemingly immutable doctrine of centralized law-making.

Before engaging in such interpretation, some further details about the period will be helpful. The fluctuations in overall central–local fiscal relations are well documented in a number of sources,[27] and can be roughly summarized as follows. First, fiscal regimes changed quickly and each was short-lived, some lasting only for one year, as a result of the government's attempt to deal with inflation, deficit, and the gradual dismantling of the planned economy all at the same time. Second, at each time, the central government agreed to different packages with different

---

[25] *Ibid.* Section 5.1.

[26] See Yasheng Huang, *Capitalism with Chinese Characteristics: Entrepreneurship and the State* (Cambridge: Cambridge University Press, 2008).

[27] See, e.g., Oksenberg and Tong, *supra* note 13; Christine P.W. Wong, 'Central–Local Relations in an Era of Fiscal Decline: The Paradox of Fiscal Decentralization in Post-Mao China' (1991) 128 *China Quarterly* 691; Wong, *supra* note 11.

provinces, ranging from very decentralized (e.g., with some provinces agreeing to make (or receive) lump sum transfers to (or from) the center, while the rest of their fiscal affairs were completely locally managed) to relatively centralized arrangements (e.g., with some provinces remitting to the center most of the revenues they collected and following the center's dictate for their expenditures). Third, from the late 1970s to the late 1980s, revenue sharing arrangements tended to allow greater revenue retention by provinces, and thus became incrementally more decentralized. Fourth, despite this, the central government opportunistically claimed certain revenue sources, and dramatically decentralized most expenditures. As a result of this and the overall decline in fiscal revenue relative to GDP, many local governments ended up in worse budgetary situations then before.[28] This complex story led some commentators in the early 1990s to write: '[It] would be inappropriate to characterize the system as evolving towards either greater centralization or decentralization … [Instead], a major theme … is the growing complexity of central–provincial budgetary arrangements.'[29]

The allocation of tax legislative power, however, remained centralized. There was no different allocation for different years, nor for different provinces. Many of the government documents in the 1980s and early 1990s cited the 1977 Measures for their procedures for provincial grants of limited tax reductions and exemptions as if they were sufficient.[30] In 1986, the 1977 Measures were incorporated by reference in the Provisional Measures on the Administration of Tax Collection,[31] the predecessor to the Law on the Administration of Tax Collection (LATC).[32] Many aspects of this early body of law on tax procedure relied on the idea of a consistent tax legal order, and the 1977 Measures stood for that order. For example, the concept of late payment fines[33] depended on knowing which tax rules impose binding obligations the breach of which would result in such fines. The 1977 Measures took the view that

---

28 *Ibid.*

29 Oksenberg and Tong, *supra* note 13, at 31.

30 This conclusion, and much of the following discussion, are based on a review of over 100 central and local government documents listed as referring to the 1977 Measures in the database www.chinalawinfo.com.

31 State Council, Guofa [1986] 48, adopted on 21 April 1986, art. 3.

32 National People's Congress, 4 September 1992, effective as amended 1 May 2001.

33 Under both the law in place then as well as current Chinese tax law, late payments fines may be imposed on overdue taxes. The fines are not merely interest charges – the rate is much higher, standing now at over 18 percent per annum – but are also distinct from penalties.

only central and provincial governments, directly or through their finance ministries/bureaus, had the authority to issue such binding rules. It was against the background of this simple and consistent position that, in 1992, the newly enacted LATC put forth the following principle: 'the imposition of a tax or the cessation thereof, the reduction, exemption, refund or additional payment of tax shall be implemented in accordance with statutes or, if the State Council is authorized by statutes to formulate relevant provisions, in accordance with the relevant provisions prescribed in administrative regulations formulated by the State Council'.[34] Some interpret this provision as reserving tax legislative power entirely to the National People's Congress and State Council, while others believe that as long as explicit procedures are followed, tax legislative power may be further delegated to other entities, including local governments. In either case, however, the provision clearly anticipated the increased centralization under the 1993 State Council decision and the post-1994 status quo.

Although the 1977 Measures clearly centralized tax legislative power, that does not mean that the provinces complied with them willingly. By the mid-1980s, many local governments and ministerial agencies were expanding tax preferences beyond what were allowed by the State Council. Tax evasion was becoming widespread, partly due to the lack of zeal in local tax collection. In response, starting in 1987, the central government launched a series of campaigns to crack down on local tax preferences. Unauthorized grants of tax reductions and exemptions were made punishable by administrative sanctions. It was in the nature of such campaigns to meet with resistance and non-compliance, and they had to be carried out repeatedly. One local government circular, for example, reported that 'some regions and agencies did not understand the importance and necessity of the State Council's [policy], were not giving it enough emphasis, and were adopting a "wait and see" attitude'.[35] Continuous admonishment was needed to forestall the renewal of unauthorized tax preferences. A 1991 State Council directive explicitly acknowledged that the centralization of tax legislative power was being questioned:

> Some believe that unifying tax law and centralizing tax power was an approach adopted when governance and order were badly lacking. Now that

---

34 LATC, art. 3.

35 Notice of the People's Government of the Ethnic Autonomous Region of Guangxi regarding Implementing the State Council's Decision to Seriously Enforce Tax Law and Discipline and Enhancing Tax Work, Guizhengfa [1987] 78, 1 September 1987.

> governance and order have been re-established, they are challenging the principles of unification and centralization, and claim that fiscal management can be loosened. Therefore, some local governments are ignoring the unity of tax law and giving tax reductions and exemptions in an unauthorized manner, expanding the scope of such reductions/exemptions, arbitrarily extending them, reducing taxes for sales of local products in other places, adding taxes for products made elsewhere and sold locally, thus engaging in local protectionism. Tax preferences for foreign investments that go beyond national policy are also appearing with frequency.[36]

The State Council issued orders against unauthorized local tax preferences almost annually all the way up to the eve of the 1994 tax reform,[37] indicating that keeping such preferences under control required high-level politicking and could not be managed as a routine task by the Ministry of Finance and tax agencies alone.

Nonetheless, the central government was able to maintain the centralization line and gradually gathered political support for it. A particularly striking manifestation of this was the central government's ability to push forward indirect tax reform despite various 'management contract responsibility systems' (MCRS) that became prevalent for state owned enterprises (SOEs) in the mid-1980s and lasted until around 1993. Under an MCRS, the managers of an SOE only had to surrender pre-contracted amounts of profit to the SOE's owners.[38] The purpose was to give managers of enterprises greater autonomy, and even though this was conceptually distinct from granting local governments greater autonomy, it was also advocated as a form of decentralization at the time. The various forms of MCRS often included income tax payments in the bargain as well, which spelled doom for the government's effort to develop an income tax system for SOEs.[39] However, it appears that the central government continued to insist that any kind of MCRS must not include contracting for indirect tax payments, which must be made 'according to law'. Specific measures were adopted for sanctioning the overstatement of expenses for enterprises that have fulfilled their contractual obligations for fixed profit payments to enterprise owners, on the

---

36 State Council, Notice Forwarding the Report of the State Administration of Taxation (SAT) regarding Further Progressing Taxation according to Law and Strengthening Tax Administration, Guofa [1991] 67, 9 December 1991.

37 State Council, Notice regarding Strengthening Tax Administration and Strictly Controlling Tax Reductions and Exemptions, Guofa [1993] 51, 23 July 1993.

38 See Wong, *supra* note 11, at 216–19.

39 *Ibid.* 218.

ground that such overstatement reduced tax and other payments to the government that is not part of the management contract.[40] In opposition to decentralizing forces that favored contracting both profit and tax payments with enterprises, the doctrine of centralization seemed to have played a role in the success of indirect tax reform.

III. SUBSTANTIVE AND RHETORICAL FUNCTION OF LAW

One reaction to the phenomenon described in the last section is to say that the uniformity of law across China should simply be assumed. The Communist Party founded the PRC as a unitary state, and centralized political leadership has always been fundamental. All discussions of centralization and decentralization take place within such a framework.[41] Responding to this reaction is beyond the scope of this chapter,[42] and instead I will consider another possible reaction. If little attention has previously been given to the allocation of tax legislative power, might it be because it is of marginal importance or even irrelevant to fiscal politics? To put it bluntly, might it not be that the social scientists have been examining the issues that really mattered in pre-1993 Chinese public finance, whereas studying the legal arrangements during this period is at best an optional exercise? This section seeks to provide evidence to refute this reaction, by examining both the substantive and the rhetorical roles played by law in central–local fiscal relations between 1977 and 1993.

What substantive roles might tax law be expected to have played in China in the 1980s and early 1990s? To think about this question, one would of course have to consider first what role taxation played during this time of economic transition. An extremely simplified answer to this

[40] See MOF and the Audit Administration, Reply to Two Specific Questions in the Implementation of the State Council's Provisional Measures on the Sanctioning of Violations of Fiscal Law and Regulations, 7 December 1988.

[41] See Xu, *supra* note 5.

[42] The basic replies are: (i) the reaction falsely assumes that centralization along certain dimensions implies centralization along other dimensions, whereas recent international research on federalism tends to find lack of correlation on the degrees of centralization along different dimensions; (ii) the reaction is factually inconsistent with the decentralization of tax legislative power before 1977.

last question might go as follows.[43] Although China settled on its course of developing a market-based economy only in the 1990s, it was already trying to liberalize its public sector in the 1980s by allowing much greater enterprise autonomy than had been possible under central planning. It was also tolerating the growth of a significant private sector. For both sectors, tax was to generate revenue for the government on the basis of autonomous enterprise decisions, in contrast to the prior regime when enterprises were government-managed and where profit could be expropriated and tax extracted simply on an administrative basis. However, for both sectors, taxation was an unfamiliar tool. Because the state had depended on the public sector for revenue for so long, finding a balance between enterprise autonomy and the assurance of revenue from that sector was difficult. How much autonomy was needed to make SOEs work was anybody's guess,[44] and it was very tempting for ministries and local governments to provide more 'autonomy' by giving tax breaks (as long as these governments could benefit from the business success of the relevant SOEs in other ways). For the private sector, the system of tax collection simply did not exist and had to be created from scratch.

In this context, three conditions arguably must be satisfied in order for the government's attempt to introduce taxation to succeed: there must be a consistent set of tax rules for parties to follow; the rules must be backed by the compulsory force of the state; and they must also be made publicly known. These three conditions are also essential features of law.[45] Consequently, a tight bond developed between tax policy and law, despite the general underdevelopment of the Chinese legal system at the time.

The main offending parties against the rules laid out in the 1977 Measures during the latter's initial years of implementation were not necessarily local governments, but ministries other than the Ministry of Finance (MOF) (and their local counterparts). These ministries had dictated the management of the enterprises in the sectors they supervised. Reflective of a mentality under the planned economy, they appeared to believe that they could also make decisions on tax matters. The MOF reviewed a small sample of 13 policy documents issued by various

---

43 See, generally, World Bank, *China: Revenue Mobilization and Tax Policy Issues and Options* (1990).

44 It turned out that enterprise autonomy alone was not enough: the creation of market competition with unregulated market prices was necessary.

45 See, generally, H.L.A. Hart, *The Concept of Law* (Oxford: Clarendon Press, 1994).

ministries relating to fiscal matters in the half-year period before February 1982, and found nine that either did not receive the consent of the MOF, or were ones that the MOF had explicitly disagreed with.[46] Against this, the State Council emphasized that only the MOF, or the State Council at the request of the MOF, could issue (national) tax rules. Neither other ministerial nor local government entities may issue rules about taxation.[47] This effort to achieve unified control over tax and budgetary matters was probably necessary given large national deficits and high risks of inflation at the time. Given this objective, it made sense to present tax rules *as law*: having specific authorities identified as the origin and ultimate interpreter of certain rules, and ensuring that these rules do not conflict, are precisely one feature that makes any set of rules *law*.

The problem of coordination was not just a problem for the central government. Local governments at the time had to make the same efforts to carry out tax policy in the presence of multiple government agencies. In these local efforts,[48] the consistency of tax rules was felt to be crucial. Finance and tax authorities repeatedly emphasized the importance of procedures for issuing and interpreting tax rules. Tax preferences must be granted through formal documents instead of on an oral basis.[49] If the taxpayer disagreed with the tax policy represented by a tax rule, it should not refuse to pay tax on the basis of that disagreement, or on the ground that it had not been instructed by the government agency that supervised it to pay the tax. All disagreements with policy may be reported through tax agencies and local governments to the central government, but before the policy was changed, it must be implemented.[50]

---

[46] MOF, Report regarding Tightening Fiscal Management and Preventing Unauthorized Revenue Reductions and Expenditure Increases, approved and released by the State Council, 26 March 1982. The offences pertained to tax reductions and exemptions as well as unauthorized increases in enterprise expenditures.

[47] Decision of the State Council regarding Balancing Fiscal Revenue and Expenditures and Tightening Fiscal Management, 26 January 1981, section 2.

[48] Tax collection in the 1980s was carried out entirely by (very often under-staffed) local tax agencies reporting to local governments.

[49] Guangxi Ethnic Autonomous Region ('Guangxi') Bureau of Finance, Report on Strengthening Unified Tax Administration, Effectively Organizing Tax Reductions and Exemptions, approved and released by the Guangxi People's Government, Guizhengfa [1981] 80, 9 May 1981; see also State Council, Decision regarding Enforcing the Taxation Order and Enhancing Tax Administration, Guofa [1988] 85, 27 December 1988.

[50] Guizhengfa [1981] 80, *supra* note 49.

A second condition believed to be necessary for introducing a new tax system was giving tax rules the backing of the compulsory force of the state. In the 1980s, the government came to recognize that tax agencies needed to be given civil powers, such as the power to carry out onsite inspections and sometimes set up checkpoints at transportation nodes, and the power to enforce against taxpayer assets and accounts, against equivalent or even more powerful government entities. There was also resistance to taxation, including riots and violence.[51] Tax collectors had to be protected from such violence. At the request of the State Council, the Ministry of Public Security issued a Notice regarding Diligently Investigating and Handling Cases of Beating Tax Agents in 1987 to local public security bureaus, which read in part:

> The focus should be on rioters targeting tax agencies and violence aimed to hurt tax collectors … [Local public security bureaus] should widely and deeply disseminate relevant provisions of the state's tax law, and publicize the importance of taxation for ensuring national fiscal revenue and developing the national economy … [Local bureaus] may recommend the publication of formal notices [against tax violence], and select typical cases to prosecute in coordination with People's Courts.[52]

The Chinese judicial system, which in the 1980s was strongly (though by no means exclusively) identified with criminal justice, makes an appearance in our story mostly in this narrow context. However, even this is already significant, in light of the fact that a prevalent alternative was to 'criticize and educate' tax evaders, or penalize them only if a case was 'serious'.[53]

A third prerequisite for the successful implementation of tax policy at the time was securing voluntary compliance through giving publicity to tax law. Administrative extractions of taxes from state-owned enterprises did not require such publicity. Enhancing voluntary compliance was particularly important because the system of tax agencies across the

---

51 State Council, Decision to Seriously Enforce Tax Law and Discipline and Enhancing Tax Work, Guofa [1987] 29, 8 April 1987.

52 Guofa [1988] 85, *supra* note 49; numerous local government documents mentioned tax protests and violence as problems that needed to be dealt with.

53 See, e.g., Guizhengfa [1981] 80, *supra* note 49 (if an enterprise refused to pay tax, the sanction may be reduced retainable profit, and one year of forgone bonus for the head officers of the enterprise).

country had yet to be adequately staffed and made operative.[54] Consequently, the law enforcement system was enlisted to publicize tax rules. It was in this context that the slogan of 'taxation according to law' (*yifa zhishui*) made one of its earliest appearances. A joint circular issued by the MOF and Ministry of Justice in 1987[55] urged the inclusion of the topic of taxation in the legal education campaigns across the country aimed at 'increasing legal consciousness' of citizens:

> Tax law is an important component of the legal system of our country. Strengthening the dissemination and education of tax law and policy, investigating and handling acts of tax evasion and tax revolt in accordance with law, maintaining the dignity of the law of the state, and guaranteeing fiscal revenue of the state, are shared responsibilities of law enforcement and fiscal agencies at different levels … [Citizens should be made to] know what is taxation and what is tax law, to understand that paying tax according to law as well as exposing and informing the government of tax evasion are honorable responsibilities of citizens, and to know what sanctions will be given to violations of tax law, so that they can understand and obey the law.

The need to associate taxation with the law was reiterated in an important directive (with 'taxation according to law' in its title) that was endorsed by the State Council in 1991.[56] In drafting the directive, the SAT expressed the concern that 'the concept of rule of law in taxation was relatively weak among Chinese citizens, who lacked knowledge and understanding of taxation. Some viewed taxation as an excessive burden, did not distinguish between taxes and fees, and indeed confused taxation with the arbitrary charging of fees.' The idea that tax was collected on the basis of rules that only a limited number of authorities could issue was thus important, in the view of tax agencies themselves, to the legitimacy of taxation.

Today, independent adjudication, along with democratic participation in legislation or rule-making, is most frequently emphasized in connection with the 'rule of law'. It should not be forgotten, however, that there are other features of legal systems that make law essential to governance. It is these other features – the way in which consistency among rules is

---

[54] Government documents from the 1980s consistently emphasized the importance of sufficiently staffing tax agencies and not cutting back on tax collection personnel.

[55] Joint Notice regarding Seriously Implementing the State Council's Decision, Strengthening Public Education regarding Tax Law, Tightening Law and Discipline within Taxation, Caishui [87] 071, 21 May 1987.

[56] Guofa [1991] 67, *supra* note 36.

achieved, the way rules secure compliance through publicity (instead of, say, bureaucratic command) and the compulsory powers of the state – that gave law an unavoidably substantive role in the development of the Chinese tax system in the 1980s and 1990s. Indeed, the idea that a tax system could develop willy-nilly, with the law as mere window-dressing, seems incoherent.

The next issue to consider is, if the legal system mattered, did the centralization of tax legislative power also matter? On the one hand, the locus of tax legislative power determined how tax rules were made and interpreted. On the other hand, centralization is not a necessary feature of legal systems. There is no reason why a decentralized system of governments could not operate on the basis of law, and the necessity of law does not translate into the necessity of centralization.

So far, we have not touched on justifications for tax centralization during the period of Chinese economic reform under examination, and it is in fact difficult to distil any rationale from the set of pronouncements declaring and enforcing the centralization doctrine. Examining these documents, it seems that the law played an important rhetorical role during policy debates at this time. In effect, law was conflated with centralization. There were many instances of this conflation. In launching the 1987 campaign to crack down on local tax preferences, for example, the State Council proclaimed: 'Tax law is the law of the State; amending tax law and changing rules regarding tax exemptions and reductions must follow legislative procedures and administrative limits, and cannot be done simply as one thinks fit.'[57] A year later, the State Council asserted again: 'The tax law of the State must be uniform, taxing power cannot be dispersed, the principle of uniform tax law must always be insisted upon and there cannot be any wavering or bending of the rules.'[58] There is a barely hidden ambiguity in the use of the word 'State' (*guojia*) in these assertions. In Chinese the term may denote either a nation/country, or abstractly (as for the English term 'state') the government authority of a geographical jurisdiction. Tax law is clearly attributable to 'the State' in

[57] Guofa [1987] 29, *supra* note 51. This particular passage went on to say: 'From now on, [to implement] any tax reductions and exemptions falling with the jurisdiction of the central government, a region or ministry must seek the opinion of the Ministry of Finance, and seek the State Council's approval. All documents regarding tax reductions and exemptions unilaterally issued by regions and ministries beyond their jurisdiction are void, the tax agencies at different levels may refuse to enforce them, and should report them to the Ministry of Finance.'

[58] Guofa [1988] 85, *supra* note 49.

the latter sense, but why must it always be national in scope? This lack of clarity was never satisfactorily resolved even in some of the more elaborate formulations that developed in the early 1990s. For instance, under the heading 'To maintain resolutely the uniformity and seriousness of tax law', the SAT argued in the 1991 directive:

> Insisting on taxation in accordance with law, unifying tax law, and centralizing taxing power are necessary requirements for developing a socialist planned commodity economy, and are the basic principles of taxation. Observance of these principles must be unwavering in all circumstances. Regulating the economic environment and rectifying economic disorder must rely on taxation in accordance with law. Fiscal contracting between central and local governments, management responsibility contracting with enterprises, and improving large and medium enterprises, must also all rely on taxation in accordance with law. Actions that violate the principles of the uniformity of tax law and the centralization of taxing powers and that indiscreetly offer tax exemptions and reductions in excess of one's authority must of necessity disturb the unified socialist market, obstruct the implementation of state industrial policy, create unfair competition among enterprises, and erode the fiscal powers of central and local governments.[59]

The passage was clearly alluding to two matters: first, that local protectionism (one technique of which was offering tax preferences to local enterprises and locally made products) had become a serious problem, and second, that both central and local governments were suffering from revenue decline. Nonetheless, it is conceptually unclear why decentralization of taxing power must necessarily obstruct inter-jurisdictional commerce or fair competition. The fiscal woes suffered by government entities at the time, which partially helped to generate local protectionism, were attributable not to decentralization in taxation, but to the extraordinary decentralization in expenditures, the fiscal decline due to the narrow bases of the existing and *nationally designed* taxes, and the central government's opportunistic grabbing of revenue sources.[60] Many of the policy decisions taken were at odds with (or at least disconnected from) the idea that there must be only one set of tax rules for the country. At best, the doctrine of centralization, in the early 1990s, became a desperate means for the central government to attempt to curtail, by

---

[59] Guofa [1991] 67, *supra* note 36. See text accompanying *supra* note 23 for a similar formulation in the 1993 State Council Decision.

[60] Wong, *supra* note 11.

administrative fiat, the unwanted and unanticipated effects of decentralization. This does not make it generally sound policy, nor does it justify the continued insistence on centralization since 1977.

Of course, it is difficult to say what would have happened if China had not centralized tax legislative power in 1977. If local governments possessed greater autonomy over taxation, would some of them have taken a more active approach to revenue collection, tried to increase as opposed to decrease taxes, or even tried more actively to develop more broad-based taxes than were available under the planned economy? The answer is uncertain. It may be that centralization was a natural approach to tax reform during this period of economic transition. The central government might have enjoyed advantages, e.g., in terms of information and the economy of scale, in designing new tax law for a new economy and, compared with local governments, it might have been the party with greater foresight in this era of radical social change. In addition, if the legal system was necessary for tax reform, the central government might have been better able to supply this good than local governments. Victor Shih has argued that because provincial jurisdictions faced a collective action problem in adopting anti-inflationary measures, the central government – and the central bureaucratic factions of the Chinese Communist Party – were able to gain political power when inflationary threats were strong.[61] To the extent that there is a natural bias towards centralization in issues of taxation, tax policy may also favor 'centralist factions' in political contest.

Be that as it may, the centralization of tax legislative power was contentious. Judging from the widespread breaches of the limits of authority the central government had laid down, it did not command political consensus. The central government defended it partly by appealing to a strategy that *was* dominant from a social perspective, namely, implementing tax policy as a matter of the rule of law. Partly by using law as a rhetorical device, the central government was able to keep at bay serious challenges to this aspect of China's political order.

---

61 Victor Shih, *Factions and Finance in China: Elite Conflict and Inflation* (Cambridge: Cambridge University Press, 2007).

IV. IMPLICATIONS FOR LEGAL AND SOCIAL SCIENTIFIC RESEARCH

The lessons that may be drawn from the legal historical analysis offered in this chapter are of both the positive and normative varieties.

From a positive perspective, the distinct history of the evolution of the centralization of tax legislative power in China is pertinent to an important methodological discussion in the study of federalism: namely, how the degree of decentralization along each of the many distinct dimensions of government authority may fail to correlate with the degrees of decentralization along other dimensions. An increasing number of social scientists have emphasized that recognizing this fact is crucial for analysing the consequences (beneficial or otherwise) of decentralization.[62] Considering the dimensions of centralization or decentralization only within the fiscal sphere, it can be seen that revenue claims and expenditure responsibilities may be decentralized to different degrees (leading to the necessity of upward or downward transfer payments). Just considering the revenue sphere, the powers of tax legislation, tax administration, and laying claims to revenue may be allocated among national and sub-national governments in significantly different manners.

In China, the degree of fiscal decentralization has often been conceived of in terms of the second and third of these three types of powers. The first power, to enact tax legislation, is often merely noted and not discussed. What we have seen, first, is that even without structural changes to China's political system, centralization along this dimension has by no means been invariant (especially considering the fluctuations before 1977). Second, between 1977 and 1993, centralization in this dimension has failed to reflect changes in the degree of centralization in other dimensions of revenue power. And third, despite the nascent status of the legal system and the culture of rule of law in contemporary China, this dimension cannot be neglected, because the importance of law to building a modern tax system in China in the 1980s and 1990s is a firm historical fact.

---

[62] See, e.g., Jonathan Rodden, 'Comparative Federalism and Decentralization: On Meaning and Measurement' (2004) 36(4) *Comparative Politics* 481; Jorge Martinez-Vazquez and Andrei Timofeev, *Decentralization Measures Revisited*, Andrew Young School of Policy Studies International Studies Program Working Paper No. 09-13 (2009); Dan Stegarescu, 'Public Sector Decentralization: Measurement Concepts and Recent International Trends' (2005) 26(3) *Fiscal Studies* 301.

Indeed, whether to assume the centralization of tax legislative power may be an important decision in social scientific modeling. For example, some political economists who argue that fiscal decentralization in the 1980s was accountable for China's remarkable economic growth also treat the tax rate and tax base (with which local politicians work) as exogenously given.[63] This implicitly assumes that the central government sets the tax rate and tax base – which is precisely what the centralization doctrine envisions. Thus, while ostensibly studying the consequences of decentralization, these theorists have introduced a basic form of centralization in their model. By contrast, some other models of fiscal federalism assume that local jurisdictions set tax rates for some taxes, and arrive at significantly different conclusions.[64] It is important to make these assumptions and their historical basis explicit, for exploring not only the consequences of decentralization but also its origins (i.e., for the theory of 'endogenous decentralization').

Beyond the accuracy of factual assumptions, there are also normative issues at stake in this analysis. From the normative perspective, the complete centralization of tax legislative power is obviously problematic because it inevitably violates one of two basic principles: (1) the rules of a tax system should be laid out in forms that have the force of law; and (2) sub-national governments should be given some discretion over some tax matters, as a part of fiscal autonomy. Both principles are sufficiently weak as to be consistent with a wide range of conceptions of proper law-making procedures and of the appropriate degree of centralization. Government rule-making can gain legitimacy in many ways. For example, parliaments can play greater or lesser roles vis-à-vis the executive branch. Similarly, the extent of fiscal decentralization can vary greatly – from much to little local discretion. To satisfy both principles, the law-making power of a sub-national government entity only has to substantially track the extent of fiscal discretion given to that entity. What is striking about Chinese institutions is that the adoption of the centralization doctrine has ensured that even these minimal principles would be violated. On the one hand, in certain historical circumstances, powerful local political factions were able to adopt tax policies that contradict national law and trespass on the authorized limits of local legislation,

---

[63] See Jin, Qian and Weingast, *supra* note 5; Roger Gordon and Wei Li, 'Provincial and Local Governments in China: Fiscal Institutions and Government Behavior' ch. 8 in Joseph Fan and Randall Morck (eds), *Capitalizing China* (University of Chicago Press, 2012).

[64] Hongbin Cai and Daniel Treisman, 'State Corroding Federalism' (2004) 88 *Journal of Public Economics* 819.

without attracting any sanctions.[65] The norms of the rule of law face serious challenges on these occasions. On the other hand, in the more common type of case, the monopoly of tax legislative power by the central government has perpetuated a situation where local political leaders look to transfer payments as well as under-regulated sources of revenue (e.g., proceeds from land sales), instead of taxation, to finance local expenditure needs. These are options generally considered to be inconsistent with fiscal autonomy.

The normative inadequacy of the centralization doctrine constitutes a basic reason for being skeptical about justifications for its adoption by China. Instead, the prominence of the doctrine may be attributable to its expediency for those political forces that benefit from nationalizing policy-making. If that is correct, one would expect that the doctrine would be contested in practice. This study of the history of the doctrine in the 1977–1993 period shows that this was indeed the case.[66] Moreover, the study shows that both central and local governments were justifiably, even if perhaps surprisingly, keen to implement tax policy within the framework of law. This means that the inadequacy of the centralization doctrine, in creating a conflict between law and the potential need for decentralization, was present from the beginning.

Even if the central government was able to get away with conflating law and centralization in the 1980s and 1990s, that is no longer the case. Starting in the late 1990s, local governments in China began pursuing unauthorized tax preferences by exploiting legal loopholes. One example is a technique called 'refund after collection', which is the opposite of the preference of Western politicians for disguising expenditures as tax cuts: local governments would return tax collected to taxpayers as a matter of expenditures, and effectively undermine tax law and prohibitions on local tax preferences, because expenditure decisions, unlike tax rules, are decentralized in China.[67] The existence of such loopholes is ultimately attributable to the fact that law, after all, is neutral between centralization and decentralization. Even if the central government was able to score some political wins in the name of law in past decades, the law as a rhetorical weapon goes only so far.

---

[65] See Ye, *supra* note 3, for a report of the recent controversy about the lack of legal basis for Chongqing and Shanghai's pilot programs in real property taxation.

[66] See Cui, *supra* note 7, at para. 5, for similar controversies and crackdowns on local tax preferences after 1993.

[67] *Ibid.*

From the perspective of the development of Chinese law, the most important implication of all this is that decoupling the concept of law from the ideology of centralization is an urgent task. How to do this systematically, plausibly and practically is a topic wide open for exploration. For developing countries, especially those that are characterized by weak legal institutions, the role of law in the evolution of Chinese fiscal federalism offers at least two points for reflection. First, a strong connection between law and taxation can be found even in a social and historical context where probably many would not have expected to see such a connection. Second, the distorted configuration of the distribution of tax legislative power in China is evidence that the locus of such power is likely to be a fundamental issue of political contention. Indeed, the example of China suggests that the issue is so fundamental that it can be viewed as a dimension of centralization distinct from all others. Both points suggest that the weakness of a country's legal institutions is insufficient reason for neglecting the law in understanding and designing the country's public finance system.

8. The globalization of tax expenditure reporting: transplanting transparency in India and the Global South

Lisa Philipps

I. INTRODUCTION

This chapter traces the rise of tax expenditure reporting in countries of the Global South, with a particular focus on India. It investigates why and how policy-makers in some low and middle income countries are now moving to adopt a budgeting practice that originated in wealthy Western nations in the 1970s. I discuss the potential advantages of this trend, but also argue that there is a need for its champions to face up to some challenges and potential disadvantages of transplanting this form of fiscal transparency into different national contexts. These include methodological and political challenges that are well known to Western observers but are seldom fully acknowledged in the literature advocating adoption of tax expenditure reporting by developing countries. In addition, the chapter questions whether generic prescriptions are sufficiently attuned to local political, economic and institutional circumstances that may diminish the value of OECD-style tax expenditure reporting to receiving countries.

Section II briefly reviews the history of tax expenditure analysis since the late 1960s and then charts the more recent campaign to encourage its implementation by developing countries. The analysis shows that international organizations, Western commentators and domestic tax policy experts have all contributed to this campaign. Advocates have tended to rely on two main types of rationale. The first is technocratic, stressing the value of tax expenditure reporting to government policy-makers seeking to craft a more efficient, equitable and administratively simple tax system which raises maximum revenues to finance state priorities. The second focuses more on democratic governance and the role of transparency in securing accountability for the allocation of public resources and distribution of tax burdens. Section II concludes by reviewing the evidence that there is indeed a modest trend toward the globalization of tax expenditure reporting.

Section III offers a case study of India's experience leading up to the publication of its first tax expenditure report in 2006 and how this report has developed through several budget cycles. The case study shows that a mix of internal and external influences were at play in bringing this budget document to India. It also compares the Indian report to Canada's tax expenditure report and finds that the Indian exercise is more robust from both technocratic and democratic perspectives. Section III highlights both the potential benefits of tax expenditure reporting in India and its limits. While the tax expenditure report provides new and valuable information and analysis, there are significant political and institutional barriers to translating this knowledge into tax reforms.

In section IV, I suggest several reasons why foreign experts and international organizations ought to choose our words carefully in recommending tax expenditure analysis to countries of the Global South. Law and development literature has documented the problems that can arise when institutional reform prescriptions are not sufficiently contextualized to local politics, economies and culture. I argue that these concerns apply with equal force to the quest for universal tax expenditure reporting. At a minimum, advocates should openly acknowledge that tax expenditure analysis remains contested and has limited political purchase in the OECD countries usually held out as models of best practice. Caution is also needed to ensure that normative biases about ideal tax policy are not smuggled in through an ostensibly technocratic exercise in transparency, thereby distorting or sidestepping the domestic policy-making processes of the receiving country. Finally, before investing scarce administrative resources in a particular model of tax expenditure reporting, developing countries should be encouraged to weigh its potential benefits and costs, including the opportunity costs of forgoing other possible activities of finance and revenue personnel. I argue that without an explicit strategy for naming, analysing and tackling these challenges as they arise in context, tax expenditure reporting is even less likely to impact positively on either policy formation or democratic accountability than in the high income countries where it was first established.

Section V concludes by summarizing the potential benefits but also the likely limitations and costs of tax expenditure reporting as a development strategy.

II. TAX EXPENDITURE REPORTING: FROM US ORIGINS TO GLOBAL RELEVANCE

Since the late 1960s tax policy analysts in the United States and other industrialized countries have drawn an analytical distinction between, on the one hand, the normal or technical rules of a tax which are designed to raise revenues in an equitable and efficient manner, and on the other, the special concessions or targeted exceptions from the normal rules which are designed to achieve other economic or social policy goals of government. Stanley Surrey, as Harvard Professor and Assistant Secretary to the US Treasury, famously coined the term 'tax expenditures' to describe this second dimension of a tax system and to make the point that these exceptional provisions should be understood not as tax rules at all but as indirect spending programs.[1] When governments wish to address market failures or stimulate changes in economic or social behavior, they can choose from a suite of policy instruments including soft or hard regulation, direct service provision, money transfers, or tax measures.[2] Surrey argued that deciding to tax a particular group or economic activity more lightly than others in order to achieve such goals is financially equivalent to providing a direct grant to the taxpayers who benefit. Thus, they should be designed and evaluated with the same care as direct spending programs.

Tax expenditure reporting is the remedy that Surrey prescribed to address the transparency problems created by delivering spending programs indirectly through the tax system. Accountability of government institutions for the expenditure of public funds is typically identified as a basic requirement of the rule of law.[3] Thus, information about the objectives, cost, target effectiveness and distributional impact of any public spending program in principle should be available for review by

---

1 See Stanley S. Surrey, *Pathways to Tax Reform: The Concept of Tax Expenditures* (Harvard University Press, 1973); and Stanley S. Surrey and Paul R. McDaniel, *Tax Expenditures* (Harvard University Press, 1985). The history of Surrey's work through the late 1960s and 1970s, much of it with Prof. Paul McDaniel, is reviewed in J. Clifton Fleming, Jr and Robert J. Peroni, 'Reinvigorating Tax Expenditure Analysis and its International Dimension' (2008) 27 *Virginia Tax Review* 437 at 439–41.

2 See Surrey, *supra* note 1, at 3; and Surrey and McDaniel, *supra* note 1, at 25–6.

3 See, e.g., Michael J. Trebilcock and Ronald J. Daniels, *Rule of Law Reform and Development: Charting the Fragile Path of Progress* (Edward Elgar, 2008) 32.

democratic institutions of the state and civil society. However, tax expenditures often escape this type of scrutiny because they are embedded within highly technical provisions of a tax law that generally need never be re-approved once enacted. Over time, these preferences and deviations from the normal tax system can come to be seen as part of a complex revenue raising structure rather than spending programs which should be costed and reviewed like any other government expenditure. Surrey's proposed solution to counteract this relative invisibility was to embed tax expenditure reporting within the budgetary process. That is, the budget should include information about the forgone revenues and other impacts associated with tax expenditures to facilitate cost–benefit analysis of individual measures and trade-offs with other uses of public money. In addition to improving transparency about the total spending budget, Surrey hoped that exposing the inequities, inefficiencies and administrative complexities of tax expenditures would provide impetus for base-broadening tax reforms.[4]

Under Surrey's influence the US government began publishing tax expenditure data in 1968.[5] Since then the basic principles and ideals of tax expenditure analysis have been accepted by many Western tax policy analysts inside and outside government and by international bodies that are influential in developing fiscal policy norms (as discussed further below). Tax expenditure reporting is a well established practice in many OECD countries, some of which require it by law.[6] It also has fierce critics. Especially in the United States, an entrenched debate persists about the basic coherence of the concept and whether it is possible in a clear and principled way to distinguish the normative tax system of a country from the exceptions to it. Surrey and McDaniel defined their benchmark tax in relation to the Schanz–Haig–Simons concept of economic income as the sum of the value of a person's consumption plus the

---

4 United States, Staff of the Joint Committee on Taxation, *A Reconsideration of Tax Expenditure Analysis*, JCX-37-08 (US Government Printing Office, 12 May 2008) 2–3. See also Surrey, *supra* note 1, at 30–33.

5 United States Treasury, *Annual Report of the Secretary of the Treasury on the State of the Finances for the Fiscal Year ended June 30, 1969* (US Government Printing Office, 1969) 330, available as of 12 February 2012, at www.archive.org/details/annualreportofse1969statiunit.

6 See, e.g., Australia's Charter of Budget Honesty Act, 1998, pt 5, div. 1, s. 12(1)(d), and the US Congressional Budget and Impoundment Control Act 1974. See also OECD, *Tax Expenditures in OECD Countries* (OECD, 2010); OECD, *Tax Expenditures: Recent Experiences* (OECD, 1996); and OECD, *Tax Expenditures: A Review of Issues and Country Practices* (OECD, 1984).

change in their net wealth over a period of time.[7] Some critics have rejected their choice of benchmark as a thinly veiled political agenda to reform the tax system in accordance with a particular model, while others argue that it is too vague to resolve the classification of many provisions.[8] In a recent comparative study of OECD countries Christopher Heady noted there is in fact significant variation among countries in the choice of benchmarks.[9] Beyond this fundamental definitional question other controversies abound over how to measure the costs, distributional impacts and behavioural effects of tax expenditures, and whether estimates of revenue forgone from tax expenditures are so uncertain and contingent that they are more likely to mislead than to enlighten the public.[10]

Despite these ongoing debates, many tax commentators accept the basic principles and ideals of tax expenditure analysis. Their most frequent lament is that it has had such limited impact on policy-making in OECD countries. Academic scholars and other budget analysts have frequently complained about the lack of depth and detail in tax expenditure reports, the failure of policy-makers to integrate tax expenditure analysis fully into budgetary decision-making or tax law design, and the rapid growth of tax expenditures in number and cost despite the availability of information about them.[11] These and other problems led

---

[7] Henry Simons, *Personal Income Taxation: The Definition of Income as a Problem of Fiscal Policy* (University of Chicago Press, 1938).

[8] See Boris I. Bittker, 'A "Comprehensive Tax Base" as a Goal of Income Tax Reform' (1967) 80(5) *Harvard Law Review* 925, and 'Accounting for Federal "Tax Subsidies" in the National Budget' (1969) 22(2) *National Tax Journal* 244.

[9] Christopher Heady, 'Tax Expenditures: Definitional and Policy Issues' in Lisa Philipps, Neil Brooks and Jinyan Li (eds), *Tax Expenditure Analysis: State of the Art* (Canadian Tax Foundation, 2011).

[10] Paul McDaniel recently reviewed and responded to these criticisms in 'The Staff of the Joint Committee on Taxation Revision of Tax Expenditure Classification Methodology: What is to be Made of a Change that Makes No Changes?', ch. 3 in Philipps, Brooks and Li, *supra* note 9. For a revealing discussion of how debate over the benchmark has undermined the political effectiveness of tax expenditure analysis, see Victor Thuronyi, 'Tax Expenditures: A Reassessment' (1988) *Duke Law Journal* 1155. For a thorough discussion of the critiques and a response in defense of tax expenditure analysis, see Fleming and Peroni, *supra* note 1, at 487–525.

[11] Some recent examples include Robin Boadway, 'The Annual Tax Expenditure Reports: A Critique' (2007) 55(1) *Canadian Tax Journal* 106; Mark Burton, 'Making the Australian Tax Expenditures Statement an Effective Policy Instrument: From Fiscal Record to Transparent Report' (2005) 8(1) *Australian Journal*

the Staff of the Joint Committee on Taxation of the US Congress to conclude in 2008 that 'Surrey's original hope that tax expenditure analysis would have a salutary effect on budget transparency (and through that, on actual budget outlays) has not been realized'.[12]

Similar disappointments have been expressed by leading international organizations, which have served as key interlocutors in the effort to globalize tax expenditure analysis. First among these is the Organisation for Economic Co-operation and Development (OECD), widely recognized as the dominant player in the formation of global tax policy norms.[13] The OECD has been critical of the proliferation of tax expenditures based on its view that the most efficient tax system in a market economy has a broad base and low rates applied neutrally to different forms of income or economic activity. It has reiterated this concern recently:

> Accounting in many countries suggests that the use of tax expenditures is pervasive and growing … At any time, the possibility that a back channel for resource allocation could lead to inefficient government 'spending' would be troubling. When many government budgets are threatened by population ageing and adverse cyclical developments [i.e., deficits], the concern is only greater.[14]

The OECD has accordingly sought to encourage critical analysis of tax concessions at the country level. For example, its Best Practices for Budget Transparency provides that '[t]he estimated cost of key tax expenditures should be disclosed as supplementary information in the budget … in order to inform budgetary choices'.[15] Importantly, it does not limit its advocacy to OECD countries. Rather, the Best Practices are

---

of Taxation 1; Edward Kleinbard, 'The Congress Within the Congress: How Tax Expenditures Distort Our Budget and Our Political Processes' (2010) 36 *Ohio Northern Law Review* 1; and Emil Sunley, 'Tax Expenditures in the United States: Experience and Practice' in Hana Polackova Brixi, Christian M.A. Valenduc and Zhicheng Li Swift (eds), *Tax Expenditures – Shedding Light on Government Spending Through the Tax System: Lessons from Developed and Transition Economies* (International Bank for Reconstruction and Development/ World Bank, 2004) 155.

[12] *Supra* note 4.

[13] For a detailed discussion of the OECD's leadership role in international tax policy standard setting, see Allison Christians, 'Networks, Norms and National Tax Policy' (2010) *Washington U Global Studies Law Review* 12.

[14] *Tax Expenditures in OECD Countries*, *supra* note 6, at 14.

[15] *OECD Best Practices for Budget Transparency* (OECD, 15 May 2001) para. 2.2.

explicitly designed as a 'reference tool for Member and non-Member countries'.[16] Thus, the OECD promotes tax expenditure reporting as a universal good. I describe its approach as technocratic because it focuses on assisting government actors to make better policy, as measured against the OECD's standards of an ideal tax system.

Both the IMF and the World Bank have reinforced the OECD's message and directed it more pointedly at low and middle income countries. Both of these bodies have more power than the OECD to intervene and produce policy change at the country level, for example through loan conditionality, surveillance reporting and provision of technical assistance to design and implement reforms. The IMF's Code of Good Practices on Fiscal Transparency says that every country's budget should disclose 'the nature and fiscal significance of central government tax expenditures'.[17] The IMF publishes reports (the so-called 'Fiscal ROSCs', Reports on Observance of Standards and Codes) on individual countries' compliance with this Code.[18] The importance of presenting tax expenditure estimates to Parliament, 'preferably as part of annual budget documentation' was reiterated recently in a Technical Guidance Note prepared by IMF staff.[19]

Policy analysts have elaborated several rationales for advocating that lower income and transition countries embrace the kinds of tax expenditure reporting practiced in high income countries. These include a mix of technocratic arguments aimed at policy-makers, and more accountability-oriented rationales that speak to democratic governance of the budget process in developing countries. Thus, World Bank analyst Schiavo-Campo warns that concessions granted through tax laws 'are not submitted to the same system of internal control and legislative authorization as

---

[16] *Ibid.* para. 4.

[17] Code of Good Practices on Fiscal Transparency (IMF, 2007) para. 3.13.

[18] The Fiscal ROSCs published to date can be viewed on the IMF's Fiscal Transparency webpage: www.imf.org/external/np/rosc/rosc.asp?sort=topic#Fiscal Transparency. For a full discussion of the IMF's limited vision of budget transparency, see Lisa Philipps and Miranda Stewart, 'Fiscal Transparency: Global Norms, Domestic Laws, and the Politics of Budgets' (2009) 34(3) *Brooklyn Journal of International Law* 797.

[19] Ian Lienert, *Role of the Legislature in Budget Processes* (IMF Fiscal Affairs Department, April 2010) 13, available as of 12 February 2012, at http://blog-pfm.imf.org/files/fad-technical-manual-9.pdf.

other expenditures', and that tax expenditure reporting 'enhances legislative scrutiny of government policy'.[20] This scrutiny is in turn expected to improve the quality of tax policy because it will expose the ineffective, inefficient and inequitable character of many tax expenditures. It could reveal, for example, that 'high-income households can benefit more than needier households from tax credits' and that the latter group would be better served by 'family allowances targeted to low-income groups'.[21] Other commentators have linked the rise of tax incentives to problems of corruption and abuse of power in developing countries. Li Swift, for example, argues that tax incentives often create avenues for avoidance or evasion by wealthier taxpayers and for discretion-wielding officials to favor powerful interests.[22] This connects to a larger concern about erosion of the state's capacity to raise revenues to finance development projects directly. For example, a study of Poland's budget provided data to show that the 'cost of tax expenditure programs … has grown much faster than direct spending programs'.[23] Tax expenditure reporting is presented as a way to counteract this alarming trend:

> with limited theoretical understanding of, and ad hoc experience with, applying tax expenditures, developing countries now confront not only revenue losses higher than they had anticipated but also the erosion of their tax bases in systems that generally have been in existence fewer than 10 years.[24]

---

20 Salvatore Schiavo-Campo, 'The Budget and Its Coverage' in Anwar Shah (ed.), *Budgeting and Budgetary Institutions* (International Bank for Reconstruction and Development/World Bank, 2007) 53, 81.

21 *Ibid.* See also Zhicheng Li Swift, Hana Polackova Brixi and Christian Vanenduc, 'Tax Expenditures: General Concept, Measurement and Overview of Country Practices' in Brixi, Valenduc and Li Swift, *supra* note 11, at 5.

22 Zhicheng Li Swift, *Managing the Effects of Tax Expenditures on National Budgets*, World Bank Policy Research Paper 3927 (May 2006) 11–13, available as of 12 February 2012, at www-wds.worldbank.org/servlet/WDSContentServer/WDSP/IB/2006/05/23/000016406_20060523092056/Rendered/PDF/wps3927.pdf. Academic scholar Wilson Prichard has similarly argued that non-transparent tax expenditures fuel corruption in developing countries. See Wilson Prichard, *Taxation and State Building: Towards a Governance Focused Tax Reform Agenda*, Institute of Development Studies, University of Sussex Working Paper 341 (2010) 33–4.

23 Carlos B. Cavalcanti and Zhicheng Li Swift, 'Poland: Reforming Tax Expenditure Programs' in Brixi, Valenduc and Li Swift, *supra* note 11, at 211.

24 *Ibid.* 1.

Liberal use of tax incentives is blamed for 'reducing these countries' capacity to assist the needs of the poor'.[25] Heavier scrutiny of tax expenditures is therefore recommended as part of a strategy to mobilize revenues for development spending in the interests of less powerful sectors of society.

Tax incentives for foreign investors and domestic industry have been particularly singled out by some commentators. For example, Richard Krever has provided a strong critique of corporate income tax incentives in Mongolia and recommended that its government implement tax expenditure analysis as part of its policy-making process.[26] In previous work Miranda Stewart and I have made a similar argument that promoting transparency about not only the costs but the distributive impact of investment tax incentives could foster democratic debate about tax policy at the country level and build domestic support for base-broadening reforms.[27]

At least one high profile NGO has also been active in calling on developing countries to publicize information about their use of tax expenditures. In 2006 the International Budget Project (IBP), an arm of the Washington-based Centre on Budget and Policy Priorities, launched its Open Budget Index, an evaluation and ranking of the degree of budget transparency in low and middle income countries. One of the many factors which forms the basis for the ranking is whether a country's budget documentation includes information on tax expenditures, and if so the quality of that information.[28] The IBP's stated reasons for advocating greater fiscal transparency are heavily focused on democratic governance rather than bringing domestic policy into line with particular OECD standards. Instead, the IBP seeks to empower civil society groups inside and outside a country to question how public funds are being used and to apply political pressure for changes they believe are needed. A recent report by Burton and Stewart for the IBP discusses concrete ways that civil society advocates can use a tax expenditure report effectively in

---

25 *Ibid*. 2.

26 Richard Krever, *Reform of the Mongolian Corporate Income Tax* (Development Alternatives, Inc. (DAI), for the USAID-financed Economic Policy Support Project, 24 September 2003) 12–14.

27 Philipps and Stewart, *supra* note 18, at 841–2.

28 See Open Budget Questionnaire, question 45, available as of 12 February 2012, at http://internationalbudget.org/what-we-do/open-budget-survey/.

order to hold governments accountable for budgetary decisions.[29] Constituencies may make different uses of available information depending on their priority issues, such as redressing poverty, fighting corruption, making government spending more efficient, ensuring foreign aid is used for its intended purposes, definancing parties to a violent conflict, or improving environmental practices.[30]

It is difficult to quantify the practical effect of expert discourses such as those discussed above. However, it does appear that tax expenditure reporting has gained some traction in some low and middle income countries in the early part of the twenty-first century. Based on data gathered by the OECD from 2007–2009, 50 per cent of OECD member countries provided a 'comprehensive table of tax expenditures' in their budget documents, while the same was true of 30 per cent of non-member countries surveyed.[31] Further, between 2006 and 2008, the International Budget Project reported improved scores on tax expenditure reporting for eight low or middle income countries, while only one country had a lower score.[32] This pattern of incremental reform continued in the 2010 survey with ten countries improving their performance, though six others received a lower grade for tax expenditure reporting than in the 2008 survey.[33] Burton and Stewart provide abundant examples and sources to show how specific developing and emerging countries

---

[29] Mark Burton and Miranda Stewart, *Promoting Budget Transparency Through Tax Expenditure Management: A Report on Country Experience for Civil Society Advocates* (3 June 2011) esp. 64–8.

[30] This diversity of political agendas is apparent from the range of testimonials by civil society advocates on the website of the Open Budget Index, available as of 12 February 2012, at http://internationalbudget.org/what-we-do/open-budget-survey/advocacy/obsa/.

[31] OECD International Database of Budget Practices and Procedures (available as of 12 February 2012, at www.oecd.org/gov/budget/database), question 35. The non-OECD countries reporting on tax expenditures in their budget documents were Argentina, Brazil, Ethiopia, Fiji, Ghana, Israel, Kenya, Latvia, Malawi, Mauritius, Moldova, Mongolia, Morocco, Papua New Guinea, Philippines, Taiwan, Tajikistan and Zimbabwe.

[32] See IBP Open Budget Index for 2006 and 2008, answers to question 45. The countries that improved their score were Argentina, Georgia, Ghana, Guatemala, India, Jordan, Kenya and Turkey. Only Papua New Guinea had a decline in its score.

[33] The ten improved countries were Chile, Colombia, Guatemala, Indonesia, Kazakhstan, Mexico, Morocco, Philippines, Russia and Ukraine. The countries receiving a lower grade for tax expenditure reporting than on the 2008 survey were Georgia, Ghana, India (down from 'a' to 'b' due to incomplete information about new tax expenditures in the budget year), Kenya, Peru and Sri Lanka.

have begun reporting data, often quite recently.[34] The impetus for such reforms is likely different in each country but Western influences of some kind are often readily apparent. In some cases international agencies or experts have pointedly recommended that a country should do more to disclose and analyse its use of tax expenditures.[35] In others, domestic experts have invoked international models and standards to help make the case for reform.[36] India provides a prime example of a country that has embraced tax expenditure reporting in a significant way in recent years.

III. TAX EXPENDITURE REPORTING IN INDIA, 2006–2011

For decades, Indian tax policy experts have been calling for greater scrutiny of tax expenditures within their country. In 1974, not long after Stanley Surrey pioneered the concept in the United States, Anand Bagchi wrote that '[n]o one familiar with the Indian tax scene would fail to perceive how urgently the Indian income tax needs [tax expenditure analysis]'.[37] A decade later, Anand P. Gupta took up the cause arguing that the Indian tax system is 'honeycombed with tax expenditures' and that 'there is no proper system of accounting' for their costs.[38] Gupta laid out glaring examples of concessions that were outdated, ineffective or prone to abuse by tax avoiders, and proposed a serious review based on the following questions:

---

[34] Burton and Stewart, *supra* note 29.

[35] See, e.g., Krever's 2003 Report on Mongolia's corporate income tax, *supra* note 26. See also International Monetary Fund, *Experimental Report on Transparency Practices: Argentina* (15 April 1999), which commented that 'published information on extrabudgetary funds, tax expenditures, and contingent liabilities is partial or unavailable' (para. 11). Based on data in their Open Budget Index Questionnaires, both Argentina and Mongolia have increased their reporting of tax expenditures since 2006.

[36] See, e.g., M. Golam Mortaza and Lutfunnahar Begum, *Tax Expenditures in Bangladesh: An Introductory Analysis* (Policy Analysis Unit, Bangladesh Bank, 2006), which draws heavily on IMF and World Bank literature in advocating that Bangladesh should improve its tracking and reporting of tax expenditures.

[37] 'Efficacy of Tax Incentives: "Tax Expenditure Analysis" and its Relevance for India' (1974) 9(24) *Economic and Political Weekly* 951 at 952.

[38] 'Management of Tax Expenditures in India' (1984) 19(47) *Economic and Political Weekly* M-122 at M-127.

> How much assistance does this tax expenditure provide? Does the activity benefiting from this tax expenditure continue to be high on the national agenda? Does the tax route continue to be the better way of assisting this activity? Has this tax expenditure been misused? ... Has it added to the costs of tax administration and made the tax system more complex and irrational? Who has benefited from it? Has it encouraged extravagance or waste? ... Has it been used to avoid or evade taxes? A periodical review along these lines would help in removing tax expenditures which serve little purpose.[39]

A series of government-appointed tax reform commissions returned to this theme repeatedly through the 1990s and early 2000s.[40] In 2002, the Kelkar Task Force Report on Direct Taxes decried what it famously called the 'exemption raj', arguing that overuse of tax incentives was distorting economic behavior, eroding revenues, draining administrative resources, and promoting corruption and abuse.[41] The Task Force concluded that tax concessions are 'not an efficient way of achieving ... developmental objectives' and recommended broadening the tax base to finance a higher level of direct expenditures on public goods 'particularly in the areas of health, education and other social infrastructure'.[42] Indian scholars also published several studies around this time criticizing the country's continued reliance on a complex web of exemptions and tax holidays in the face of abundant evidence of misuse and other active harms to the fairness and efficiency of the tax system.[43]

The passage of the Fiscal Responsibility and Budget Management Act (FRBM) in 2003 contributed to the momentum for tax expenditure

---

39 *Ibid.* M-130.

40 See the Reports of the Tax Reforms Committee headed by Raja Chelliah (1991–1993), the Shome Committee and the Kelkar Task Force on Direct Taxes (2002), as discussed in Amaresh Bagchi, R. Kavita Rao and Bulbul Sen, *Raising the Tax-Ratio by Reining in the 'Tax Breaks': An Agenda for Action*, National Institute of Public Finance and Policy Working Paper No. 54 (December 2005), available, as of 12 February 2012, at www.nipfp.org.in/newweb/sites/default/files/wp05_nipfp_tr_038.pdf.

41 Vijay L. Kelkar *et al.*, *Report of the Task Force on Direct Taxes* (New Delhi, 27 December 2002) 11–12 and 64–113, available as of 12 February 2012, at www.prsindia.org/uploads/media/DTC%20Bill/kelkar%20direct%20taxes.pdf.

42 *Ibid.* 12.

43 See, e.g., Bagchi, Rao and Sen, *supra* note 40; Amaresh Bagchi, R. Kavita Rao and Bulbul Sen, *Tax Breaks for the Small Scale Sector* (May 2006); and M. Govinda Rao and R. Kavita Rao, *Trends and Issues in Tax Policy and Reform in India* (October 2005).

reporting.[44] While the FRBM does not require tax expenditure reporting per se it sets out targets for deficit reduction and requires more generally that the central government 'shall take suitable measures to ensure greater transparency in its fiscal operations in the public interest'.[45]

The Indian Ministry of Finance released its first tax expenditure report with the Union Budget of 2006–2007, providing estimates of the revenue cost of various concessions to corporations, cooperatives and individuals.[46] It also analysed the gap between statutory and effective corporate tax rates and how the effective rate varied among larger and smaller corporations depending on the generosity of tax concessions available to them.[47] This is notable because many OECD countries, including Canada, do not attempt any such distributive analysis in their tax expenditure reports but simply estimate the aggregate cost of each concession.[48] The tax expenditure exercise was repeated in 2007–2008 along with the following celebratory comment in the budget:

> A tax expenditure or a revenue foregone [*sic*] statement was laid before Parliament for the first time during Budget 2006–07 … It was well received by all quarters and gave rise to constructive debates on the entire gamut of issues concerning fiscal policy. It also lent credence to the Government's intention of bringing about transparency in the matter of tax policy and tax expenditures.[49]

The government's third tax expenditure report, released with the 2008–2009 budget, expanded the distributive analysis by comparing effective

---

[44] Fiscal Responsibility and Budget Management Act, No. 39 of 2003, *Gazette of India* (2003).

[45] *Ibid.* s. 6. I am indebted to Dr Pinaki Chakraborty of the National Institute for Public Finance and Policy for assistance in making this link.

[46] Receipts Budget, Annex 12, Tax Expenditure under the Central Government Tax System, 2004–05, available as of 12 February 2012, at http://indiabudget.nic.in/ub2006–07/rec/annex12.pdf.

[47] *Ibid.* tables 1 and 2.

[48] The Canadian Department of Finance Tax Expenditure Reports from 1995 to 2011 were available as of 12 February 2012, at www.fin.gc.ca/purl/taxexp-eng.asp. In late 2011 the Parliamentary Budget Officer for the first time released tables showing the distribution of personal tax expenditures among income groups and provinces of Canada. See Office of the Parliamentary Budget Officer, *2011 Reference Tables for Tax Expenditure Distributional Analysis* (Office of the Parliamentary Budget Officer, 11 November 2011) (data are for taxation year 2009), available as of 12 February 2012, at www.parl.gc.ca/PBO-DPB/documents/2011_Reference_Tables_Note_EN.pdf.

[49] Union Budget 2007–08, Receipts Budget, Annex 12, Revenue forgone under the Central Tax System: Financial Years 2005–06 and 2006–07, 45.

tax rates in different industrial sectors. It found that the corporate tax burden was higher on public companies than privately owned ones, and higher on the manufacturing sector than the service sector.[50] The report concluded with the following openly normative statement:

> the amount of revenue foregone [*sic*] continues to increase year after year. As a percentage of aggregate tax collection, revenue foregone [*sic*] remains high even though a declining trend is noticeable. This trend reflects the success of the tax reforms undertaken by the Government during the last four years. Moderate tax rates and base expansion are the two essential elements of such tax reforms.[51]

The 2009–2010 and 2010–2011 Statements of Revenue Forgone have adopted a sterner and less self-congratulatory tone:

> As a percentage of aggregate tax collection, revenue foregone [*sic*] remains high and shows an increasing trend as far as Corporate Income-tax is considered for the financial year 2007–08. In case of indirect taxes the trend shows a significant increase for the financial year 2008–09 due to reduction in customs and excise duties. Therefore, it is necessary to reverse this trend to sustain the high tax buoyancy.[52]

Again, this commentary is strikingly more directive about policy than anything in the Canadian tax expenditure report, which generally provides only brief, anodyne statements about the government's stated policy objectives for each relieving provision, and omits any comment on trends in the number or cost of tax concessions as a proportion of overall spending.[53] Exceptionally, where legislation or government undertakings require, the report may offer a closer analysis of a particular provision.[54]

Further, unlike the Indian tax expenditure report, the Canadian version is not delivered as part of the federal budget but as a free-standing

---

50 Union Budget 2008–09, Receipts Budget, Annex 12, Revenue forgone under the Central Tax System: Financial Years 2006–07 and 2007–08, 45–7.

51 *Ibid.* 58.

52 Union Budget 2009–10, Receipts Budget, Annex 12, Revenue forgone under the Central Tax System: Financial Years 2007–08 and 2008–09, at 58. See also Union Budget 2010–11, Receipts Budget, Annex 12, Revenue forgone under the Central Tax System: Financial Years 2007–08 and 2008–09, at 57.

53 See, e.g., Department of Finance Canada, *Tax Expenditures and Evaluations 2011* (2012), available as of 12 February 2012, at www.fin.gc.ca/taxexp-depfisc/2011/taxexp11-eng.pdf.

54 See, e.g., the discussion of the public transit tax credit in the 2011 report, *ibid.* 48.

document released at a different time of the year and with little fanfare on the Finance Department website. Burton and Stewart note that one possible rationale for releasing a tax expenditure report well in advance of the annual budget is to provide citizens and parliamentarians with information that can be considered in the context of pre-budget consultations and advocacy.[55] In Canada this would make sense if the tax expenditure report was coordinated with the government's fall Economic and Fiscal Update which sets the stage for pre-budget consultations.[56] However this is not the practice and the most recent report was released on 9 January 2012, following the conclusion of parliamentary budget consultations.[57] While Canadian federal budgets generally include projected costs for any newly announced tax expenditures, the failure to treat the full report covering all tax expenditures as a budget document means that Canada does not meet OECD or IMF standards of best practice in this area. As reiterated by the OECD in 2010, '[o]ne basic standard of tax expenditure reporting is that data be included in the budget' as this facilitates the essential comparison with direct expenditure data.[58] Nor has Canada participated to date in the Open Budget Survey of the IBP. In all these respects, the Indian record is superior.

The value of India's report in stimulating discussion and evaluation of tax subsidies seems incontestable. No doubt the methodology, coverage and findings of its report can be subjected to critical analysis and improvement as in any country. Indeed the most recent Open Budget Index has downgraded India from 'a' to 'b' on the quality of its reporting, citing a lack of complete information on new tax expenditures proposed in the current budget year.[59] Nonetheless, compared to having no report and even compared to a country like Canada where tax expenditure reporting has a longer history, it is evident that India's Finance Ministry has improved the transparency of India's budget with this report and has

---

55 Burton and Stewart, *supra* note 29, at 26.

56 *Tax Expenditures and Evaluations 2011*, *supra* note 53. The Fiscal and Economic Updates were available as of 12 February 2012, on the Department of Finance website at www.fin.gc.ca/access/statement-eng.asp.

57 The House of Commons Standing Committee on Finance released its report on pre-budget consultations in December 2011: *Pre-Budget Consultations 2011*, available as of 12 February 2012, at www.parl.gc.ca/CommitteeBusiness/CommitteeHome.aspx?Cmte=FINA&Language=E.

58 *Tax Expenditures in OECD Countries, supra* note 6, at 45.

59 International Budget Project, Open Budget Questionnaire, India September 2009, question 45, available as of 12 February 2012, at http://internationalbudget.org/wp-content/uploads/2011/04/India-OBI2010QuestionnaireFinal.pdf.

generated new evidence to inform policy-making, legislative debate and civil society advocacy. While fully acknowledging these benefits, I suggest it would be wrong to conclude that all low and middle income countries should necessarily follow this same path, or even that India should necessarily continue its current efforts in the same form in future. In the balance of this chapter I will argue that in weighing the value of a tax expenditure report, developing countries should also consider certain implicit costs and risks involved in adopting a budgetary practice pioneered in high income countries.

IV. UNIVERSALIZING TAX EXPENDITURE ANALYSIS: SOME CAUTIONARY NOTES

In this section, I suggest there is a need for more critical evaluation of tax expenditure reporting as a strategy for advancing development goals in particular countries. It is difficult to argue against transparency at a general level, and this is precisely the problem. Tax expenditure reporting is often recommended to developing countries in a way that suggests it is an unmitigated positive, with no downside risks or contingencies that depend on local circumstances. As a result there is very little space for governments to question the wisdom of this advice or offer reasons why they have chosen not to adopt tax expenditure reporting, without damaging their own credibility as nations that are committed to good governance. This universalism sits uneasily with the broader law and development literature which has cautioned against externally driven reform efforts that are not attuned to local history and political economy. Trebilcock and Daniels make this point neatly:

> Optimal institutions generally, including legal institutions in particular, will often be importantly shaped by factors specific to given societies, including history, culture, political traditions and institutional culture. This in turn implies some degree of modesty on the part of the external community in promoting rule of law or other legal reforms in developing countries and correspondingly a larger role for 'insiders' with detailed local knowledge.[60]

Similar concerns have been voiced in studies of tax reform in developing countries. Richard Bird, for example, emphasized the folly of attempting to design one-size-fits-all tax policy for developing countries, arguing

---

[60] *Supra* note 3, at 12.

that '[t]o be relevant, policy recommendations need to be geared specifically to the prevailing circumstances and objectives of that country'.[61] Further, Stewart and Jogarajan have written about the role of international experts and organizations in prescribing substantive tax reforms for developing countries and the difficulty of implementing prescriptions that do not enjoy domestic political support.[62] Based on these studies, we should also be skeptical about imposing a generic best practice relating to tax expenditure reporting that is based largely on the experience and tax policy norms of high income OECD countries.

It would be far too simplistic to suggest that transparency standards are always foisted on developing countries from outside. Domestic governments have varying degrees of autonomy to determine their own budget processes. In the case of India, as discussed in section III, the Union government's decision to publish a tax expenditure report followed a decades-long internal campaign by Indian tax policy experts. It was not simply a foreign idea brought to India by Western-dominated international financial institutions. In fact India has worked to insulate itself from many of the most coercive economic restructuring pressures those institutions have applied to other Global South countries. In particular, it has pointedly not borrowed from the IMF since the Asian Financial Crisis of the early 1990s. Nonetheless, even in India it would also be wrong to ignore the influence of outside tax and governance expertise.

First, it is notable that in writing about tax expenditures in the 1970s and 1980s, Indian commentators borrowed heavily from the writings of US experts. More recently, tax reformers have also acknowledged the influence of international norms in setting the direction of domestic policy. Thus, the Kelkar Task Force commented:

> In a world of increasingly mobile and frictionless international flow of capital, outward looking national governments soon realised that getting a share of competitive global capital necessitated keeping the tax rates low and tax rules simple – in line with global trends ... At the beginning of the 21st century, some truths about taxation have become self-evident ... if the objective is to have transparent, efficient and feasible tax administration, then the structure of all taxes should comprise common elements. These are low rates, few nominal rates, a broad base, few exemptions, few incentives, few surcharges, few temporary measures.[63]

---

[61] Richard M. Bird, *Tax Policy and Economic Development* (Johns Hopkins University Press, 1992) 17.

[62] M. Stewart and S. Jogarajan, 'The International Monetary Fund and Tax Reform' (2004) *British Tax Review* 146.

[63] Kelkar Task Force on Direct Taxes, *supra* note 40, at 67.

In their bid to compete in global markets for investment and trade, Indian policy-makers have also understood the value of receiving public praise from international agencies about India's progress on economic reforms. In particular, the IMF's Fiscal ROSC reports are used by investment analysts to guide investment location decisions, and by credit rating agencies in rating sovereign debt.[64] Formally speaking, these reports are prepared only at the request of a government and are published only with its permission. The Fiscal ROSC on India, from 2001, noted that while the Union Budget met many of the requirements of the Code of Good Practices on Fiscal Transparency, 'there is no information on tax expenditures'.[65] In the years following the Fiscal ROSC, IMF papers continued to criticize India's pervasive use of tax incentives and exemptions, arguing that they distort investment decisions, erode revenues and constrain growth.[66] Similarly the World Bank's 2003 report on India stated:

> Services and agriculture need to be brought into the tax net, and lower tax rates must be complemented with the elimination of exemptions. Exemptions doubled from 1996 to 2002/3.[67]

Given these kinds of highly visible statements, the Indian government's decision to embrace tax expenditure reporting should not be seen as entirely home grown but rather as a combined product of external and internal norms and politics. In other countries where international donors and agencies have more direct leverage, the potential disadvantages or risks of importing tax expenditure analysis may be greater.

At least three such risks can be identified. The first is that advocates may overstate the effectiveness of tax expenditure reporting as a strategy either to improve policy or to strengthen democratic oversight of the budget. This might be seen as a relatively mild downside that does no active harm to the receiving country. However, I argue it is more troubling in light of a second risk that with tax expenditure reporting, and particularly the identification of a benchmark norm, a country may also import ideas about what constitutes good tax policy. That is, it may function indirectly to expose countries to criticism for making tax policy

---

64 See Philipps and Stewart, *supra* note 18, at 812–15.

65 IMF Fiscal ROSC for India, 2001, para. 16. This gap has since been remedied, as discussed in section III above.

66 See, e.g., Hélène Poirson, *The Tax System in India: Could Reform Spur Growth?*, IMF Working Paper WP/06/93 (2006) 15; and IMF Survey 7 August 2006, vol. 35, No. 15, 238.

67 World Bank, *India: Sustaining Reform, Reducing Poverty* (14 July 2003) 53.

choices that depart from received international standards. Finally, the production of tax expenditure reports consumes valuable staff time and energy. Given the challenges that many developing countries face to administer their budget and revenue collection processes, new demands should not be added on a mere hope that some benefit may flow. Each of these disadvantages or risks is elaborated below.

A. Exaggerating the Potential of Tax Expenditure Reporting to Effect Change

Surrey and other early tax expenditure theorists had high hopes that greater transparency would trigger more rational policy-making. This same hope is evident in the recent literature calling on developing countries to adopt tax expenditure reporting, as reviewed above in section II. What is less fully conveyed is how difficult it has proven to be in practice for OECD countries such as the United States, Canada and the United Kingdom to make lasting reductions in the number or size of their tax expenditures.[68] Often politically easier to pass into law than direct expenditures, they also tend to evade critical review and evaluation once enacted.[69] In making the case for transparency there is perhaps a natural tendency to focus on its potential benefits. What the advocates of tax expenditure reporting often understate, however, are the political barriers and costs to changing certain parts of the tax code that may be widely viewed as an entitlement or as supporting a culturally valued way of life, or that may be defended vigorously by narrow constituencies who benefit from concessions.

Recent tax reform debates in India demonstrate the challenges of effecting base-broadening tax reform. The draft Direct Tax Code of 2009 proposed significant changes to the personal and corporate income tax of the sort that would appeal to many OECD-style reformers. These included eliminating deductions for home mortgage interest and reducing special treatment for capital gains, while using the increased revenue to reduce the general tax rate.[70] After approximately a year of consultation

---

68 For a review of trends in ten countries, see *Tax Expenditures in OECD Countries, supra* note 6, ch. 4.

69 *Ibid.* 31–4. See also Christopher Howard, 'The Politics of Tax Expenditures in Wealthy Democracies' in Philipps, Brooks and Li, *supra* note 9, at para. 7:1; and Edward D. Kleinbard, 'The Congress within the Congress: How Tax Expenditures Distort our Budget and our Political Processes' (2010) 36 *Ohio Northern University Law Review* 1.

70 For an overview, see KPMG LLP, *Direct Tax Code 2009 – Highlights*.

in which the government reportedly received more than 1,600 representations, a 2010 reform proposal was released with a much scaled back vision.[71] Home mortgage deductions and capital gains relief will remain largely as is, as will tax rates.[72] The 2010 Bill has been further delayed by a lengthy review in the parliamentary Finance Committee during which taxpayer and profession groups advocated additional changes.[73] The Finance Minister has announced a further, indefinite delay while he considers the Finance Committee's recommendations.[74]

If the 2009 proposals were in fact defeated in part by interest group lobbying, India certainly would not be alone in that experience. In Canada the 1967 report of the Carter Commission which proposed a move away from source-based taxation toward a comprehensive tax base met a similar set of compromises following intensive advocacy by the business, investment and tax professional communities.[75] The point in both cases is that the process of tax reform ultimately has little to do with what technocratic information is available to policy makers or the public, and much more to do with a society's political economy at a particular historical juncture. This is a key reason why tax expenditure reporting in many OECD countries has not succeeded in containing the number or cost of these measures, and why Western tax scholars are now grappling with the question of what other institutional changes could be introduced

---

[71] See KPMG LLP, *Update on India's Direct Tax Code Bill* (November 2010). The 2010 Direct Taxes Code was introduced in the Lok Sabha as Bill No. 110 of 2010 on 30 August 2010, and if passed was to become effective as of 1 April 2012 (cl. 1(3)) (available as of 12 February 2012, at http://164.100.24.219/BillsTexts/LSBillTexts/asintroduced/DTC%20%28110%20of%202010%29%20To%20be.pdf).

[72] For a summary, see KPMG LLP, *Direct Taxes Code – 2010,* available as of 12 February 2012, at www.kpmg.com/in/en/whatwedo/tax/pages/directtaxcode.aspx.

[73] See Standing Committee on Finance (2011–12), Fifteenth Lok Sabha, *The Direct Taxes Code Bill, 2010*, Forty-ninth Report (New Delhi: Lok Sabha Secretariat, March 2012).

[74] Prasanta Sahu and Anant Vijay Kala, 'India Direct-Tax Law May Be Revised' *The Wall Street Journal*, 28 August 2012, available as of 26 November 2012, at http://online.wsj.com/article/SB10000872396390444506004577617342103767070.html.

[75] See Leslie T. MacDonald, 'Why the Carter Commission Had to be Stopped' in Neil Brooks (ed.), *The Quest for Tax Reform* (Carswell Company Ltd, 1988) 351; and Linda McQuaig, *Behind Closed Doors: How the Rich Won Control of Canada's Tax System … And Ended Up Richer* (Penguin Books Canada Ltd, 1987).

to discipline the use of the tax system as a spending instrument.[76] Given that tax expenditure reporting is not a costless exercise, countries would be well advised to weigh the benefits and identify clear objectives and strategies for using a tax expenditure report to inform policy or public debate.

B. Importing Tax Policy Ideas Through the Benchmark Norm

The second concern is that in adopting tax expenditure analysis a government may implicitly endorse a set of assumptions about what its tax and broader fiscal system ideally should look like. A tax expenditure is by definition a deviation from normal or benchmark tax rules. Many of the classic writings and OECD prescriptions assume the broadest possible tax base as the norm, with fully neutral treatment of different sectors, taxpayers and forms of production and consumption. They also assume that tax-based programs can and should be replaced by direct government spending if this will achieve the goals of the program more effectively and transparently. These background assumptions are acknowledged to represent an ideal model rather than practical reality even by OECD-based analysts. They may be even less appropriate in a low income country with a large impoverished population, highly uneven industrial development, and limited or non-existent public safety net. That is, tax concessions designed to protect basic consumption of the poor or to support particular development objectives may be more justified or at least harder to replace with direct spending programs in low income countries than in wealthy ones.

This tension was captured, for example, in the reactions of one Indian commentator to the Kelkar reports. Economist and senior civil servant Madhav Godbole praised the Task Force's recommendation that a rigorous cost–benefit analysis be applied to any proposed new tax expenditures.[77] He went on, however, to object to its proposed reduction of tax concessions for saving, educational expenses and medical expenses as overly harsh. With respect to the first of these he pointed out:

---

[76] See, e.g., Burton, *supra* note 11; Mark Burton, 'Capturing Contemporary "Democracy": The Shortcomings of Australian Tax Expenditure Management and their Ideological Foundations' in Philipps, Brooks and Li, *supra* note 9, at para. 7:1; and Edward D. Kleinbard, 'Tax Expenditure Framework Legislation' (2010) 63 *National Tax Journal* 353.

[77] Madhav Godbole, 'Task Force Reports on Direct and Indirect Taxes: Some Issues' (2002) 37(49) *Economic and Political Weekly* 4884 (7–13 December 2002).

> there is no social security net in India unlike in a number of other countries. Drawing lessons from disparate countries on the important question of tax exemption for saving instruments and making them applicable to India may therefore be counter-productive. There is certainly room for rationalization of some of the existing incentives ... but to go to the other extreme and abolish all incentives altogether, as suggested by the task force, is certainly neither warranted nor will it be in the national interest.[78]

Similarly, Joosung Jun defends generous tax expenditures in South Korea as the most rational tax structure for that country, not because they encourage desirable economic behaviours but because they make the tax burden more equal between workers in the formal and informal sectors, thereby stemming tax evasion and encouraging taxpayers to enter the formal economy.[79] He rejects the standard international prescription to eliminate tax preferences, arguing that their base-protection effects offset any revenue or efficiency costs which in his view are 'overstated'.[80]

The need to define a benchmark that suits the domestic context does not go entirely unrecognized by Western-based experts. World Bank analyst Li Swift, for example, acknowledges that the benchmark norm may need 'some modification ... corresponding to specific economic conditions in transition and developing countries'.[81] Likewise, there is an active debate among tax scholars in the West about whether developing countries should be discouraged outright from using tax incentives to promote investment and growth, or whether the main focus should be on better design of incentives to prevent abuse and achieve state goals more effectively.[82] Yet these nuances are side-stepped in much of the literature that promotes tax expenditure reporting by developing countries, and a zero-incentive norm is implicitly or explicitly adopted as the universal ideal benchmark against which a tax system should be evaluated.[83]

---

78 *Ibid.* 4886.

79 Joosung Jun, 'Korea's Tax System: A Growth-Oriented Choice' in Roger H. Gordon (ed.), *Taxation in Developing Countries* (Columbia University Press, 2010) 220, 245–6.

80 *Ibid.* 245.

81 *Supra* note 22, at 19.

82 See, e.g., Reuven Avi-Yonah and Yoram Margalioth, 'Taxation in Developing Countries: Some Recent Support and Challenges to the Conventional View' (2007–2008) 27 *Virginia Tax Review* 1.

83 Yariv Brauner makes a similar point in 'International Trade and Tax Agreements May Be Coordinated, But Not Reconciled' (2005–2006) 25 *Virginia Tax Review* 251, esp. 297–302, where he argues against using a country's tax expenditure report to determine if it has subsidized exports contrary to the WTO, because we should not expect a consensus among (or even within) countries

Countries may also be drawn to a broad benchmark because it is the simplest to define. Doing so, however, may place domestic policy-makers on the defensive when their tax systems are then evaluated by these same outside agencies. In this way, without explicitly imposing any particular tax policy, it may impinge on a country's policy autonomy.

C. Increasing Administrative Burdens

Tax expenditure reporting requires an investment of time by expert staff. While these costs may be negligible to a high income country with a large civil service, their significance for other countries should not be discounted. For example, Li Swift cautions that 'It takes at least two years to develop a basic tax database for initial estimating [of?] tax expenditures. Therefore, any development relating to tax database for this purpose must be planned and begin as soon as possible.'[84] Many developing countries have only modest staff resources available to manage their budget processes.[85] In a particular case, the preparation of tax expenditure reports may not be worth its opportunity costs. Case studies on tax reform and development have identified a list of other priority investments that countries should make in order to strengthen their tax systems, many of which focus on improving administrative capacity rather than analysing or refining tax policy.[86] As Richard Bird has underlined, tax administration challenges render many policy prescriptions for developing countries impractical.[87]

Strengthening tax administration may require investing in information technology and human capital through training and better pay to retain skilled staff. Further, tax personnel are increasingly called upon to participate in international fora where treaties, soft law norms and strategies for countering tax avoidance and evasion are being negotiated or discussed.[88] Especially because developing countries have not yet

---

about how to define the benchmark or normal tax system, nor are measurements of the cost of tax expenditures sufficiently reliable or comparable to direct subsidies.

[84] Li Swift, *supra* note 22, at 22.

[85] See Richard Allen, *The Challenge of Reforming Budgetary Institutions in Developing Countries*, IMF Working Paper WP/09/96 (May 2009).

[86] See Trebilcock and Daniels, *supra* note 3, at 212–35.

[87] See Bird, *supra* note 61, at 189–93.

[88] For an overview of these fora, see UN Social and Economic Council, *Strengthening of Institutional Arrangements to Promote International Cooperation in Tax Matters, including the Committee of Experts on International Cooperation in Tax Matters: Report of the Secretary General* (18 March 2011).

attained an equal place at the table in global tax governance, it is important that they participate and make their perspectives heard wherever possible.[89] The leaders of finance departments and revenue agencies in developing countries will often have to make difficult choices about how best to deploy limited human and operational resources. In this context, it is not obvious that gathering, analysing and reporting tax expenditure data provides the best value for money.

V. CONCLUSION

This chapter examines the rise of tax expenditure reporting in countries of the Global South, and particularly within India as an emergent economic power, and describes the sources of international and domestic expertise that have actively called for this type of reform. While recognizing the potential benefits of greater transparency, I also suggest that more critical reflection is needed about its potential risks and costs for particular countries. My critique extends the point made by other tax scholars, that generic reform prescriptions of international bodies may be poorly adapted to the local circumstances of developing countries, and may impinge on their political autonomy to set tax policy. As Allison Christians has written:

> International tax policy formulation has almost exclusively been the purview of experts from developed countries, despite periodic efforts to achieve some measure of participation by less developed countries. As a result, the economic, social, and legal context of these less developed countries may be too easily overlooked as international consensus evolves regarding the strategies nations should employ to raise revenues in the context of a global economy.[90]

Tax expenditure reports may fall into this trap. They may also be far less effective than hoped at stimulating policy change or improving transparency and oversight, as the experience of high income countries such

---

[89] See Allison Christians, 'Tax Policy in a Time of Crisis: Policy Leadership from the OECD to the G20' (2010) 5 *Northwestern Journal of Law and Social Policy* 19, for a critical analysis highlighting the historical exclusion of non-OECD countries from international tax policy-making processes and the continuing difficulty for poor countries of gaining voice through the G20 or other global governance institutions.

[90] *Global Trends and Constraints on Tax Policy in the Least Developed Countries*, University of Wisconsin Legal Studies Research Paper Series, Paper No. 1086 (2009) 31.

as Canada shows. Moreover, tax expenditure reporting consumes resources which might be better deployed in some other fashion, like detecting avoidance, negotiating tax treaties or smoothing compliance for taxpayers.

As a regulatory norm, transparency often avoids controversy and escapes critical analysis because it presents a relatively value neutral and non-interventionist approach to governance. For the same reasons it may appear to transcend local differences and provide a model for universal reform. There are good reasons to support greater transparency about tax expenditures. However, exactly what should be transparent, to what ends and for whose benefit are political questions that should be answered to some extent at the level of national budget institutions. This chapter has also identified the need for countries to analyse whether the potential benefits of tax expenditure reporting outweigh the costs to them. When developing countries do embark on tax expenditure reporting they are well advised to consider their own objectives, priorities and resources and to design the exercise to fit these.

PART IV

Tax equity, redistribution and aid

9. International equity and human development

Anthony C. Infanti

I. INTRODUCTION

When we speak of 'equity' in tax policy circles, what usually springs to mind is interindividual equity; that is, the concern within a tax system of taxing similarly situated taxpayers similarly ('horizontal' equity) and taxing differently situated taxpayers in an appropriately differentiated fashion ('vertical' equity). In their seminal essay, Richard and Peggy Musgrave approached tax equity from a broader perspective and considered how the international context both complicates questions of inter-individual equity and 'creates the additional problem of equity among states and nations'.[1] The Musgraves had earlier labeled this latter problem – and titled their 1972 essay discussing it – 'inter-nation equity'.[2]

In that essay, the Musgraves added a new dimension to the discussion of tax equity by viewing the concept through an international lens. In this chapter, I add a new dimension to the Musgraves' discussion of tax equity, building on my earlier work critiquing the US domestic tax equity debate.[3] There, I viewed tax equity through a critical lens and highlighted the debate's overweening focus on the economic dimension of individuals. Here, I lay that same critical lens over the Musgraves' international lens in

[1] Richard A. Musgrave and Peggy B. Musgrave, 'Inter-nation Equity' in Richard M. Bird and John G. Head (eds), *Modern Fiscal Issues: Essays in Honor of Carl S. Shoup* (1972) 63.

[2] E.g., Peggy B. Musgrave, *United States Taxation of Foreign Investment Income: Issues and Arguments* (1969) 130–33; see Kim Brooks, 'Inter-nation Equity: The Development of an Important but Underappreciated International Tax Policy Objective' in *Tax Reform in the 21st Century: A Volume in Memory of Richard Musgrave* (2009) 471, 472 and note 2.

[3] Anthony C. Infanti, 'Tax ~~Equity~~' (2008) 55 *Buff. L Rev.* 1191.

considering the role that tax equity might play in advancing human development.

Strong parallels exist between the US domestic tax equity debate and the internation equity debate. In this chapter, I first observe how discussions of internation equity track established notions of inter-individual equity. Internation equity has distinctly 'horizontal' and 'vertical' aspects to it, and the 'vertical' aspect of internation equity – like its interindividual equity counterpart – focuses entirely on the economic dimension of people. Although commentators sometimes chafe at the economic focus of internation equity, they have failed to break out of this constraint.

Continuing to trace the parallels between these debates, I then describe how they are plagued by a tax 'exceptionalism' that acts like a set of blinders limiting the horizons of debate. I argue that it is time to remove these blinders and recognize the larger foreign policy and development context within which the internation equity debate is situated. This is important because the larger debate over development has been undergoing a similar transformation from a narrow focus on economic growth and per capita income to a wider focus on human development.

I next offer some initial thoughts on how countries might reform their international tax rules to embrace a wider focus on human development. I close with a description of the advantages of expanding the internation equity debate to address both economic *and* non-economic lines of difference among nations in an effort to encourage all countries to advance human development, especially for the most vulnerable among us.

II. INTERNATION EQUITY

A. The Musgraves' Description

In their 1972 essay, the Musgraves explain internation equity with the help of a simple case involving multiple countries. For the Musgraves, the crux of internation equity lies in determining the appropriate allocation of national gain or loss among these countries: 'Let X, a resident of A, invest in B. Income earned thereon constitutes a national "gain" to country A. If country B taxes income earned by X, the gain accruing to country A as a nation is reduced. This is the issue of inter-nation equity.'[4]

[4] Musgrave and Musgrave, *supra* note 1, at 68.

Whether this national gain or loss is accompanied by a gain or loss to country A's treasury is a different question, because that 'is a matter of intra-nation transfer between treasury and individual and does not affect the existence of national gain or loss'.[5] Thus, the subject of internation equity is nations – not individuals – and the crux of internation equity is 'whether and how' the country of source will tax.[6]

In exploring the question of whether and how the source country will tax, the Musgraves explored four different approaches: (1) benefit taxation, (2) source taxation, (3) national rental charges and (4) redistribution. A brief summary of each of these four approaches follows.

First, under the benefit principle, 'each jurisdiction would charge for services which it has rendered'.[7] The Musgraves summarily dismissed the idea of allocating taxing jurisdiction based on the benefit principle because '[m]ost taxes are not imposed on a benefit basis'.[8]

Second, the Musgraves concluded that residency-based taxation 'has no bearing on inter-nation equity' because '[s]uch national gain as country A derives is obtained by it whether A's treasury imposes a tax or not'.[9] In contrast, source-based taxation is relevant to internation equity because it permits a country 'to tax income which results from activities undertaken in its borders. That is to say B is permitted to tax X's income and thus to appropriate part of A's national gain'.[10] If a country imposes tax based on the source of income, the Musgraves argue that a rule of non-discrimination should apply; that is, 'B should tax income received by X as if it were received by B's own residents'.[11]

Third, turning from a legal to an economic perspective, the Musgraves discuss the possibility that, were it resource rich but capital poor, country B might justifiably argue that it is entitled to 'obtain a rental or royalty share in A's gain over and above the addition to its labor income'.[12] This national rental would take the form of a tax but would be imposed outside country B's domestic tax system. In essence, the levy would constitute 'an *in rem* tax on operations by foreigners'.[13]

---

5 *Ibid.*
6 *Ibid.* 69.
7 *Ibid.* 70.
8 *Ibid.* 71.
9 *Ibid.*
10 *Ibid.*
11 *Ibid.* 72.
12 *Ibid.* 73.
13 *Ibid.*

Finally and most directly relevant to this chapter, the Musgraves turned to the possibility that internation equity might serve 'as an instrument of international redistribution'.[14] As they explain, '[w]ith a highly unequal distribution of resource endowments and per capita income among countries and in the absence of an adequate method for dealing with the problem, an appropriate pattern of tax-imposed national gains and losses might be used to secure some degree of adjustment'.[15] The Musgraves proposed a uniform rate schedule for corporate taxation that would, by international agreement, apply in all capital-importing countries.

The rates would not be reciprocal, as are the withholding tax rates in current tax treaties. Rather, the rates 'would be related inversely to per capita income in the capital-importing country and directly to per capita income in the capital-exporting country. This would improve the relative position of low-income countries.'[16] Thus, at one extreme, the Musgraves proposed applying a rate of 60 percent where the per capita income of the capital-exporting country was greater than US$1,000 and the per capita income of the capital-importing country was less than US$250. At the other extreme, the Musgraves proposed applying a rate of 10 percent where the per capita income of the capital-exporting country was less than US$250 and the per capita income of the capital-importing country was greater than US$1,000.

B. Observations

1. 'Horizontal' versus 'vertical' internation equity

This fourth approach is quite distinct from the prior three. To borrow the familiar terminology used in domestic discussions of tax equity, the first three approaches (i.e., benefit taxation, source taxation and national rental charges) all have a 'horizontal' flavor to them. Indeed, when discussing the situation where income is derived from a combination of activities in several different countries, the Musgraves advocate the adoption of 'taxation ... on an international basis' with formulary apportionment to allocate the tax on those profits among the several countries that can claim to be their origin.[17]

In contrast, the fourth approach (i.e., redistribution) has a 'vertical' flavor to it. It does not concern the competing claims of similarly situated capital-importing countries to a share of the profits generated within their

---

14 *Ibid.* 74.
15 *Ibid.*
16 *Ibid.*
17 *Ibid.* 84.

respective territories. Instead, it concerns the allocation of the tax base between differently situated capital-exporting and capital-importing countries. The fourth approach thus recognizes the reality that all states are *not* situated equally and that 'states will vary significantly in their resources and power'.[18]

The Musgraves highlight the distinctive nature of the fourth approach when discussing the multiple-source-country situation. They qualify their advocacy of formulary apportionment by stating that there should be an 'allocation of proceeds on an apportionment basis among the participating countries, *making allowance for distributional considerations*'.[19] In other words, in keeping with the first three approaches, there should be a horizontal allocation of the tax base among the several source countries. But that horizontal allocation should then be altered to take account of the vertical differences in per capita income levels between these source countries.

The first three approaches to internation equity all view the nations connected to the generation of income as co-equal sovereigns competing for their fair portions of a shared tax base. The fourth approach expands this view to recognize that these nations comprise groups of people, some of which are economically better off than others. It further acknowledges that the economic differences between these groups might properly influence what is considered to be a fair sharing of the tax base. This represents a marked shift away from viewing nations connected with the generation of income as a homogeneous group of sovereigns vying to exercise their taxing jurisdiction to a (slightly) more nuanced view of them as heterogeneous groups of people with different resource endowments and average levels of income.

2. Focus on per capita income

The focus on income in describing the redistributive aspect of internation equity is worth further exploration. The Musgraves explicitly recognize that nations, like individuals, are different from one another. But the only differences that the Musgraves deem relevant to their analysis are along the lines of resource endowments and per capita income. And in their proposal, they collapse even these two lines of difference into one. The Musgraves' proposed sliding scale of tax rates uses per capita income as

---

[18] Diane Ring, 'Democracy, Sovereignty and Tax Competition: The Role of Tax Sovereignty in Shaping Tax Cooperation' (2009) 9 *Fla. Tax Rev.* 555 at 558.

[19] Musgrave and Musgrave, *supra* note 1, at 85 (emphasis added).

the only metric for determining whether and how redistribution should occur.

Although Peggy Musgrave often revisited and refined this seminal articulation of internation equity in her later work,[20] she has never returned in any sustained way to the redistributive aspect of internation equity.[21] Other commentators have followed her lead. In one of the most in-depth treatments of internation equity, Nancy Kaufman focuses on questions of division of the tax base among co-equal sovereigns and merely mentions the redistributive aspect of internation equity.[22] Other commentators focus exclusively on horizontal allocation of the tax base and make no mention at all of the redistributive aspect of internation equity.[23]

---

[20] Brooks, *supra* note 2, at 480–87.

[21] E.g., Peggy B. Musgrave, 'International Tax Differentials for Multinational Corporations: Equity and Efficiency Considerations' in Carl S. Shoup (ed.), *The Impact of Multinational Corporations on Development and on International Relations* (1974) 43, 46–8; Peggy B. Musgrave, 'The OECD Model Tax Treaty: Problems and Prospects' (1975) *Colum. J World Bus.* (Summer) 29, 36–7; Peggy B. Musgrave, 'Fiscal Coordination and Competition in an International Setting' in Lorraine Eden (ed.), *Retrospectives on Public Finance* (1991) 276, 294–6; Peggy B. Musgrave, 'Substituting Consumption-based Direct Taxation for Income Taxes as the International Norm: A Comment' (1992) 45 *Nat'l Tax J* 179 at 180–81; Peggy B. Musgrave, 'Consumption Tax Proposals in an International Setting (2000) 54 *Tax L Rev.* 77; Peggy B. Musgrave, 'Interjurisdiction Equity in Company Taxation: Principles and Applications to the European Union' in Sijbren Cnossen (ed.), *Taxing Capital Income in the European Union: Issues and Options for Reform* (2000) 46, 59; Peggy B. Musgrave, 'Sovereignty, Entitlement, and Cooperation in International Taxation' (2001) 26 *Brook. J Int'l L* 1335 at 1340; Peggy B. Musgrave, 'Combining Fiscal Sovereignty and Coordination: National Taxation in a Globalizing World' in Inge Kaul and Pedro Conceição (eds), *The New Public Finance: Responding to Global Challenges* (2006) 167, 175–7 (hereinafter Musgrave, 'Combining Fiscal Sovereignty').

[22] Nancy H. Kaufman, 'Fairness and the Taxation of International Income' (1998) 29 *Law and Pol'y Int'l Bus.* 145, 191–2, 203 (hereinafter Kaufman, 'Fairness'); see Nancy H. Kaufman, 'Equity Considerations in International Taxation' (2001) 26 *Brook. J Int'l L* 1465.

[23] E.g., Rifat Azam, 'E-commerce Taxation and Cyberspace Law: The Integrative Adaptation Model' (2007) 12(5) *Va. JL and Tech.* 23 at 32, 36, 97; William B. Barker, 'An International Tax System for Emerging Economies, Tax Sparing, and Development: It Is All about Source!' (2007) 29 *U Pa. J Int'l L* 349; Klaus Vogel, 'Worldwide vs. Source Taxation of Income: A Review and Re-evaluation of Arguments (Part III)' (1988) 11 *Intertax* 393 at 398, 400, 401.

Approaching the question of redistribution directly – but failing to address the Musgraves' contribution to the literature – Ilan Benshalom provides a limited moral or philosophical basis for global wealth redistribution through the international tax regime.[24] Benshalom eschews cosmopolitan or statist approaches to global distributive justice and proposes an alternative, 'relational-distributive' approach that relies upon economic relationships as the foundation for global wealth redistribution.[25] Yet, even without directly addressing the Musgraves' conceptualization of internation equity, Benshalom proposes a framework that nonetheless relies upon nations' relative incomes as the cornerstone for determining whether a relational-distributive duty exists.[26]

Similarly, Diane Ring has approached the redistributive aspect of internation equity in the context of discussing the role of sovereignty in the tax competition debate.[27] Ring strongly questions whether internation equity can play any role in the debate over tax competition because 'firm foundations for a generally accepted vision of inter-nation equity have yet to be established'.[28] When Ring does eventually consider a 'realistic' application of internation equity claims to the tax competition debate, her focus is entirely on the economic dimension of states.[29] She speaks of the possibility of 'expand[ing] upon some of the accepted thinking on human rights to encompass more clearly defined economic rights'.[30] Ring's concern here is not with human rights generally but with the redistribution of wealth from higher income countries to lower income countries in an effort to ensure a baseline of economic subsistence.[31]

Other commentators addressing issues of internation equity have adopted the same singular focus on income.[32] Working within this

---

24 Ilan Benshalom, 'The New Poor at Our Gates: Global Justice Implications for International Trade and Tax Law' (2010) 85 *NYU L Rev.* 1.

25 *Ibid.* 9–36.

26 *Ibid.* 59.

27 Ring, *supra* note 18.

28 *Ibid.* 583.

29 *Ibid.* 590.

30 *Ibid.*

31 *Ibid.*

32 E.g., Reuven S. Avi-Yonah, 'Globalization, Tax Competition, and the Fiscal Crisis of the Welfare State' (2000) 113 *Harv. L Rev.* 1573 at 1648–51; Jinyan Li, 'Improving Inter-nation Equity Through Territorial Taxation and Tax Sparing' in Arthur J. Cockfield (ed.), *Globalization and Its Tax Discontents: Tax Policy and International Investments* (2010) 117; Yoram Margalioth, 'Tax Competition, Foreign Direct Investments and Growth: Using the Tax System to Promote Developing Countries' (2003) 23 *Va. Tax Rev.* 161 at 192–7, 201–2;

framework, some commentators have even noted the possibility that the international tax regime may work a form of 'reverse redistribution', with lower income countries ceding a portion of their tax base under some circumstances to higher income countries.[33]

Thus far, Kim Brooks has made the only contribution to the literature on internation equity that attempts to break with an unbending focus on per capita income.[34] She approaches the question of revenue allocation between high and low income countries from a feminist perspective and explores how that perspective might support allocating a greater share of revenue to low income countries. Focusing on the role of tax treaties in the international tax regime, Brooks observes:

> There are a wide range of ways feminists might approach tax treaties as a tool for tempering the unregulated market: they could be used to compensate low-income states for the prevalent abuses perpetuated by corporations resident in high-income states; they might be used to allocate increased international tax revenue to states that actively promote women's equality; and, finally, they might be used to punish corporate taxpayers who act in ways that erode or hamper women's equality.[35]

Among her particular suggestions, Brooks proposes allocating a larger share of tax revenues to a low income country that 'better advances women's equality' or imposing a tax penalty on multinational companies that 'fail to adopt pay equity'.[36] Though these suggestions do not so narrowly focus on per capita income, they do incorporate and perpetuate the general income-centric focus of internation equity by furnishing no more than a feminist justification for the redistribution of wealth from high to low income countries.

Ruth Mason, 'Tax Expenditures and Global Labor Mobility' (2009) 84 *NYU L Rev.* 1540 at 1590–91, 1593–9; Adam H. Rosenzweig, 'Harnessing the Costs of International Tax Arbitrage' (2007) 26 *Va. Tax Rev.* 555 at 600–608.

[33] E.g., Aldo Forgione, 'Clicks and Mortar: Taxing Multinational Business Profits in the Digital Age' (2003) 26 *Seattle UL Rev.* 719 at 762, 766–7; Jinyan Li, 'The Rise and Fall of Chinese Tax Incentives and Implications for International Tax Debates' (2007) 8 *Fla. Tax Rev.* 669 at 707–11.

[34] Kim Brooks, 'Global Distributive Justice: The Potential for a Feminist Analysis of International Tax Revenue Allocation' (2009) 21 *Can. J Women and L* 267.

[35] *Ibid.* 290–91.

[36] *Ibid.* 291, 292.

III. TAX BLINDERS

A. Tax Exceptionalism

Discussions of internation equity, like discussions of interindividual equity, largely seem to occur in a tax vacuum. For instance, inter-individual equity debates in the United States proceed on the assumption that the tax laws form a closed system, even though their 'larger purpose is to allocate the burden of funding our government and of paying for public services'.[37] Tax is viewed as separate and apart from (and, therefore, wholly unconcerned with) other areas of the law – not to mention the spending side of the fiscal system and domestic social systems more generally. Thus, as it is sometimes said in the United States, tax is treated as 'exceptional'.

Viewing the world wearing tax blinders, US commentators generally ignore the larger context in which the tax system operates and, consequently, ignore all differences among taxpayers other than differences in amount or type of income.[38] These commentators thus fail to take account of other forms of difference (e.g., race, ethnicity, gender, sexual orientation and physical ability) that 'have served, and continue to serve, as the basis for invidious discrimination that already imposes heavy burdens on its victims'.[39] Elsewhere, I have urged US commentators to take a holistic view of the allocation and apportionment of burdens in American society. More pointedly, I urged them to 'begin to offer competing ideas about what makes a tax system fair' that take into account the non-tax burdens imposed by American society on groups that have traditionally been subordinated along lines other than class.[40]

Debates about internation equity are similarly plagued by tax exceptionalism. For example, US commentators seem to view international tax as being separate and apart from international law. Tellingly, Reuven Avi-Yonah begins his essay 'International Tax as International Law' with the question: 'Is international tax law part of international law?'[41] He then candidly states that one of his aims in writing the essay is 'to

---

[37] Infanti, *supra* note 3, at 1195.
[38] *Ibid.* 1200.
[39] *Ibid.* 1196.
[40] *Ibid.* 1197.
[41] Reuven S. Avi-Yonah, 'International Tax as International Law' (2004) 57 *Tax L Rev.* 483.

persuade international tax lawyers and international tax academics that their field is indeed part of international law'.[42]

Likewise, US commentators only rarely acknowledge that international tax forms part of a nation's foreign policy. Notably, Michael Graetz has recognized that '[f]oreign policy concerns have long played an important role in U.S. international tax policy'.[43] Indeed, he has neatly summarized this history, which extends from China trade corporations in the 1920s to Western Hemisphere trade corporations in the 1940s to Subpart F rules targeting developing countries in the 1960s – not to mention the denial of foreign tax credits to those who invested in South Africa during apartheid and, even now, to those who participate in boycotts of Israel.[44] Graetz also pointed out that '[f]oreign policy objectives may influence decisions about which countries to enter or cancel tax treaties with and the appropriate parameters of treaty concessions'.[45] Graetz further observed that, if tax were to be used as a means of redistributing income among nations, then '[t]ax policy, of course, would have to be coordinated with other policies such as foreign policy and debt forgiveness'.[46]

In the same vein, it is rare to find US commentators discussing the idea that international tax provisions may constitute foreign aid or assistance. Obviously, tax sparing, which the United States has consistently rejected, is widely viewed as a form of foreign aid.[47] Less obviously, David Pozen has highlighted how US tax expenditures relating to non-profit organizations can be reconceptualized as a hidden form of foreign aid or assistance.[48]

Of particular interest here, unilateral departures from a country's exercise of source tax jurisdiction can be conceptualized as tax expenditures.[49] For example, it has been suggested that the US portfolio interest

---

42 *Ibid.*

43 Michael J. Graetz, 'Taxing International Income: Inadequate Principles, Outdated Concepts, and Unsatisfactory Policies' (2001) 54 *Tax L Rev.* 261 at 307.

44 *Ibid.* 307–8.

45 *Ibid.* 310.

46 *Ibid.* 301 note 165.

47 E.g., OECD, *Tax Sparing: A Reconsideration* (1998) 16, 19; Kim Brooks, 'Tax Sparing: A Needed Incentive for Foreign Investment in Low-Income Countries or an Unnecessary Revenue Sacrifice?' (2009) 4 *Queen's LJ* 505 at 518–21; Yariv Brauner, 'A Framework for an Informed Study of the Realistic Role of Tax in a Development Agenda' (2010) 42 *U Brit. Colum. L Rev.* 275 at 315.

48 David E. Pozen, 'Hidden Foreign Aid' (2007) 8 *Fla. Tax Rev.* 641.

49 Allaire Urban Karzon, 'Tax Expenditures and Tax Reform' (1985) 38 *Vand. L Rev.* 1397 at 1408–11 (reviewing Stanley S. Surrey and Paul R.

exemption might be classified as a tax expenditure.[50] Canada actually does classify its unilateral (as opposed to treaty-based) departures from its non-resident withholding tax as tax expenditures.[51] Australia likewise classifies its unilateral (as well as certain of its treaty-based) departures from its non-resident withholding tax as tax expenditures.[52] Such reductions in a source country's non-resident withholding tax inure to the benefit of (i.e., provide aid to) the residence country, which is permitted to retain that much more of the national gain produced by its residents' investments in the source country.

Similarly, the most common methods for mitigating double taxation – the foreign tax credit and the exemption from tax of foreign source income – can also be conceptualized as tax expenditures. For instance, it has been suggested that the US foreign tax credit might be classified as a tax expenditure when compared to a baseline of allowing only a deduction for foreign taxes.[53] In fact, Canada includes its foreign tax credit on a list of arguable tax expenditures.[54] The US exclusions from gross income for (1) certain income earned by US citizens residing

McDaniel, *Tax Expenditures* (1985)). It is worth noting that the discussion of tax expenditures in the text below makes implicit assumptions about the baseline international tax regime, including the relationship between source and residence taxing jurisdiction and whether certain tax provisions constitute tax expenditures (and, therefore, hidden foreign aid) as compared to that baseline. There are some, for example, Nancy Kaufman, who would argue that the current international tax regime does not provide assistance to lower income countries, but works a redistribution in the opposite direction. See *supra* note 33 and accompanying text. For an argument that tax sparing is not a concession to the source state but a recognition of the source state's jurisdiction over an item of income, see Luís Eduardo Schoueri, Chapter 5.

50 Karzon, *supra* note 49, at 1411–13; see Avi-Yonah, *supra* note 32, at 1598 note 91.

51 Department of Finance Canada, *Tax Expenditures and Evaluations 2010* (2010) 21 (hereinafter *Tax Expenditures*); *Tax Expenditures: Notes to the Estimates/Projections 2010* (2010) 77–8.

52 Commonwealth of Australia, *Tax Expenditures Statement 2010* (2011) 68–9, 72, 205–6.

53 Pozen, *supra* note 48, at 652 note 41 (citing Office of Management and Budget, Executive Office of the President of the United States, *Budget of the United States Government: Fiscal Year 2008: Analytical Perspectives* (2007) 316; and Boris I. Bittker, 'Accounting for Federal "Tax Subsidies" in the National Budget' (1969) 22 *Nat'l Tax J* 244 at 250 note 15).

54 *Tax Expenditures*, *supra* note 51, at 16.

abroad and (2) income of US residents from sources within certain US possessions are already classified as tax expenditures.[55]

If recast as tax expenditures, both the credit and exemption methods of mitigating double taxation may be seen as providing a benefit to source countries. For instance, if the United States in its capacity as a residence country were to allow its citizens and residents no more than a deduction for income taxes levied by a source country, then it would deter investment abroad by its citizens and residents. Under such a regime for the mitigation of double taxation, US citizens and residents would not invest capital abroad unless the foreign investment produced an after-foreign-tax return greater than the pretax return on a US domestic investment.[56] Accordingly, the more generous methods of mitigating double taxation (i.e., the foreign tax credit and exemption methods) facilitate or even encourage investment abroad when compared to a deduction baseline and, from that perspective, provide a form of foreign aid to source countries.

Wearing their tax blinders, commentators contributing to the inter-nation equity debate generally ignore the larger foreign policy framework in which the international tax rules are situated. They concomitantly ignore the possibility that a nation's international tax rules can operate to provide foreign aid or assistance to other countries – whether intentionally or unintentionally and whether consistently or inconsistently with the nation's larger foreign policy framework. Ignoring this larger context, they (like their counterparts in US domestic tax equity debates) tend to focus on a single (economic) dimension of nations – per capita income – when considering questions of internation equity.

B. Removing the Tax Blinders

By framing discussions of redistribution solely in terms of relative per capita income, commentators replicate on the international level a domestic tax equity debate rendered insipid by its one-dimensional focus on economic class. The only difference between the domestic and international debates about redistribution is that commentators contributing to the international debate speak of high and low income 'nations'

[55] Office of Management and Budget, Executive Office of the President of the United States, *Budget of the United States Government: Fiscal Year 2012: Analytical Perspectives* (2010) 241 at 257; Staff of Joint Committee on Taxation, No. JCS-3-10, 111th Cong., *Estimates of Federal Tax Expenditures for Fiscal Years 2010–2014* (Comm. Print 2010) 32, 34.

[56] Musgrave and Musgrave, *supra* note 1, at 70.

(rather than high and low income 'taxpayers'). This may lend the terms of the international debate a comfortable feel and, by focusing on numbers, may even lend it the veneer of objectivity that so many tax academics seem to yearn for. Nevertheless, a narrow focus on per capita income is both problematic and outdated.

As Klaus Vogel long ago explained, 'equity reasoning can never be based on a single set of presumptions. In a complex world, it is necessary to consider multiple aspects.'[57] By removing our tax blinders, we can recognize that internation equity is just one component of each country's foreign policy framework, and, more specifically, of its development policy. Furthermore, Vogel's words echo those of contributors to the development literature who have argued in favor of expanding its own traditionally narrow focus on economic growth to encompass additional dimensions in an effort to make the idea of development more meaningful.

For example, Amartya Sen singles out 'identifying development with the growth of gross national product ... or with the rise in personal incomes' as examples of 'narrower views of development'.[58] Instead, Sen persuasively argues that:

> An adequate conception of development must go much beyond the accumulation of wealth and the growth of gross national product and other income-related variables. Without ignoring the importance of economic growth, we must look well beyond it.
>
> The ends and means of development require examination and scrutiny for a fuller understanding of the development process; it is simply not adequate to take as our basic objective just the maximization of income or wealth, which is, as Aristotle noted, 'merely useful and for the sake of something else'. For the same reason, economic growth cannot sensibly be treated as an end in itself. Development has to be more concerned with enhancing the lives we lead and the freedoms we enjoy. Expanding the freedoms that we have reason to value not only makes our lives richer and more unfettered, but also allows us to be fuller social persons, exercising our own volitions and interacting with – and influencing – the world in which we live.[59]

---

[57] Klaus Vogel, 'The Search for Compatible Tax Systems' in Herbert Stein (ed.), *Tax Policy in the Twenty-first Century* (1988) 76, 84.

[58] Amartya Sen, *Development as Freedom* (1999) 3.

[59] *Ibid.* 14–15; see *ibid.* 3, 8–9, 90, 131, 290–92.

IV. EXPANDING THE HORIZON

Other participants in debates over development policy have likewise expanded their horizons beyond economic growth and per capita income. For example, in the first Human Development Report (HDR) in 1990, an independent team working under the auspices of the United Nations Development Programme (UNDP) introduced the Human Development Index (HDI) in an effort to move past the development literature's narrow focus on economic growth and expand the scope of development measures.[60] The 1990 HDR stated that '[t]he basic objective of development is to create an enabling environment for people to live long, healthy and creative lives'.[61] The 2010 HDR contains a more refined conceptualization of human development:

> Human development is the expansion of people's freedoms to live long, healthy and creative lives; to advance other goals they have reason to value; and to engage actively in shaping development equitably and sustainably on a shared planet. People are both the beneficiaries and drivers of human development, as individuals and in groups.[62]

This people-centered conceptualization of human development is strongly grounded in Amartya Sen's capability approach,[63] which focuses on 'the "capabilities" of persons to lead the kind of lives they value – and have reason to value'.[64] Applying this approach to the development

---

[60] Amartya Sen, 'Introduction' to U.N. Development Programme, *Human Development Report 2010* (2010) vi, vi (hereinafter '2010 HDR'). The HDRs typically contain a caveat that they do not necessarily reflect the views of the UNDP but only those of the team that produced them. For example, the 1990 HDR contains the following caveat in its foreword: 'The views expressed in this Report are those of the team and not necessarily shared by UNDP or its Governing Council or the member governments of UNDP. The essence of any such report must be its independence and its intellectual integrity.' William H. Draper III, 'Foreword' to U.N. Development Programme, *Human Development Report 1990* (1990) iii, iv. The independence of the authors of the HDRs is considered to be one of the great strengths of these reports. Desmond McNeill, '"Human Development": The Power of the Idea' (2007) 8 *J Hum. Dev.* 5 at 11–12.

[61] 2010 HDR, *supra* note 60, at 12.

[62] *Ibid.* 22.

[63] *Ibid.* 16; see Amartya Sen, 'Capability and Well-Being' in Martha Nussbaum and Amartya Sen (eds), *The Quality of Life* (1993) 30.

[64] Sen, *supra* note 58, at 18.

context, Sen 'treats the freedoms of individuals as the basic building blocks'.[65]

Sen views individual freedoms as having both a constitutive and an instrumental role in development.[66] He explains the constitutive role of freedom as follows:

> The constitutive role of freedom relates to the importance of substantive freedom in enriching human life. The substantive freedoms include elementary capabilities like being able to avoid such deprivations as starvation, undernourishment, escapable morbidity and premature mortality, as well as the freedoms that are associated with being literate and numerate, enjoying political participation and uncensored speech and so on.[67]

But freedom is not only the 'primary end' of development but also its 'principal means'.[68] Thus, freedoms also have a role to play in contributing, 'directly or indirectly, to the overall freedom people have to live the way they would like to live'.[69] Sen groups instrumental freedoms into five basic categories: political freedoms (e.g., civil rights, democracy and freedom of the press), economic facilities ('opportunities ... to utilize economic resources for the purpose of consumption, or production, or exchange'), social opportunities (e.g., education and health care), transparency guarantees (i.e., the openness necessary for mutual trust), and protective security (i.e., social safety net).[70]

A. Human Development Index

To better measure human development in keeping with Sen's approach, the HDI combines information along three different dimensions. Recognizing that income has a role (but not the only role) to play in development, the HDI considers (1) per capita income, (2) schooling (both mean years of schooling and expected years of schooling), and (3) health (life expectancy at birth).[71] The HDI is meant to rival 'the handy usability of the crude GNP', 'but, unlike GNP, without being oblivious of everything other than incomes and commodities'.[72] Yet, as Sen himself

---

65 *Ibid.*
66 *Ibid.* 18–19, 36–40, 246.
67 *Ibid.* 36.
68 *Ibid.*
69 *Ibid.* 38.
70 *Ibid.* 38–40.
71 2010 HDR, *supra* note 60, at 13 Fig.1.1, 15 box 1.2.
72 Sen, *supra* note 60, at vi.

cautions, 'the huge breadth of the human development approach must not be confused, as it sometimes is, with the slender limits of the HDI'.[73]

The 2010 HDR marked the twentieth anniversary of the HDI's introduction. The team writing the 2010 HDR took this occasion to engage in some retrospection and found that there 'is the lack of a significant correlation between economic growth and improvements in health and education'.[74] For instance, the 2010 HDR compared and contrasted two countries, China and Tunisia, to demonstrate the disconnect between economic growth and improvements in health and education:

> In 1970 a baby girl born in Tunisia could expect to live 55 years; one born in China, 63 years. Since then, China's per capita GDP has grown at a breakneck pace of 8 percent annually, while Tunisia's has grown at 3 percent. But a girl born today in Tunisia can expect to live 76 years, a year longer than a girl born in China. And while only 52 percent of Tunisian children were enrolled in school in 1970, today's gross enrolment ratio is 78 percent, considerably higher than China's 68 percent.[75]

These findings confirm Sen's insights more than a decade earlier regarding 'the dissonance between income per head … and the freedom of individuals to live long and live well'.[76] In fact, the 2010 HDR concluded that 'human development is different from economic growth and … substantial achievements are possible even without fast growth'.[77]

Economic measures may not only be limiting but also misleading. Per capita income, for instance, is nothing more than a country's average income. Averages such as this can mask as much – or sometimes more – than they reveal.[78] In the case of income, averaging can mask profound levels of inequality in a society – and, of course, will completely miss inequalities along other lines (e.g., health, education, employment, and

---

[73] *Ibid.*

[74] 2010 HDR, *supra* note 60, at 4; see *ibid.* 46–64 (explaining the data and reasoning supporting this conclusion). The 2010 HDR draws a distinction between levels of income and health and education, on one hand, and changes in income and health and education, on the other. There is a positive correlation between a nation's level of income and its level of health and education; however, there is no significant correlation between change in income and change in health and education. *Ibid.* 47.

[75] *Ibid.* 47.

[76] Sen, *supra* note 58, at 5; see *ibid.* 5–6, 43–9, 108–10, 285.

[77] 2010 HDR, *supra* note 60, at 5.

[78] *Ibid.* 87.

social acceptance).[79] Indeed, in discussing the ways in which average income can be misleading, the 2010 HDR points to the United States as an example of a country where 'mean income is almost a third higher than median income, and the gap is growing'.[80] The 2010 HDR further points to gaps of similar size in Italy and New Zealand and even larger gaps in Côte d'Ivoire, Liberia and Zambia.[81]

B. Additional Dimensions

To address such concerns, the 2010 HDR introduced a refined version of the HDI, the Inequality-adjusted HDI (IHDI).[82] After taking inequality into account, 'the global HDI of 0.62 in 2010 would fall to 0.49, which represents a drop from the high to the medium HDI category'.[83] In 2010, the average loss in HDI due to inequality was 22 percent, and the losses ranged from a low of 6 percent to a high of 45 percent.[84]

A few examples may help to underscore the impact of inequality on measuring human development. Taking inequality into account, the United States would see its HDI drop by more than 11 percent (from 0.902 to 0.799), and it would fall nine places in the HDI ranking.[85] The Republic of Korea, another high income country and member of the Organisation for Economic Co-operation and Development (OECD),[86] would see its HDI drop by nearly 17 percent (from 0.877 to 0.731), and it would fall 18 places in the HDI ranking.[87] Brazil, an upper-middle income country,[88] would see its HDI drop by 27 percent (from 0.699 to 0.509), and it would fall 15 places in the HDI ranking.[89]

The 2010 HDR also introduced a more refined measure of gender inequality, the Gender Inequality Index (GII).[90] The GII takes account of three dimensions: (1) women's reproductive health (through maternal mortality ratios and adolescent fertility rates); (2) women's empowerment

---

79 Sen, *supra* note 58, at 107–10.
80 2010 HDR, *supra* note 60, at 72.
81 *Ibid.*
82 *Ibid.* 7.
83 *Ibid.*
84 *Ibid.* 87.
85 *Ibid.* 152.
86 World Bank, *World Bank List of Economies* (2011).
87 2010 HDR, *supra* note 60, at 152.
88 World Bank, *supra* note 86.
89 2010 HDR, *supra* note 60, at 153.
90 *Ibid.* 89–94.

(through national parliamentary representation and educational attainment); and (3) women's labor force participation.[91] As measured by the GII, the average loss in achievement for the ten countries closest to gender equality was 23 percent while the average loss in achievement for the ten countries farthest from gender equality was 79 percent.[92]

Again, a few examples will help to underscore the impact of gender inequality on measuring human development. The United States ranks fourth in the HDI but only 37 in the GII, with a 40 percent loss in achievement due to gender inequality.[93] Qatar, a high income country,[94] ranks 38 in the HDI (placing it in the very high human development category) but ranks 94 in the GII, with a 67 percent loss in achievement due to gender inequality.[95] More startlingly, Saudi Arabia, a high income country,[96] ranks 55 in the HDI (placing it in the high human development category) but ranks 128 in the GII, with a 76 percent loss in achievement due to gender inequality.[97] Mexico, an upper-middle income country,[98] ranks 56 in the HDI (also placing it in the high human development category) but ranks 68 in the GII, with a nearly 58 percent loss in achievement due to gender inequality.[99]

There is a strong correlation 'between gender inequality and the loss due to inequality in the distribution of the HDI'.[100] Yet, this measure fails to capture other dimensions of gender inequality, including occupational segregation, the gender wage gap, and the experience of non-elites as well as women's 'time use, access to assets, domestic violence and local-level empowerment'.[101]

C. Yet Further Dimensions

The 2010 HDR candidly recognizes the limits of its measures, stating that, 'as with any aggregate measure and international comparison, it simplifies and captures only part of what human development entails'.[102]

---

91 *Ibid.* 91 Fig. 5.3.
92 *Ibid.* 93.
93 *Ibid.* 156.
94 World Bank, *supra* note 86.
95 2010 HDR, *supra* note 60, at 156.
96 World Bank, *supra* note 86.
97 2010 HDR, *supra* note 60, at 157.
98 World Bank, *supra* note 86.
99 2010 HDR, *supra* note 60, at 156.
100 *Ibid.* 93.
101 *Ibid.* 92, 94.
102 *Ibid.* 13.

Thus, the purpose of the HDI and the related measures discussed above 'is not to build an unassailable indicator of well-being – it is to redirect attention towards human-centred development and to promote debate over how we advance the progress of societies'.[103] Among other dimensions that the 2010 HDR acknowledges are important to human development are human rights and the political and social empowerment of groups of people, sustainability of production and impact on the environment, wellbeing, the availability of decent work, and addressing threats to the human development that has been achieved.[104] In fact, the 2010 HDR included six new statistical tables that cover these additional dimensions.[105]

Moreover, the OECD has highlighted the increasing recognition that 'development and human rights are interdependent and mutually reinforcing'.[106] It has identified a clear trend among aid agencies to adopt, develop and refine human rights and development policies.[107] In collecting and reviewing the experiences of a number of these aid agencies with human-rights-based approaches to development,[108] the OECD recognized the advantages of a human rights perspective in development work.[109]

In its review, the OECD noted how human rights have impacted tax reform – and interindividual equity – in developing countries.[110] The OECD called attention to the work of the UK Department for International Development (DFID) in Peru. As part of a larger project addressing the causes of poverty in Peru, DFID promoted 'a focus on equity and accountability – rather than simply efficiency – into revenue policy and administration' by 'promoting the perspective that when citizens pay taxes, not only is it a duty but it also creates rights'.[111] Thus, DFID 'set out to ensure that resources reached excluded groups, on the expenditure side; and promoted the perspective that paying taxes is not only a duty but also creates rights, on the revenue-creation side'.[112] Given the people-centered nature of human rights discourse and the ways in

---

103 *Ibid.*
104 *Ibid.* 17–19, 22, 85 tbl. 5.1.
105 *Ibid.* 137.
106 OECD, *The Development Dimension: Integrating Human Rights into Development* (2006) 17.
107 *Ibid.* 26.
108 *Ibid.* 3–4.
109 *Ibid.* 20–21.
110 *Ibid.* 19, 43.
111 *Ibid.* 44; *see ibid.* 117–22.
112 *Ibid.* 120.

which a human rights focus can draw attention to the plight of marginalized groups, it is little wonder that '[h]uman rights have … become an important part of the literature on development'.[113]

Recent empirical research from the World Bank further buttresses the notion that economic growth does not guarantee advances in human rights. Put differently, 'political/civil liberties and good governance are not a "luxury good": the process of economic development does not itself automatically ensure improved governance, civil liberties, and control of corruption'.[114] Indeed, this research supports the conclusion that '[t]he causality direction is from improved governance to economic development, not vice versa'.[115] Consequently, there is no 'automatic virtuous circle', and 'specific interventions and policies on governance and [first-generation human rights] are required at every stage'.[116]

Although 'there is no consensus about development policy', the foregoing discussion illustrates that 'new trends are emerging', including an increasing recognition that there is more to development than economic growth and per capita income and that 'captur[ing] the "missing" dimensions … is increasingly feasible'.[117]

V. TAX AND HUMAN DEVELOPMENT

It is time for these new trends to penetrate the internation equity debate. To begin expanding our horizons, commentators must first leave behind tax exceptionalism and recognize that discussions of redistribution and internation equity are no more than the tax aspect of a larger debate about development policy. Our blinkered debates about internation equity, like the larger debates about development policy before them, have traditionally focused on per capita income. But, as the new trends in the development debate highlight, per capita income is just one of many lines of difference among nations that should be considered in formulating international tax policy. Not only can participants in the internation equity debate come to better appreciate the importance of the multiple dimensions of human development, but, as the 2010 HDR illustrates,

---

113 Sen, *supra* note 58, at 227.

114 Daniel Kaufmann, 'Human Rights and Governance: The Empirical Challenge' in Philip Alston and Mary Robinson (eds), *Human Rights and Development: Towards Mutual Reinforcement* (2005) 352, 382.

115 *Ibid.*

116 *Ibid.*

117 2010 HDR, *supra* note 60, at 19–20.

there are measures available for them to actually incorporate the human development approach into proposals intended to further internation equity.

In keeping with the human development approach, the redistributive aspect of internation equity can – and ought to – involve more than the shifting of financial resources from higher income 'developed' countries to lower income 'developing' countries in an effort to shore up their per capita incomes. But expanding the focus of internation equity beyond economic growth requires more than simply fashioning arguments for enhanced forms of redistribution that incorporate non-economic (e.g., feminist, social or strategic) considerations.[118] Such arguments still operate within the linear framework of redistribution from higher to lower income countries.

In the remainder of this section, I offer proposals that embody a notion of internation equity that promotes human development. These proposals are an initial step toward fashioning a more robust notion of internation equity freed of its tax/economic blinders. Certainly, commentators could – and, hopefully, will – craft other proposals that advance human development in more ambitious ways. Indeed, the principal aims of this chapter are to influence the direction of the internation equity debate and to lay the groundwork for future work integrating tax and development policy. With that background, let us turn to a discussion of the proposals.

A. Reality Check

A single assumption undergirds these proposals, namely, that, given our extant international tax regime, nations can already be seen as providing development assistance to each other through the tax expenditures embedded in their international tax rules.[119] As discussed above, both departures from a source country's non-resident withholding tax and a residence country's mitigation of double taxation through the foreign tax

---

118 E.g., Brooks, *supra* note 34; Karen B. Brown, 'Missing Africa: Should U.S. International Tax Rules Accommodate Investment in Developing Countries?' (2002) 23 *U Pa. J Int'l Econ. L* 45.

119 This is, of course, not to say that development assistance should be run through tax expenditures rather than provided directly, but rather to (1) acknowledge the reality that such assistance may already be provided through the tax laws, and (2) where appropriate, encourage better targeting of that assistance so as to further human development. Cf. Avi-Yonah, *supra* note 32, at 1640; Brooks, *supra* note 47, at 549; Brauner, *supra* note 47, at 312. It is also not to say that these proposals could not be adopted even were it concluded that these provisions do not constitute tax expenditures at all. See *supra* note 49.

credit or exemption methods can be conceptualized as tax expenditures that provide aid to other countries. In this light, we will consider exercises of source and residence taxing jurisdiction in turn, with related proposals advanced for each.

Before reaching that discussion, however, it is important to state a caveat. Once it is recognized that countries can provide foreign aid through their international tax rules, each country must decide whether it is in a position to provide such aid. Especially for countries that (1) underperform in terms of human development and (2) provide little (if any) direct foreign development assistance, it may be that scaling back or eliminating international tax expenditures is the most appropriate step to take. The forgone revenue may be better spent furthering development at home rather than abroad. If, however, tax expenditures that provide 'hidden' foreign aid are to continue, then it will be necessary to consider how these rules might better target assistance to further human development.

Furthermore, though I have, on occasion, used the United States as an example in this chapter, these proposals are drafted broadly and are not meant to be limited in their application to any one country. In fact, the incentive created by these proposals for all countries (regardless of income level) to advance human development will only grow more powerful as more countries adopt them. Concomitantly, the pressure will grow on non-adopting countries (assuming that they choose to retain their international tax expenditures) to adhere to an emerging international tax norm of targeting 'hidden' foreign assistance so as to further human development.

B. Source Taxation

In considering how much tax to levy on non-residents, a source country might choose to adopt a sliding scale of withholding tax rates, whether through domestic law or its network of tax treaties, that varies depending on how the taxpayer's country of residence does in terms of advancing human development. As a first step, this sliding scale could be implemented through domestic law. A short target timeframe could be specified within which all existing tax treaties would be renegotiated to comport with the sliding scale, perhaps based on bands of withholding tax rates built into the statutory sliding scale in order to accommodate some reduction in the statutory rate as a treaty concession without crossing from one level in the statutory sliding scale to another. Naturally, future tax treaties would be negotiated from the outset to comport with the sliding scale.[120]

As described below, such a sliding scale could easily be tied to the measures of human development in the annual HDRs, such as the HDI, the IHDI and the GII. These indices, though neither perfect nor all-encompassing in their scope, provide a measure of human development that is just as handy as, but more meaningful than, per capita income.[121] An added benefit of these measures is that they are produced by a team that works independently of the United Nations, thereby limiting concerns about political influence in the creation of the indices.[122] And, of course, these indices can always be replaced or supplemented as more refined or complete measures of human development arise.

For instance, the source country could afford the lowest withholding tax rates to residents of countries that (1) appear in the HDI's 'very high human development' category (to reward those already doing well) or are among the highest scorers in the 'HDI improvement rank' (to reward those making the greatest strides even if they are not yet among the best overall), and (2) experience losses in HDI due to inequality (as measured by the IHDI) and in achievement due to gender inequality (as measured by the GII) below a specified threshold.[123] This would result in the source country ceding more of the national gain (i.e., providing more foreign aid) to the residence country as it performs better in the HDR's

---

120 Indeed, the treaty negotiation process could provide an additional means for expanding the web of countries adopting these proposals. A treaty partner's firm resistance to adopting the sliding scale approach would not, however, present a problem because reciprocity in withholding rates is by no means an inexorable feature of tax treaties. See, e.g., Convention for the Avoidance of Double Taxation, the Prevention of Fiscal Evasion with respect to Taxes on Income, and the Encouragement of International Trade and Investment, United States–Trinidad and Tobago, Art. 12, 9 January 1970, 22 U.S.T. 164, 177–8 (limiting the Trinidad and Tobago tax on dividends to a maximum rate of 25 percent, but imposing no limit on the US statutory withholding tax rate on dividends).

121 See Gustav Ranis *et al.*, 'Human Development: Beyond the Human Development Index' (2006) 7 *J Hum. Dev.* 323 (demonstrating that a broader set of measures is necessary to assess a fuller definition of human development than the basic one employed for purposes of the HDI, but concluding that the HDI is superior to both per capita income and under-five mortality rates as a measure of a fuller definition of human development).

122 *See supra* note 60.

123 2010 HDR, *supra* note 60, at 143–60.

human development measures. In this way, the source country would encourage all countries whose residents invest capital there to work to advance human development.

Conversely, the highest withholding tax rates could be applied to residents of countries that either (1) appear in the HDI's 'low human development' category and fare poorly in the 'HDI improvement rank', or (2) experience losses in HDI due to inequality (as measured by the IHDI) and in achievement due to gender inequality (as measured by the GII) above a specified threshold. This would result in the source country retaining a greater share of the residence country's national gain as it performs more poorly in the HDR's human development measures. This would serve as encouragement to the affected residence countries to pay greater attention to advancing human development. Withholding tax rates in between the highest and lowest rates could be applied to residents of countries falling in between these extremes.

Countries would move among the different levels of withholding tax rates as the measure of their human development changes over time.[124] Accordingly, as a country whose residents were subject to the highest withholding tax rates improved in the various measures of human development, the withholding tax rates imposed on its residents would be reduced under the sliding scale. Some underperforming countries might not (at least initially) respond to this encouragement any more than they respond to the segments of their own populations who are bearing the brunt of their lack of human development. Residents of these countries would be punished for this inaction by being subject to persistently high withholding tax rates – and appropriately so. The marginalized and disadvantaged in these countries are not likely to be among those making investments abroad. To the contrary, only those with wealth and advantage, who are, directly or indirectly, benefiting from their country's underdevelopment, would be making investments abroad. Perhaps the tangible, personal effect of a penalty tax on the segments of the population more likely to be heard by those in power (or to themselves

---

[124] There is little reason to be concerned about complexity arising from the possibility of annual changes in withholding rates. For instance, the Internal Revenue Service annually publishes treaty-rate withholding tables for use by withholding agents and could do the same for a sliding scale of rates. *Withholding of Tax on Nonresident Aliens and Foreign Entities*, IRS Publication No. 515 (2011). Moreover, governments can combat abusive 'rate shopping' through stringent limitation on benefits provisions similar to those already employed to combat 'treaty shopping'.

be part of the power structure) will eventually serve as an incentive for change.

Once change is made and the measure of a country's human development improves, the withholding tax would be correspondingly reduced. At first blush, there seems to be an 'upside-down' quality to the aid provided through this sliding scale of withholding rates, as the benefit of reduced rates goes to those who are wealthy enough to make investments abroad. But keep in mind that the benefit of these lower rates only comes if those with wealth and power ensure that the lot of the disadvantaged in their countries is improving. In this way, it is the necessary obverse of the penalty tax imposed on those same individuals when they fail to improve the lot of the disadvantaged in their countries. More importantly, by ceding a greater share of the national gain, the source country allows the residence country to claim a greater share of the gain through taxation for use in ongoing development efforts.

C. Residence Taxation

A similar sliding scale could be applied by residence countries to their own citizens and residents when determining how to mitigate double taxation. A number of methods exist for mitigating double taxation. A residence country can (1) adopt worldwide taxation accompanied by a credit for foreign taxes paid; (2) exempt foreign source income from tax; or (3) provide a deduction for foreign taxes paid.[125] Some countries, like the United States, use a combination of these methods.[126]

In their 1972 essay, the Musgraves asserted that internation equity concerns only source-based (and not residence-based) taxing jurisdiction. Yet, as Peggy Musgrave later noted, 'the country of residence, as the residual taxing authority, has control over the total tax burden on the foreign-source income of its resident taxpayers'.[127] How a residence country divides the residual national gain from foreign investment between the taxpayer and its treasury will undoubtedly influence where its residents invest.[128] In this way, the residence country can affect which source countries will be able to lay claim to a portion of the national gain

---

[125] Paul R. McDaniel, 'The U.S. Tax Treatment of Foreign Source Income Earned in Developing Countries: A Policy Analysis' (2003) 35 *Geo. Wash. Int'l L Rev.* 265 at 267.

[126] IRC ss. 164(a)(3); 901(a), (j); 911.

[127] Musgrave, 'Combining Fiscal Sovereignty', *supra* note 21, at 168–9.

[128] Mihir A. Desai and James R. Hines, Jr, 'Evaluating International Tax Reform' (2003) 55 *Nat'l Tax J* 487 at 491.

generated by its residents' foreign investments. This channeling effect of residence taxation impacts the redistributive aspect of internation equity.

A residence country could encourage investment in source countries doing well in terms of human development by exempting income sourced in those countries from tax. It could discourage investment in source countries doing poorly in terms of human development by providing no more than a deduction for foreign taxes paid (or for the worst offenders, by denying relief from double taxation). For countries falling in between these extremes, it could choose among the following options:

(a) provide a foreign tax credit;
(b) provide an exemption from tax, but take the exempt income into account in determining the rates applicable to the resident's taxable income – so-called exemption with progression;[129]
(c) employ some form of tax sparing; or
(d) some combination of these (or other) methods.

In this way, the residence country would encourage all source countries seeking capital investments from its residents to work to advance human development.

As with the sliding scale of non-resident withholding tax rates, this sliding scale of methods for mitigating double taxation would reward (i.e., target aid to) countries doing well in terms of human development and encourage underperformers to pay greater attention to advancing human development. At its heart, this is no more than a special application of general notions of efficiency in the international tax context. Typically, efficiency debates in the international tax context are phrased in terms of capital-export, capital-import or national neutrality.[130] Rather than being concerned with reducing or eliminating investment-allocation, competitive or tax-revenue distortions, this sliding scale of methods for mitigating double taxation would revolve around reducing or

---

129 Kaufman, 'Fairness', *supra* note 22, at 150 note 31.

130 Anthony C. Infanti, 'Spontaneous Tax Coordination: On Adopting a Comparative Approach to Reforming the U.S. International Tax Regime' (2002) 35 *Vand. J Transnat'l L* 1105 at 1114–15. Capital-ownership neutrality, which is a more recent approach to international efficiency and is based on 'the principle that world welfare is maximized if the identities of capital owners are unaffected by tax rate differences', could be achieved in the unlikely event that all countries harmonized their international tax rules. Desai and Hines, *supra* note 128, at 488; see *ibid.* 494–6, 499; Charles H. Gustafson *et al.*, *Taxation of International Transactions: Materials, Text and Problems* (2011) 22.

eliminating distortions in human development. In essence, the residence country's approach to international tax efficiency would serve as a means of furthering internation equity. For once, efficiency would become the servant of equity rather than equity being subservient to – or even worse, subsumed by – efficiency.[131]

Naturally, some lower income (and even some higher income) countries might not fare well in terms of the amount of 'hidden' aid received under a sliding scale system for mitigating double taxation. (At this juncture, it is worth recalling the earlier examples of higher income countries that have fared poorly in the IHDI and GII, including the United States and some of its major trading partners.) Again, this may be an entirely appropriate result. If a country is not significantly advancing human development, it is not likely to be an appropriate target for (direct or indirect) development assistance given the strong possibility that any assistance might not actually be used to advance development.

Furthermore, given the lack of a significant correlation between economic growth and advancing human development (recall the comparison of China and Tunisia above), any reduction in assistance should not unduly limit a country's ability to achieve real advances in human development and obtain more favorable treatment under the sliding scale, leading to greater levels of 'hidden' aid that could then be used to even further advance human development. Thus, far from creating a vicious circle in which low levels of human development lead to tax deterrents to foreign investment that impede advances in human development, this sliding scale can create a virtuous circle in which advances that cost little in monetary terms can lead to foreign direct investment that can increase the resources available to devote to development efforts.

More ambitious countries might take into account additional dimensions of human development not captured by the HDI, IHDI and GII. These countries could turn to the HDR's additional statistical tables containing information regarding empowerment, sustainability and vulnerability, human security, perceptions of individual wellbeing, measures of civic and community wellbeing, and decent work – especially if those measures are further refined in coming years.[132] Other sources of relevant information include Amnesty International's annual human rights report and the International Lesbian, Gay, Bisexual, Trans and Intersex Association's (ILGA) annual report on state-sponsored homophobia.

---

131 Infanti, *supra* note 130, at 1115; Infanti, *supra* note 3.

132 2010 HDR, *supra* note 60, at 164–83, 188–91.

Whatever metrics a country chooses, some value judgements will necessarily be involved – whether they are judgements made by others (e.g., if the HDR indices and statistical tables are used) or by the country itself (e.g., if Amnesty International's or ILGA's raw data is used). As Amartya Sen has explained, this is not a drawback, but a strength, of the human development approach.[133] Even real-income measures entail value judgements, however concealed or implicit they might be.[134] In a similar vein, Kim Brooks observes, 'That the application of a concept of inter-nation equity requires value judgments is rarely explicitly recognized in the literature, and yet the lack of traction that the concept has had for policy-makers and scholars must be at least partly explained by that realization.'[135] She continues, 'The mistake, then, is thinking that inter-nation equity is something other than a tool for beginning that conversation.'[136] In this regard, the advantage of the human development approach is in rendering these value judgments transparent and explicit so that they can be subjected to 'public scrutiny, criticism, and correction'.[137]

VI. ADVANTAGES OF AN EXPANDED HORIZON

In closing, I describe several of the advantages of widening the focus of the internation equity debate to encompass both economic *and* non-economic lines of difference among nations in an effort to promote human development.

First, a wider focus would make the internation equity debate more meaningful. As described above, economic growth may be a means of furthering human development, but it is not the end of human development. Yet, the tax literature too often ignores other aspects of human development in favor of a nearly exclusive focus on economic growth.[138] By refocusing the debate on the ends to be achieved through development, commentators will better be able to locate the tax aspects of development in the larger human development picture.

---

133 Sen, *supra* note 58, at 30–31, 79–81; Amartya Sen, 'Development Thinking at the Beginning of the XXI Century' in Louis Emmerij (ed.), *Economic and Social Development into the XXI Century* (1997) 531, 542–4.

134 Sen, *supra* note 58, at 30–31, 79–81; Sen, *supra* note 133, at 542–4.

135 Brooks, *supra* note 2, at 492.

136 *Ibid.* 493.

137 Sen, *supra* note 133, at 544.

138 E.g., Brauner, *supra* note 47, at 280, 291–307, 321.

Second, embracing multiple lines of difference among nations represents a welcome break from the linear view of internation equity as being concerned only with redistribution from higher to lower income countries. In this linear view, higher income 'developed' countries (who are assumed to have already arrived at the end of the development path) pass money back to the lagging, lower income 'developing' countries to aid them in their progress toward the ultimate destination of being 'developed' (i.e., having high per capita income). In contrast, advancing human development is a concern for *all* countries.

Amartya Sen has clearly made the case that human development is not only a concern for lower income countries but for all countries, including higher income countries.[139] We are all engaged in the process of advancing human development along different tracks and in different ways.[140] That is precisely why the reform proposals considered in the previous section make no distinction between countries based on their status as high or low income; rather, each country adopting a sliding scale would apply that scale to *all* other countries. Given its inclusion as a component of the HDI (and IHDI), income would be a factor in determining where a country falls in the sliding scale, but, importantly, it would only be one among a number of different factors influencing that position.

Third, even though the human development approach applies to all countries, it 'is first and foremost an ally of the poor' and disadvantaged.[141] As described above, averages (like per capita income) homogenize populations and can mask profoundly disturbing levels of inequality in a society. For instance, high income countries (e.g., Saudi Arabia and Qatar) show some of the greatest losses in achievement due to gender inequality. In contrast to such averages, the human development approach 'put[s] people at the centre'.[142] Given the social justice focus of redistribution and internation equity, it is important that the human development approach helps us to bring the most vulnerable – for example, the poor, the disabled, women, ethnic and racial minorities, and sexual minorities – out of the shadows and into the center of the internation equity debate.[143]

Fourth, situating the internation equity debate in a wider context allows us to quickly address two criticisms that have been leveled at the notion

---

139 Sen, *supra* note 58, at 6, 21–4.

140 *Ibid.* 126–7, 240–42, 285, 297–8.

141 *Ibid.* 144.

142 2010 HDR, *supra* note 60, at 2; *see also* Sen, *supra* note 58, at 18.

143 See 2010 HDR, *supra* note 60, at 5–6.

of international redistribution. These two criticisms relate to: (1) the lack of a normative basis for redistribution, and (2) the inability to differentiate between 'worthy' and 'unworthy' recipients of assistance.[144] Both of these criticisms are products of the unduly narrow focus on per capita income in the extant internation equity debate.

Once the internation equity debate is situated in the broader development context, it becomes clear that normative grounding for a more robust notion of internation equity can be found in Sen's capability approach and his related exposition of the advantages of a freedom-based approach to development.[145] In addition, the OECD has observed that '[t]he intrinsic value of human rights offers development actors an explicit normative and analytical framework, grounded in a consensual global legal regime. The framework can be adapted to different political and cultural environments.'[146] Moreover, '[a]ll states party to the relevant international human rights instruments have a duty to promote and protect human rights, including through international co-operation'.[147]

In terms of differentiating between 'worthy' and 'unworthy' recipients of assistance, Ilan Benshalom has posited the problem as follows:

> Simply put, in a world where North Korea can spend money without asking Japan for any authorization and can even use it to prepare for a war against Japan, the Japanese will not be willing to engage in any cross-border redistribution of wealth, regardless of North Korean poverty and the reasons for it.[148]

A more robust notion of internation equity that aims at advancing human development could be used to sort out 'worthy' from 'unworthy' recipients of development assistance. Those with a record of promoting advances in human development (as evidenced in the HDI, IHDI, GII or other measures) could easily be targeted for greater aid than those without such a record.[149]

---

144 Benshalom, *supra* note 24; Ring, *supra* note 18, at 586–9.

145 Sen, *supra* note 58, at 54–86; see *ibid.* 18–19.

146 OECD, *supra* note 106, at 20.

147 *Ibid.* 28.

148 Benshalom, *supra* note 24, at 5–6.

149 This approach also has an advantage over Kim Brooks' suggestion to provide negotiated assistance through tax treaties with countries that evidence a commitment to the Millennium Development Goals (MDGs). Brooks, *supra* note 34, at 296–7. The MDGs are too narrow in their focus because they concentrate on selected human development priorities and completely ignore others (e.g.,

As noted above, there is still no consensus regarding development policy, and the UNDP's Human Development Reports and their formulation of the HDI and other measures are not without controversy.[150] However imperfect these measures might be, using them to take account of additional dimensions of human development beyond just economic growth is a step in the right direction, especially when per capita income is itself far from a perfect measure of human development. Moreover, the lack of a broad consensus on development policy is no reason to ignore the emerging trend toward recognizing that there is more to human development than just economic growth and per capita income and that 'captur[ing] the "missing" dimensions ... is increasingly feasible'.[151]

Tax commentators do not shy away from discussions of efficiency merely because there are competing notions of international efficiency (i.e., capital-export, capital-import, national and 'capital-ownership' neutrality) and a lack of consensus about which notion should prevail.[152] To the contrary, commentators routinely advocate policy prescriptions based on their preferred version of international efficiency in an effort to persuade others of their correctness. There should be a similar lively debate in which commentators air their competing ideas about how internation equity and development fit together. After all, Sen has underscored the importance – and great benefit – of public dialogue about human development:

> In line with the importance I [i.e., Sen] attach to the role of public discussion as a vehicle of social change and economic progress ... this work is presented mainly for open deliberation and critical scrutiny ... If my arguments arouse any interest, and lead to more public discussion of these vital issues, I would have reason to feel well rewarded.[153]

I can only express a similar hope for a rewarding public discussion regarding the formulation of a more robust notion of internation

---

'inequality and process freedoms'). 2010 HDR, *supra* note 60, at 17. Furthermore, Brooks seems to contemplate targeting assistance based on a 'commitment' to the MDGs, whereas using the HDI, IHDI, GII and other output-based measures could facilitate targeting development assistance at countries that are already successfully advancing human development (rather than merely promising to do so at some point in the future).

150 2010 HDR, *supra* note 60, at 15–22.

151 *Ibid.* 19–20.

152 Gustafson *et al.*, *supra* note 130, at 20–22.

153 Sen, *supra* note 58, at xiii–xiv.

equity – one that advances the interests of all people, especially the traditionally disadvantaged, and not just the interests of some homogenized 'average' person who inhabits a one-dimensional economic plane of existence.

10. The role of developed world tax incentives in microfinance

Charlene D. Luke*

I. INTRODUCTION

Microfinance institutions provide the poor with access to financial tools – such as credit, savings accounts, or insurance – that more affluent individuals often take for granted. The best-known microfinance tool is microcredit, which is the provision of small loans to foster entrepreneurial activity. Microcredit has been among the most lauded of development tools. In 2006, one of microcredit's pioneers, Muhammad Yunus, and the institution he founded, the Grameen Bank, were awarded the Nobel Peace Prize.[1] Given the promised benefits, the tax policy approach of developed nations to microcredit would seem to be rather obvious: create generous tax incentives that will result in greater resources for these worthy institutions.

Professional and scholarly opinions about microcredit's benefits and future have, however, become increasingly divided.[2] In particular, theoretical and empirical scholarship questions the claims that originally catapulted microcredit to its star status. Microcredit promised to be a

* I thank the contributors to this volume and in particular the editors, Yariv Brauner and Miranda Stewart, for their comments and suggestions. I also thank my research assistants Robert Braxton, Justin Bryan and Rachel Espey.

1 See Ananya Roy, *Poverty Capital: Microfinance and the Making of Development* (Routledge, 2010) 89–137 (exploring perceptions about microcredit inside Bangladesh and the trajectory of Bangladeshi microcredit institutions, including Grameen Bank); Muhammad Yunus, *Banker to the Poor* (PublicAffairs, 2007) (describing foundation and development of the Grameen Bank); David Hulme, 'The Story of the Grameen Bank: From Subsidized Microcredit to Market Based Microfinance' in David Hulme and Thankom Arun (eds), *Microfinance: A Reader* (Routledge, 2009) 163.

2 See generally Beatriz Armendáriz and Jonathan Morduch, *The Economics of Microfinance: Second Edition* (MIT Press, 2010).

self-sustaining development tool that would allow virtually any individual to use entrepreneurial activities as a path out of poverty. While microcredit does appear to provide important benefits, it can no longer credibly be viewed as a panacea or, to put it more bluntly, as the 'hand up' to end virtually all 'hand outs'. Thus, given the risk of privileging flawed narrative claims, caution is needed in deploying tax subsidies to support microcredit that go beyond those that already exist.

While microcredit's star has dimmed, microfinance tools beyond microcredit – for example, microsaving and microinsurance – may be poised to take microcredit's place in the development firmament.[3] Using the tax policy of developed countries to accelerate that process could yield benefits, but again, caution is warranted given the relative youth of some of these products.

This chapter sets out in section II a brief description of microcredit, including a discussion of the debate about subsidy in microcredit. In section III, the chapter next discusses how tax law in the developed world, using United States law as the example, already interfaces with the structure of microcredit. The main focus of this discussion is on the application of tax incentives for charitable giving and how these may be applied to subsidize microcredit. Finally, this chapter in section IV discusses microfinance tools beyond microcredit and discusses current and possible future tax policy with respect to these tools.

II. MICROCREDIT

The archetypal microcredit narrative remains that told by Mohammed Yunus. In 1976, Yunus began visiting a village near the university at which he taught to enhance his understanding of the economic lives of the poor and to see whether he 'could help them directly in any way'.[4] On one of these outings he met a woman who would toil for hours each day making bamboo stools to sell. He saw that this woman, though clearly hard working and exhibiting great entrepreneurial spirit, was unable to generate a profit sufficient to move out of extreme poverty

---

[3] For a general discussion of microfinance, see Armendáriz and Morduch, *supra* note 2; Brigit Helms, *Access for All: Building Inclusive Financial Systems* (World Bank Publications, 2006); Joanna Ledgerwood, *Microfinance Handbook: An Institutional and Financial Perspective* (World Bank Publications, 1999); David Hulme and Thankom Arun (eds), *Microfinance: A Reader* (Routledge, 2009).

[4] Yunus, *supra* note 1, at 45.

because she had to borrow to purchase the raw materials at a relatively high interest rate. In Yunus's words:

> Her children were condemned to live a life of penury, of hand-to-mouth survival, just as she had lived it before them, and as her parents did before her. I had never heard of anyone suffering for the lack of *twenty-two cents*. It seemed impossible to me, preposterous. Should I reach into my pocket and hand Sufiya the pittance she needed for capital? That would be simple, so easy. I resisted the urge to give Sufiya the money she needed. She was not asking for charity. And giving one person twenty-two cents was not addressing the problem on any permanent basis.[5]

This encounter marked the beginning of Yunus's path toward founding the Grameen Bank. The themes contained in this story continue to permeate the framing of microcredit. Microcredit is intended to provide poor individuals the means to grow out of poverty through their entrepreneurial efforts. The narrative emphasizes self-improvement and self-sustenance, and it also exhibits an inspiring faith about the entrepreneurial skills of individuals and the benefits of entrepreneurial labor. Finally, the story hints that microcredit offers an approach that could be expanded widely to address poverty directly and in a lasting way.

Whether the tax policy of developed countries has a significant role to play in the support of microcredit depends first on whether there is a place for subsidy in microcredit and, to a lesser extent, on the nature of subsidy that would be appropriate. As may be expected given the emphasis on self-reliance within the microcredit community, the role of subsidy in microcredit is the most divisive issue in the larger microcredit discourse. Microcredit institutions, nearly universally, claim that they reject subsidy and are, or will soon be, self-sustaining. Thus, as an initial matter, the subsidy debate focuses on what should or should not count as self-sustenance. Beyond the discussion over subsidy semantics, the more crucial questions are whether the benefits of subsidy outweigh its costs and whether subsidy dollars would be better spent on other programs. While it is well-established that many microcredit institutions depend on subsidy, despite their protestations to the contrary, whether or not subsidy should continue to play a role is far from settled.[6]

A complete discussion of the debate over microcredit subsidy is beyond the scope of this chapter, but even brief consideration of the issue

---

5 *Ibid.* 48.

6 Armendáriz and Morduch, *supra* note 2, at 322–5 (describing use of subsidies by the Grameen Bank).

will serve to illustrate the complexities involved as well as to provide additional background on the operation of microcredit institutions. At a basic level, the divide over the role of subsidy in microcredit can be described as a disagreement over whether the word 'banker' or 'poor' should be emphasized in Mohammed Yunus's phrase 'Banker to the Poor'. Those who emphasize 'banker' argue that the way to get the best overall results is to charge interest rates that will cover all administrative costs and provide a profit incentive for furnishing the loan capital. Advocates of this approach argue that only through charging market interest will credit supply be sufficient to meet demand and be targeted to the poor who are best positioned to use the funds in business. Thus, this approach aims at reaching the poor, but argues that more poor can be reached more efficiently using market interest. This market-oriented, for-profit approach is frequently called the 'financial systems' approach, the name given to it by Marguerite Robinson, one of its prominent advocates.[7] Microcredit appears to be trending toward increased commercialization and the financial systems approach.

On the other hand, microcredit institutions that emphasize the word 'poor' in the phrase 'Banker to the Poor' are often called 'poverty lending' institutions, a term also originated by Marguerite Robinson.[8] Poverty lending institutions still charge interest but do so at rates that are often sufficient only to cover recurring administrative costs and not capital or risk-related non-recurring costs. These loans provide an implicit interest rate subsidy to their clients. To varying degrees, poverty lending institutions rely on donor capital for non-recurring costs. Poverty lending institutions frequently speak of access to credit in the language of human rights and argue that the interest charged should facilitate profit maximization by the poor rather than by the lender.[9] At the same time, however, poverty lending microcredit institutions also aspire to be 'hand up' rather than 'hand out' institutions. Thus, they work to be free of donor capital (and donor interference).[10]

---

[7] Marguerite S. Robinson, *The Microfinance Revolution: Sustainable Finance for the Poor* (World Bank Publications, 2001) 8–45.

[8] *Ibid.*

[9] See Muhammad Yunus with Karl Weber, *Building Social Business: The New Kind of Capitalism that Serves Humanity's Most Pressing Needs* (Public Affairs, 2010) 13 ('common human decency forbids' pursuing profit maximization from the poor); Yunus, *supra* note 1, at 207 (advocating an economic system 'that would allow each man or woman to explore his or her economic potential'). See also Roy, *supra* note 1, at 23–5.

[10] Yunus, *supra* note 1, at 249 ('charity is no solution to poverty').

Final resolution of whether the financial systems, or poverty lending, microcredit approach is best seems unlikely given the implicit value judgements underlying each of the approaches. Empirical researchers, such as those affiliated with MIT's Abdul Latif Jameel Poverty Action Lab, have recently argued that the way forward is to discover what works through empirical testing, particularly randomized controlled trials.[11] For example, in their recent book, *Poor Economics*, Abhijit V. Banerjee and Esther Duflo argue that 'whether particular instances of aid did some good or not'[12] should determine whether a technique should be replicated, expanded, modified or abandoned; automatic dismissal or embrace of a potential poverty alleviation technique out of adherence to an underlying, pre-existing belief should be avoided.

The starkest contrast between financial systems institutions and poverty lending institutions is in the interest rates. Grameen Bank, an institution in the poverty lending tradition, generally charges annual interest of 20 percent; financial systems institutions may set annual interest rates range from 80 to over 100 percent.[13] While a contrast can be set up relatively easily, assessing the meaning of these interest rates is much more difficult and depends to some extent on their relation to a market rate of interest. The debate about the meaning of these interest rates relates to the tax policy issues discussed in the next section because interest rates largely determine the extent to which a microcredit institution operates on a subsidy basis (the poverty lending model), or alternatively, operates on commercial terms (the financial institutions model). In turn, US tax incentives are generally only available to institutions providing charity, in the subsidy sense of the word.

---

[11] Abhijit V. Banerjee and Esther Duflo, *Poor Economics: A Radical Rethinking of the Way to Fight Global Poverty* (PublicAffairs, 2011) 14–16; Dean Karlan and Jacob Appel, *More than Good Intentions: How a New Economics is Helping to Solve Global Poverty* (Dutton Adult, 2011) 27–33.

[12] Banerjee and Duflo, *supra* note 11, at 4–5. See also Karlan and Appel, *supra* note 11, at 28 ('Find individual programs that work, and support them. Find programs that don't work, and stop doing them.').

[13] See Daryl Collins, Jonathan Morduch, Stuart Rutherford and Orlanda Ruthven, *Portfolios of the Poor: How the World's Poor Live on $2 a Day* (Princeton University Press, 2009) 132; Yunus, *supra* note 9, at 13. Interest rates, however, will not necessarily provide a clear signal of the mission of the underlying institution, as even some NGOs charge nearly 40 percent, while some commercial microcredit banks charge less than 20 percent. Armendáriz and Morduch, *supra* note 2, at 249–50. See also Karlan and Appel, *supra* note 11, at 65 (rates can be as high as 82 percent even among non-profit organizations).

The microcredit narrative arguably starts with a story about market failure.[14] Microcredit loans are intended to provide capital for entrepreneurial activities and not for personal consumption. Microcredit institutions make small business loans to poor individuals, who would not be readily accepted as clients by more traditional lending institutions because of the difficulty in setting an appropriate interest rate. Traditional lending methods require a relatively good understanding of the borrower's risk of default – both the risk that a disproportionate number of inherently untrustworthy individuals will want to borrow (the adverse selection problem) and that individuals will subsequently fail to take adequate care in managing their financial lives to assure available funds for repayment (the moral hazard problem). Further, collection from defaulters would be difficult given the relative poverty of the client. Finally, the administrative costs associated with originating and servicing tiny loans are relatively large. The rates at which a traditional lender would be willing to lend could be so high that such a lender would risk not only a public relations debacle over usury charges but also could drive out the best, least risky clients if they are more comfortable with the terms on the loans available to them from family, friends and even moneylenders.[15]

Microcredit's original innovation was to create methods for working around the commercial market's failure to provide adequate credit supply to the poor. These methods allow for administrative economies of scale while converging on a zero default goal. Microcredit default rates are commonly very low, generally around 2 percent.[16] A significant amount of the discussion surrounding microcredit has been about which method components are essential to a zero default goal and, of course, whether this is a helpful goal in the first instance.[17] While that discussion as well

---

[14] Armendáriz and Morduch, *supra* note 2, at 29–59.

[15] *Ibid.*; Banerjee and Duflo, *supra* note 11, at 161–6; Collins *et al.*, *supra* note 13, at 133; Karlan and Appel, *supra* note 11, at 113.

[16] On occasion, microcredit loan portfolio quality has declined dramatically. For example, Grameen Bank suffered setbacks in the late 1990s, which were exacerbated by flooding disasters. Grameen II was also a response to this crisis. Collins *et al.*, *supra* note 13, at 70–71, 75–81; Yunus, *supra* note 1, at 235–41.

[17] Armendáriz and Morduch, *supra* note 2, at 97–162; Banerjee and Duflo, *supra* note 11, at 174–8; Karlan and Appel, *supra* note 11, at 126–39; Erica Field and Rohini Pande, 'Repayment Frequency and Default in Microfinance: Evidence from India' (2008) 6 *Journal of the European Economic Association* 501; Benjamin Feigenberg, Erica M. Field and Rohini Pande, *Building Social Capital through Microfinance*, National Bureau of Economic Research, Working Paper No. 16018 (2010), available at www.nber.org/papers/w16018; Erica Field, Rohini

as spontaneous local variations have triggered some differences among the methods of microcredit institutions, it remains possible to sketch a generic profile of microcredit methods.

A traditional microcredit program requires both group lending and group liability. In group lending, loans are not disbursed to individuals unless they are part of a group of individuals, each of whom takes out a loan. Group liability requires that each member of the group be jointly and severally liable for all of the loans taken by group members. In its most strict form, default on any loan by a member of the group means no future loans for all members of the group, though this appears to be rarely enforced.

Multiple groups are combined into a larger unit, often called a center; in some variations, each group will also be jointly and severally liable for all the groups in the same center. The groups are required to attend weekly center meetings together, and loan payments are made at these meetings, with public announcement of the results. These sessions begin almost immediately on commencement of the loan, because the payment schedule typically calls for a payment within a week of loan receipt. Many microcredit institutions require not only mandatory weekly loan payments but also mandatory weekly savings deposits, which then secure the debt, at least in part. Loan cycles are generally one year, with early repayments only allowed starting at six months. New clients are advanced only a very small amount, with the amount of credit typically ratcheting upward with each successful loan cycle completion.

To the extent that a microcredit institution achieves very low default rates the microcredit institution may be closing the gap between a market rate and a subsidized rate. That is, since any return on very low risk debt would also be low, the amount of subsidy may not be all that large. Poverty lending institutions tend to adhere more closely to traditional microcredit mechanisms, such as group lending, than do more commercialized lenders. In effect, some of the reduction in interest rate is paid for by the clients through increased rigidity and inconvenience of the loan method.

The inflexibility of the group lending method may explain why there appears to be continued demand for moneylender loans. In contrast to stereotypically grim portrayals of moneylenders, local moneylenders may actually be less intimidating than a microcredit institution because they

---

Pande and John Papp, *Does Microfinance Repayment Flexibility Affect Entrepreneurial Behavior and Loan Default?*, Centre for Micro Finance Working Paper Series No. 34 (2009), available at www.povertyactionlab.org/sites/default/files/publications/EFieldDoesMicrofinanceRepayment%20.pdf.

are a familiar part of the landscape or part of the borrowers' extended social network. Moneylenders may also offer greater flexibility and convenience.[18] Qualitative empirical research suggests that actual moneylender rates often end up being much lower than advertised.[19] Thus, while for-profit microcredit institutions and their advocates may point out that their rates are markedly lower than those charged by moneylenders the differences may be less than they appear on their face.[20]

In summary, the lines between subsidized, market and above-market interest rates are inherently difficult to assess, even more so when the intended clientele is a vulnerable population. Even if rough dividing lines can be determined, the significance of the dividing lines will also be difficult to ascertain. This makes it problematic to determine the extent of subsidy in different types of microcredit and the benefits provided by that subsidy. On the larger questions – the relationship of microcredit benefits to their costs, to other poverty alleviation programs, or to non-intervention – the evidence remains limited.[21] Recent empirical studies using randomized controlled trials suggest that microcredit provides greater profits to individuals who are already engaged in entrepreneurial activities or who already have some entrepreneurial skills or capital while providing less income gains to more vulnerable groups, including women.[22] These studies so far tend to reinforce an already existing trend

---

18 Banerjee and Duflo, *supra* note 11, at 161–6; Collins *et al.*, *supra* note 13, at 70–71, 151–3.

19 Collins *et al.*, *supra* note 13, at 134–44.

20 Robinson, *supra* note 7, at 13–15, 170–222.

21 Armendáriz and Morduch, *supra* note 2, at 325–41.

22 See Banerjee and Duflo, *supra* note 11, at 168–71; Karlan and Appel, *supra* note 11, at 73–80; Suresh de Mel, David McKenzie and Christopher Woodruff, 'Returns to Capital in Microenterprises: Evidence from a Field Experiment' (2008) 123 *Quarterly Journal of Economics* 1329; Dean Karlan and Jonathan Zinman, 'Expanding Credit Access: Using Randomized Supply Decisions to Estimate the Impacts' (2010) 23 *Review of Financial Studies* 434; Abhijit Banerjee, Esther Duflo, Rachel Glennerster and Cynthia Kinnan, *The Miracle of Microfinance? Evidence from a Randomized Evaluation* (2009), available at http://econ-www.mit.edu/files/4162. These studies did seek to measure non-income indicators of wellbeing, but an expansion along such lines is likely warranted. See Amartya Sen, *Development as Freedom* (Anchor, 1999). Women are more likely than men to repay their loans. For a discussion of the scholarship on gender and microfinance, see Armendáriz and Morduch, *supra* note 2, at 211–34; Erica Field, Seema Jayachandran and Rohini Pande, 'Do Traditional Institutions Constrain Female Entrepreneurship? A Field Experiment on Business Training in India' (2010) 100 *American Economic Review: Papers and Proceedings* 125 (May); Naila Kabeer, 'Conflicts Over Credit: Re-evaluating the

toward increased commercialization of microcredit, that is, towards a 'financial systems' approach.[23] Although the trend may, however, be toward for-profit microcredit, it seems likely that poverty lending institutions will continue to be an important feature of the microcredit landscape for the foreseeable future.

III. DEVELOPED WORLD TAX INCENTIVES AND MICROCREDIT

This section takes as a working assumption that there is continued need for subsidy in microcredit and turns to discussing the role of developed country tax incentives in subsidizing this form of poverty relief. As already discussed, the primary area for subsidies is in the poverty lending microcredit model. Poverty lending microcredit institutions provide at least two potential areas for subsidies: (1) contributions for non-recurring costs, and (2) loans of funds for on-lending to the clients.

A central developed world tax incentive is the subsidization of charitable contributions to charitable organizations. In the United States, there are currently no specific tax incentives for microfinance. However, because of the scope for charitable contributions contained within the poverty lending model, current tax policies for charitable giving already provide some incentives in support of microcredit institutions. This section focuses on the tax incentives available in the United States, but similar incentives are present throughout the developed world.[24] In the United States, the two principal charitable-giving tax incentives are (1) exemption from the income tax for qualifying non-profit organizations, and (2) tax reductions (income, gift and estate) for individuals who make contributions to qualifying charitable organizations.

Considerable scholarship has been devoted to questioning the general benefits of these US charitable tax incentives, particularly whether the incentives actually alter behavior and increase public welfare.[25] Such

---

Empowerment Potential of Loans to Women in Rural Bangladesh', reprinted in Hulme and Thankom, *supra* note 3, at 108.

[23] Armendáriz and Morduch, *supra* note 2, at 239–64.

[24] See Sigrid J.C. Hemels, 'Are We in Need of a European Charity? How to Remove Fiscal Barriers to Cross-Border Charitable Giving in Europe' (2009) 37 *Intertax* 424.

[25] See, e.g., Brian Galle, 'Keep Charity Charitable' (2010) 88 *Texas Law Review* 1213; Mark P. Gergen, 'The Case for a Charitable Contributions Deduction' (1988) 74 *Virginia Law Review* 1393.

broad policy concerns have, however, not (yet) led to a general retrenchment of tax incentives for charitable giving. The previous section discussed the debate and the level of uncertainty about the extent of the benefits of poverty lending microcredit. It is, however, argued here that it would be problematic, at this stage, to reframe the tax incentive rules in the developed world in a way that would place obstacles in the path of poverty lending institutions.[26] To do so would subject microcredit to a higher standard of proof of benefit than that required for numerous other aid programs, whose benefits are also hotly debated.[27] On the other hand, without better evidence about both the benefits of charitable incentives and of microcredit it would also be problematic to custom-tailor incentives so as to privilege poverty lending microcredit. A final question is whether the form of the subsidy found in poverty lending microcredit requires new developed world tax incentives in order to put it on an even footing with other poverty reduction missions. In addressing these issues, the stated preferences of poverty lending institutions should also be considered since, as discussed above, these institutions generally eschew subsidy in form, if not always in substance.

A. Cash Donations to Public Charities

The US tax law contains highly complex rules for obtaining income, gift and estate tax reductions for making charitable contributions.[28] Individual states may provide further incentives. Only the US federal income tax rules for cash contributions to public charities will be outlined here, not only because these rules are relatively simple but also because they illustrate the general nature of the US charitable contribution incentives and provide sufficient context for the discussion contained in this chapter.

Cash contributions made to public charities reduce the income tax of individuals who elect to itemize deductions rather than take a standard

---

[26] Microcredit is not solely utilized in the developing world; Grameen America, for example, has brought microcredit to the United States. Yunus, *supra* note 9, at xi.

[27] See, e.g., William Easterly, *The White Man's Burden* (Penguin, 2006); William Easterly (ed.), *Reinventing Foreign Aid* (MIT Press, 2008).

[28] For discussion of these rules, see, e.g., Boris I. Bittker and Lawrence Lokken, *Federal Taxation of Income, Estates, and Gifts: Second/Third Edition* (Thomson Reuters, 2011) para. 35.1 *et seq.*, para. 100.1 *et seq.*, para. 130.1 *et seq.*; Boris I. Bittker, Martin McMahon and Lawrence Zelenak, *Federal Income Taxation of Individuals* (3rd edn, Thomson Reuters, 2011) para. 25.01 *et seq.*; Frances R. Hill and Douglas A. Mancino, *Taxation of Exempt Organizations* (Thomson Reuters, 2010).

deduction. The standard deduction in 2012 for married individuals filing jointly was US$11,900 and for a single individual was US$5,950.[29] The combination of the standard deduction threshold and the deductibility mechanism itself means that the tax incentive is generally stronger for more affluent individuals subject to higher income tax rates. For example, a 100 dollar deduction would be worth nothing in terms of tax savings to someone who does not itemize but worth 35 dollars to an itemizer in the 2012 top US tax bracket.[30] Cash donations are, however, deductible only to the extent they do not exceed 50 percent of an individual's income for the year; contributions that exceed this percentage threshold are carried forward for up to five subsequent taxable years.[31] Because these percentage limitations apply to all taxpayers regardless of tax bracket, they do not alter the deduction's tilt toward a more valuable tax benefit for those in higher tax brackets.[32]

A US income tax deduction is available only if the contribution is made to a qualifying organization. Contributions made to specific individuals, whether made directly or by using a charitable organization as a conduit, are not deductible.[33] Thus, a charitable organization soliciting funds through the use of compelling stories about particular individuals would need to specify that contributions are made to the organization and that the individual stories represent the type of, rather than the specific, individuals who the donor will be assisting through her contribution.

Adherence to numerous formal and substantive rules is required before an organization will qualify as a tax-exempt public charity. The US Tax Code provides that the organization must be 'organized and operated

---

29 See Internal Revenue Service News Release IR-2011-104 (20 October 2011).

30 Charitable contributions are currently not an adjustment to the US alternative minimum tax (though prior to 1993, certain types of in-kind contributions did cause adjustments). Internal Revenue Code s. 57. See Omnibus Budget Reconciliation Act of 1993, Public Law No. 103-66 s. 13171(a), 107 Statutes at Large 312 (repealing adjustment relating to donation of appreciated capital gain property). The top alternative minimum tax bracket rate is, however, lower than that under the general income tax (28 percent as compared to 35 percent). Internal Revenue Code s. 1(i) and s. 55(b). As a result, on occasion it may be advantageous to postpone charitable contributions to years when the alternative minimum tax would not be applicable.

31 Internal Revenue Code s. 170(d)(1)(A).

32 See Miranda Perry Fleischer, 'Generous to a Fault? Fair Shares and Charitable Giving' (2008) 93 *Minnesota Law Review* 165 at 192–6.

33 See Bittker *et al.*, *supra* note 28, at para. 25.01[1].

exclusively for ... charitable ... purposes'.[34] Income earned by the charitable organization may not inure to charity insiders or be for the private benefit of other individuals. Failure to follow the prohibitions on private inurement and private benefit may result in sanctions or even loss of tax exemption.[35]

Charitable organizations may participate in unrelated businesses, but they are taxed on such businesses,[36] and over-indulgence in unrelated activities could also lead to a loss of exemption. The line between successful adherence to charitable mission and impermissible mission drift is not always clear. Joint ventures between a US tax-exempt entity and a for-profit entity raise additional concerns regarding whether the US tax-exempt entity is adequately adhering to its mission.[37] Much of the existing US authority on such joint undertakings involves charitable hospitals. These authorities tend to focus particularly on the extent to which the tax-exempt entity retains control, including not only control over adherence to charitable mission but also the extent to which its assets will be at the disposal of the for-profit organization.[38]

In the case of microcredit, whether an organization exhibits exemption-qualifying adherence to a charitable mission would largely turn on the intended recipients of the loans and on the loan terms they receive, including the extent of interest rate subsidy. The more commercial the terms, then the more likely the organization would not qualify as having a charitable purpose under US tax law. Thus, a poverty lending micro-credit institution generally would adhere to the charitable purpose required to qualify for US income tax exemption whereas a financial systems microcredit organization would not. Having impoverished individuals as the clientele (whether or not well-intentioned) is insufficient for US exemption if the terms offered to such individuals are commercial rather than subsidized.[39]

---

34 Internal Revenue Code s. 501(c)(3). See also *ibid.* s. 509 (rules for distinguishing between private and public 501(c)(3) charities).

35 See *ibid.* s. 4958; Treasury Regulation s. 1.501(c)(3)–1(f).

36 Internal Revenue Code s. 511 *et seq.*

37 See Revenue Ruling 2004-51, 2004-1 *Cumulative Bulletin* 974; Revenue Ruling 98-15, 1998-1 *Cumulative Bulletin* 718.

38 As a result, participation by a tax-exempt organization as a passive partner with limited liability generally does not raise the same concerns. For a more thorough discussion of joint arrangements between tax-exempt and for-profit enterprises, see John R. Washlick, 'Joint Ventures Involving Tax-Exempt Organizations' (2007) 478 *BNA Tax Management Portfolio*.

39 See Revenue Ruling 74-587, 1974-2 *Cumulative Bulletin* 162 (low-cost loans to assist impoverished community); Revenue Ruling 70-585, 1970-2

The income tax deductibility of charitable contributions made for the benefit of non-US institutions or projects is subject to additional scrutiny. First, only contributions made to a US tax-exempt institution qualify for deductibility, so a direct contribution to a non-US microcredit organization would not be deductible under the US income tax.[40] Contributions intended for non-US programs may still be deductible, but only if the US tax-exempt institution retains sufficient control over the non-US program. Such control could, for example, be maintained if the US institution created a foreign subsidiary through which to administer its non-US projects. The US tax-exempt institution could also retain sufficient control of disbursements made to unrelated non-US institutions by reviewing and approving particular projects, retaining discretion regarding whether to provide further funds, and keeping oversight over the use of already committed funds.[41]

The emphasis in US tax law on the US charity's retention of control underlines the influence of US donors, even though the appropriateness of donor influence is an area of heated disagreement within development aid discourse. De-emphasizing US donor control in US tax law could be desirable. For example, the United States could extend income tax deduction parity to various non-US charitable organizations.[42] Extending such parity only with respect to poverty lending microcredit institutions could be a place to start such a de-emphasis on donor control, but, again

Cumulative Bulletin 115 (below-cost housing qualified as charitable purpose; housing provided at cost did not qualify even though purpose was to build affordable housing).

[40] Internal Revenue Code s. 170(c)(2)(A) (2011). Some treaties may contain provisions overriding this limitation. See Revenue Procedure 59-31, 1959-2 *Cumulative Bulletin* 949. The US estate and gift tax regimes do, however, allow for direct, deductible donations to non-US charitable organizations. See Treasury Regulation s. 20.2055-1(a) (estate tax deduction); Treasury Regulation s. 25.2522(a)-1(a) (gift tax deduction).

[41] See Revenue Ruling 63-252, 1963-2 *Cumulative Bulletin* 101, as amplified by Revenue Ruling 66-79, 1966-1 *Cumulative Bulletin* 48. US law prohibits support for organizations designated as terrorist organizations, some of which may provide microcredit. Internal Revenue Code s. 501(p) (2011).

[42] The Court of Justice of the European Communities recently took a step in this direction by extending parity of treatment within the EU. Case C-318/07, *Hein Persche* v. *Finanzamt Lüdenscheid* [2009] PTSR 915, available at www.bailii.org/eu/cases/EUECJ/2009/C31807.html. With thanks to Pasquale Pistone for this observation. Articles 12 and 16 of the proposed Common Consolidated Corporate Tax Base would extend parity not only to Member States but also to certain qualifying third countries.

caution is warranted in setting microcredit apart from the multitude of other development programs.

B. Loans

The below-market interest rates of poverty lending institutions provide a second potential area for tax incentives. Individuals or institutions in the developed world already provide capital for loans to microcredit clients; for example, any individual in the United States may use the Internet to loan funds for on-lending to microcredit clients.[43] Because of the low default rates present in poverty lending microcredit institutions, the loan principal is almost certain to be returned to the lender. If for some reason the loan principal is not returned, the loss should be deductible at that time.[44]

In these loan arrangements, the US lender also provides a current subsidy by agreeing to forgo the interest she would have collected by placing her funds elsewhere. This subsidy is not deductible under current US tax law, but this lack of deduction is consistent with the US Treasury's decision not to tax imputed interest on below-market loans to charitable institutions.[45] A US taxpayer making a below-market loan to a US charity could be taxed on the imputed interest should the US Treasury alter its position; if imputed interest were taxed, such taxation would, however, then allow for an immediate charitable deduction, generally producing a tax wash. The lack of a deduction for the forgone interest is also consistent with general US charitable tax policy. For example, providing rent-free use of property or free services is not

---

[43] See, e.g., www.kiva.org (non-profit). Compare www.microplace.com (for profit).

[44] Internal Revenue Code s. 166 allows a short-term capital loss deduction for the bad debt losses of creditors making loans for personal or investment reasons; US individuals loaning money to non-profit (or for-profit) microcredit organizations would generally fall into this category of creditors. See Sarah B. Lawsky, 'Money for Nothing: Charitable Deductions for Microfinance Lenders' (2008) 61 *Southern Methodist University Law Review* 1525 at 1533–4. In order to utilize the bad debt loss deduction, the debt must be wholly worthless. In some cases, depending on the donative intent of the lender, the structure of the loan, and the timing of the lender's forgiveness of microcredit loan principal, the cancellation of debt could instead be characterized as a charitable contribution.

[45] Treasury Regulation s. 1.7872-5T(b)(9) (as amended in 1988) (no imputed interest if aggregate gift loan to charitable organization does not exceed US$250,000).

deductible, but the imputed rent or wage income also does not generate taxable income.

The treatment of the loan principal presents some opportunity for additional tax incentives. Sarah Lawsky has proposed allowing an immediate deduction for microcredit loan principal, followed by a subsequent income inclusion when (if) it is repaid.[46] Such a route could provide the taxpayer with time-value-of-money benefits and thus provide an incentive that is focused on poverty lending microcredit institutions. Such an approach could, however, raise concerns that tax-exempt institutions promoting microcredit are being unjustifiably favored over other tax-exempt organizations, which might also benefit from a rule allowing deduction of principal for below-market loans made to the institution. Of course, on-lending is the *raison d'être* of microcredit, whereas it is not common in other tax-exempt institutions. Still, given the debate over microcredit interest rates, the extent of subsidy in them and the benefits of microcredit, discussed above, it is argued here that the current treatment of developed country taxpayer loans to microcredit institutions – no taxation of imputed interest and deduction for loss of principal – seems sufficient.

C. Financial Systems Microcredit

As discussed above, in contrast to poverty lending institutions, financial systems microcredit institutions would fail to qualify as tax-exempt institutions because they operate as commercial, for-profit businesses. Investment in financial systems, for-profit microcredit by a US individual or institution would be subject to the same US tax treatment as other taxable investments. For example, because a US individual is taxed on worldwide income, interest or dividend payments made to her by such a microcredit organization (or by an intermediary microcredit investment vehicle) would be fully taxable in the United States, though she would be able to seek relief from double taxation should she also have paid tax on the interest in a non-US jurisdiction.[47] Individuals investing in for-profit microcredit institutions through qualifying retirement funds would be able to defer paying tax on income earned through such investments until such funds are withdrawn.[48] In short, for-profit microcredit institutions

---

46 Lawsky, *supra* note 44, at 1540.

47 See Internal Revenue Code s. 61(a)(4) and (a)(7) (gross income includes interest and dividends); *ibid.* s. 164(a)(3) (deduction for foreign taxes); *ibid.* s. 901 *et seq.* (foreign tax credit alternative to foreign tax deduction).

48 See *ibid.* s. 401 *et seq.*

do not appear to be singled out for better or worse tax treatment than other investments by US individuals in international businesses.

While beyond the scope of this chapter, the tax policies internal to developing countries and vis-à-vis developed countries also raise interesting issues. For example, more thought should be given regarding the extent to which the home country of a for-profit microcredit institution may be providing implicit subsidies to that institution, for example, by not taxing, purposely or not, microcredit clients on the returns from their entrepreneurial activities. A related issue is, to the extent microcredit profits cross international borders, whether the home country is able to withhold a fair share of the tax revenue on paid returns before they pass into the developed world.[49] These issues warrant further research in the context of particular developing countries.

IV. BEYOND MICROCREDIT: MICROGRANTS, MICROSAVING AND MICROINSURANCE

The development and popularity of microcredit, in spite of its possible shortcomings, has prompted inquiries into whether and how additional microfinance tools should be delivered to the poor. The trend toward commercialization of microcredit has increased the importance of finding alternative financial tools that will provide benefits for even the poorest individuals. This section briefly considers three of these tools: microgrants, microsaving and microinsurance. Scholarly attention is increasingly turning to analysis of these tools, but the volume of research has yet to reach that devoted to microcredit.

A. Microgrants

Microgrants formalize a poverty reduction technique that has been around since time immemorial: the direct contribution of cash or assets to the poor. Formalization of the process allows for delivery through an institution offering access to other poverty reduction tools and programs. The microgrant may come with some strings attached, for example, attending training, signing up for a microsaving account, or enrolling children in school, but is otherwise relatively free of constraints.[50] The idea often is

---

49 With thanks to Allison Christians for this observation.

50 The benefits of entrepreneurship training are also the subject of scholarly study. See Dean Karlan and Martin Valdivia, *Teaching Entrepreneurship: Impact*

that these grants will prepare individuals to advance to more sophisticated financial tools, such as microcredit. Because these programs recognize that some individuals are better suited than others for microcredit, they are not inconsistent with a financial systems approach to microcredit. Thus, for-profit institutions may support outreach programs using such micro-grants in order to cultivate future clientele for microcredit (and also possibly avoid the 'microshark' label). Whether such programs are effective remains to be established, but some promising study results have been obtained.[51]

Because microgrants are outright subsidies, the tax incentives for charitable contributions readily apply. In the United States, cash contributions would be deductible so long as they were made to a qualifying US tax-exempt institution and satisfy the control and other tests, as discussed above. Charitable solicitations for microgrant assistance could readily incorporate individual narratives, although, as described in the section on cash contributions generally, under US law direct earmarking for a particular individual would have to be avoided to maintain deductibility. Care would also be required to the extent such programs involve partnerships with for-profit institutions looking to expand client base or improve image.

B. Microsaving

Microsaving accounts permit the poor to deposit tiny amounts of cash in a safe place – amounts that could be well below the minimum deposit requirements of many commercial banks.[52] Whereas the microcredit narrative is centered on fostering entrepreneurship, microsaving is intended also as a means of smoothing consumption. That is, access to microsaving provides enhanced stability and regularity by enabling the

---

of Business Training on Microfinance Clients and Institutions (2010), available at http://karlan.yale.edu/p/TeachingEntrepreneurship_revision_jan2010.pdf.

[51] Armendáriz and Morduch, *supra* note 2, at 334–6; Banerjee and Duflo, *supra* note 11, at 211–12, 219–20; Abhijit Banerjee, Esther Duflo, Raghabendra Chattopadhyay and Jeremy Shapiro, *Targeting the Hard-Core Poor: An Impact Assessment* (2010), preliminary working paper, available at http://econ-www.mit.edu/files/6645.

[52] Armendáriz and Morduch, *supra* note 2, at 192; Banerjee and Duflo, *supra* note 11, at 78–81. Debt is often used as an alternative 'savings' vehicle allowing individuals to pay back loan principal and interest in small increments. Stuart Rutherford with Sukhwinder Arora, *The Poor and their Money: Microfinance from a Twenty-first Century Consumer's Perspective* (Practical Action, 2009) 15–36.

poor to save up sums for necessary, but lumpy, purchases such as medical care. Large purchase needs, particularly emergency purchase needs, have a destabilizing effect on the life of a poor individual. Too many such events or a single, large event can set back an individual for years or even a lifetime.[53]

Given the benefits of saving, the question then becomes whether the poorest can afford to save given their daily budget constraints. Anecdotal and more systematic research suggests that the poor are able to afford to save and desire to save.[54] For example, in some areas, poor individuals pay significant fees for the ability to store their small savings in a relatively secure manner.[55] Microsaving may also afford women an important tool for gaining control over household finances,[56] which they may be more likely to use for household expenditures on health and education benefits.[57]

The largest obstacle to saving among the poor appears to be the same obstacle faced by individuals worldwide: the difficulty of committing to and following through on plans to put money aside for anticipated necessities, let alone for a rainy day. It is easy to agree to 'save more tomorrow', but when tomorrow becomes today, the saving is put off even further into the future.[58] Recommendations for commitment devices aimed at gently nudging individuals to follow through on their own expressed preferences have become routine in the United States. Current research on microsaving aims to find out which types of commitment devices work best in assisting the poor in meeting their own goals.

In the United States, automatic withholding is often put forward as an effective commitment device. For example, individuals in the United States may be automatically enrolled by their employers in a retirement savings plan. While the individual could opt out, any tendency to procrastinate would work to keep the individual saving. Wage withholding

---

53 Banerjee and Duflo, *supra* note 11, at 134–41.

54 Collins *et al.*, *supra* note 13, at 95–131; Robinson, *supra* note 7, at 224–48.

55 Collins *et al.*, *supra* note 13, at 21–2.

56 Karlan and Appel, *supra* note 11, at 272.

57 Armendáriz and Morduch, *supra* note 2, at 334–6; Banerjee and Duflo, *supra* note 11, at 126–8.

58 Richard H. Thaler and Shlomo Benartzi, 'Save More Tomorrow: Using Behavioral Economics to Increase Employee Saving' (2004) 112 *Journal of Political Economy* S164. See also Richard H. Thaler and Cass R. Sunstein, *Nudge: Improving Decisions about Health, Wealth, and Happiness* (Yale University Press, 2008).

mechanisms would obviously be more difficult to implement in the developing world, but simple, automatic savings reminders may help. Increasingly, mobile phones make such reminders easy to provide in many regions, and such reminders may even be linked to instant banking services.[59] Strong restrictions on withdrawal are another option, but may be problematic in the developing world given the severe liquidity restraints that can operate in the lives of the poor.[60] Restrictions that function to move the temptation out of sight rather than prohibit access show some promise.

One possible avenue to explore, which would also provide an opportunity to involve donors, is the use of matching funds.[61] Some research on US individuals suggests that such funds can provide an important motivational tool.[62] Contributions of such funds would be governed by the same rules discussed in the section on microcredit; as a result, the donors would contribute to the organization, which would control the allocation of the matching funds, rather than contributing directly to specific individuals.

Institutions seeking contributions for fostering savings by the poor should have no trouble demonstrating a charitable purpose under US law, though once again, the contributions would have to remain under control of a US tax-exempt institution to be deductible. Donor funds could also potentially be used to pay administrative costs. Microsaving as a financial product does, however, differ from microcredit in that it is generally subject to many more regulatory requirements. The ability to accept saving deposits implies the need for greater institutional security, for example, through reserve requirements.[63] Because of these regulatory requirements, it may be necessary for a non-profit microfinance institution to form a partnership with an existing commercial bank.

C. Microinsurance

Microinsurance could help mitigate the financial volatility frequently experienced by impoverished individuals. While microinsurance is

---

[59] Banerjee and Duflo, *supra* note 11, at 189.

[60] Armendáriz and Morduch, *supra* note 2, at 194.

[61] Banerjee and Duflo, *supra* note 11, at 191–204; Karlan and Appel, *supra* note 11, at 165. With thanks to Diane Ring for this suggestion.

[62] Esther Duflo, William Gale, Jeffrey Liebman, Peter Orszag and Emmanuel Saez, 'Saving Incentives for Low- and Middle-Income Families: Evidence from a Field Experiment with H&R Block' (2006) 121 *Quarterly Journal of Economics* 1311.

[63] Armendáriz and Morduch, *supra* note 2, at 194.

widely seen as tool that would be of great benefit to the poor, it may also prove to be the most difficult to implement.[64] Insurance allows for an individual to shift a portion of her risk of experiencing a particular loss to a group. Pricing this benefit requires that the individuals within the group face diverse probabilities of the covered risk occurring and that the probability of the risk occurring to any one person in the group in a given year be determinable. In addition, problems similar to those affecting the provision of credit also affect the provision of insurance. Individuals with hidden information about their exposure to the risk could threaten the financial stability of the insurance group (the adverse selection problem). Individuals could also undermine the insurance group if they take less care as a result of knowing that they no longer bear all of the risk of their behavior (the moral hazard problem). And, of course, fraud in making insurance claims is also a problem.[65]

Commercial insurance companies must expend many resources in pricing and monitoring their products. A sense of the difficulty of crafting microinsurance is suggested by the lack of close, informal insurance substitutes. That is, while informal versions of microcredit, microgrants and microsaving are common among the poor, true insurance pools almost never arise without formal financial intermediation. Although village 'insurance' may exist, it is generally a form of saving and self-insurance rather than an example of true risk-pooling insurance.[66]

Microcredit solutions to pricing problems cannot be readily imported into microinsurance because far more complex behaviors than repayment would have to be monitored.[67] For example, microinsurance on livestock and crops has been plagued by false claims of loss. The insurer could, for example, refuse payment on a claim made on dead livestock unless the dead animal is produced, but the administrative costs would likely be insurmountable and could still be insufficient to stop false claims. In

---

64 See *ibid.* 195–203 (providing overview of microinsurance); Warren Brown, 'Microinsurance: The Risks, Perils, and Opportunities' reprinted in Hulme and Thankom, *supra* note 3, at 171.

65 See Banerjee and Duflo, *supra* note 11, at 148–9; Charlene D. Luke and Aviva Abramovsky, 'Managing the Next Deluge: A Tax System Approach to Flood Insurance' (2012) 18 *Connecticut Insurance Law Journal* 1 (article proposing flood loss safety net and describing current problems in US flood insurance system).

66 Banerjee and Duflo, *supra* note 11, at 144–7; Collins *et al.*, *supra* note 13, at 70–71, 75–81 (discussing prevalence of self-insurance but noting exception found in South African burial societies).

67 Armendáriz and Morduch, *supra* note 2, at 195–203.

Poor Economics, Banerjee and Duflo report on one attempt to get around this problem through a requirement that the insured produce the ear of the dead cow. Rather than ensuring the sustainability of the insurance product, the requirement triggered a market in cow ears.[68] Rainfall insurance has shown promise as providing an indirect form of crop insurance that can be more easily monitored.[69] Each event or item to be insured is, however, likely to require its own individual solution.

Because microinsurance is only beginning to emerge, the possible role of tax incentives is also not certain. At the same time, because of its relative newness, the potential field for donor cash is also wide open. For example, donations could have potential use in supporting micro-insurance research, reducing start-up and other administrative costs, enhancing reserves or funding reinsurance for microinsurers. Donor-supported reinsurance or enhanced reserves could allow a microinsurer to survive the steep learning curve in providing microinsurance coverage.

The potential uses for donated funds suggested above are aimed at fostering the financial stability of microinsurance institutions. Providing incentives targeted to the clients of microinsurers may also be useful because, just as with microsaving, microinsurance raises commitment problems. That is, even when insurance is demonstrably a wise purchase decision, it can be difficult for individuals to commit to making their premium payments, particularly if budget constraints are strong. Further, the purchase of insurance may require contemplation of events that are unpleasant or difficult to conceptualize.[70] Insurance also assumes a relatively sophisticated understanding of coverage limits and terms. Thus, even if microinsurance is made available, take-up rates may be low for some types of risk and dissatisfaction with the resulting policies a strong possibility.[71] The difficulties could prove to be similar to those encountered by development programs aimed at getting individuals to be vaccinated or use mosquito nets because individuals may have difficulty discerning the benefits when they occur far in the future.[72] Subsidization of microinsurance premiums or other incentives to encourage purchase should be considered, but with care taken in determining whether such a subsidy works. Empirical research suggesting that a small side incentive

---

68 Banerjee and Duflo, *supra* note 11, at 149.

69 Armendáriz and Morduch, *supra* note 2, at 199–201.

70 See Luke and Abramovsky, *supra* note 65.

71 Banerjee and Duflo, *supra* note 11, at 153–4.

72 The debates over whether vaccines or mosquito nets should be subsidized are legendary. *Ibid.* 48–50, 57–68.

can lead to significant increases in vaccine take-up rates could, for example, be tested in the microinsurance area.[73]

While there seems to be ample room for donated funds in establishing microinsurance, once again it seems unnecessary to create new, specific tax incentives for microinsurance. General charitable contribution provisions should provide adequate inducement to donors.[74] The complexity involved in pricing microinsurance will, however, likely require the expertise of commercial insurers. Because such insurers are unlikely to be interested in providing the coverage themselves, alliances between microinsurers and commercial insurers seem a necessity.[75] As with microsaving, and to a much lesser extent with microgrants, the continued development of microfinance tools beyond microcredit seems almost certain to require microfinance institutions to seek the expertise of or investment by for-profit, commercial institutions. In the United States such alliances could benefit from clarification of the existing authorities on the tax-exempt status of charitable organizations that partner with for-profit institutions, since, as discussed in the section on microcredit, relatively few authorities exist in this area and those that are available tend to focus on health care ventures.

V. CONCLUSION

The question of the extent to which developed world tax incentives should be used to support microfinance requires a decision about the role of subsidy in microfinance. The role of subsidy is, however, central to the debate about the future of microcredit and seems likely also to trigger conflicting viewpoints in newer microfinance tools, such as microinsurance.

---

[73] *Ibid.* 62–3 (describing pilot programming leading to sevenfold increase in immunizations by providing 2 pounds of dried beans as incentive).

[74] This assumes that the insurance-providing activity would qualify as a charitable one. US tax law does, for example, deny tax exemption to an organization if a 'substantial part of its activities consists of providing commercial-type insurance'. Internal Revenue Code s. 501(m) (2011). Thus, if an organization furnished microinsurance but charged its customers commercial rates instead of below-cost rates, the organization would not qualify for US tax exemption.

[75] Collins *et al.*, *supra* note 13, at 2 (describing the need for such alliances and pointing out that '[s]uch partnerships are already under way around the world'); Brown, *supra* note 64, at 176–84.

The microcredit debate is instructive as an example of the need to exercise caution in designing customized tax incentives. Microcredit's initial promise as a poverty panacea has not stood the test of time. Had tax policy been custom-tailored to privilege a particular style of microcredit in the early days, this could ultimately have made it more difficult to arrive at a more pragmatic assessment of microcredit's strengths and weaknesses. At a more general level, strong tax incentives provided by the developed world could have a problematic, unilateral influence over solutions crafted in the developing world.[76]

Empirical research may eventually provide a clearer picture of how donor contributions are performing, which may then prompt a more nuanced discussion about the values that should be used in prioritizing those contributions. Until then, custom-tailoring new tax incentives in the developed world to support microfinance in the developing world seems ill-advised given the current microfinance landscape. Existing charitable tax contribution incentives likely already provide significant support while being flexible enough to provide space for the continuing innovation of microfinance.

---

[76] See Easterly, *White Man's Burden*, *supra* note 27, at 6 (arguing for 'Searchers' over 'Planners' because '[a] Planner believes outsiders know enough to impose solutions. A Searcher believes only insiders have enough knowledge to find solutions, and that most solutions must be homegrown').

PART V

Tax cooperation

11. Geographical boundaries of tax jurisdiction, exclusive allocation of taxing powers in tax treaties and good tax governance in relations with developing countries

Pasquale Pistone*

I. INTRODUCTION

Despite the absence of international customary law in tax matters,[1] the geographical boundaries of tax jurisdictions have reached common standards worldwide. Global income taxation in the country of residence (with some slight variations related to citizenship-based exercise of taxing rights involving in particular the United States) is generally accepted, thus justifying the right of a country to levy its taxes on income produced outside its territory whenever said income is derived by one of its residents (or, if applicable, citizens). General liability to tax on worldwide income is then combined with a more limited liability to tax in the country where income is sourced, giving rise to an exposure to international (juridical) double taxation. Relief for double taxation through exemption or credit removes (in full or part) or prevents the perceived negative effects of such phenomenon on cross-border income, but also alters the international conditions of neutrality and inter-nation equity.[2]

* Member of the Junge Kurie of the Austrian Academy of Sciences.

1 There is, however, a contemporary discussion over this issue. See, e.g., Reuven Avi-Yonah, *International Tax as International Law* (New York: Cambridge University Press, 2007); but see Brian D. Lepard, *Customary International Law: A New Theory with Practical Applications* (New York: Cambridge University Press, 2010).

2 For a recent survey of the economic discourse, see, e.g., J. Becker and C. Fuest, 'The Taxation of Foreign Profits: The Old View, the New View and a

This chapter will not address those issues in a general way, but only from the perspective of ascertaining whether, to what extent and on what grounds the mechanisms of taxing jurisdiction should be reconsidered in relations with developing countries. The focus is here on income taxation and the analysis is carried out from a legal perspective, but also taking into account policy considerations, with a view to enhancing international tax justice and a fair allocation of taxing rights in relations with developing countries. In this context, previous (multidisciplinary) academic writing of the author constitutes the starting point of this chapter, even when its content is not reproduced hereby.[3]

This chapter focuses attention on the OECD Model Tax Convention, which is often assumed to represent the internationally accepted (or 'best')[4] tax treaty practice, in order to find out whether its suitability to become the worldwide standard is also appropriate to regulate relations with developing countries. Afterwards, the analysis will continue on alternative clauses on the allocation of taxing powers, which could apply in the framework of all developing countries' treaties. Before drawing some conclusions, the outcome of the analysis will be reviewed from the perspective of good tax governance, in order to find out whether some

---

Pragmatic View' (2011) 46(2) *Intereconomics* 92; K. Bilicka and C. Fuest, *With Which Countries Do Tax Havens Share Information?*, EUI Working Papers, RCSAS 2012/06, available at www.eui.eu/RCSAS/Publications/.

[3] P. Pistone, 'Tax Treaties with Developing Countries: A Plea for New Allocation Rules and a Combined Legal and Economic Approach' in M. Lang, P. Pistone, J. Schuch, C. Staringer and M. Zagler (eds), *Tax Treaties from a Legal and Economic Perspective* (IBFD Publications, 2010) 413–39; P. Pistone, 'Rasgos fundamentales del Proyecto de Modelo de Convenio para América Latina' in A. Mazz and P. Pistone (eds), *Reflexiones en torno a un modelo latinoamericano de convenio de doble imposición* (Fundación de cultura universitaria Montevideo, 2010) 57–76; P. Pistone and T. Goodspeed, 'Rethinking Tax Jurisdictions and Relief from International Double Taxation with Regard to Developing Countries: Legal and Economic Perspectives from Europe and North America' in M. Zagler, *International Tax Coordination: Virtues and Pitfalls* (Abingdon: Routledge, 2010) 13–36.

[4] The author perceives an overwhelming influence of the OECD Model Tax Convention on tax treaties also beyond the boundaries of its member states as a kind of implicit result of an assumption, which is questionable as such, that it represents the expression of the most advanced tax treaty practice. Although this is most usually the case for tax treaty policy of its member states, the author doubts that this may also be true for other countries. Consequently, this chapter will focus on ascertaining whether and to what extent the clauses contained in the OECD Model Tax Convention could be desirable also from the perspective of non-OECD countries, with special emphasis on developing countries.

separate standards should be set in relations with developing countries and, in the affirmative, on the basis of what parameters.

II. THE OECD 'BEST' TAX TREATY PRACTICE AS AN INTERNATIONAL TAX STANDARD

It is well known that several good arguments support global taxation of income in the country of residence. The need to adapt the levying of taxes to the personal situation of taxpayers (in connection with the ability-to-pay principle) in at least one tax system seems of particular importance for personal income tax purposes with a view to achieve compliance with equality and secure fairness of taxation regardless of where income tax liability arises. The ability-to-pay principle plays a more limited role for income taxes levied on other legal persons, such as companies, since such taxes generally apply on the basis of proportional rates and therefore fairness in taxation can be achieved when income is compartmentalized among different taxing jurisdictions.

The existence of different tax rates across the various jurisdictions alters tax neutrality at the international level and creates considerable scope for tax arbitrage, strengthening the importance of (potentially undesirable) international tax planning. Various economic studies – also taking into account relief methods, even in the presence of tax treaties – have come to the conclusion that taxation, in general, and tax treaties, in particular, have a limited impact on foreign direct investment (FDI) locational decisions.[5] This chapter does not question whether such studies are technically correct. However, the author perceives that the economic analysis of tax treaties very frequently streamlines their clauses on the basis of the ones that are included in Model Tax Conventions, rather than of those that are actually contained in bilateral tax treaties that are negotiated globally.[6] Recent comprehensive legal studies carried out on tax treaties around the world[7] show that significant differences can still be recorded across treaties.

Contrary to what is commonly believed, treaties concluded with or between non-OECD countries do not necessarily follow the UN Model

[5] See, e.g., R. Davies, 'Tax Treaties and Foreign Direct Investment: Potential versus Performance' (2004) 11(6) *International Tax and Public Finance* 775.

[6] See the reports in Lang *et al.*, *supra* note 3.

[7] See P. Pistone, 'General Report' in M. Lang, P. Pistone, J. Schuch and C. Staringer, *The Influence of the OECD and UN Model Conventions on Bilateral Tax Treaties* (Cambridge: Cambridge University Press, 2012) 1 *et seq.*

Tax Convention, which has gradually lost its importance over the years. Depending on the concrete outcome of negotiation of the single articles contained in such bilateral treaties, there can be an influence of specific clauses included in the UN or OECD Model Tax Conventions, but also ad hoc compromises that are acceptable for the contracting parties. Accordingly, there seems to be a disconnect between the limited attention paid by (legal and economic) academic writing to specific bilateral treaties at the global level[8] and the real pattern, which concretely steers international tax planning and business decisions of multinational enterprises around the world. The more tax treaty clauses depart from the patterns of Model Tax Conventions, the more we get into a domain surrounded by uncertainty, where problems of positive and negative conflicts of taxing jurisdiction are likely to arise. Such scenarios can give rise to undesirable problems, such as double taxation and double non-taxation, but also facilitate international routing of income for the purpose of minimizing the tax burden. The latter phenomenon is not a problem as such, but should be taken into due account when setting the rules for the allocation of taxing rights in cross-border situations and analysing it.

Furthermore, the overall international tax scenario has significantly changed from a legal perspective when compared to the one existing when the foundations of global worldwide liability to tax were laid. The author will now briefly illustrate such difference.

Global income taxation, if combined with relief for foreign taxes through the credit method, was conceived in order to secure capital export neutrality and thus a sort of level playing field that at least prevented business from choosing to operate abroad rather than domestically, for tax driven reasons.[9] Rather than being an extraterritorial taxation of income, it is personal-based taxation levied on any resident who derives income regardless of its actual geographical source, thus allowing for a parallel exercise of taxing jurisdiction to the one of the country that taxed income as such, i.e., on an objective basis and regardless of who

---

[8] Most legal studies are carried out in the form of single commentaries of one or more provisions contained in one or more bilateral treaty of a given country, thus precluding a global vision of the legal boundaries and implication of clauses included in bilateral treaties.

[9] However, the use of the ordinary credit method for relieving international juridical double taxation does not achieve neutrality with domestic competitors of the state of residence when foreign sourced taxes are higher than the ones applying in the country of residence of the investor.

derives it.[10] Besides contributing to international juridical double taxation, this mechanism established a theoretical justification for the exercise of tax prerogatives of capital exporting countries beyond their borders. This prevents capital flows towards lower tax jurisdictions and reduces the leverage of multinational enterprises to negotiate tax holidays with countries needing to import capital. Further, it even allows capital exporting countries to levy their tax on foreign sourced income on top of the tax paid in countries of source, when the latter ones are below the amounts corresponding to the worldwide liability to tax on the residence basis.

The interesting feature of such theories and the underlying foundations of the credit method, when applied to relations with capital importing, or developing, countries, is that, for the purpose of preventing concessions being made to multinational enterprises, it justifies an expansion of the sovereignty of developed countries. Accordingly, developed countries end up interfering with tax policy decisions of the developing countries, turning any tax advantage for international investors (who are usually resident in such developed countries) into a relative advantage, where credit for lower foreign taxes can become an additional source of revenue for the state of residence.

North American (in particular US)[11] academic writing has traditionally opposed the various types of notional tax credit, such as tax sparing and matching credit, which generally prevent consistency with the goals of their foreign tax credit based international tax regimes, but (especially in

---

[10] The concept of parallel exercise of taxing jurisdiction is perhaps not particularly known outside the European Union. The European Court of Justice developed it when differentiating between cases of subjective and objective links to tax sovereignty and concluding that juridical double taxation arising in such context is the outcome of a disparity between the way in which two states exercise their taxing powers.

[11] See, e.g., S. Surrey, representations to the US Senate, Double Taxation Convention with Pakistan: Hearing Before the Committee on Foreign Relations, 85th Cong. Second Sess. (1957). For the history of the position, see R. Kuhn, 'United States Tax Policy with Respect to Less Developed Countries' (1963) 32 *George Washington Law Review* 262. For recent reiterations of the opposition to tax sparing, see, e.g., D. Rosenbloom, 'Trends in Tax Treaties between the United States and Developing Countries' in *UN Draft Model Taxation Convention: Proceedings of a Seminar held in Copenhagen in 1979 during the 33rd Congress of the International Fiscal Association* (Boston: Kluwer, 1979) 19; and Y. Brauner, 'A Framework for an Informed Study of the Realistic Role of Tax in a Development Agenda' (2010) 42 *University of British Columbia Law Review* 275.

the case of tax sparing) in fact preserve tax policy decisions of the developing country.

The use of the exemption method for relieving cross-border juridical double taxation, especially in North American (in particular, economic) tax literature, is often a synonym for a proposal for territorial taxation,[12] since applying the exemption method, the residence state refrains from exercising its taxing jurisdiction on foreign-sourced income and in effect, renders the taxing powers of the state of source final and exclusive. However, it is interesting to consider the use of this method in respect of losses as well as income. As a result of several decisions of the European Court of Justice (ECJ), the use of this method in the European Union has often justified shifts of foreign-sourced temporary losses in and out of the state of residence jurisdiction,[13] as well as shifting of final losses.[14] This shows that an exact equivalence between a territorial system and a worldwide system with exemption does not exist. The latter method implies the existence of a direct legal link with the taxing jurisdiction of the state of residence of a given taxpayer for all income and losses regardless of their geographical origin, while the former method does not.[15] Accordingly, any legal analysis taking European Union law into account should conclude that the failure to take into account foreign losses does not generate any violation of the non-discrimination principle insofar as the tax system is a purely territorial one. However, the same

---

[12] For a recent articulation, see, e.g., Technical Explanation of the Ways and Means Discussion Draft Provisions to Establish a Participation Exemption System for the Taxation of Foreign Income (26 October 2011) (known as the 'Camp Proposal'); and M. Desai, C. Foley and J. Hines, Jr, *Tax Policy and the Efficiency of U.S. Direct Investment Abroad* (30 June 2011), available at SSRN: http://ssrn.com/abstract=1875750, or http://dx.doi.org/10.2139/ssrn.1875750.

[13] See Case C-157/07, *Krankenheim am Wannsee* [2008] ECR I-08061, ECJ, judgment of 23 October 2008.

[14] See Case C-446/03, *Marks & Spencer* [2005] ECR I-10837, ECJ, judgment of 13 December 2005. However, the ECJ has taken a different view in Case C-337/08, *X Holding* [2010] ECR I-012015, judgment of 25 February 2010, para. 21, expressing the view that no violation of fundamental freedoms arises from the failure of the Dutch fiscal unity regime to allow for temporary import of losses from a foreign subsidiary. This view was criticized in tax literature for being potentially inconsistent with other ECJ case law. See, among others, the Opinion Statement of the CFE Taskforce on the *X Holding* case, submitted in January 2011, available at www.cfe-eutax.org.

[15] See CFE, Opinion Statement of the CFE ECJ Taskforce on losses compensation within the EU for individuals and companies carrying out their activities through permanent establishments, submitted in July 2009, available at www.cfe-eutax.org.

conclusion would not be true if a worldwide system with exemption applies.

From the late 1980s onwards, a general reduction of the controls and restrictions on free movement of capital and payments globally has affected the original framework in which global income taxation was conceived. In Europe, this was gradually combined with their full liberalization in a context where (primary and secondary) supranational law provides for non-discriminatory relief of cross-border economic double taxation, the reduction or elimination of withholding taxes and a general reduction in corporation taxes. This new European framework allows for greater tax planning flexibility. In the presence of genuine structures (from the perspective of staff, premises and equipment)[16] in a different EU Member State from the state of residence, this opens up the entitlement to treaty benefits of such country and allows for a genuine routing of investment in and out of third countries (i.e., non-members of the European Union).

Those who are familiar with the impact of EU law on cross-border taxation also know that controlled foreign company (CFC) and similar types of anti-deferral tax legislation cannot entirely neutralize such tax planning schemes if these are not found to involve abusive practices. The current legal scenario in the European Union generates a flexible pattern for international tax planning decisions, which may lead business to operate from or through a given country and to repatriate a lower tax burden to the country from which the capital investment originated.

In this changed context, the author argues that it now makes less sense to evaluate the impact of a given bilateral tax treaty in isolation, because side routes may be taken by the taxpayer that allow income to flow where it is most conveniently taxed at the cross-border level. A good example of this situation concerns the double tax treaty between Brazil and Germany. Germany made the decision to terminate this treaty for various reasons, including the fact that the tax concessions (including notional credit) made by Germany to foster economic development of Brazil were no longer justified in the light of the current economic development of the latter country. Although this could be held in theory to be a correct decision, backed up by a technically consistent analysis of the concrete situation, in reality, international tax planning made various alternative options for income to flow between the two countries with a similar tax burden. In particular, other Brazilian tax treaties in force, such

---

[16] See Case C-196/04, *Cadbury Schweppes* [2006] ECR I-07995, ECJ, judgment of 12 September 2006, para. 67.

as the one with Austria, have a similar content and include notional credit. Setting up a genuine structure in Austria may therefore allow a German resident company to apply similar tax conditions on cross-border income, due to the advantages applicable under the Austria–Brazil Tax Treaty and the EU Parent–Subsidiary Dividend Directive.

The scenario is different in some countries, such as the United States, which have erected legal fences to international tax planning, combining a broad application of CFC legislation, limitation on benefits (LOB) clauses and deferral of the deduction of losses. Such strong unilateral measures may prove effective, but often have disproportionate (also deterrent) effects and add further complexity and cost to the worldwide scenario. This is particularly evident in the case of LOB clauses. Their extreme complexity may deter someone from exercising the entitlement to the benefits of a tax treaty, which is made subject to burdensome procedures for the taxpayer, who will otherwise bear the negative consequences.

From a European law perspective, artificial structures that are set up essentially to circumvent the liability to tax (or otherwise obtain undue advantages from it) and that are therefore abusive, are not entitled to the application of the benefits of supranational law and can be countered at the national level.[17] But the reaction to such abusive practices should not exceed what is strictly limited to effectively counter them[18] or otherwise harm the effective enjoyment of a given right in a genuine situation.[19]

---

[17] Case C-264/96, *ICI* [1998] ECR I-04695, ECJ, judgment of 16 July 1998, para. 28; Case C-110/99, *Emsland-Stärke* [2000] ECR I-11569, ECJ, 14 December 2000, para. 38. See further on this P. Pistone, 'Abuse of Law in the Context of Indirect Taxation: From (before) Emsland-Stärke 1 to Halifax (and Beyond)' in S. Vogenauer and R. de la Feria (eds), *Prohibition of Abuse of Law: A New General Principle of EU Law?* (Oxford: Hart Publishers, 2011) 381–93.

[18] The settled case law of the ECJ has acknowledged the relevance of the principle of proportionality (and suitability) for EU law in all fields of taxation since the late 1990s. See on this Joined Cases C-286/94, C-340/95, C-401/95 and C-47/96, *Garage Molenheide BVBA and others* [1997] ECR I-07281, ECJ, judgment of 18 December 1997, paras 45–7 (proportionality); and Case C-264/96, *ICI* [1998] ECR I-04695, ECJ, judgment of 16 July 1998, para. 28 (suitability).

[19] According to settled ECJ case law (see Joined Cases C-6/90 and C-9/90, *Francovich* [1991] ECR I-05357, ECJ, judgment of 19 November 1991), the exercise of a right granted by EU law could not be made subject to burdensome conditions. See further on this in P. Pistone (ed.), *Legal Remedies in European Tax Law* (Amsterdam: IBFD Publications, 2009).

In such context the author wonders whether, and to what extent, an alternative approach to such problems could (or should) be followed. In general, the author believes that the era of global tax law is spreading throughout the world a kind of global norm concerning the exercise of taxing jurisdiction. This is significantly aggregating the approach of national governments around what is regarded as the expression of an international best practice, and is leading country legislatures to harden such practices into statutory provisions. The role of the OECD is particularly important in the creation of what is often regarded as the internationally accepted 'best' tax practice. This process can reduce the scope for tax arbitrage and gradually lead to a more homogeneous exercise of national tax jurisdictions on cross-border situations. However, the author is uncertain as to whether this path is also suitable for relations between OECD and non-OECD countries, or between non-OECD countries. Accordingly, the view is held that treaties based on the OECD Model should be considered to represent no more than international best practice for countries that share the policy goals of the OECD, being its member states. This position is supported by various further reasons.

First, all OECD countries contribute to building up the rules that best reflect their common international tax policy goals. In compliance with the indications by the OECD and thanks to their usually stronger negotiation power, coupled with the increasing technical authoritativeness of the OECD Model worldwide, OECD countries are generally successful in applying OECD standard clauses in their bilateral tax treaties.

Second, insofar as non-OECD countries do not actively participate in working parties that elaborate the arguments underlying the OECD Model Convention and its Commentaries, a problem of lack of representation may arise.[20] Such a problem is not a democratic deficit in strict terms, since we are dealing here with a mere model convention and all such countries voluntarily decide whether or not to follow the OECD standards in their bilateral treaties, which enter into force only after being signed and duly ratified. However, the deficit of representation arises

---

[20] Even when a country is represented in the OECD as an observer, its power of persuasion as an observing country is limited and may not be significantly different from its power to influence its own bilateral tax treaties. A significant economic power or an otherwise important country will be able to influence the content of its bilateral tax treaties and other treaties that may affect it regardless of input within the working parties, and weaker powers may have insignificant influence even if they fully participate and timely express their observations. For some countries, the cost of maintaining significant presence within OECD working parties is not insignificant.

insofar as one considers that such countries do not in fact contribute to determine the content of treaty clauses that build up the internationally accepted tax practice and are then included in their bilateral treaties. It seems a kind of *prendre ou laisser* game, which softly erodes national sovereignty through tax treaties that search for the myth of the international 'best practice' tax treaty network. Despite the undeniable merits of the work of the OECD in drafting tax treaties and technical commentaries, this phenomenon, if seen from the perspective of the rest of the world, may appear as a kind of new colonialism, through which a club of countries steers the worldwide order. Especially since the UN Model appears to have declined in importance worldwide in recent times, this phenomenon is possibly also enhanced by the total absence of a worldwide dialogue on tax treaties beyond the OECD pattern.

This scenario, on the one hand, often pushes capital importing countries to accept treaty rules even when going against their policy goals, and on the other hand, pushes net capital exporting countries to try and approximate their international tax rules to those of the OECD group of countries, which they soon hope to join, as a recognition of their increased economic wealth and power.

The author suggests that although global normative pressures lead to an emphasis on a tax treaty policy that reconciles the primary goals of a country with a close watch on the measures applied by other competitors, non-OECD countries should start to consider what their respective policies have in common, be they capital importing countries or net capital exporting countries, in order to establish a constructive dialogue with OECD countries that enhances fairness of international allocation rules. This approach would bring together a number of countries that are generally known as (and still are called in economic literature) 'developing countries'. The author concedes that the homogeneous composition of this group of countries is fading away, ceding pace to specific groups of countries that have considerably increased their GDPs and role in worldwide policy, such as the BRIC(S) countries (Brazil, Russia, India, China (and South Africa)), or that may be better considered as economies in transition, such as for instance the CIVET(S) (Colombia, Indonesia, Vietnam, Egypt, Turkey (and South Africa)) countries.[21] The dividing line between these categories becomes even thinner if one considers that countries like Mexico and Chile have joined the OECD, thus apparently

[21] Besides the economic features, additional elements could be taken into account, such as, e.g., the fact of being members of the G20 or of other international or regional country groups.

sharing its tax treaty policy goals although they have many features in common with BRICS or other developing countries.

Despite the current multifaceted nature of non-OECD countries, the author still believes that a constructive dialogue among these countries on international tax policy, under the general label of 'developing' countries, could identify some common features that such jurisdictions share, as opposed to those of 'developed' countries, which generally match the boundaries of OECD membership. This equivalence should be deemed to exist only at a first level of approximation, since some OECD countries have shown their intention to diversify their international tax policy position on specific tax treaty issues, as is the case of Chile and Mexico concerning the application of new Article 7 of the OECD Model Convention.[22] Furthermore, OECD countries that are also Member States of the European Union will be obliged to take a position that complies with their supranational law and that may in some cases not necessarily match with the position that would represent the internationally accepted practice in line with the OECD standards, such as in the case of the reaction to abusive practices.

III. SOME IDEAS FOR AN ALTERNATIVE ALLOCATION OF TAXING POWERS

This section of the chapter proceeds to consider some ideas for an alternative allocation of taxing powers in tax treaties that would better suit developing countries that have a goal of economic development. An example from another context that takes this approach is Article 66.2 of the TRIPS (Trade-Related Aspects of Intellectual Property Rights) Agreement[23] which aims to stimulate developed countries to provide incentives in their own countries that would support economic development in least-developed countries in the specific field of the transfer of intellectual property and intangibles. Tax treaties seem to go in the opposite direction to this approach, since they not only refrain from supporting

---

[22] See OECD, Attribution of Profits to Permanent Establishments (2010), and Art. 7 of the 2010 OECD Model Tax Convention. The reservations appear at the end of the commentary to Art. 7.

[23] TRIPS Agreement, Art. 66.2: 'Developed country members shall provide incentives to enterprises and institutions in their territories for the purpose of promoting and encouraging technology transfer to least developed country members in order to enable them to create a sound and viable technological base.' See www.wto.org/english/tratop_e/trips_e/t_agm7_e.htm.

this goal, but in fact run against it. As the previous section of this chapter has indicated, the current approach in tax treaties may an outcome of a combination of factors, including the asserted limited impact of tax treaties on economic development (as put forward by economic theories) and the protective attitude of capital exporting countries, in particular OECD member states, towards an exercise of their sovereignty that at least achieves full capital export neutrality for them.

The current situation could be questioned from the perspective of preserving an effective tax sovereignty of capital importing countries and their international tax policy decisions. There may be a latent conflict between current international treaty 'best practice' and the ideal goals of international tax justice, that is, a fair allocation of taxing powers between countries, regardless of how strong their negotiation powers can be when concluding a tax treaty. The establishment of some deeper level of international tax justice is a fundamental prerequisite for allowing developing countries to raise sufficient financial resources, based on the exploitation of their territory and economic resources arising from it, to fund their national budget. In other words, the author supports the idea that there could be a change from a policy of constant and endless 'charitable' or aid subsidies to developing countries from OECD member states, to a new policy that allows capital importing countries to run on their own feet and fund their economic development with sound tax policies coupled with proper revenue from economic resources located on their territory.

Worldwide income taxation was for long coupled with the spirit of comprehensive income taxation, including an effective integration of taxes levied on companies with the ones levied on their shareholders. Over the past few years, effective integration is being replaced in various areas of the world by schedular systems with predetermined levels of relief at corporate and shareholder levels. Furthermore, schedular taxation of income is picking up in various areas of the world (in particular in Europe), applying on an optional or compulsory basis on some categories of income, which are moved out of the traditional concept of global income for various groups of taxpayers.

In this context one may wonder whether it still makes sense, in particular for legal persons other than individuals, to plead for a global assessment of the ability to pay in the country of residence, especially insofar as one considers that splitting income among the various countries would allow an exercise of the taxing sovereignty that more closely reflects the reasons for operating on a given market and achieves some level playing field between all operators who are active in a given market. This outcome will be examined in particular as regards its potential effect on relations with developing countries, because the purpose of this chapter is to find out whether the existing pattern of international taxation can be changed in a context that pursues a stronger international tax justice in the presence of asymmetrical flows of income and capital.

In theory, this result can be achieved by acting at two different levels. First, one could keep the existing rules on the allocation of taxing powers and enact the change at the level of rules for relieving from double taxation. Accordingly, compensatory relief can be replaced with a tax sparing and exemption system. Second, and alternatively, the existing rules on the allocation of taxing powers can be replaced by a stronger rule in favour of exclusive jurisdictional allocation rules, at least insofar as a stronger link arises with the jurisdiction of source or residence, with the aim of achieving some overall balance at the level of the whole tax treaty. The latter option would retain shared taxing powers between the treaty contracting states, whenever there are no sufficient grounds for making the taxing powers of a contracting state prevail over those of another state. This alternative approach would prevent double taxation from occurring and leave it up to a state to take the final decision as to whether and to what extent its taxing powers should be exercised.

In principle, one could argue that an exclusive allocation of taxing powers can favour, per se, all cases of double non-taxation, in particular making it possible to attract international capital through tax holidays, thus giving rise to a race to the bottom. However, this traditional reluctance should now be examined in a context where offshore regimes are being made the target of approaches to eliminate harmful tax competition and where transfer pricing and fiscal transparency rules (through enhanced exchange of information on cross-border situations) are becoming increasingly effective. In this context, one should also consider that any partial or full relinquishing in the exercise of the taxing jurisdiction of a country should be left to the sovereign policy decision of such country, which could also consider it as part of a way to compensate some potential disadvantages that foreign investors could face in its territory. This could be the case for business income invested in initiatives of countries with insufficient infrastructure or higher costs of production (for instance due to transport costs, or other reasons), as is often the case for developing countries. From such a perspective, eliminating double taxation across jurisdictions, governed through international tax coordination measures contained in tax treaties, could contribute to simplify the taxation of cross-border situations and remove potential for disputes and arbitrage, and also re-establish a framework for a more consistent tax policy for developing countries.

The author considers the international tax treatment of business income to be a very good example to test this alternative approach in relations with developing countries. At present, tax treaties (in particular after the release of the 2010 edition of the OECD Model Convention) seem to support a potential development towards an exclusive allocation of taxing powers. Income attributable to a permanent establishment should follow the separate entity theory and be taxed as if it belonged to a different taxpayer from its head office. Likewise, business income in the absence of a permanent establishment, or attributable to the head office, has always been exclusively taxable in the state of residence of the taxpayer. In such situation, when drafting the first Latin American Model Tax Convention (in fact a multilateral non-self executing convention) for the Latin American Institute of Tax Law (ILADT),[24] the author has supported the view that business income should be exclusively taxed in the state where the business entity was situated, namely, that of its head office or of its permanent establishment. In the latter situation this implies that the state of the head office would entirely refrain from any interference with what the state of the permanent establishment would do as to the exercise of its taxing jurisdiction, also precluding any temporary shifts of losses following recapture, as would be required in the European Union in the case of exemption.

The ILADT Model Latin American Convention has applied this same method to other categories of income, such as income from employment and pensions. However, it retains shared taxing powers in respect of types of income where no prevailing link to a taxing jurisdiction could be set, for example, in the case of the various types of passive income. In such situations, however, it allowed shared taxing powers in a way that also preserved the right of the source country to levy its own taxes on income derived from the exploitation of a source situated on its territory. Accordingly, the ILADT Model Convention steers clear of a policy of reducing withholding taxes in the country of source and holds instead to a homogeneous level of source taxation in order to preserve the right of such country to exercise its jurisdiction. While doing so, it also significantly reduces the scope for international tax planning strategies.

---

[24] ILADT, Modelo de Convenio para América Latina, Instituto Colombiano de Derecho Tributario, Cartagena, 2010. See further the preliminary studies on this in A. Mazz and P. Pistone (eds), *Reflexiones en torno a un modelo latinoamericano de convenio de doble imposición* (Fundación de cultura universitaria Montevideo, 2010). The Multilateral Convention was approved by the Latin American Institute of Tax Law on 7 September 2012.

Exemption would not be an appropriate solution for passive income, which is only partly taxed in the state of source. However, in the author's view neither would a credit be appropriate, unless the use of treaty clauses with shared taxing powers can be combined with a notional credit that would prevent the state of residence from interfering in tax policy decisions of the source country.

IV. GOOD TAX GOVERNANCE

Good tax governance is essential to increase the tax revenue of developing countries and enable them to dispose of sufficient financial resources to carry out the activities that are needed for a sound running of the state and economic development. Good tax governance has been increasingly referred to in the statements by the OECD[25] and the European Union[26] from different perspectives, but its content is still hard to define with exact certainty.

In particular, the OECD is making constant reference to good tax governance in the framework of the project on global fiscal transparency, which currently involves a very large group of taxing jurisdictions from around the world engaged in the Global Forum. Global fiscal transparency supplements the establishment of good tax governance, insofar as it allows each country to effectively exercise its sovereignty on cross-border situations falling within the boundaries of its jurisdiction. Accordingly, an efficient system for exchanging tax information worldwide is an essential tool for developing countries to effectively establish good tax governance and to counter international abusive practices.[27]

---

[25] See http://oecd.org/tax/transparency.

[26] See COM(2009)201 and SEC(2010)426.

[27] Many developing countries would also find an interest in countering abusive practices, especially when it is taken into account that capital flight from said countries to tax havens may be related to issues of public interest such as corruption and money laundering. Such an interest is well exemplified by a recent request of the Indian Supreme Court to have access to the list of Indian nationals included in the database containing the personal details of persons holding investments in Liechtenstein which had already been provided by Germany to the Indian tax authorities. Except for such circumstances in which tax authorities can fairly easily detect what relevant information should be requested, there seems to be a general problem of building technical capacity and skills for tax authorities of developing countries to efficiently operate on the request of information in cross-border situations. Accordingly, it would be

In EU law, good tax governance within the EU internal market should involve a level playing field for competition in tax matters, which combines efficiency with equity and sustainability, while countering any phenomenon of harmful tax competition. Its external dimension has been required in relations with developing countries since the EU Parliament requested in 2009 a commitment to pursue good tax governance by such countries, as a condition for receiving EU financial donations.[28]

The question arises as to whether the standards of good tax governance applicable in developing countries ought to match the standards of EU and OECD countries, or whether by contrast they may or should apply in a different way. In general, good management of public resources is essential to good administration, no matter what the context. Within the European Union, in particular after the EU Charter of Fundamental Rights became binding, good administration is not to be measured only in terms of efficiency, but also from the perspective of protection of basic rights of taxpayers and motivation of the acts of tax authorities.[29] Strictly speaking, the requirement of good tax governance within the EU internal market should set the grounds for an external EU notion applicable to this field. However, the traditional consistency between internal and external legal dimensions seems to fail here, especially if one considers that donations by the European Union are aimed at fostering economic growth and development, rather than at establishing an area of economic integration that becomes similar to the EU internal market.

---

reasonable not just to conduct a campaign towards setting up tools for exchanging information, but also instructing tax authorities of non-OECD countries to use them.

[28] See European Parliament, Committee on Economic and Monetary Affairs, *Report on Promoting Good Governance in Tax Matters*, 2009/2174(INI) (2 February 2010), where, at para. 22, the following proposal can be found: '[The European Parliament] [u]rges the EU to implement a consistent approach to good tax governance in the context of the European Neighbourhood Policy, the enlargement policy and the development cooperation policy'. In this respect, the Explanatory Statement to the original draft version of the same Report (2009/XXXX(INI), 21 October 2010) clarifies that 'Financial incentives which are available under the 10th European Development Fund to a number of Caribbean and Pacific Countries are also effective instruments to encourage the adoption of the principles of good tax governance.' Such a remark appears to be in line with conclusions reached by the G20 Summit of 2 April 2009 where a review of bilateral aid programmes was mentioned among the possible incentives to ensure compliance with the global standards of fiscal transparency.

[29] See in particular EU Charter on Fundamental Rights, Art. 41.

If one then combines both the EU and OECD perspectives on the core issue of governance, the following view may be held. Insofar as good governance is the ability to take independent decisions that are consistent with a specific desirable policy goal, good tax governance for developing countries should aim at pursuing economic development specifically relevant to these countries, and beyond the goals that can be more attractive to OECD and EU countries. The different context should also make good tax governance more heavily concentrate on sustainable practices of fiscal transparency, rather than on best practices of OECD and EU countries, which could, in some cases, be too sophisticated to handle by tax authorities of developing countries.

For the purposes of this chapter, the author suggests that the key question is whether the existing tax treaties can be instruments to achieve the goals of good tax governance for developing countries. In principle, different views could be held in this respect, according to the relevant specific aspect or clause contained within tax treaties.

For instance, if one keeps the emphasis on issues of fiscal transparency, the current internationally accepted tax standard set within the framework of the Global Forum on fiscal transparency can exceed in the short run an affordable dimension for developing countries. For example, a developing country tax administration could be required in response to an information request, to provide more detailed information than it could possibly be able to handle or, in turn, need to request in respect of its own tax system. Some kind of simplified version of the existing standards could therefore prove a more proportionate instrument for enhancing an effective and immediate impact on good tax governance for such countries.

However, one cannot deny that in the medium and long-term perspective, enhanced transparency will be to the advantage of the entire world and bring the sphere of international taxation to a multilateral common standard, which could be included in some international agreement applicable worldwide.[30] This conclusion does not deny that the flow of information in relations between a developing country and an OECD country could prove to be asymmetrical, thus creating more costs than benefits for the former country. Especially considering the fact that this situation would possibly expose taxpayers of the developing country to bear a higher burden to pay a larger number of hours of tax officials of such country, one may therefore wonder whether solutions based on

---

[30] For a more detailed discussion on international developments in this area, see Miranda Stewart, Chapter 13.

servicing fees for supply of information could be introduced in tax treaties with developing countries, in particular when the supply of such information could be tailored and require the carrying out of a specific inquiry by the developing country. The author therefore welcomes pragmatic solutions of the type that Australia recently included in the Memorandum of Understanding of some of its treaties,[31] or in the new treaty signed between Argentina and Uruguay,[32] which do not move away from an execution in good faith of treaty obligations and achieve a fairer outcome in relations with (or between) developing countries.

Another example could be transfer pricing methodologies and the supply of information in this context. Arm's length standards can sometimes be rather difficult to determine with absolute certainty. Relations with developing countries could therefore be more appropriately handled by applying, for example, predetermined margins within transfer pricing, regardless of whether they meet arm's length standards in all circumstances.

On the other hand, incorporating good tax governance standards into general tax treaties with specific reference to distributive rules, that is, rules governing the distribution of taxing rights among contracting states,[33] may prove more challenging. The shared allocation of taxing powers, in particular for cases of relief from double taxation by the credit method, can entail a significant number of calculations and a critical tax auditing activity for the state of residence, which a developing country is not always able to effectively carry out. Certainly, developing countries would find themselves more frequently in the position of states of source and less in that of states of residence. However, this would not prevent them from seeking a more simplified approach, which could be easier to handle. Schedular relief methods (including notional types, such as tax sparing) or exemption could prove to be more appropriate for this reason. However, as was pointed out earlier in this chapter, an exclusive

---

[31] In particular, where unilateral flows of information can arise, the requested state only incurs ordinary cost, whereas the counterpart bears all extraordinary cost, such as for carrying out research, copying of documents, engaging experts, interpreters or translators, conveying documents to the requested party, costs for litigation or obtaining deposition or testimony.

[32] The treaty was signed on 23 April 2012 and includes a clause in Art. 8, according to which extraordinary cost will be borne by the requesting contracting state. This is in line with the Model Tax Information Exchange Agreement of 2006 developed by the OECD.

[33] With reference to the OECD Model as well as the UN Model, these rules are included in Chapter III, 'Taxation of Income', which encompasses Arts 6 to 21.

allocation of taxing powers could eventually be an even easier option to handle, since each country would have to determine whether its connection with income is stronger than that of the other country and, in the affirmative, proceed further with levying its taxes on a given income, regardless of what the other contracting state would do.

An additional dimension for good tax governance in tax treaties with developing countries could also arise from the perspective of how much they comply with the goal of securing high standards of international tax justice. This perspective would measure the allocation of taxing powers in such a way that countries take care of fairness in the exercise of their taxing powers among the various relevant elements that measure their successful attitude concerning the achievement of their policy goals. As discussed in the previous section, one may wonder whether the current international scenario achieves such fairness.

In consequence, one should consider whether we should equate the OECD Model standards for tax treaties as 'best' international tax practice for all countries. Regardless of the extent to which one would agree on the technical reliability of such standards, from the perspective of developing countries, the issue remains that OECD standards in fact pursue typical policies of capital exporting countries. Can a developing country consider such standards as entirely satisfactory from its own point of view? The author doubts that an affirmative answer could be reasonably argued in this respect. And yet, the OECD Model Convention is currently being used by a significant number of countries, including non-member states of the OECD, as the universal basis for negotiating tax treaties. From such perspective it seems unlikely that a developing country could pursue good tax governance by the mere fact of sticking to the OECD standards, in particular when it comes to the allocation of taxing powers.

It must be remembered that national tax rules can also have an immediate impact on good tax governance standards. For our purposes one could refer to the geographical boundaries of tax jurisdiction from a different perspective than the one that was taken into account earlier in this chapter. Stretching the boundaries of a tax jurisdiction too far will certainly have an immediate positive repercussion on the levying of taxes, but it would also potentially increase the possibility of positive conflicts of taxing jurisdiction between various countries, going beyond the traditional source–residence conflict and making the possibility of residence–residence conflicts significantly higher than it would be otherwise.

One matter to consider is whether there could be specific issues for developing countries arising from the context of domestic rules and their geographical boundaries? A negative answer could in this case be justified, since any immediate impact could be more related to the application of a given domestic measure, than to the proper peculiarities of the relations with developing countries. Accordingly, applying CFC legislation could allow a country to set up broader boundaries to its taxing jurisdiction, which would apply to income derived by foreign controlled subsidiaries situated in tax havens, regardless of whether such country is to be considered as a developing country. Likewise, applying CFC legislation in a developing country of residence of the parent would raise similar issues, as happens in an increasing number of developing countries which apply this type of rules.

Good tax governance should, however, also have a procedural dimension, affecting the relations of tax authorities with taxpayers. Such a dimension should enhance the collection of taxes through an increased cooperation with taxpayers. This can imply that obtaining information in advance by taxpayers and allowing them to find safe havens through an *ex ante* analysis of the relevant facts would give rise to win–win situations, in which taxpayers are not challenged by tax authorities and tax authorities spend fewer hours in auditing and have higher returns through voluntary compliance. However, developing countries should also make sure that this does not compromise the protection of taxpayers' rights. This can also have immediate repercussions on tax treaties, which include clauses on exchange of information that usually relegate taxpayers to a kind of secondary dimension, thus depriving them of an active role in the handling of data that directly affect them. Accordingly, treaties with a more precise definition of taxpayers' rights would undoubtedly enhance the goals of good tax governance.

V. CONCLUSION

In the current era of global taxation, there has been inadequate attention paid to building a specific framework for international tax that is relevant for developing countries. The author suggests that so-called 'best' international tax practices are not appropriate to apply whenever significant asymmetries arise in relations between two countries. Several issues of this kind arise in tax treaties with developing countries, which also show different priorities in terms of international tax policy from the ones that are clearly set within the main source of international tax treaty rules, being the OECD Model Tax Convention.

Tax treaty rules could be utilized as instruments for achieving international tax justice if new priorities are included in them, which would put the emphasis on a stronger protection of the interests of developing countries. We need to reconsider economic theories concerning international taxation in a context of liberalized movement of capital, and in which the existing discrepancies between diverse bilateral tax treaties can allow international tax planning to achieve a tax efficient repatriation of income from foreign investment even where capital export neutrality would in principle be protected by foreign tax credit for direct flows.

Accordingly, the author suggests that the time has come to reconsider the very foundations of relief of double taxation, specifically the foreign tax credit, as this mechanism allows capital exporting countries to levy their taxes on top of the tax levied by capital importing countries and neutralize their tax policy decision under the pretext of preventing multinational enterprises from negotiating tax holidays. From this perspective, the author pleads for a reconsideration of rules on the allocation of income. The author argues in favour of a framework of exclusive allocation of taxing powers (based on the closer link of a type of income with a tax jurisdiction of either contracting state), and prevention of international double taxation by this means, as the rule for a simplified framework of tax treaties in relations with or between developing countries. One example of this kind of approach can be found in the ILADT Latin American Model Convention discussed above. This Model also does away with the traditional opposition to notional credits and enables a wider use of exemption in all cases when the closer link with a jurisdiction cannot be established, in such a way as to give a contracting state exclusive taxing powers on given types of income.

Further, the author believes that developing countries should only follow the internationally accepted tax treaty practice arising from the OECD Model Convention insofar as this allows them to achieve consistency with their own key objectives, thus ensuring consistency from a good tax governance perspective applied to internation relations. This conclusion also applies in respect of relations between developing countries and EU Member States that require a commitment to pursue good tax governance.

12. Tax activists and the global movement for development through transparency

Allison Christians

I. INTRODUCTION

Activists around the world are calling on governments to require public disclosure of information about how much and where in the world multinational companies pay taxes. Their goal is to awaken public attention to the systemic undertaxation of multinationals, to show that this undertaxation is connected to development failure in poor countries, and to convince law-makers that the public has an interest in changing this paradigm. In their quest for tax transparency, the activists are inserting themselves in an elite policy-making arena that has traditionally been closed both to them and to the countries on whose behalf they seek change. Tax transparency challenges the tax policy norms developed within this arena, while the activists' demand for non-governmental participation in tax governance challenges the institutional foundations of contemporary international tax policy-making.

This chapter identifies and explores the rise of a global tax transparency movement, what it reveals about global governance in tax law, and how it seeks to alter the substance of tax policy norms and the process of tax policy-making. The discussion begins with a profile of the identity and goals of global tax transparency activists. It then examines three ways these activists have gone about the task of pursuing tax reform: appeal to multinational companies, appeal to national legislatures, and appeal to the international tax community through the institutional architecture of the Organisation for Economic Co-operation and Development (OECD), a 34-member 'rich nations' club'.[1] It analyses

[1] See, e.g., Haig Simonian and Maria Fekter, 'Iron Lady steeled for "solid programme" to reduce debt', *Financial Times*, 27 September 2011; James

what these pathways to reform reveal about who defines tax policy in an economically, socially and politically integrated world. The chapter concludes by exploring how worldwide demand for transparency and non-governmental participation in international tax policy decision-making could impact global tax governance.

II. WHO ARE TAX TRANSPARENCY ACTIVISTS AND WHAT DO THEY SEEK?

The past several years have produced a global financial crisis, coordinated cross-country bail-outs of large financial and commercial interests, increased budget gaps and attendant budget-cutting in rich countries, and intensified public concern about poverty and inequality around the world.[2] Over the same period, many multinational companies have reported record profits on their worldwide operations while apparently enjoying vanishing tax burdens.[3] International tax transparency activism has arisen as a global phenomenon against this backdrop.[4] Tax transparency activists seek to ask and answer the question: how is it that the world's largest profit centers are contributing so little to public revenue needs, especially in poor countries? This is an empirical question on the part of activists – an information quest rather than a call for change.[5] But normative goals clearly animate the quest. Uncovering and analysing these normative goals begins with an exploration of how tax transparency activism came about.

Arnold, 'What is the OECD for?', *BBC News*, 30 April 2003, available at http://news.bbc.co.uk/2/hi/business/2987887.stm.

[2] For an overview, see, e.g., '2011 Revisited: Charting the Year', *The Economist*, 31 December 2011, available at www.economist.com/node/21542191.

[3] See discussion *infra* notes 48 to 51.

[4] For a discussion of the general nature and character of transparency initiatives, see Mark Fenster, *The Transparency Fix: Advocating Legal Rights and their Alternatives in the Pursuit of a Visible State* (9 January 2012), available at http://ssrn.com/abstract=1918154.

[5] It is by no means the first time tax information has been sought with respect to corporations in the United States or elsewhere. For a discussion of the US experience with corporate tax disclosure as a national policy, see Richard D. Pomp, 'The Disclosure of State Corporate Income Tax Data' (1993) 22 *Capital University Law Review* 373.

A. Origins of Tax Transparency Activism

The quest for tax transparency began as a campaign by a few discrete anti-corruption activist groups. It has grown into a global tax transparency movement with support around the world from non-governmental organizations (NGOs), government officials, business representatives and other members of 'civil society' – loosely defined as individuals and groups with no direct political or economic stake in the tax rules that apply to multinationals.[6]

The first mover was Global Witness, a US and UK-based watchdog group that is concerned about the connection between foreign investment, government corruption and armed conflict in resource-rich but underdeveloped countries.[7] In a 1999 report, Global Witness argued that government officials in Angola were diverting tax revenues from oil producers for personal gain, mainly by funding ongoing war, rather than using it for the public good.[8] Global Witness specifically blamed underdevelopment on corruption, and corruption on the lack of transparency regarding the taxation and other payments made by multinationals to officials in Angola. The group sought international action to impose transparency, arguing that the public in Angola was unable to impose it themselves due to social, political and economic controls.[9]

Global Witness' 1999 report garnered widespread interest and support from individual activists, NGOs and watchdog groups involved in monitoring the social justice aspects of natural resource extraction,

---

[6] See, e.g., World Bank, 'Civil Society Organizations', available at http://web.worldbank.org/WBSITE/EXTERNAL/TOPICS/CSO/0,,contentMDK:20127718~menuPK:288622~pagePK:220503~piPK:220476~theSitePK:228717,00.html. The term 'civil society' is ambiguous and is used inconsistently, sometimes including any non-governmental member of society, including business and industry, and other times excluding profit-oriented enterprises. For a discussion, see Laura G. Pedraza-Farina, *Conceptions of Civil Society in International Law-Making and Implementation: A Theoretical Framework* (6 March 2012), available at http://ssrn.com/abstract=2017312. In this chapter, references to civil society generally encompass the latter approach, that this designation encompasses members of society that are both non-governmental and not primarily profit-oriented enterprises, such as businesses and industry groups.

[7] See Global Witness, 'About Us', available at www.globalwitness.org/about-us.

[8] Global Witness, *A Crude Awakening* (1 December 1999), available at www.globalwitness.org/library/crude-awakening.

[9] *Ibid.* 4.

including Bono, Mo Ibrahim, George Soros, Oxfam and Transparency International UK.[10] These activists formed a coalition to advocate tax information disclosure. They issued further reports and launched two significant campaigns in 2002: Publish What You Pay (PWYP) and the Extractive Industries Transparency Initiative (EITI).[11] PWYP and EITI are interconnected initiatives that explicitly link confidentiality in tax payments and resource royalties to ongoing poverty in autocratic countries.[12]

As tax transparency developed into a global campaign through the PWYP and EITI coalition, other activists sought to expand these principles to all multinationals, in all industries. In 2003, Richard Murphy, a UK accountant, economist and tax justice activist, issued a paper calling for broad PWYP-style disclosure rules for all publicly traded companies.[13] He sought disclosure of global corporate structure, inter-company prices and tax payments made in every jurisdiction in which companies do business. Murphy later called these principles country-by-country reporting (CBCR), and he became an active proponent of the effort to introduce CBCR as a global policy reform measure.[14] A growing number of international NGOs became supporters of CBCR, including some of those that had already been active in PWYP, as well as the Task Force on Financial Integrity and Economic Development,[15] the Tax Justice Network,[16] ActionAid UK[17] and Christian Aid.[18]

---

10 See, e.g., William MacNamara and Christopher Thompson, 'EU closer to US-style financial reform', *Financial Times*, 3 March 2011, available at www.ft.com/intl/cms/s/0/32b8327e-45ce-11e0-acd8-00144feab49a.html#ixzz1FcK0UAYW.

11 The founding members of PWYP also included the Catholic Overseas Development Agency, the Open Society Institute and Save the Children UK. Publish What You Pay, 'History', available at www.publishwhatyoupay.org/about/history; EITI, 'History of EITI', available at http://eiti.org/eiti/history.

12 See PWYP, 'About "Objectives"', available at www.publishwhatyoupay.org/about/objectives.

13 Richard Murphy, *Reporting Turnover and Tax by Location, Association for Accountancy and Business Affairs Limited* (2003), available at www.richard.murphy.dial.pipex.com/A%20New%20International%20Accounting%20Standard.pdf.

14 Murphy has employed traditional media, such as articles and editorials in mainstream newspapers, as well as online and social media to advance his views on tax justice. See Tax Research UK, www.taxresearch.org.uk/Blog/; The Tax Justice Network, www.taxjusticenet.org.

15 Task Force on Financial Integrity and Economic Development, www.financialtaskforce.org/about/overview/ ('a consortium of governments and

Expanding the movement for tax transparency beyond the resource (extractive industry) sector enabled CBCR proponents to identify broader connections between the taxation of multinationals, development in poor countries and the fiscal health of countries in general. While Global Witness and the resource sector activists identified corruption as the main perpetrator of fiscal problems and underdevelopment in poor countries, CBCR activists seek to connect both the underdevelopment of poor countries and the deteriorating fiscal situation in rich and poor countries alike to the systemic undertaxation of multinationals.[19] This frames undertaxation of multinationals as not only a problem for poor countries, but also a global problem that threatens the ability of all countries to tax effectively. Moreover, it frames the problem as one that is not limited to corruption or lack of compliance on the part of business or government, but rather as a rule of law problem, located in the foundational tax structure that every nation employs. CBCR activists thus characterize confidentiality in tax transactions among multinationals and governments as a generalized problem for development, whether or not these transactions involved legal payments and whether or not they were connected to corruption per se.

Some of these groups embraced tax transparency for its own sake, as a guard against 'venal states and unscrupulous officials'.[20] Others, such as ActionAid UK and Christian Aid, began to include tax transparency as a cause, packaged with other appeals to justice and human rights, including 'just and democratic governance', to be pursued on a global basis.[21]

---

research and advocacy organizations [that] focuses on achieving greater transparency in the global financial system for the benefit of developing countries').

16 Tax Justice Network, www.taxjusticenet.org. The Tax Justice Network is a British-based organization that was founded by Richard Murphy and John Christensen in 2003. See Memorandum and Articles of Association, available at www.taxjustice.net/cms/upload/pdf/TJN__Memorandum_Filed.pdf.

17 ActionAid UK, 'How to Stop Tax Dodging', available at www.actionaid.org.uk/102021/how_to_stop_tax_dodging.html.

18 Christian Aid, *Accounting for Change: Shifting Sands* (November 2010), available at www.christianaid.org.uk/images/accounting-for-change-shifting-sands.pdf.

19 See, e.g., Christian Aid, *supra* note 18, at 1.

20 Fenster, *supra* note 4, at 3.

21 See, e.g., ActionAid UK, *Annual Report 2010* (2010) 9, available at www.actionaid.org.uk/102636/where_did_your_money_go_in_2010.html (adding tax disclosure to its list of causes that include advocacy on behalf of women's rights, rights to education, security and food).

B. Informational and Political Goals

The immediate goal of the tax transparency movement is to expand public knowledge about the global profits earned by multinationals, but the ultimate goal is to spur widespread tax reform movements as societies react to the knowledge so obtained. Activists seek to present as an empirical fact a global fiscal compromise that systemically allows multinationals to escape taxation in ways that are foreseeable and expected, if not deliberately intended by law-makers. CBCR activists may uncover corruption and non-compliance by business and government as a feature of this global compromise, but that is not the only or perhaps even the primary target. Instead, they seek to expose the legal and institutional structure that allows multinationals to escape taxation even under full compliance with all applicable tax laws. This is a substantive expansion of the transparency goals sought under the PWYP regime. There, the goal is to expose collaborations between business and governments that foster corruption and non-compliance with tax laws; under CBCR, the goal is also to expose collaborations between business and governments that foster undertaxation of multinationals as a matter of systemic design.

The chosen mechanism for knowledge expansion is to overcome existing rules that either safeguard the confidentiality of tax information or otherwise introduce complexity in ways that impede assessment of a company's financial situation even when information is publicly available. The confidentiality and complexity to be overcome lies in current legal disclosure standards, which require multinationals to publish only limited and piecemeal information about their operations. No one country requires multinationals to provide a globally comprehensive picture of their geographic operations, inter-company transfers or tax payments.[22] As a result, multinationals use various complex financial strategies and multijurisdictional structures to locate profit in ways that are often difficult (practically or politically) for their home or headquarters countries to track, and all but impossible for the public to monitor or understand.[23]

---

22 See, e.g., Lynnley Browning, 'Insight: Microsoft use of low-tax havens drives down tax bill', *Reuters*, 27 July 2011, available at www.reuters.com/article/2011/07/27/us-microsoft-tax-idUSTRE76Q6OB20110727.

23 Richard Murphy, *Country by Country Reporting: Holding Multinational Corporations to Account Wherever They Are* (June 2009), available at www.financialtaskforce.org/wp-content/uploads/2009/06/Final_CbyC_Report_Published.pdf.

Tax transparency is offered as the solution to this systemic problem. For example, under CBCR standards, multinational companies would disclose their worldwide geographic locations, the names of all of their subsidiaries in these locations, their market and inter-company commercial and financial transactions, their labor costs and employee numbers, their assets in each country, their tax assessments and payments in each country, and additional technical tax details.[24] CBCR is thus not tax policy reform but instead is accounting disclosure reform, to be implemented through securities regulations applicable to large public corporations in their home-base countries.[25] Most governments already collect some of this information, such as inter-company pricing practices and actual tax payments made by companies to the home government even if they do not permit its public disclosure. But tax transparency activists also seek information that governments do not necessarily collect, sometimes notoriously so, such as chains of corporate ownership, the identity of beneficiaries, and the payment of taxes to foreign countries.[26]

The legal challenge for achieving disclosure is whether any of this information, whether currently collected by governments or not, constitutes '[p]ublic business [that] is the public's business', as to which the public has 'the right to know'.[27] In most cases, national corporate privacy laws suggest that it is not: tax information is typically protected from public scrutiny by strict confidentiality rules.[28] Certain persons who are deemed to have a 'material interest' in a specific taxpayer's return, such as, in the case of corporations, 'any bona fide shareholder of record owning 1 percent or more of the outstanding stock of such corporation', are entitled to obtain such returns.[29] However, public disclosure of any information obtained under this exception is prohibited, even if lawfully

---

[24] See, e.g., Christian Aid, *supra* note 18, at 2 (setting out specific information to be disclosed); Tax Justice Network, *Country-by-Country Reporting: How to Make Multinational Companies More Transparent* (March 2008), available at www.taxjustice.net/cms/upload/pdf/Country-by-country_reporting_-_080322.pdf.

[25] Richard Murphy, 'Why is Country-by-Country Financial Reporting by Multinational Companies so Important?', available at www.taxresearch.org.uk/Documents/CountrybyCountryReporting.pdf.

[26] See, e.g., Kelly Carr and Brian Grow, 'Special Report: A Little House of Secrets on the Great Plains', *Reuters*, 28 June 2011.

[27] Fenster, *supra* note 4, at 19.

[28] In the United States, for example, tax information is protected pursuant to federal statute, with high penalties for disclosure. IRC s. 6103. Canada has a similar rule. See Canada Income Tax Act of 1985 ss. 239(2.2), 241.

[29] IRC 6103(d)(e)(1)(D)(iii).

obtained by the shareholder. The prohibition cannot be overcome by freedom of information requests.[30] Placing new reporting requirements under securities compliance rules rather than within the tax code would overcome this problem.[31] Accordingly, it is within securities regulations, and not tax codes, that tax transparency activists seek to counter the confidentiality status quo as a matter of both government policy choice and business practice.

Transparency proponents suggest that numerous constituencies would use the information gathered through more comprehensive tax disclosure requirements to make better-informed market decisions. Perhaps the primary intended audience for this use of tax transparency is investors, who would ostensibly have more information to make informed choices with respect to investing in 'unstable regimes, tax havens, war zones, and other sensitive areas'.[32] In the United States, giving shareholders access to corporate tax information by making corporate tax returns public records was an early feature of the modern corporate income tax, but it was quickly overcome under pressure from business lobbyists.[33] Reviving tax transparency as a matter of shareholder interest places the issue squarely within the corporate social responsibility paradigm, in which activists hope to alter what they perceive as negative corporate behavior by enlisting the power of public and consumer opinion.[34] Similarly targeted constituencies include workers, suppliers and customers, who would have more information about the social attributes of entities with which they seek to transact.[35] Although opponents of transparency often dismiss this appeal, recent empirical research suggests that the market

---

30 5 USC 552(b)(3) (exception from Freedom of Information Act disclosure for information otherwise protected by statute).

31 See, e.g., Steven Mark Levy, 'How the FBAR is Used' in *Federal Money Laundering Regulations, Banking, Corporate and Securities Compliance* (2003, rev. 2011) ch. 10.04.

32 Raymond Baker, 'Foreword' in Murphy, *supra* note 23, at 4.

33 See 44 Congress Rec. 4000 (1909) (Senate debate in the Payne-Aldrich Tariff Act of 1909, the predecessor of the current US corporate income tax system); Pomp, *supra* note 5, at 387–8 (discussing the efforts of the Illinois Manufacturing Association to prevent corporate tax disclosure).

34 See, e.g., Christen Broecker, 'Better the Devil You Know: Home State Approaches to Transnational Corporate Accountability' (2008) 41 *New York University Journal of International Law and Politics* 159.

35 Murphy, *supra* note 23, at 14–16; see also Lisa Misol, 'Private Companies and the Public Interest: Why Corporations Should Welcome Global Human Rights Rules', Human Rights Watch, *World Report 2006*.

responds positively to firms that are identified as meeting corporate social responsibility goals.[36]

Even so, the appeal to the market for information raises the specter that information flow can have unintended consequences on the behavior of market participants. In the brief historical US experience with corporate tax disclosure, opponents argued that publishing corporate tax returns failed to increase revenue, encouraged tax evasion,[37] and served to give business rivals something of value to the detriment of the taxpayer.[38] A similar phenomenon is seen in the corporate social responsibility world. For example, a campaign that successfully induces change in one company or region may fail because another company or region 'pick[s] up where their more socially responsible competitors had left off, and even significantly improv[es] their profitability vis-à-vis their foreign competitors as a result of their decision not to adopt and adhere to corporate codes of conduct'.[39] No empirical data has been compiled to determine the extent to which these potential costs would outweigh the potential benefits of disclosure.

Transparency advocates have not articulated direct solutions to these potential unintended consequences, but this may be because market participants are not the only audience, and may not even be the primary audience, for tax transparency. Instead, the broader audience for the information to be gathered through tax transparency appears to be an informed tax-paying public that uses its collective political influence to name and shame multinationals as specific contributors to underdevelopment. CBCR thus identifies 'stakeholder groups', such as those supporting PWYP and CBCR, as the primary users of information, who will use it to 'monitor corrupt practices, corporate governance, tax payments, and world trade flows'.[40] CBCR also identifies citizens in developing countries, who would have more oversight with respect to who owns the companies that are trading in their countries, and what these companies are actually paying in taxes.[41] The clear goal is to activate social pressure

---

[36] See Ioannis Ioannou and George Serafeim, *The Impact of Corporate Social Responsibility on Investment Recommendations*, Harvard Business School Working Paper 11-017, available at www.hbs.edu/research/pdf/11-017.pdf.

[37] Pomp, *supra* note 5, at 392, citing Sidney Ratner, *Taxation and Democracy in America* (1967).

[38] 'Cost of publicity scored in Treasury', *New York Times*, 3 September 1925, 1 (citing Treasury Secretary, Andrew Mellon).

[39] Broecker, *supra* note 34.

[40] Raymond Baker, 'Foreword' in Murphy, *supra* note 23, at 4.

[41] CBCR opponents reject these claimed benefits, as discussed below.

both on multinationals that seem to avoid paying an appropriate share of taxation on a global scale, as well as on governments that seem to avoid insisting that such a share be paid. As one extractive industry representative put it, 'morality has entered the tax lexicon and … the naming and shaming of companies in the media, … are difficult [developments] for multinational companies'.[42]

C. Precedent for the Power of Public Engagement

There is reason to anticipate that tax transparency would provoke negative public reaction. One example is found in the copper mining industry in Zambia, where the government has been collecting revenues of just 0.6 per cent of profits each year.[43] A leaked tax audit that led to the publication of this low tax burden on a highly profitable industry created moral pressure on mining operators in Zambia, who were quickly labeled 'tax dodgers' by the media.[44] Strictly speaking, these companies were not dodging tax, but were compliant with the tax rules imposed upon them by Zambia. The problem is that these obligations seemed too low in the mind of the public. The undertaxation of its mining industry thus generated moral pressure on Zambia's government itself: media stories about the low taxation of the copper mining companies created embarrassment for the country and the government faced institutional pressure from the International Monetary Fund to address the situation.[45]

---

[42] Paul Skinner, 'Managing the Tax Affairs of a Multi National Company in a Globalising World' (notes of speech delivered 10 January 2006), at www.riotinto.com/media/18435_presentations_2311.asp.

[43] See SCIAF, 'Zambia', available at http://sciaf.live.visionwt.com/ where_we_work/africa/zambia; Counter Balance, *The Mopani Copper Mine, Zambia: How European Development Money has Fed a Mining Scandal* (December 2010), available at www.counterbalance-eib.org/wp-content/uploads/2011/03/Mopani-Report-English-Web.pdf.

[44] See joint press release by Centre for Trade Policy and Development (CTPD), Counter Balance, Eurodad, Oxfam and Tax Justice Network, 'Mopani Copper Mines is dodging taxes in Zambia', 10 February 2011, available at www.ctpd.org.zm/index.php?option=com_content&view=article&id=133:mopani-copper-mines-is-dodging-taxes-in-zambia&catid=66:blogs&Itemid=124.

[45] Mutale Kapekele, 'Government saving face on mine tax issue', *The Zambia Post Online*, 15 June 2011, available at www.postzambia.com:3128/post-read_article.php?articleId=21201; 'IMF urges Zambia to up mine taxes to fight poverty', *Lusaka Times*, 5 March 2010, available at www.lusakatimes.com/2010/03/05/imf-urges-zambia-to-up-mine-taxes-to-fight-poverty/.

While Zambia's low tax rates on copper mining provided a specific point of focus for development-oriented activists, the connection between the undertaxation of multinationals and deteriorating fiscal conditions in the rich world is creating a more generalized pressure on a global scale. The emerging international prominence of the tax transparency movement coincides with other grassroots efforts, such as the 'Uncut' and 'Occupy' movements, which have mobilized public agitation against the rules that allow multinationals to escape their tax obligations.[46] UK Uncut began as a protest against the propensity of some of the European Union's richest citizens and corporations to legally escape their tax obligations even as governments were calling for major social program cuts to counter mounting fiscal crises.[47] Momentum quickly spread throughout the world, with affiliated Uncut groups forming at the national level in the United States, Canada, Europe and Australia, as well as at the sub-national level with affiliate state- and city-based groups.[48] The Occupy movement picked up on and further expanded the social

---

[46] See, e.g., Cristobal Young, 'Momentum for a millionaire's tax', *Boston Review*, 7 December 2011, available at www.bostonreview.net/BR36.6/cristobal_young_occupy_movement_future.php; Allison Kilkenny, '"We're Not Broke": The Movement that Helped Spark Occupy Wall Street', *The Nation*, 13 January 2012, available at www.thenation.com/blog/165635/were-not-broke-movement-helped-spark-occupy-wall-street.

[47] UK Uncut, www.ukuncut.org.uk/.

[48] For a few examples, see US Uncut, www.usuncut.org/; Canada Uncut, http://canadauncut.net/; Australia Uncut, www.facebook.com/pages/Australia-Uncut/191927247514953; Portugal Uncut, http://portugaluncut.blogspot.com/; Greece Uncut, www.facebook.com/greeceuncut; US Uncut Wisconsin, www.facebook.com/usuncutwi; US Uncut Wisconsin-Milwaukee, www.facebook.com/pages/US-Uncut-WisconsinMilwaukee/199736063379233; US Uncut Florida, www.facebook.com/pages/US-Uncut-Florida/136622739740210. US Uncut was formed after a small group of activists in the United States heard about the UK Uncut Movement and decided to join the protest. Interview with Joanne Gifford, cofounder of US Uncut, 21 September 2011, notes on file with the author; see also Dominic Rushe and Matthew Taylor, 'UK Uncut inspires US groups to attack cuts and tax avoidance', *The Guardian*, 25 February 2011, available at www.guardian.co.uk/uk/2011/feb/25/uk-uncut-us-groups-cuts. For the article that inspired the movement in the United States, see Johann Hari, 'Vision: Everyday Brits are in revolt against wealthy tax cheats: can we do that here?', *AlterNet*, 5 February 2011, available at www.alternet.org/teaparty/149806/vision%3A_everyday_brits_are_in_revolt_against_wealthy_tax_cheats_–_can_we_do_that_here/.

influence of the rhetoric and ideas from the Uncut movement, making the taxation of multinationals a front page news item.[49]

These groups have been responsible for public protests involving hundreds of thousands of individuals responding to media reports of undertaxation of businesses juxtaposed with large cuts to social programs.[50] Because of tax confidentiality, journalists often cannot clearly demonstrate the fact of non-payment of taxes, nor why taxes are underpaid despite reported profits, and it is likely that many of the protestors have little or no understanding of the tax rules at play. In one case, a company representative for General Electric, one of the major names implicated in the Uncut protests, felt compelled to respond to the criticisms but offered incoherent and contradictory explanations, leading to increased confusion with little resolution in the public discourse.[51] This kind of interplay may explain why so much protest has been activated by anecdote: publication of stories abound that involve allegations of tax dodging by well-known global companies such as Verizon, Apple and Google. Bono, one of the supporters of EITI and PWYP, has

---

[49] Kilkenny, *supra* note 46.

[50] See, e.g., Jerome E. Roos, '100,000 rally against austerity in Portugal – in pictures', *Roarmag.org*, http://roarmag.org/2011/10/100000-rally-against-austerity-in-portugal-in-pictures/; US Uncut Minnesota, 'Occupy Wall Street movement reports 80 arrested today in protests', *ABC News*, 24 September 2011, available at http://usuncutmn.blogspot.com/2011/09/occupy-wall-street-movement-reports-80.html; Rae Gomes, 'Love the iPhone, hate the tax cheat: US Uncut protests Apple, and Apple gets aggressive', *AlterNet*, 8 June 2011, available at www.alternet.org/vision/151252/love_the_iphone,_hate_the_tax_cheat%3A_us_uncut_protests_apple,_and_apple_gets_aggressive_/.

[51] David Kocieniewski, 'GE's strategies let it avoid taxes altogether', *New York Times*, 24 March 2011, available at www.nytimes.com/2011/03/25/business/economy/25tax.html?_r=1&scp=3&sq=ge&st=cse; Jake Tapper, 'General Electric paid no federal taxes in 2010', *ABC News*, available at http://abcnews.go.com/Politics/general-electric-paid-federal-taxes-2010/story?id=13224558. For a discussion of GE's contradictory responses, see Kim Peterson, 'GE Chief Defends Company's 2010 Tax Bill', *MSN Money*, 1 April 2011, available at http://money.msn.com/top-stocks/post.aspx?post=a0b9a8f0-4c1a-4387-b76f-dc71e05e90d0 (reporting that GE'S Jeffrey Immelt stated that '[l]ike any American, we do like to keep our tax rate low … but we do it in a compliant way and there are no exceptions', but that 'the company appeared to contradict itself. First, spokeswoman Anne Eisele told AFP that "GE did not pay U.S. federal taxes last year because we did not owe any". But the same spokeswoman told Business Insider that GE did pay U.S. federal income tax in the form of prepayments – and when the final 2010 tax bill is determined this fall, the company may have to pay more.').

himself been the target of public scrutiny in response to publication of his own group's offshore tax avoidance strategies.[52]

Through these anecdotes, the tax transparency movement brought international tax avoidance to prominence in the public imagination. The rise of the movement itself illustrates that continued tax confidentiality has social costs, not least of which is a crisis of confidence in the tax system itself. Public protest may also take other, less visible forms, such as an increase in direct appeals to governing representatives.[53] The surge of public interest in the tax transparency, Uncut and Occupy movements suggest that the public will likely react with anger to the information disclosed through tax transparency. On the other hand, there is some concern that the publication of tax information will act as an information guide to other taxpayers, who will be emboldened to increase their own legally sanctioned tax avoidance strategies as a result.

The tension between confidentiality and compliance has long been a subject of tax policy debate. In an early US example, Horace Greeley argued that the US civil war-era practice of publishing income tax information 'has gone far toward equalizing the payments of income tax by the rogues with that of honest men'.[54] Those in favor of protecting privacy argue that increased disclosure of tax information would provide taxpayers with both incentive and a roadmap to decreasing their own taxes, while impeding the ability of governments to maintain an image of the tax system as an even-handed instrument of the rule of law.[55] Those in favor of more transparency argue that tax information disclosure either increases or has negligible effects on compliance.[56] Insufficient empirical evidence has been marshaled to support a clear answer for the question.

---

[52] Adam Gabbatt, 'U2 Glastonbury tax protest: activists condemn "heavy-handed" security', *Guardian*, 25 June 2011, available at www.guardian.co.uk/music/2011/jun/25/u2-bono-tax-protest-glastonbury.

[53] In the United States, there is evidence of such increased 'citizen advocacy' over the past decade. Congressional Management Foundation, *Communicating with Congress: How Citizen Advocacy is Changing Mail Operations on Capitol Hill* (2011), available at www.congressfoundation.org/storage/documents/CMF_Pubs/cwc-mail-operations.pdf ('most congressional offices have seen a 200–1,000% increase in constituent communication volume in the past decade').

[54] Richard F. Janssen, 'Income tax snooping through history', *Wall Street Journal*, 6 May 1970.

[55] See, e.g., Joshua Blank, 'In Defense of Individual Tax Privacy' (2011) 61 *Emory Law Journal* 265 (focusing only on individual, not corporate, taxpayers).

[56] See, e.g., Stephen Mazza, 'Taxpayer Privacy and Tax Compliance' (2003) 51 *University of Kansas Law Review* 1065; Marjorie E. Kornhauser, 'Doing the

An experiment with greater disclosure might provide a source of data for necessary analysis, but the contemporary public discourse over tax transparency suggests that lack of empirical evidence will not impede strong advocacy on either side.

Having asserted a need for transparency to create public oversight and participation in future tax reforms, the question for activists is how best to achieve disclosure. Longstanding national protections for confidentiality of tax and financial data present legal obstacles to reform, while an entrenched and organized constituency with high stakes in preserving the status quo present political obstacles. Activists need to navigate ways to overcome these. They also need to determine whether their goals can be achieved by overcoming the legal and political obstacles in only one or a few countries, or whether global reforms are necessary, and if the latter, how this can be achieved in a world of independent sovereign states. The strategies invoked by tax transparency activists to date illuminate these ongoing challenges.

III. THREE PATHWAYS TO REFORM

Tax transparency activists have taken three distinct yet interrelated pathways to tax information disclosure. First, they have tried to overcome political obstacles by appealing directly to multinational companies, seeking voluntary adoption of global disclosure commitments. Second, they have tried to overcome legal obstacles by appealing to national legislators to enact new disclosure laws that circumvent existing confidentiality rules. They have done this both in the countries that serve as headquarters for multinationals (typically rich countries) and those that serve as hosts for multinational activities (especially in the extractive industries, typically very poor countries). Finally, they have tried to overcome both political and legal obstacles by appealing to the international tax community, namely, an elite global network of tax officials and international business interests that define global tax policy in the form of 'soft' tax law – norms and standards delivered through models, reports and guidance.

Full Monty: Will Publicizing Tax Information Increase Compliance?' (2005) 18 *Canadian Journal of Law and Jurisprudence* 1.

A. Appeal to Multinationals: Voluntary Compliance

The first pathway to tax transparency is to identify the multinational taxpayer itself as the best source of tax information. The 1999 Global Witness report took this approach, calling upon resource-rich countries, companies engaged in the extraction of minerals and fossil fuels, and industry watchdog groups to work together to end the secrecy that fostered corruption.[57] EITI and PWYP, the initiatives that ultimately arose from Global Witness's advocacy work, both seek voluntary disclosure on the part of multinationals regarding payments made in connection with extraction activities, including tax and royalty fees.[58]

Transparency activists have had some success in their direct appeal efforts. Rio Tinto, one of the world's largest mining conglomerates, was an early adopter of PWYP standards and its directors attribute its commitment to transparency to the theory that transparency translates into greater profitability in the long term. As one director put it, 'We do subscribe to EITI; we subscribe to open transparent taxes. We have actually been the first of the big mining companies to publish our taxes on a country by country basis. And again educate and inform everyone about the benefits of stable fiscal regimes, leading to stable investment regimes, leading to more spending.'[59] The World Bank reports that 'Fifty of the world's largest oil, gas, and mining companies support and participate in the EITI process – through their operations in implementing countries, their international commitments, and their industry associations.'[60]

Appealing to companies to voluntarily disclose their own tax practices may make transparency initiatives more palatable to those concerned with confidentiality as a legally protected right, but voluntary disclosure presents major challenges in terms of verifying that the information

---

[57] Global Witness, 'A Crude Awakening', *supra* note 8, at 13.

[58] EITI and PWYP both supplement the international movement to eliminate corporate bribery of elected officials, which in the United States culminated in the Foreign Corrupt Practices Act of 1977 (FCPA). EITI and PWYP are broader than the FCPA in that the FCPA is intended to end illegal payments of bribes, kickbacks and the like to government officials, while EITI and PWYP focus on all payments to foreign governments, including legal ones.

[59] 'Rio Tinto 2011 Interim Results, Q&A Transcript', available at www.riotinto.com/documents/FinancialResults/Rio_Tinto_2011_Interim_Results_QA_transcript.pdf.

[60] World Bank Group, *Voices of Transparency* (World Bank, 2011), available at http://siteresources.worldbank.org/INTOGMC/Resources/EITI_Final_Brochure.pdf.

divulged is both truthful and comprehensive.[61] The lack of enforcement mechanisms implied by voluntary compliance is likely to lead to under-reporting of information that may be interpreted as negative by the public, and over-reporting of the converse. If voluntary disclosure becomes a marketing exercise, the activists' goals would not be realized. One way to mitigate this result is to enlist the voluntary cooperation of governments in overseeing the voluntary disclosure, in partnership with the multinationals. EITI activists have sought this cooperation by appealing to legislators in the United States, Canada, Australia and elsewhere to enact PWYP standards on a national basis.

B. Appeal to National Legislators: Unilateral Adoption of Standards

A decade after the initial Global Witness Report, PWYP activists appeared to achieve success in achieving national legislative reform that would mandate transparency. In early 2009, the Canadian Parliament considered Bill C-300, An Act Respecting Corporate Accountability for the Activities of Mining, Oil, or Gas Corporations in Developing Countries.[62] Later that year the US Senate considered a similar bill, entitled the Energy Security through Transparency Act of 2009.[63] Both bills called for regulatory disclosure reform by way of PWYP principles as well as cooperative effort by the government through international institutions and the EITI to gain international consensus in disclosure rules.

After extensive lobbying by the extractive industries in each country, both bills failed.[64] Nevertheless, in 2010, the US Congress passed a

---

61 Thus while Rio Tinto advertises its EITI-compliant partnerships with Mongolia, Guinea and Mozambique, the media in Zimbabwe reports that Rio Tinto has not extended the same efforts there. See 'Rio Tinto 2011 Interim Results', *supra* note 59, at 9; Veneranda Langa, 'Mining companies should divulge earnings', *Newsday Zimbabwe*, 29 August 2011, available at www.newsday.co.zw/article/2011-08-29-mining-companies-should-divulge-earnings.

62 John McKay, 'John McKay's Bill C-300 on corporate accountability passes 2nd Reading, moves to Committee Stage' (23 April 2009), available at www.johnmckaymp.on.ca/newsshow.asp?int_id=80507.

63 S.1700, Energy Security through Transparency Act of 2009, 111th Congress, 1st Session, 23 September 2009, available at http://thomas.loc.gov/cgi-bin/query/z?c111:S.1700.

64 For an overview of the Canadian mining industry response to Act 300, see Fasken Martineau, 'Sharp Criticism for Bill C-300: Lawyers Tell Parliamentary Committee Private Member's Bill Threatens Canada's Minerals Industry' (26

PWYP initiative in the form of a two-page addendum to the Dodd-Frank Wall Street Reform Act, a bill designed to compensate for the lax regulation that had been pinpointed as the cause of the 2008–2009 economic crisis in the United States.[65] Commentators suggest that the extractive industry was caught by surprise by the inclusion of PWYP in the bill.[66] The industry has since engaged in an aggressive campaign to prevent the implementation of the law by forestalling the issuance of necessary regulations, which were due to be in place by 15 April 2011 but are still forthcoming.[67] Such regulations, if they are ever issued, are now expected to eviscerate the disclosure requirements to such an extent as to make them ineffective. However, the news of successful passage of legislation in the United States, no matter how toothless in the absence of

---

November 2009), available at www.fasken.com/firm-opposes-bill-c-300-in-ottawa/; Prospectors and Developers Association of Canada (PDAC), 'Corporate Social Responsibility in the Mineral Industry', *Issues and Advocacy*, available at www.pdac.ca/pdac/advocacy/csr/index.html (explaining the role PDAC played in opposing the passage of Act 300). For an overview of the US mining industry opposition to S.1700, see Ken Silverstein, 'As oil pours into Gulf, oil industry fights anti-corruption measure', *Harpers*, 11 May 2010, available at http://harpers.org/archive/2010/05/hbc-90007021 (explaining the opposition of the American Petroleum Institute, a trade association that represents the US oil and gas industry).

65 H.R. 4173, Dodd-Frank Wall Street Reform and Consumer Protection Act of 2010, s. 1504; see also Publish What You Pay, 'The Cardin-Lugar Amendment (Dodd-Frank 1504)', available at www.publishwhatyoupay.org/about/stock-listings/cardin-lugar-amendment-dodd-frank-1504.

66 See, e.g., Daniel Firger, 'Lifting the Resource Curse: Will Dodd-Frank Do the Trick?' (28 September 2010), available at http://industry-news.org/2010/09/28/daniel-firger-lifting-the-resource-curse-will-dodd-frank-do-the-trick-2/; Rebekah J. Poston and Carine M. Williams, *Extraction and Compliance: New Reporting Requirements for Issues Involving Oil, Natural Gas or Minerals, Thomson Reuters Accelus*, 3 November 2010, available at www.complinet.com/dodd-frank/news/analysis/article/extraction-and-compliance-new-reporting-requirements-for-issuers-involving-oil-natural-gas-or-minerals.html.

67 See, e.g., Rep. Barney Frank *et al.*, Letter to the Securities and Exchange Commission, 12 February 2012, available at www.sec.gov/comments/s7-42-10/s74210-162.pdf (correspondence from Members of the US House of Representatives who support the extractive industry revenue transparency provision, expressing their concern that 'the Commission is far behind in meeting the statutory deadline' and stating that '[m]oreover, we are aware of efforts by industry to press the SEC to throw out a year and half of important work and start the rulemaking process anew, or to release a watered down rule that does not reflect the statutory language as well as the legislative intent of Section 1504').

regulatory implementation, created some international momentum in Europe[68] and is bolstered by the recent adoption by Australia of a pilot EITI program entitled the Mining for Development Initiative.[69]

There is precedent for disclosure of at least some tax details in the United States, historically at the federal level but also based upon state practice. Nationally, the public has had varying levels of access to tax information throughout US history, with current standards of confidentiality being the most restrictive.[70] While the US states generally reflect the federal stance, the state of Wisconsin stands out as an exception.[71] Specifically, for a US$4 fee per disclosure, any resident of Wisconsin may obtain information about the amount of net income tax or gift tax reported by another Wisconsin individual or corporation.[72] The law presents a few barriers to disclosure. First, the requesting person must provide the exact name and address of the company for which the information is requested, so that existing confidentiality surrounding these details will prevent any tax information from being revealed.[73] Second, the information so obtained may not generally be divulged to

---

68 See, e.g., William MacNamara and Christopher Thompson, 'Shell chief's warning on Dodd-Frank', *Financial Times*, 2 March 2011, available at www.ft.com/intl/cms/s/0/f5dcb758-450a-11e0-80e7-00144feab49a.html#axzz1 a4W6lVt8.

69 Commonwealth of Nations, notes on 2011 Commonwealth Heads of Government Meeting, Perth, 28–30 October 2011, available at www.dfat.gov.au/intorgs/commonwealth/index.html; Press Office, Prime Minister Julia Gillard, Launch of Australia Mining Initiative, available at www.pm.gov.au/press-office/launch-australian-mining-initiative.

70 See Congressional Research Service, *Legislative History of Tax Return Confidentiality: Section 6103 of the Internal Revenue Code of 1954 and its Predecessors* (1974); Pomp, *supra* note 5.

71 No other state has a general disclosure rule like Wisconsin's, but a few states have restricted disclosure rules. For example, Iowa and Maine permit limited disclosure for legislative research purposes, and in Massachusetts, information about whether an individual or company has filed a tax return in the state can be obtained upon request (no actual return data may be disclosed, however). See Robert Ellis Smith, Compilation of State and Federal Privacy Laws 65–66, 2002, 2011 Supplement.

72 Wisconsin State 71–78 (2).

73 This barrier is similar to a specific information request made under a tax treaty or tax information exchange agreement with another country. See, e.g., Lee A. Sheppard, 'Don't Ask, Don't Tell, Part 4: Ineffectual Information Sharing', 122 *Tax Notes*, 23 March 2009, 1411; Michael J. McIntyre, 'How to End the Charade of Information Exchange', 56 *Tax Notes International*, 26 October 2009, 255.

another person, effectively preventing the publication of tax information received under request.[74] Yet the statute makes clear that nothing prevents the disclosure of information lawfully obtained from being published in a newspaper or spoken in a public address.

In practice, even this bare minimum of tax disclosure illustrates how information enables advocacy. In Wisconsin, public interest advocates employed the disclosure rule to demonstrate that many well-known and well-respected companies with a heavy local presence do not pay any taxes to the state.[75] To comply with the statute, the advocates have employed public speaking as a primary medium, relying on journalists to take an interest in the stories sufficient to publish the underlying data. This exposure, despite its limitations, attracted the attention of national journalists, who used the information as a means of exploring the distribution of tax burdens within the state as well as in the United States as a whole.[76]

While it is difficult to measure the social and political impact of this kind of advocacy, the example illustrates the concept that peer pressure can be a powerful tool for change. It is not surprising, then, that tax transparency advocates have identified another source of peer pressure as a target for their advocacy campaigns, namely, the international community of tax experts associated with the OECD.

Despite its exclusive membership, this institution's work on tax matters has made it a de facto world tax organization, and it asserts itself as a provider of 'soft law' – internationally accepted standards that may lack the force of law but nevertheless compel law-like adherence by both member and non-member states.[77] The OECD's central role in creating global tax policy lies in its unique institutional capacity for facilitating networking among elite national tax officials and professionals.[78] Its

---

[74] Wisconsin State 71–78 (1) ('This subsection does not prohibit publication by any newspaper of information lawfully derived from such returns or claims for purposes of argument or prohibit any public speaker from referring to such information in any address').

[75] See Institute for Wisconsin's Future, 'Who Does Not Pay Taxes', available at www.wisconsinsfuture.org/.

[76] See David Cay Johnston, 'Wiping out Wisconsin taxes', *Reuters*, 26 August 2011, available at http://blogs.reuters.com/david-cay-johnston/2011/08/26/wiping-out-wisconsin-taxes/.

[77] See Allison Christians, 'Hard Law, Soft Law, and International Taxation' (2007) 25 *Wisconsin International Law Journal* 325.

[78] See, e.g., Yariv Brauner, 'An International Tax Regime in Crystallization' (2003) 56 *Tax Law Review* 259 (identifying the OECD as the key source of international coordination).

main contribution is to produce non-binding norms around which nations can converge.[79] The OECD accordingly describes itself as a 'market leader in developing [tax] standards and guidelines'.[80] As the world's foremost source of 'soft' tax law, the OECD appears to be the most likely forum from which tax transparency activists could launch a global campaign.

C. Appeal to the International Tax Community: Engaging Soft Law

The first signs that CBCR advocates sought international attention emerged in the United Kingdom in 2009, when the UK Tax Minister, Stephen Timms, introduced the concept of CBCR to a tax conference audience. He presented CBCR as a relatively new, grassroots issue that had gained sufficient interest for international policy-makers to consider.[81] Timms argued that in order for CBCR to have a serious chance of being implemented by national governments, it would require international discussion.[82] Subsequently, after an Anglo-French summit, the British Prime Minister and French President suggested that CBCR be debated internationally within the OECD.

The OECD responded by including CBCR on the agenda of a January 2010 meeting of the OECD Global Forum on Transparency and Exchange of Information for Tax Purposes. Stephen Timms used the 2010 meeting of the Global Forum to support discussion of CBCR by the OECD on the grounds that 'there should be transparency about where companies earn their profits and where they pay their tax'. Timms stated that the OECD ought to issue multinational guidelines through a process of discussion among governments, multinationals and civil society, in order to define a standard that would then become globalized through the OECD's soft law channels.[83] As a result, by mid-2010, CBCR had

---

[79] OECD, *The OECD's Current Tax Agenda 2008* (2008) 74–5; see also Sophie Ashley, 'OECD may detract from UN TP work', *Transfer Pricing Week*, 17 May 2011; Tax Justice Network, 'OECD may detract from UN work' (19 May 2011), available at http://taxjustice.blogspot.com/2011/05/oecd-may-detract-from-un-work.html; Tax Justice Network, 'UN versus OECD: not a football match' (23 June 2011), available at http://taxjustice.blogspot.com/2011/06/un-versus-oecd-not-football-match.html.

[80] OECD, *The OECD's Current Tax Agenda 2008*, *supra* note 79.

[81] ActionAid UK takes much of the credit for inciting Timms to this action. See *supra* note 17.

[82] Stephen Timms, Remarks at OECD Tax and Development Conference, Paris, 27 January 2010.

[83] *Ibid.*

arrived on the international stage. Its presence on the OECD's tax agenda launched the activists and their goals into the public consciousness, and prompted a swift response from the international community.

The OECD set up a task force to discuss the issue of CBCR. However, prior to the first meeting, the OECD published a critique of CBCR by William Morris.[84] Morris, the director of tax policy at General Electric (GE) and a well-known international tax lobbyist, is highly visible within the OECD transnational tax network.[85] GE has been labeled by the media as an aggressive tax dodger over several years, so perhaps it is not surprising that its senior tax advisor would take a strong position in opposition to a reform proposal which might force his company to divulge information about the company's tax planning strategies.[86] The publication of Morris's criticism two months prior to the initial meeting of the task force appears to have served mainly as a framing exercise for the OECD's subsequent work.[87]

Morris introduced several arguments in opposition to CBCR. Each of these arguments reflects those made by the extractive industry in its campaign against PWYP, with adjustments to counter specific goals Morris identified as being those of CBCR advocates. Morris' first argument was for the futility of additional disclosure. CBCR would be futile, he argued, first because governments and the public already knew whatever they needed to know about industry tax practices, so that CBCR would not reveal anything new, and second because even if additional

---

84 William Morris, 'Is Country-by-Country Reporting the Answer?' (2010) *OECD Observer* (March) 278.

85 Morris is Senior International Tax Counsel and Director of Tax Policy at GE. In addition, Morris is the Vice Chairman of the Business and Industry Advisory Committee (BIAC) to the OECD, a member of the Tax Policy Group of Business Europe, Chairman of the European Tax Policy Forum and, most recently, Chairman of the Tax Committee at the Confederation of British Industry, 'the UK's top business lobbying organization' according to its own website. Mr Morris previously served as the Associate International Tax Counsel in the Office of Tax Policy of the US Treasury from 1995 until 2000, where he worked on international tax issues including deferral rules.

86 See *supra* note 51.

87 See, e.g., Erving Goffman, *Frame Analysis: An Essay on the Organization of Experience* (1974); David Snow and Robert Benford, 'Framing Processes and Social Movements: An Overview and Assessment' (2000) 26 *Annual Review of Sociology* 11; Kim Fisher, 'Locating Frames in the Discursive Universe', 2 *Social Research Online* 3, available at www.socresonline.org.uk/2/3/4.html; Michael T. Maher, 'Framing: An Emerging Paradigm or a Phase of Agenda Setting' in Stephen D. Reese, *Framing Public Life: Perspectives on Media and our Understanding on the Social World* (2001).

information should come to light, poor countries would be too administratively feeble to make effective use of it.[88] Morris highlighted the futility of the regime against the unnecessarily burdensome compliance costs it would entail. These costs would be unsupported in his view, since companies already generally try to get compliance 'right'.[89] This statement echoes those made by extractive industry representatives, including corporate officers who have voluntarily adopted PWYP in their own reporting and advocate on its behalf more broadly.[90]

Morris then argued that CBCR poses a risk that firms will 'respond'.[91] While he did not state what response was anticipated, the implication was clear: if one country adopts CBCR, multinationals will flee to another country that does not. This argument has been used consistently by lobbyists to resist tax reform efforts in myriad contexts in the United States.[92] It was also put forth by the extractive industries in the United States and Canada to terminate the 2009 PWYP legislative efforts in these two countries.[93]

There is a basic internal inconsistency in this argument. Either CBCR will be futile, unnecessary and useless to shareholders and governments alike, or it will be so effective and useful that it will cause multinationals to realize they can no longer expect to pay nominal or no taxes in these countries. Both cannot simultaneously be true. Given the level of industry opposition to disclosure, the success of CBCR appears to be the more likely case.

It seems problematic that the OECD would pre-emptively attack CBCR using its newsletter as a platform for industry self-interest presented as observation or commentary. But perhaps what is most striking about Morris's article is the way it frames the issues surrounding CBCR so narrowly. There is no acknowledgement in this article of the

---

88 See Morris, *supra* note 84.

89 *Ibid.*

90 See Skinner, *supra* note 42.

91 *Ibid.*

92 See, e.g., Impact of US Tax Rules on International Competitiveness: Hearing Before the H. Comm. on Ways and Means, 106th Congress 64 (1999) (statement of Fred F. Murray, Vice President for Tax Policy National Foreign Trade Council, Inc.), available at http://frwebgate.access.gpo.gov/cgi-bin/getdoc.cgi?dbname=106_house_hearings&docid=f:66775.pdf.

93 See Martineau, *supra* note 64 (detailing Canadian mining industry opposition to PWYP in Canada); Silverstein, *supra* note 64 (detailing US extractive industry opposition to PWYP in the United States).

reasons why CBCR advocates seek disclosure reform as a substantive matter, and why they seek an oversight role for civil society in international tax matters as a procedural one. By placing the focus purely on estimated costs and predicted outcomes of increased disclosure for companies and, perhaps, governments, the article misses completely the more fundamental significance of the CBCR movement for transparency in global tax policy-making. This frames the debate about disclosure within the narrow confines of expected behavioral responses of firms and governments to rule change, and refuses to engage with the potentially much more important social and cultural impact that occurs upon the increased availability of information about the taxation of multinationals.

This narrow framing is particularly troublesome in its apparent impact on subsequent OECD study of the subject, which consistently treats the potential social and cultural impacts of CBCR as unnecessary or impossible to assess and therefore not worthy of detailed study. Two months after the OECD Observer article was published, the OECD convened a working group to discuss the issue, and tasked a drafting group to report on the dialogue. The 38-page report, called a 'preparatory note', repeated the narrow focus of the Morris article, discussing at length the predicted costs and outcomes of revised disclosure rules, but leaving aside 'the issue of whether greater transparency could aid public debate on appropriate tax policy' for the reason that this impact would be 'very difficult to assess' because the political discourse would involve 'differing arguments, [that] can be used more or less responsibly'.[94] The preparatory note presents this description as self-evident, and does not explain why the social or cultural impact of information disclosure would be any more or less difficult to assess, or more or less prone to differing arguments than the debate about how disclosure would impact firms or governments or both. The preparatory note was then re-issued as a 46-page report, which purported to present a more detailed consideration of the issue.[95] The report in fact added very little

---

[94] OECD Informal Task Force on Tax and Development, Preparatory Note from the Sub Group on Transparency in Reporting Financial Data by Multinational Corporations, 17 March 2011, available at www.oecd.org/dataoecd/57/4/47521678.pdf.

[95] Oxford Centre for Business Taxation, *Transparency in Reporting Financial Data by Multinational Corporations* (July 2011). This report was authored by a group chaired by Michael Devereaux that included members from Oxford University, the OECD, ActionAid UK, Christian Aid, Rio Tinto, PricewaterhouseCoopers, University of North Carolina and William Morris of GE.

to the analysis, repeating almost verbatim the entirety of the preparatory note, and therefore again dismissing the social and cultural aspects of disclosure advocacy as incapable of assessment without further comment.

This narrow frame is an unfortunate outcome for those interested in the connection between taxation and development, since it intentionally omits, and perhaps even prevents, any discussion about what may be the most important aspect of law and legal change, namely, the social or cultural context in which the law constantly redefines itself. By confining the CBCR discussion to the behavioral impacts of firms and governments, the discussion locks out the very group that is animating the call for change, and chooses to ignore the reasons for this group to seek access as a procedural matter. As a result, the OECD treatment of the subject of transparency entirely and willfully omits all discussion of the oversight role being demanded by civil society as well as why civil society is demanding this role at all. This is a loss for international tax policy discourse, and it particularly underscores the problem of under-representation of poor countries in the soft tax law regime. The underlying goals of the CBCR movement deserve closer inspection, as they hold a key to understanding global tax governance.

IV. IMPLICATIONS FOR GLOBAL TAX GOVERNANCE

In their quest to seek an active participatory role for civil society in matters of international tax policy, tax transparency activists have revealed some enduring structural problems in the development of international tax policy discourse. They have shown that the concerns of poor countries are all but ignored, and they have revealed the extent of control wielded by multinational companies over the global tax policy environment. These characteristics create an institutionally enforced narrowness in international tax policy perspectives.

CBCR proponents seek to alter this institutional structure at the international soft law level, but as they try to move the OECD forward in constructive dialogue, they illustrate the inherently exclusive nature of the OECD, with full participation limited to officials and tax professionals from the world's richest countries. Despite its claim to international consensus, the OECD's main feature is its exclusive membership.[96] Poor countries have always been excluded from full participation.[97]

In recent years the OECD's exclusivity evidently became problematic: it was no longer plausible to claim to be the voice of international consensus when its membership excluded some of the world's biggest and most dynamic economics, including China, India and Brazil.[98] In 2007, the OECD decided to invite some non-member countries to limited and tightly prescribed participation. This was effected through a multi-tier system, in which some countries, such as Brazil, China and India, would be invited into 'enhanced engagement' with the organization, while others would be invited to 'observe' various OECD projects either on an ad hoc basis or regularly, according to internally determined criteria.[99] The OECD suggests both that these roles are similar to full participation, and that in some cases, this level of participation could lead to full membership. The former claim cannot be verified, since OECD meetings are not currently open to observation by the press or other disinterested observers. However, it is clear that accession to full membership has not to date been granted to any of the countries that have been invited to participate on a limited basis, and the view of commentators is that non-member countries can hope for no more than 'second tier' status in the institution.[100]

If the marginalization of poor countries is a troubling factor of OECD exclusivity, it is at least visibly so; by contrast, the marginalization of civil society is another, less obvious aspect of OECD exclusivity. Because it originated as a quasi-governmental organization, the OECD has traditionally limited direct participation by NGOs in its work. It created two internal institutions, the Business and Industry Advisory

---

[96] The membership includes the United States, United Kingdom, Canada, Australia and Western Europe, but no countries in Africa, and very few in South America and Asia. OECD, 'Members and Partners', available at www.oecd.org/document/25/0,3746,en_36734052_36761800_36999961_1_1_1_1,00.html.

[97] In the past, many poor countries were excluded from direct participation because they were viewed as represented through their colonial ties to Europe.

[98] Allison Christians, 'Taxation in a Time of Crisis: Policy Leadership from the OECD to the G20' (2010) 5 *Northwestern Journal of Law and Social Policy* 19.

[99] See OECD, 'Members and Partners', *supra* note 96; OECD Global Relations, 'Non-Member Participation in Formal OECD Bodies', available at www.oecd.org/pages/0,3417,en_36335986_36339055_1_1_1_1_1,00.html.

[100] Arthur Cockfield, 'The Rise of the OECD as Informal "World Tax Organization" Through National Responses to E-Commerce Tax Challenges' (2006) 8 *Yale Journal of Law and Technology* 136 at 185–6.

Counsel to the OECD (BIAC), and the Trade Union Advisory Council to the OECD (TUAC), as liaison groups, tasked with representing the voice of business and labor, respectively, in OECD discussions.[101] In tax policy matters, however, BIAC (currently headed by William Morris) has taken a dominant role, while TUAC has been generally silent.[102]

This has left most OECD tax working parties composed solely of rich-country government officials and business representatives. To the extent that government's job is to represent the voice of civil society, which presumably includes workers, the working party model theoretically represents all viewpoints. But in practice, it is clear that business interests take precedence and are most heavily represented in OECD discussions. This is clear from conversations with industry insiders; it is also suggested by the authorship of many OECD-commissioned reports.

Tax transparency activism is significantly undermining the OECD's claim to universality in consensus building. In demanding a seat at the bargaining table where the OECD intended to discuss CBCR, CBCR activists implicitly expressed a concern about who in society is represented by OECD participants, including the government officials charged to act in the interest of their countries as a whole. Thus CBCR proponents 'conceptualized the state as something distinct from the public, as an entity that at once represents its citizens but is distant from them'.[103]

Tax transparency activism ultimately challenges two assumptions that had heretofore legitimized the OECD's work: first, that government officials represent civil society in their countries, and second, that government officials are working toward the OECD's stated mission, 'to promote policies that will improve the economic and social well-being of people around the world'.[104] If the first of these assumptions held true, there might be little need for civil society to intervene in OECD deliberations. The fact that CBCR advocates seek a place for themselves in OECD deliberations distinct from their country representatives suggest that the first assumption is not held by a growing number of people, including those who are directly represented through the membership of

---

[101] OECD, 'Relations with Business and Labor', available at www.oecd.org/document/53/0,3746,en_2649_34495_1910965_1_1_1_1,00.html.

[102] See Christians, *supra* note 98 (discussing the make-up of OECD working groups and committees).

[103] Fenster, *supra* note 4, at 17.

[104] 'About the Organisation for Economic Co-operation and Development', available at www.oecd.org/pages/0,3417,en_36734052_36734103_1_1_1_1_1,00.html.

their countries in the OECD.[105] OECD reports on the transparency initiative simply do not engage with this issue.

Whether and how the inclusion of civil society in OECD discourse also advances the cause for poor countries in the soft tax law order remains to be seen. If the representativeness of civil society by national officials is challenged, the assumption that the OECD is working toward universally beneficial policies also seems vulnerable. If so, the presence of civil society from rich countries serves to underscore just how imperative it is that either the OECD create a way for poor countries to meaningfully participate in OECD activities, or that the OECD relinquish its grip on international tax in order to allow a more inclusive forum to take its place.[106] To the extent that the message of tax transparency activism is the same message poor countries would bring if they were able to participate as full members in international tax policy circles, transparency advocates may serve in a temporary proxy role for direct participation by poor countries in the OECD.

V. CONCLUSION

The tax transparency movement seems to fundamentally demonstrate, in a way that other tax policy reform efforts have not, that pressure on the system must be applied from without. The movement suggests that individuals and leaders currently involved in tax policy governance cannot be counted on to concentrate on distributing the tax burden in a way that comports with broader social values. It remains to be seen whether awakening public attention to multinational tax planning will provoke sufficient political attention to compel paradigmatic change.

For such change to take place, activists would need not only to activate the release of relevant and usable tax information, but also to engage scholars to examine this data and establish the extent to which and the reasons why multinationals are undertaxed. They would need to indelibly connect that undertaxation, and the policies that create it, to development

---

105 See, e.g., Steve Charnovitz, 'The Illegitimacy of Preventing Civil Society Participation' (2011) 36 *Brooklyn J Int'l L* 891 ('In my view, the value-added from NGOs on the international plane is that they correct for the pathologies of governments and [international organizations]').

106 See Christian Aid, *supra* note 18, at 5 (if an international tax transparency standard is perceived 'as an imposition from the North, it may serve to undermine trust, and points to the need for the genuine engagement of these countries in developing a standard').

failure in poor countries. Finally, they would have to convince lawmakers in rich countries and poor countries alike that the public has an interest in changing this paradigm. Each of these steps will present enormous challenges and many will involve vigorous opposition. The alternative is acquiescence to a global status quo with which fewer and fewer are satisfied, a status quo that includes severe strains on governments and growing pressure on social systems in rich and poor countries. In this context, tax transparency seems a plausible starting point in the quest to understand and empower the engines of economic development and prosperity throughout the world.

13. Global tax information networks: legitimacy in a global administrative state

Miranda Stewart

I. INTRODUCTION

Many commentators have traced the historical and more recent developments in transnational tax information exchange.[1] In a global era, national tax administrators must cooperate with each other and work to build transnational institutions and networks that give them the capacity to enforce tax laws in respect of multinational and mobile capital and labour. This chapter discusses whether national tax administrators are, finally, beginning to achieve the levels of transnational tax cooperation required to maintain national tax sovereignty. This chapter then explores the question of legitimacy of transnational tax information networks, which will be crucial for the long-term sustainability and effectiveness of transnational tax administrative cooperation.

[1] Sol Picciotto, *International Business Taxation as a Study in the Internationalization of Business Regulation*, Law in Context series (London: Weidenfeld and Nicolson, 1992:); Michael Keen and Jenny E. Ligthart, 'Information Sharing and International Taxation: A Primer' (2006) 13 *International Tax and Public Finance* 81; Steven A. Dean, 'The Incomplete Market for Tax Information' (2008) 49(1) *Boston College Law Review* 1; T. Schenk-Geers, *International Exchange of Information and the Protection of Taxpayers* (Alphen aan den Rijn: Kluwer Law International, 2009); Jan Wouters and Katrien Meuwissen, *Global Tax Governance: Work in Progress?*, Working Paper No. 59 (Leuven Centre for Global Governance Studies, February 2011); V. Tanzi and H.H. Zee, 'Can Information Exchange be Effective in Taxing Cross-Border Income Flows?' in K. Andersson, P. Melz and C. Silfverberg (eds), *Modern Issues in the Law of International Taxation* (Stockholm: Kluwer Law International, 2001); Sara K. McCracken, 'Going, Going, Gone ... Global: A Canadian Perspective on International Tax Administration Issues in the Exchange-of-Information Age' (2002) 50 *Canadian Tax Journal* 1869.

There have been calls for the establishment of a world tax organization or similar institution that would instigate a form, whether limited or expansive, of international administration of cross-border tax issues.[2] This has not yet been achieved. However, this chapter argues that we can observe national tax agencies taking another path towards effective global tax information exchange (and other forms of administrative cooperation). This alternative path comprises the building of transnational tax administrative networks between national tax agencies, under the direct, or indirect, authority of state governments. Thus, as in the case of shipping regulation, we observe a gradual process of 'regulation up', as national tax agencies begin to institutionalize processes of global regulation in taxation.[3] This chapter also argues that such a networked, governance approach is preferable to adopting an alternative suggestion made recently by Steven Dean that countries could seek to constitute a 'robust market' for tax information (even if that could be achieved).[4]

Legitimacy of transnational cooperation may be assessed in a number of different ways; that is, there may be several different sources of legitimacy. This chapter adopts the approach of Robert Baldwin to the problem of legitimacy in governmental action in general.[5] It also draws on some of the literature on accountability in a global context.[6] An overarching issue of global legitimacy concerns the range of countries (and their citizens) that may ultimately benefit from such administrative cooperation. In particular, it is important to ask how developing countries

---

[2] Vito Tanzi, 'Is there a Need for a World Tax Organization?' in A. Razin and E. Sadka (eds), *The Economics of Globalization: Policy Perspectives from Public Economics* (New York: Cambridge University Press, 1999); Adrian Sawyer, *Developing a World Tax Organisation: The Way Forward* (Fiscal Publications, 2009).

[3] Samuel Barrows, 'Racing to the Top … at Last: The Regulation of Safety in Shipping' in Walter Mattli and Ngaire Woods (eds), *The Politics of Global Regulation* (Princeton University Press, 2009) 189.

[4] Dean, *supra* note 1, at 21.

[5] Robert Baldwin, *Rules and Government* (Oxford University Press, 1995); a survey of approaches to regulatory legitimation is in Bronwen Morgan and Karen Yeung, *An Introduction to Law and Regulation* (Cambridge University Press, 2007) ch. 5.

[6] Lawrence Tshuma, 'Hierarchies and Government versus Networks and Governance: Competing Regulatory Paradigms in Global Economic Regulation' (1999) *Law, Social Justice and Global Development*, Issue 1999-1; (2000) 9(1) *Social and Legal Studies* 115; Ruth Grant and Robert O. Keohane, 'Accountability and Abuses of Power in World Politics' (2005) 99(1) *American Political Science Review* 29.

are currently, and might in future, participate in and benefit from the development of transnational tax administrative networks.

This chapter focuses on transnational tax information exchange networks. However, other aspects of tax administrative cooperation are also increasing, including assistance in investigation, enforcement and collection of taxes and the building and management of enhanced relationships between governments and multinational business. In the long run, it seems likely that these other forms of tax cooperation may become even more important than tax information sharing. However, the ability to obtain information has been essential to the extraction of revenues that produced the success of the 'tax state'.[7] The need for tax information has increased over time both within countries and across borders, as the numbers of taxpayers, types of tax, levels of taxation and bureaucratic capacity to administer complex tax systems has increased. National bureaucratic tax agencies established systems for accessing and managing information and collection of tax, hand in hand with the development of corporate capitalist enterprise in the last century, in the context of what some have termed 'regulatory capitalism'.[8] For example, pay-as-you-go employee withholding, corporate tax instalment systems, tax file numbers, computerized data matching utilizing information from corporations and banks, and sophisticated risk-based audit systems have enabled developed country tax agencies to collect significant tax revenues from businesses and individuals.

National tax laws in most developed countries grant wide information-gathering powers to revenue agencies, empowering them to demand information from taxpayers, or third parties (such as banks, employers or contractors), about their own or others' income, assets and financial transactions.[9] In Australia, the tax authority may request or subpoena information, attend premises and seize papers, in a 'fishing expedition'

---

7 Christopher Hood, 'The "Tax State' in the Information Age' in T. Paul, J. Ikenberry and J. Hall (eds), *The Nation-State in Question* (Princeton University Press, 2003) 213; Dean, *supra* note 1.

8 John Braithwaite, *Regulatory Capitalism: How it Works and Ideas for Making it Work Better* (Edward Elgar, 2008); Richard Higgott, 'Public Goods, Global Governance and Private Actors: Learning from the WTO' in G. Fraser-Moleketi (ed.), *The World We Could Win* (IOS Press, 2005) 18 at 28; D. Levi-Faur, *The Global Diffusion of Regulatory Capitalism*, Annals of the American Academy of Political and Social Science (2005).

9 A recent survey of the US and European rules is in Roman Seer and Isabele Gabert (eds), *Mutual Assistance and Information Exchange* (IBFD, 2010).

without a direct link to a tax assessment.[10] In spite of these wide powers, it is much more difficult for tax agencies to obtain the information that the state needs when income, dealings, assets or taxpayers are across borders. Since the 1970s, increased mobility of investment, tax residence and labour, and a growing number of 'tax havens' with zero or low tax rates, has created a growing problem of international tax evasion and avoidance by both corporations and individuals.

Developing countries have, in general, been less successful at collecting and utilizing tax information of resident and foreign individuals and businesses to generate revenue. There are many reasons for this.[11] Whatever the reasons, one consequence is that it will be more difficult for developing countries to participate in transnational tax information exchange, or to benefit from information obtained in such exchanges.

II. DIPLOMATIC BILATERALISM COMPARED TO NETWORKED GOVERNANCE

Globalization is perceived as reducing the role and capability of nation states. Linda Weiss, a theorist of economic globalization processes, has suggested that new technologies of transnational regulation may have the ultimate effect of extending 'the state's capacity to govern'.[12] Transnational tax administrative cooperation has a long history; indeed, the first bilateral tax treaty concerned information exchange.[13] However, international tax cooperation since the early twentieth century was established in a mode of diplomatic bilateral negotiation, rather than more widespread cooperation. As such, tax cooperation has lagged behind some other aspects of global cooperation.

In 1992, Sol Picciotto identified international cooperation between tax administrations as having 'increasingly come to play a key role in the

---

[10] Income Tax Assessment Act 1936 (Cth), ss. 263 and 264.

[11] The issue of how to improve tax governance and administration in developing countries is now widely acknowledged and discussed, see R. Bird and M. Casanegra de Jantscher (eds), *Improving Tax Administration in Developing Countries* (Washington, DC: IMF, 1992); and recently Wilson Prichard, *Taxation and State Building: Towards a Governance Focused Tax Reform Agenda*, Institute of Development Studies Working Paper 2010/341 (2010).

[12] Linda Weiss, 'The State-Augmenting Effects of Globalization' (2005) 10(3) *New Political Economy* 345.

[13] Sunita Jogarajan, 'Prelude to the International Tax Treaty Network: 1815–1914 Early Tax Treaties and the Conditions for Action' (2011) 31(4) *Oxford Journal of Legal Studies* 679.

coordination of national taxes on international business'.[14] However, he concluded that there was, at best, only an 'embryonic world tax administration'.[15] Tax administrators were too 'heterogenous, informal and over-secretive' and were reluctant to concede even a small encroachment on their discretionary negotiating power so as to enable 'minimal provisions for procedural fairness' of taxpayers.[16] Picciotto also identified a lack of legitimacy and accountability in the ad hoc attempts of states to cooperate in tax matters. States reciprocally resolved some individual tax conflicts but failed to cooperate more broadly in a way that might have collectively reinforced 'the effectiveness and harmony of national taxation as applied to international business'.[17]

In 2000, John Braithwaite and Peter Drahos also identified the failures of the international tax regime compared to other forms of international business regulation. They observed an international tax structure of 'polycentric, regulatory diversity' between 'rogue fiscal sovereigns', rather than any coherent regime of cooperation.[18] Tax administrative cooperation had grown over time, but it remained in the diplomatic mode of 'reciprocal bargaining in the national interest'.[19] The bilateral, ad hoc, cooperation of states was inadequate to deal with the monocentric complexity of multinationals with the ability to plan tax outcomes across hundreds of subsidiaries and different jurisdictions. Consequently, they concluded that there had been 'a genuine erosion of state sovereignty' in respect of taxation, as a result of economic globalization.[20]

Braithwaite and Drahos expressed hope that the OECD's Harmful Tax Competition project,[21] which officially commenced in 1998, could generate momentum towards a multilateral tax solution. However, the Harmful Tax Competition project, which many consider to have failed in achieving its ambitious goals, did not achieve a consensus on aspects related to minimum tax rates or a harmonized basis, or even on some features of tax havens that should be forcibly outlawed by member

---

[14] Picciotto, *supra* note 1, at 250.

[15] *Ibid.* 255.

[16] *Ibid.* 255 and 282.

[17] *Ibid.* 305.

[18] John Braithwaite and Peter Drahos, *Global Business Regulation* (Cambridge University Press, 2000) 106–7.

[19] Picciotto, *supra* note 1, at 306.

[20] Braithwaite and Drahos, *supra* note 18, at 109.

[21] OECD, *Harmful Tax Competition: An Emerging Global Issue* (Paris: OECD, 1998); OECD, *The OECD's Project on Harmful Tax Practices: The 2004 Progress Report* (Paris: OECD, 2004).

states.[22] Similarly, within Europe, the debate about corporate tax harmonization or competition continues without an easy resolution.[23] Both the OECD and the European Commission have turned their attention towards transnational tax information exchange and cooperation.

Before examining transnational tax information networks, it is useful to explain a little more about the concept of a network.[24] Ann-Marie Slaughter's definition of a global governance network is useful: she defines it as 'a pattern of regular and purposive relations among like government units working across the border that divide countries from one another and that demarcate the "domestic" from the "international sphere"'.[25] In this process, the nation state disaggregates into separate, functionally distinct parts, which work directly with their counterparts abroad. The state does not 'disappear' but its separate parts, such as tax agencies or subdivisions, participate in 'a dense web of relations that constitutes a new transgovernmental order'.[26]

Transnational tax administrative networks therefore involve multiple actors such as different government agencies, supranational fora or organizations, and non-governmental actors, in particular multinational enterprises or banks, who each have their own goals and strategies and who participate together in complex bargaining processes.[27] Bargains may be achieved because the actors in a network are *interdependent*, that is, they depend on each other's resources to achieve their own goals and have some common interests.

---

22 Jason Sharman, *Havens in a Storm: The Struggle for Global Tax Regulation* (Ithaca, NY: Cornell University Press, 2006); Sunita Jogarajan and Miranda Stewart, 'Success or Failure?' (2007) 22 *Australian Tax Forum* 3; Michael C. Webb, 'Defining the Boundaries of Legitimate State Practices: Norms, Transnational Actors and the OECD's Project on Harmful Tax Competition' (2004) 11 *Review of International Political Economy* 4 at 787. An exhaustive survey of subsequent developments is in the series of articles by David Spencer in (2010) 21(6) *International Taxation* (August).

23 G. Nicodème, 'Corporate Tax Competition and Coordination in the European Union: What Do We Know? Where Do We stand?' in G. Gregoriou and C. Read (eds), *International Taxation Handbook* (London: Elsevier, 2007).

24 Tshuma, *supra* note 6.

25 Ann-Marie Slaughter, *A New World Order* (Princeton University Press, 2004) 14.

26 Tshuma, *supra* note 6, at 130.

27 Walter J.M. Kickert, Erik-Hans Klijn and Joop F.M. Koppenjan (eds), *Managing Complex Networks: Strategies for the Public Sector* (London: SAGE Publications, 1997) xvii; David Coen and Mark Thatcher, 'Network Governance and Multi-level Delegation: European Networks of Regulatory Agencies' (2008) 28 *Journal of Public Policy* 49.

It has been suggested that a transnational network in taxation is established in the global processes of tax policy development and transmission involving international institutions such as the OECD and IMF, tax experts and (mostly) developed country governments, contributing to the development of international and domestic tax law and norms.[28] This policy network has achieved significant cooperation in avoiding double taxation between jurisdictions and has had a significant influence in the spread of tax policy norms around the globe. Even where successes have been achieved, however, these networks are not always an unqualified good. A network is by definition closed or exclusive. It may fail if, for example, participants act competitively rather than cooperatively; if common goals are vague or insufficiently productive for each actor; if some important actors are absent; if the presence of some actors discourages others; if there is an absence of commitment; or if there is a lack of crucial information about goals, means and actors.[29] As explained by Christians, developing countries, to date, have been excluded from global tax policy networks. Coercion may operate within or alongside the networks, so that the international tax policy norms established operate in the interests of wealthier or more powerful states and privilege particular values, such as efficiency, over other values such as distributional justice and democratic national processes. More fundamentally, as Braithwaite and Drahos argue, these tax policy networks have so far failed to achieve a genuine cooperative international tax solution that would enable the allocation and collection of a base level of adequate tax revenues across states. They have operated in the interests of capital rather than of governments and citizens.

Networks of national tax regulators may be established in three different ways:[30] (1) within the context of established international organizations; (2) under the umbrella of an overarching agreement negotiated by governments; or (3) informally between agencies, outside any legal framework, arising 'spontaneously from a need to work together to address common problems'.[31] Transnational tax information exchange networks are established in all three ways, but it is clear that they are becoming increasingly legalized and institutionalized.

---

[28] Allison Christians, 'Networks, Norms and National Tax Policy' (2010) 9 *Wash. U Global Stud. L Rev.* 1.

[29] Kickert *et al.*, *supra* note 27, at 9.

[30] Ann-Marie Slaughter, 'Global Government Networks, Global Information Agencies and Disaggregated Democracies' (2003) 24 *Michigan Journal of International Law* 1041.

[31] *Ibid.* 1049.

Many countries have also stepped up their national investigations of the offshore investments and activities of individuals and corporations, and some countries are seeking in the process to expand their national tax information capabilities unilaterally beyond their borders. The paramount example is the US Foreign Account Tax Compliance Act (FATCA), expected to become operational on 1 January 2013.[32] Similarly, bilateral negotiations, such as those still ongoing between the US and Swiss governments relating to the UBS bank scandal and similar scenarios, have a particular and limited scope in relation to the specific country tax agencies and taxpayers.[33] These developments are not addressed in this chapter.

III. MODES OF TRANSNATIONAL TAX INFORMATION EXCHANGE

A web of multilateral and bilateral treaties now provides the legal authority for cooperation between national tax agencies. Picciotto traced the development of transnational tax cooperation, including the role of bilateral double taxation agreements (DTAs); various proposals for information exchange and mutual assistance established early in the twentieth century that were watered down in actual implementation; and the OECD Model Treaty provisions on exchange of information (Article 26), mutual agreement (Article 25) and mutual enforcement (Article 27), the last being included in only a few treaties by 1992. He also noted the establishment of informal groups of tax administrators from different countries, and the beginning of simultaneous tax audits and spontaneous information exchange; attempts at multilateral cooperation in the European Community and between it and OECD member states; the ad hoc use of the competent authority procedure for settling transfer pricing adjustments; and small steps towards international arbitration of tax matters.

Transnational tax information exchange is also facilitated by the expansion of 'soft' international processes, involving many countries as well as supranational organizations and non-government organizations

---

[32] Hiring Incentive to Restore Employment Act of 2010, Pub. L. 111–157 (HR 2847), Title V Subtitle A. See detail in Dean Marsan, Parts I, II, III, *Taxes* (July, August and September 2010).

[33] A recent update is in Walter H. Boss and William M. Sharp, Sr, 'The Swiss–US "Turnover" Ground Rules: A Technical Update', *Tax Notes*, 7 November 2011.

such as the Tax Justice Network, or business lobby groups such as the European Society of Banks. This part examines the increased 'legalization' through three main modes of transnational tax information exchange, including the role of developing countries: bilateral DTAs; Tax Information Exchange Agreements (TIEAs); and the Multilateral Convention on Tax Administrative Assistance. Not surprisingly, the most well-established institutional and legal mechanisms for transnational information exchange are within the European Union. These developments are addressed elsewhere and will not be discussed here.[34] Some of these mechanisms date back to the 1970s, but as for the other processes discussed in this part, the implementation of substantive information exchange obligations only gained momentum within the last decade. The EU Savings Directive, which came into effect on 1 July 2005 has the most institutionalized system of transnational tax cooperation established to date.[35]

A. Information Exchange under Double Taxation Agreements

Most DTAs are based on either the OECD Model[36] or the UN Model,[37] which are now both frequently revised and updated. It is estimated that there are around 3,000 bilateral DTAs globally, establishing a web of legal authority for bilateral transnational information exchange.

As explained in detail by Dean, early Model DTAs had relatively broad tax information exchange provisions.[38] However, both the obligation and form of information exchange were narrowed during the formalization of the OECD DTA Model after the Second World War, including by removing the obligation for automatic exchange.[39] Since the 1970s, the Models and many bilateral DTAs have gradually expanded the possibilities for exchanging information and this process has dramatically accelerated in the last decade.[40] Today, the OECD claims that a 'universally agreed' international standard on tax information exchange is set out

---

[34] Seer and Gabert, *supra* note 9, at 5; Schenk-Geers, *supra* note 1.

[35] Directive 2003/48/EC of 3 June 2003 on taxation of savings income in the form of interest payments.

[36] OECD Model Tax Convention on Income and Capital, available at www.oecd.org ('OECD Model').

[37] United Nations Model Double Tax Convention between Developed and Developing Countries ('UN Model'), UN doc. ST/ESA/PAD/SER.E/21, most recently revised in 2001, available at www.un.org.

[38] Dean, *supra* note 1, at 39.

[39] *Ibid.* 43.

[40] Schenk-Geers, *supra* note 1, at 92.

in the revised OECD Model Article 26 (2006) and its Commentary, and in its Model TIEA.[41] The UN Model Article 26 is in essentially the same terms as the OECD Model.[42] OECD Model Article 26.1 now sets out the basic rule as follows:

> The competent authorities ... shall exchange such information as is foreseeably relevant for carrying out the provisions of this Convention or to the administration or enforcement of the domestic laws concerning taxes of every kind and description imposed on behalf of the Contracting States, or of their political subdivisions or local authorities.

The latest version of OECD Model Article 26 expands and generalizes the legal authority for information exchange in some important ways compared to prior versions. First, information exchange is not limited to residents of either contracting state, so that a contracting state could seek information relating to a third country resident, if foreseeably relevant to that state's tax administration or enforcement. The information need not have any relevance to the third country resident's tax position; the OECD gives an example of a 'triangular' situation involving parent and subsidiary companies in which a third party resident subsidiary's income derived in contracting state A could be relevant to the tax position of the parent company resident in contracting state B, which may seek the information.[43] Second, Article 26 authorizes information exchange relating to all taxes, not simply the taxes on income and capital covered by most DTAs. Third, the exchange of information is mandatory and cannot be declined 'solely because the information is held by a bank, other financial institution, nominee or person acting in an agency or fiduciary capacity or because it relates to ownership interests in a person' (Article 26.5). As a result of this clause, the G20 made its widely reported claim, in one of its first major statements about cooperation, that 'the era of bank secrecy is over'.[44]

---

41 See statements at OECD, www.eoi-tax.org and www.oecd.org/tax/transparency.

42 Revised Article 26 (2009) and Revised Commentary (2008) finalized for inclusion in the next version of the UN Model, pursuant to decisions taken by the UN Committee of Experts on International Cooperation in Tax Matters, E/29008/45, E/C.18/2008/6 (2008), available at www.un.org.

43 OECD, Model Commentary on Article 26, available at www.oecd.org/taxation.

44 G20, Global Plan for Recovery and Reform: The Communiqué from the London Summit, 2 April 2009, available at www.g8.utoronto.ca/g20/.

The OECD Model Article 26 and bilateral DTAs do not contain details about processes of information exchange. However, the accompanying Commentary and Manual on Information Exchange identify three main ways in which information may be exchanged:[45] (1) on request of a contracting state, with a particular case in mind; (2) automatically, being the systematic transmission of bulk data related to various taxpayers and types of income; and (3) spontaneously, where the transmitting state identifies information that it considers may be useful or relevant to the other contracting state. A key development is expansion of the automatic exchange of taxpayer information between tax administrations. The Commentary also discusses other techniques of cooperation that involve information sharing, including simultaneous tax examination, tax audits abroad, and industry-wide sharing and exchange. Under the authority of DTA clauses, some national tax administrations have developed informal cooperative networks, such as the Joint International Tax Shelter Information Centre (JITSIC), established by a Memorandum of Understanding between Australia, Canada, the United States, the United Kingdom and Japan (China is an observer).[46]

The actual provisions in current bilateral DTAs vary significantly. Treaties may have *grande* or *petite* (broad or narrow) information exchange clauses, depending on the date of negotiation and preferences of the contracting states. Narrower treaties often limit exchange to 'necessary' information for specific taxes and sometimes only for the purposes of the treaty (this is the historic Swiss position).[47] Most older DTAs do not contain the provision overriding bank secrecy, while some limit the forms of information exchange.

Bilateral DTA negotiation is time-consuming, ad hoc and linked to various economic and political pressures so that bilateral DTA provisions will contain a fragmented and variable coverage of the OECD 'international standard' for some time to come. Even so, this variance should not be overstated. Significant renegotiation of DTAs, or the addition of Protocols incorporating an updated provision, is underway in many countries.[48] Countries are also increasingly adopting treaty terms that

---

[45] OECD, *Commentary and Manual on the Implementation of Exchange of Information Provisions for Tax Purposes*, approved by the OECD Committee on Fiscal Affairs on 23 January 2006, available at www.oecd.org/taxation.

[46] Joint International Tax Shelter Information Centre Memorandum of Understanding, available at www.irs.gov/pub/irs-utl/jitsic-finalmou.pdf.

[47] Schenk-Geers, *supra* note 1, at 96.

[48] For example, India currently has more than 80 DTAs, including 19 recently negotiated DTAs and 23 renegotiations or Protocols to existing DTAs

facilitate generalization of treaty rules, including most favoured nation treatment, national treatment, and non-discrimination. More fundamentally, the formal tax information exchange obligations in bilateral DTAs are gradually being overtaken by the Multilateral Convention on Mutual Assistance in Tax Matters (see below).

B. Tax Information Exchange Agreements and the Global Forum

The OECD has spearheaded the campaign for negotiation of Tax Information Exchange Agreements (TIEAs), with the main purpose of enabling countries (to date, mostly but not exclusively developed countries) to access information about their own residents' offshore investment activities in and through tax havens. The TIEA project grew out of the OECD's Harmful Tax Competition project and initially made slow progress. In 2002, the OECD released its Model TIEA and accompanying Commentary; up until 2008, there had been only 44 TIEAs signed. While familiar global players, including the OECD and European Union (EU), are key players in this process, two new political forums have grown up that have been essential in leading the process. First, the G20. Between the G20 summit on 15 November 2008, which strongly supported the project, and the G20 summit in Cannes on 4 November 2011, 700 TIEAs were signed, primarily between developed countries and tax havens or 'offshore finance centre' countries.[49] Triggers for this massive increase in TIEAs include the Liechtenstein, Luxembourg and UBS bank scandals,[50] and the global financial crisis that has increased governmental concern about fiscal deficits and revenue leakage. The identified jurisdictions were each required to sign 12 TIEAs with other governments in order to get off the list. Ultimately, it was expected that tax havens would sign agreements with all country governments who wanted such an agreement. In an illustration of the scale of TIEA negotiation, Australia has,

(see http://law.incometaxindia.gov.in/DIT/intDtaa.aspx). On 11 December 2011, India and Australia signed a Protocol that updates the information exchange article and includes additional provisions for mutual assistance and enforcement of tax debts in the 1991 Australia–India DTA: available at www.treasury.gov.au.

49 The full list of countries is available at www.oecd.org/tax/transparency.

50 T.A. van Kampen and L.J. de Rijke, 'The Kreditetbank Luxembourg and the Liechtenstein Tax Affairs: Notes on the Balance between the Exchange of Information between States and the Protection of Fundamental Rights' (2009) *EC Tax Review* 2008-5, 221; and see references *supra* note 1.

since 2008, negotiated 32 TIEAs or similar agreements[51] and India has negotiated 17 TIEAs.[52]

The second important political player is the newly established Global Forum on Transparency and Tax Information Exchange.[53] The Global Forum was established initially by the OECD in response to concerns expressed by tax haven countries, which sought a voice in the coercive process of listing tax havens and requiring TIEA negotiation. It now has a membership of 116 countries, plus the European Union and 11 international organizations (including the OECD and United Nations) as observers; this is the broadest and most inclusive membership of all international tax organizations. The Global Forum was restructured at its meeting in Mexico in 2009 to give all country members an equal vote, even though technically it remains a program initiated by the OECD. Member countries contribute to administrative costs, with the bulk of funding coming from OECD member countries. Currently, the Global Forum is guided by an 18-member steering group previously chaired by Australia, and now by South Africa.

The Global Forum initially tracked and policed the signing of TIEAs; it has now moved on to a detailed process of peer review of domestic country laws of member states to ensure that these will enable the practical implementation of TIEAs, for example, by modifying bank secrecy laws and empowering the revenue agency to take appropriate information collection and transmission activities.[54] However, the Forum is a 'soft' institution in the sense that it has no rule-making or administrative power of its own and is not supported by any multilateral treaty or other delegated legal authority.

In its Progress Report of 10 November 2010, the OECD stated that all countries in the Global Forum have now committed to and 'substantially

---

51 See ATO, www.ato.gov.au/businesses/content.asp?doc=/content/00161158.htm.

52 *Supra* note 48.

53 Global Forum, www.oecd/tax/transparency. Wouters and Meuwissen, *supra* note 1, survey the growing role of international political forums in tax cooperation.

54 To date, the Forum has initiated more than 80 peer reviews; see Information Brief, 4 November 2011, available at www.oecd.org/dataoecd/32/45/43757434.pdf.

implemented' the 'internationally agreed tax standard' for TIEAs.[55] The OECD defines this standard as follows:[56]

> exchange of information on request in all tax matters for the administration and enforcement of domestic tax law without regard to a domestic tax interest requirement or bank secrecy for tax purposes. It also provides for extensive safeguards to protect the confidentiality of the information exchanged.

The standard is in some respects lower than that in the OECD Model DTA, as it is limited to exchange upon request and does not encompass automatic exchange; bank secrecy is also only lifted in the limited circumstances set out in the TIEA itself. However, through the TIEA process, this more limited standard now applies across a much wider range of countries than bilateral DTAs. The sheer speed of TIEA negotiation has meant a mass produced approach is inevitable. However, the Model TIEA is also being combined with OECD Model Article 26 in novel ways, as happened in the recently negotiated DTA Protocol between Turkey and Bahrain.[57] The two countries have 'created a hybrid method of exchanging information by mixing two models designed by [the] OECD' because of the particular features of their tax systems, which were very different (Bahrain, for example, does not have an individual income tax).[58]

A feature of TIEA negotiation is that it is being conducted *outside* the formal, diplomatic channels traditionally utilized by countries in negotiating DTAs, and in some cases outside the strict legal processes required for implementation. In the United States, the standard DTA procedure requires a Presidential signature and ratification by a two-thirds majority of the Senate before the treaty can take effect in law.[59] In contrast, the negotiation of TIEAs has generally been carried out at a lower level of formality and TIEAs are treated as secondary in status and not set before the Senate. In Australia, a DTA is negotiated by Treasury officials in a secretive diplomatic process, and is not binding until it is signed, ratified

---

55 OECD, *Progress Report on the Jurisdictions Surveyed by the OECD Global Forum in Implementing the Internationally Agreed Tax Standard* (10 November 2010), available at www.oecd.org/tax/transparency.

56 *Ibid.* note 1.

57 Cihat Oner, 'A Different Approach to the Agreement on Exchange of Information in Tax Matters (Turkey has Secretly Approved Model Tax Agreement)' (2009) 37 *Intertax* 483.

58 *Ibid.* 492.

59 US Constitution, Art. II, Sec. 2, Cl. 2 and IRC s. 7852(d).

and incorporated into domestic legislation by statutory enactment.[60] However, TIEA negotiation has been delegated to the Australian Taxation Office, which has also cooperated with the New Zealand revenue agency in negotiating TIEAs with tax havens in the Pacific region, and a streamlined implementation process has been enacted. The Nordic countries have established a collective, cooperative approach to TIEA negotiation.[61] The TIEA process and the Global Forum thus both directly engage national tax bureaucracies with each other within delegated bounds, as a task that forms part of the general course of tax administration. Similarly, implementation and enforcement of TIEAs will be a tax administrative matter that will require dedicated expertise in country revenue agencies.

C. Multilateral Convention on Tax Administrative Assistance

In 1988, the OECD and the Council of Europe developed a Multilateral Convention on Mutual Administrative Assistance in Tax Matters. Gradually, some EU and OECD member states signed the Convention and it entered into force on 1 April 1995. It did not achieve widespread implementation and a significant number of key states failed to sign or ratify it (for example, the United Kingdom did not sign until 2007). The Convention was not open to signature by other countries.

In relation to tax information exchange, the Convention overlaps significantly with existing bilateral DTAs and TIEAs. Article 1 sets out the different types of information exchange that are discussed in the OECD Model Article 26 Commentary and Manual on Exchange of Information: on request, automatic and spontaneous exchange. In other areas, the Multilateral Convention generalizes and expands existing tax administrative cooperation mechanisms. The Explanatory Report to the Multilateral Convention expresses the ambitious scope of the Multilateral Convention:

> This instrument is framed so as to provide for all possible forms of administrative co-operation between States in the assessment and collection of taxes, in particular with a view to combating tax avoidance and evasion. This

---

[60] Generally in the International Tax Agreements Act (1986, Cth).

[61] See www.norden.org/en/nordic-council-of-ministers/councils-of-ministers/council-of-ministers-for-finance-mr-finans/tax-information-exchange-agreements/.

> co-operation ranges from exchange of information to the recovery of foreign tax claims.[62]

A key objective was stated by the G20 'to make it easier for developing countries to secure the benefits of the new cooperative environment'.[63] In 2010, a Protocol was agreed that opened up the Convention to non-OECD or EU member states and made other amendments to expand the scope of the Convention. The Protocol entered into force on 1 June 2011. At the G20 meeting on 4 November 2011, all remaining G20 countries except China, signed the Convention, in a highly visible commitment.[64] Consistent with its commitment to international tax cooperation, India has now ratified the Convention and Costa Rica recently became the first Central American signatory. It seems likely that this strong momentum for expansion of the Multilateral Convention will continue. By 26 October 2012, a total of 32 countries had signed the Convention. Most, but not all, are developed countries. However, only 18 countries have ratified it and implemented it into domestic law. A process to become a party to the Convention has been established which requires a decision by consensus of existing parties. Factors to be taken into account will include confidentiality rules and practices of the applicant country (which may be a high threshold that is difficult to meet in some cases) and its membership of the Global Forum (which is open to all).

The Indian Minister for Finance, Mr Gopalan, expressed to the G20 the hope that the Convention will facilitate widespread automatic exchange of information between signatories.[65] It seems likely that automatic information exchange is the way of the future for much international tax administration and, as noted above, it is also applied under the OECD Model Article 26 (but not the TIEA Model). However, the Multilateral Convention does not mandate automatic exchange. Rather, this requires a separate 'mutual agreement' between two or more parties in relation to types of information and processes of such automatic exchange (Article 6).

---

62 OECD/EU, 'Revised Explanatory Report for Convention of 1988 and Amending Protocol of 2010', para. 3, available at www.oecd.org.

63 G20 Leaders Summit, Financial Regulation Session, Remarks by Angel Gurria, OECD Secretary General, Cannes, 4 November 2011, available at www.oecd.org.

64 *Ibid.*

65 Gopalan, cited in http://chinaepress.com/tag/bank-secrecy/ (4 November 2011).

Two other aspects of the Multilateral Convention are worth noting. First, the Convention establishes a 'coordinating body' of representatives of the competent authorities (national revenue agencies) to 'monitor the implementation and development of this Convention, under the aegis of the OECD' (Article 24.3). The Explanatory Report suggest that this body should 'encourage the formulation of uniform solutions to problems in the application and interpretation of the provisions … by furnishing its opinion on questions of application' in a general manner.[66] Second, the Explanatory Report envisages that national revenue agencies should establish dedicated divisions to manage transnational tax information exchange and other assistance. It emphasizes the need for 'direct and speedy contacts' between tax administrations as being 'the only way to make the assistance effective'. It identifies trends in this direction already, and proposes that the establishment of 'a single, central body' in each tax agency to manage transnational tax assistance is also needed because of concerns about taxpayer confidentiality and secrecy, which is only waived under the conditions established by the Convention.[67] In Australia, the recommendation for a centralized information repository and dedicated committee to manage information needs, collection and use within the Tax Office has now been adopted.

In addition to the Multilateral Convention, there have recently been negotiated a number of regional, multilateral agreements in tax administrative cooperation. These include the SAARC Limited Multilateral Agreement on Avoidance of Double Taxation and Mutual Administrative Assistance in Tax Matters, signed in 2005 and in force since 19 May 2010, which contains a provision for information exchange, although this is not as broad as the Multilateral Convention or OECD Model (for example, it does not explicitly override bank secrecy or set out types of exchange).[68] It also provides for regional training, meetings and mutual assistance between tax officers of the different national tax agencies. In 2009, the African Tax Administration Forum (ATAF) was launched with initial membership of 25 African countries.[69] Tax authorities of Serbia, Montenegro, Slovenia and both parts of Bosnia (the former Yuogslavia) signed on 19 March 2011 a regional cooperation agreement to clamp down on tax evasion and the grey economy. These developments are promising, but such cooperation is still in its early stages.

---

[66] OECD/EU, *supra* note 62, paras 239–40.

[67] *Ibid.* para. 245.

[68] South Asian Association for Regional Cooperation, between Bangladesh, Bhutan, India, the Maldives, Nepal, Pakistan and Sri Lanka.

[69] See www.ataftax.net/; the fourth meeting was concluded on 6 March 2012.

IV. TRANSNATIONAL TAX INFORMATION NETWORKS AS GOVERNANCE

Dean has suggested that a market-based solution to tax information exchange may be the best approach, if a supranational organization cannot be achieved, at least for wealthy governments such as the United States.[70] He describes the current exchange by governments, of, say, 'lists of taxpayer-specific information' by governments, as an incomplete market, comprising 'barter' or 'acquisition' exchanges.[71] However, this mischaracterizes current modes of tax information exchange. Diplomatic agreement making, although it can be analysed as a political bargain, is clearly not a market transaction, even at a barter level. The negotiation of current tax information exchange provisions has taken place in most instances within the context of an overall bilateral bargain for a DTA, which is not itself solely explainable by tax matters, but is likely to be a response to the entire bilateral political dynamic between the two states. The negotiation of TIEAs and the Multilateral Agreement on tax cooperation has taken place within a broader global political context, under auspices of the G20, and again, not in any particular tax information 'market' as such.

A market comprises multiple elective ad hoc interactions based on a *price* decision, between competitive and self-interested actors.[72] Yet there is no assessment by national tax agencies as to the relative market value, or price, of tax information exchanged under the various modes discussed in section III above. Rather, there is an *obligation* either to provide specific information requested, or under agreed administrative processes to supply certain automatic exchanges of particular types of information defined by category (not by value). The obligation exists even if the other jurisdiction *never* asks for tax information in return. Indeed, the limited evidence available to date suggest that countries likely fail to obtain full value from tax information and are unlikely to know the true value of any

---

70 Dean, *supra* note 1.

71 *Ibid.* 5.

72 The difference between networks and markets is discussed by Miles Kahler and David Lake, 'Economic Integration and Global Governance: Why So Little Supranationalism?' in Walter Mattli and Ngaire Woods (eds), *The Politics of Global Regulation* (Princeton University Press, 2009) 242, 248.

specific information.[73] The mere fact that from time to time information has been *acquired* by a country government for a sum of money does not demonstrate the existence of a market, but only that a (usually) disaffected individual who is (usually) doing an illegal or even criminal activity, is prepared to give up data, presumed to be valuable, for an amount of cash that suits them as an individual. It is arguable that rather than a market for tax information, what should be required instead is the opposite – a price on tax haven status. Where countries can achieve it, this has in fact been the result: in Europe, originally Belgium, Austria and Luxembourg refused to exchange information under the Savings Directive, for a 'price' of withheld tax revenues remitted to resident investor country fiscs, in exchange for the privilege of operating as a tax haven with effective bank secrecy.

While the current system is not even an 'incomplete' market for tax information exchange, it is possible to *envisage* some form of market for tax information. Dean suggests, for example, that tax haven countries could agree to provide tax information in exchange for, say, cash payments from various (presumably, wealthy) governments. To the extent that tax havens rely on the privacy of investors for their successful existence, and further, that the information once provided then loses its value substantially (as the names of individual taxpayers, for example, will be valuable even if there is no evidence that they invest offshore in every tax year) then they are unlikely to be willing to give up tax information at an affordable price.

Even if such a market could be established, it is suggested here that the implications would be overwhelmingly negative. First, it is difficult to see how such a market for information could be confined to exchanges between tax haven countries and rich countries. Private individuals, or disaffected governmental agents, as already happens to some extent, would likely participate in the market. Governments would likely lose control of tax information of private individuals; taxpayer privacy concerns are discussed below.

Second, in an auction or market for tax information (would information be sold to the highest bidder, and only once or multiple times?), it seems likely that developing countries might well be unable to afford to obtain the information, even if developed countries could establish a

[73] Dean suggests that countries could carry out revenue estimates indicating the value of exchanged tax information, *supra* note 1, at 52; however, experience to date suggests that such estimates are likely to have little relation to reality.

suitable price. If one of the goals of transnational tax administrative cooperation is to enable all countries to collect appropriate tax revenues, this is a problem. Third, even if tax havens could be induced to part with tax information for a price, in exchange for retaining their 'haven' status, this would simply reinforce such countries in their 'haven' status, rather than aiming to encourage them to develop other modes of economic development for the benefit of citizens.

Nonetheless, Dean makes an important point regarding the asymmetries that are apparent in the current international tax regime. In particular, small 'haven' countries are scarcely likely to want, or need, tax information from large countries. Yet, under the current system, they bear the burden of implementation of substantial tax information collection regimes. How is the exchange of information to be funded for small and poor countries? Is not 'exchange' a misnomer for the current process in which tax havens are being gathered into the global tax administrative system: what is in it for them? The OECD Model TIEA makes some provision for the cost of collecting relevant tax information. The provision by developed countries, which seek information, of funds to pay for the costs of collection of that information by tax haven countries could be a way in which these countries may benefit from tax information exchange networks.

Ultimately, the question is not whether a 'market' can be established (in any event this would, itself, require regulation) but rather, what *forms of regulation* of transnational tax information exchange will best fit the purposes and aspirations of all governments and citizens. Obtaining tax information is only one step towards the real goal of collection of adequate tax revenues and an effective and fair division of the global tax base. It is difficult to see how a tax information market could develop further into a 'market' for cooperative tax collection or mutual assistance in tax debts. A broader view is needed of transnational tax cooperation. Identifying transnational tax information networks can help us understand the incremental process of constructing transnational tax cooperation. Networks share some features of hierarchical (bureaucratic) government and of market exchange and communication. However, networks do not rely on a price decision but on shared trust and generalized reciprocity premised on common problems and public interest among participants. Networks have some of the advantages suggested by Dean for a 'market' approach, in particular they enable diversity, innovation and the development of local or particular solutions. The networking of national tax bureaucracies, and the increased legalization of transnational tax information networks, is producing a hybrid mode of global tax governance.[74]

V. LEGITIMACY AND EFFECTIVENESS

The analysis of transnational tax information networks as a form of governance has important implications for their legitimacy and efficacy in operation. This part examines different legitimacy claims for such networks, drawing on the work of Baldwin, who identifies five different types of governmental legitimacy claim.[75] Baldwin suggests that legitimacy claims may be based on: (1) the implementation of a legislative mandate; (2) accountability of the bureaucratic agency to a democratic or parliamentary institution; (3) procedural fairness or due process in carrying out the regulatory tasks of the agency; (4) professional expertise in the agency; and (5) efficiency in regulation. It is possible to debate the merits of these five types of legitimacy claims – for example, different views might be taken of the relative weight of different claims, the potential for overlap between types of legitimacy claim (for example, expertise and effectiveness), and for conflict between them (for example, a trade-off between efficiency and due process). Baldwin's overall approach suggests, usefully, that 'what matters is the collective justificatory power of the five forms of claim', so that 'where strong claims can be made under all five heads (a rare event) then a high level of legitimacy is assured'.[76]

A. Legislative Mandate

The well-recognised need for a legal basis for imposing taxation suggests that it is particularly important for governments to work towards establishing clear and general legal authority for transnational tax cooperation. Tax agencies traditionally exercise hierarchical, bureaucratic (Weberian) delegated legal authority. However, in networked governance, the participants share authority or constitute it through their interactions, so that

[74] Kahler and Lake, *supra* note 72, at 249; Tshuma, *supra* note 6, at 131.
[75] Baldwin, *supra* note 5, at 41. See also the discussion of paradoxes of national and global sovereignty and enhanced, transparent webs of global regulation in Braithwaite and Drahos, *supra* note 18, ch. 26.
[76] Baldwin, *supra* note 5, at 49.

'networked governance entails migration of authority to the policy network, but no formal delegation'.[77]

A supranational tax organization formally constituted under a treaty would have clear delegated authority from states, under the terms of the treaty. However, legal authority for tax agencies to act cooperatively on particular terms can also be established through a network of legally binding treaties. Section III above traced the increased scope, standardization and coverage of bilateral and multilateral treaties on tax information exchange, as well as some early steps in establishing coordinating or administrative bodies to oversee treaty operation. Applying a principal–agent model, national tax administrators operating in transnational tax networks act under this delegated legal authority from their own states.

However, given the multitude of different legal sources for tax cooperation, there is currently some confusion and overlap in the different sources of legal authority for tax administrative cooperation. In particular, where only informal and secret networks are relied upon, or where the legal authority is very brief (for example, the provisions supporting exchange of information in some bilateral DTAs are short and opaque), then there may be no apparent legal basis for some forms of administrative action. Over time, the standardization of treaties, in particular multilateral treaties or those based on models, will facilitate cooperation while enhancing formal legal accountability. The establishment of a 'coordinating body' for the Multilateral Convention and the recent revival of the United Nations SubCommittee on Taxation, may both assist in establishing a broader, global legal authorization for transnational tax administration.

B. Democratic Accountability

The second claim of legitimacy relates to the accountability of tax information networks to democratic institutions and the public more broadly. This could also be described as 'participatory accountability'.[78] Achieving such legitimacy requires, at a minimum, transparency of governmental action. Just as national legislatures and publics seek to ensure accountability of national tax agencies by requiring the provision to legislatures of annual statistics, reporting on process and outcomes, budgets and reports on costs and revenue raised, this collection of data is also required for accountability in transnational tax governance.

77 Kahler and Lake, *supra* note 72, at 248.
78 Grant and Keohane, *supra* note 6, at 37.

Until very recently, such data has been lacking about tax information exchange. Keen and Ligthart noted in 2006 that 'very little is known about the extent, nature or, especially, the effectiveness of international information sharing. Most countries treat information on the extent and use of information sharing with considerable confidentiality.'[79] Where reporting has been done, for example in respect of the EU Savings Directive, there have been significant gaps and there is no current obligation on member states to provide the data.

This situation is gradually changing. First, the OECD has been increasingly open about the process of DTA and TIEA negotiation and about the operation of the Global Forum, publishing all relevant documents including peer reviews. In particular, in Europe, proposed amendments to the Savings Directive will significantly strengthen the data collection and reporting by national governments to the European Commission.[80] Third, as discussed below, national agencies are beginning to track, audit and report on processes and outcomes of tax information exchange and this will be facilitated as tax agencies establish specific offices or sections to manage transnational cooperation.

As transnational tax information networks become increasingly integrated and bureaucratized, a new gap in accountability may appear. Ideally, the tax officers of particular nations working in the network would be accountable for the successful administration of the tax information network *as a whole*, and not only to their own tax agency and government. The European Commission may perform this overarching reporting function through collection, analysis and reporting of statistics, providing accountability to the European Parliament and to member states. The coordinating body of the Multilateral Convention has potential to perform this role for a global agreement on tax administration, but this potential has not yet been realized.

C. Expertise

Professional expertise in taxation is frequently claimed as a very significant justification and basis for action by governments, supranational agencies such as the OECD, or, indeed, individual academic 'experts', as

---

[79] Keen and Ligthart, *supra* note 1, at 94.

[80] Proposal for a Council Directive amending Directive 2003/48/EC on taxation of savings income in the form of interest payments, COM(2008)727, final version published on 4 March 2011, available at http://ec.europa.eu.

I have observed elsewhere.[81] In the arena of tax information exchange, the OECD and European Commission claim the level of expertise necessary to coordinate such processes, while at a national level, developed countries claim administrative expertise including sufficient computing systems and secure data storage, as well as legal and financial expertise to identify and utilize relevant data. As already noted, this claim is much more difficult to sustain for developing country tax administrations, especially low income countries which include some tax havens. As noted in section IV above, developed countries may need to bear both the cost and administrative burdens of the transnational tax information exchange network. This makes sense as, at least initially, developed countries will benefit more from tax information exchange.

D. Efficiency and Effectiveness

Are transnational tax information networks *efficient*? This legitimacy claim has two meanings, the first being the sense of *efficacy* (the achievement of regulatory outcomes in a cost-effective manner) and the second being economic *efficiency* as an independent value. Are transnational tax information networks *effective* in achieving tax revenue collection in terms of cost, compliance and administrative burden and are they *efficient* in the sense of not impeding the global market? In respect of the latter claim, it is to be expected that if tax information exchange networks successfully track and raise revenue from cross-border investment flows, this will deter those forms of investment that rely on illegal, secret or tax-free status (that is, after all, the purpose of the regulatory exercise). The concern of many banks and financial markets is that tax information obligations will become so significant as to deter legitimate movement of capital. There is no evidence that tax information exchange has had this effect as yet. Furthermore, there are much greater regulatory shifts occurring in the international bank environment since the Global Financial Crisis, so that the impact of tax information exchange is likely to be minor compared to other regulatory requirements.

Data is lacking about efficacy measured by tax revenue raised for national tax agencies, although some claims on this basis are being made. The Cannes G20 summit was told by the OECD: 'We know that 20 countries have taken advantage of this more transparent environment, putting in compliance initiatives which have already yielded €14 billion

[81] Miranda Stewart, 'Global Trajectories of Tax Reform' (2003) 44(1) *Harvard J International Law* 139.

in additional revenues from more than 100,000 wealthy tax payers who had hidden assets offshore and that there's more in the pipeline.'[82] Not surprisingly, €10 billion was in Europe; €2 billion in the United States and the remaining €2 billion divided between Asia Pacific/Africa (which includes Australia and New Zealand), and Latin America. In spite of this claim (and it must be remembered that these amounts are small compared to the trillions of euros in global capital flows every day), other sources suggest that revenue performance, so far, is disappointing. Reports on performance of the EU Savings Directive for the first period from 2005–2008 indicated revenue collection and effects on European savings markets significantly lower than expected.[83] The revenue reported was 'of an order far removed from the dimensions quite frequently discussed', when compared to the total estimated volume of savings and interest income.[84]

In Australia, a recent report on effectiveness of automatic information exchange noted the expanding volume of data exchanged in the last few years but observed that 'compliance exercises undertaken [using exchanged data] ... have typically achieved low measurable outcomes'.[85] Successful transmission and – more importantly – use and protection of large quantities of taxpayer data is not an easy matter. It is heavily dependent on technological, computing and administrative capacity in the particular countries and there is significant potential for error in transferring large quantities of data and a risk of embarrassing loss or disclosure of confidential taxpayer information. There are also, of course, limitations in these studies of effectiveness, however, it remains crucial that governments continue to seek to evaluate the outcomes of tax information exchange and report the results to citizens.

---

[82] OECD, 'Tax: Global Forum Delivers Concrete Results to the Cannes G20 Summit' (26 October 2011), available at www.oecd.org/document/7/0,3746,en_21571361_44315115_48940615_1_1_1_1,00.html.

[83] European Commission, *Report*, COM(2008)552 final, 2.

[84] Deutsch Bank Research, *EU Savings Directive: One Piece in the Puzzle of Cross-Border Tax Policy* (22 June 2009) 5. German withholding tax revenues (less than €200 million) and interest income declared (roughly €1.5 billion) were far lower than Bundesbank estimates of bonds held abroad that should generate interest income worth roughly €435 billion. And see Thomas Hemmelgarn and Gaetane Nicodeme, *Tax Co-ordination in Europe: Assessing the First Years of the EU-Savings Taxation Directive*, CESIFO Working Paper No. 2675 (June 2009).

[85] Australian National Audit Office (ANAO), *The Management and Use of Double Taxation Agreement Information Collected through Automatic Exchange*, Performance Audit Report No. 34 2009–10 (2009) 20, available at www.anao.gov.au.

E. Due Process and Taxpayer Rights

The most important type of legitimacy claim to be addressed in the context of transnational information exchange at its current juncture is that of due process (procedural fairness or taxpayer rights). To date, most information exchange has concerned individuals who invest (or hide assets and income) across borders. Many have expressed concerns about how to protect taxpayer rights and privacy where information is provided to other countries. One reason for slow progress in establishing transnational tax information networks in the first place, expressed by the League of Nations, was a fear that countries were establishing 'an extension beyond national frontiers of an organised system of fiscal inquisition'.[86] Some concerns about privacy may be more perceived than real, but a key issue is legitimacy of the nascent transnational tax bureaucracy, so it is crucial that the system is perceived to be fair.

There are many facets of this aspect of legitimacy, and I refer to only a few issues here. First, in terms of legal provisions regarding the protection of taxpayer rights, all of the treaties discussed in section III above contain provisions addressed to due process in obtaining data and the protection of taxpayer privacy and confidentiality of taxpayer information. For example, under OECD Model Article 26.2, the requesting state must promise to provide protection equivalent to that provided at a national level to all data received, while the supplying state must comply with its own national laws of both procedural fairness and confidentiality in obtaining and supplying the data. The information can be disclosed to oversight bodies, and must be used only for stated purposes of tax assessment (unless otherwise agreed by the parties).

However, the treaties rely on national tax laws to protect taxpayer confidentiality. There is no overarching enforcement or surveillance of the protection accorded by national laws in respect of transnational information exchange. For developing countries, these systems and laws may require significant enhancement. Even if the effectiveness of information protection within particular countries is accepted, the lack of a harmonized approach across all treaties generates a complex web of jurisdictions and different laws applicable to taxpayers. Further, treaty provisions on information exchange are worded in a variety of ways. It has been suggested by Schenk-Geers that secrecy obligations be standardized in the Model Article on information exchange.[87] There are

---

86 League of Nations 1927, 1928, quoted in Picciotto, *supra* note 1, at 251.
87 Schenk-Geers, *supra* note 1.

other due process issues that also warrant more detailed examination. Tax information exchange treaty provisions do not provide for taxpayer notification that a government is seeking information about them to provide to another country, or is providing data to the third country from various records. The Protocol to the Multilateral Convention empowers but does not require the contracting party states to inform nationals before transmitting information about them to another country.[88] Another issue relates to the forum for appeal if a taxpayer is concerned that either due process in transnational income gathering has not been carried out, or that privacy is breached. This issue is discussed in the Multilateral Convention and revised Commentary, but will need to be addressed in more detail in the future.

As transnational information exchange becomes more widespread and involves developing countries and multilateral exchange, or even the establishment, in time, of central repositories of information, this will become of increasing concern. Concerns will also increase as processes such as automatic information exchange become more typical. The European Data Protection Supervisor has expressed concerns about the expansion in administrative cooperation for the 'rights and interests of natural persons involved', as a consequence of the Protocol expanding the Multilateral Convention on tax assistance.[89]

A related concern is the use by national tax agencies of illegally obtained data in criminal and civil proceedings against taxpayers. The Luxembourg and Liechtenstein cases illustrate the risk that data can become available 'for purchase' either from paying agents such as banks, or from tax administration officials themselves, or can be illegally accessed through search and seizure actions. This raises the question whether governments should refuse to utilize illegally obtained data. The balance between the national tax agency and individual taxpayer rights (in an era of bank secrecy) appeared to fall on the side of the tax agency in these cases. However, regularization of data processes is important both for reasons of public perception and for practical reasons of the ability to use such data in civil and criminal prosecutions of tax fraud. Dean acknowledges that a market in tax information might cause problems for taxpayer rights such as privacy.[90] As we have seen in respect to governmental use of illegally obtained data, including from

---

[88] OECD/EU, *supra* note 62, new Art. 4.

[89] Opinion of the European Data Protection Supervisor on the proposal for a Council Directive on administrative cooperation in the field of taxation (2010/C 101/01) 101/02.

[90] Dean, *supra* note 1, at 64.

third countries, tax information does have a price, but privacy is lost in the process. The analysis of tax information exchange as a market, rather than a governmental activity, would likely place the focus on *efficiency* (efficacy) of tax information exchange at the expense of other aspects of legitimacy.

Cockfield has suggested that it is time for a 'global taxpayer bill of rights' as a means of increasing trust and confidence in the tax administration.[91] In 2003, the OECD produced a Practice Note on Taxpayer Rights and Obligations.[92] An opportunity exists now for the OECD and Global Forum to strengthen their legitimacy claims in transnational tax information exchange by embedding simple and streamlined taxpayer protection rules and obligations in legal documents, in particular in the Multilateral Convention.

VI. DEVELOPING COUNTRIES AND TRANSNATIONAL TAX INFORMATION NETWORKS

This chapter argues that hybrid transnational solutions are being developed for tax information exchange and that the rapidly expanding arena of formal legal, institutional and informal processes of information exchange is beginning to operate successfully as a networked tax bureaucracy. Questions remain about how far transnational tax networks extend beyond the old mode of reciprocal bilateralism and to what extent they remain 'purely informational' in character, so that nation states remain essentially in competitive bilateral relationships and resist sharing authority or more expansive administrative powers.[93] Questions also remain about legitimacy of transnational tax information networks, in particular in respect of due process (taxpayer rights), effectiveness and inclusiveness of the networks.

The issue of *who* gets to participate in – and benefit from – transnational tax information networks is crucial. In spite of the dramatic

---

[91] Arthur J. Cockfield, 'Protecting Taxpayer Privacy under Enhanced Cross-border Tax Information Exchange: Toward a Multilateral Taxpayer Bill of Rights' (2010) 42 *University of British Columbia Law Review* 419.

[92] OECD Centre for Tax Policy and Administration, *Taxpayer Rights and Obligations, Practice Note* (General Administrative Principles GAP002). See also OECD, *Taxpayer Rights and Obligations: A Survey of the Legal Situation in OECD Countries* (27 April 1990).

[93] Kahler and Lake, *supra* note 72.

developments of the last few years, these networks are far from global in reach. Most tax information exchange and cooperation is taking place between developed country tax administrations and, where other countries are involved (such as tax havens), in the interests of developed country fiscs. Keen and Ligthart observed that 'information exchange with developing countries is small – even though Sweden has bilateral double taxation treaties with 62 of them'.[94] The Multilateral Convention holds real promise, however the process of admission of new country signatories means that significant work in administrative capacity building will be required for many developing countries before they are likely to be admitted as parties to the Convention.

The revenues raised from tax information networks are so far relatively modest. It is not clear whether this is because there is not revenue there; because tax evaders are constantly 'one step ahead' (and recalcitrant jurisdictions provide havens for evaders); or because the successful utilization of tax information requires a significant improvement in operations and processes of national tax agencies. Tax information exchanged across borders does not itself guarantee increased revenues but is only one step towards more effective transnational tax cooperation. It will be crucial in future for national tax administrators to collaborate in establishing transnational tax 'handles' or mechanisms by which tax assessments can be enforced and tax can actually be collected. Supranational organizations including the OECD and Global Forum must also take further steps to enhance national and international legitimacy, as this is essential for the success of transnational tax administrative cooperation.

94 Keen and Ligthart, *supra* note 1, at 100.

Bibliography

ActionAid UK, *Annual Report 2010* (2010), available at www.actionaid.org.uk/102636/where_did_your_money_go_in_2010. html

ActionAid UK, *How to Stop Tax Dodging* (2010), available at www.actionaid.org.uk/102021/how_to_stop_tax_dodging.html

Ahmad, E. and Stern, N. (eds), *The Theory and Practice of Tax Reform in Developing Countries* (New York: Cambridge University Press, 1991)

Alarie, B., *Price Discrimination in Income Taxation: Defending Half-Hearted Anti-Avoidance* (26 March 2011), available at http://ssrn.com/abstract=1796284

Allen, R., *The Challenge of Reforming Budgetary Institutions in Developing Countries*, IMF Working Paper WP/09/96 (May 2009)

Altshuler, R. and Grubert, H., *The Three Parties in the Race to the Bottom: Host Governments, Home Governments and Multinational Companies*, CESifo Working Paper Series No. 1613 (December 2005), available at http://ssrn.com/abstract=875308

Altshuler, R., Grubert, H. and Newlon, T.S., *Has U.S. Investment Abroad Become More Sensitive to Tax Rates?*, NBER Working Paper No. W6383 (January 1998), available at http://ssrn.com/abstract=226131

Armendáriz, B. and Morduch, J., *The Economics of Microfinance* (2nd edn, Cambridge, MA: MIT Press, 2010)

Ashley, S., 'OECD may detract from UN TP work', *Transfer Pricing Week*, 17 May 2011

Australian National Audit Office (ANAO), *The Management and Use of Double Taxation Agreement Information Collected through Automatic Exchange Performance Audit*, Report No. 34 2009-10, available at www.anao.gov.au

Avi-Yonah, R.S., 'Globalization, Tax Competition, and the Fiscal Crisis of the Welfare State' (2000) 113 *Harvard Law Review* 1573

– 'International Tax as International Law' (2004) 57 *Tax L Rev.* 483

– *International Tax as International Law: An Analysis of the International Tax Regime* (New York: Cambridge University Press, 2007)

Avi-Yonah, R.S. and Clausing, K.A., *Reforming Corporate Taxation in a Global Economy: A Proposal to Adopt Formulary Apportionment*, Hamilton Project Discussion Paper 2007-08, (Brookings Institution, 2007), available at www.brookings.edu/research/papers/2007/06/corporatetaxes-clausing

Avi-Yonah, R.S. and Margalioth, Y., 'Taxation in Developing Countries: Some Recent Support and Challenges to the Conventional View' (2007–2008) 27 *Virginia Tax Review* 1

Azam, R., 'E-commerce, Taxation and Cyberspace Law: The Integrative Adoption Model' (2007) 12 (5) *Va. JL and Tech.* 23

Bagchi, A., 'Efficacy of Tax Incentives: "Tax Expenditure Analysis" and its Relevance for India' (1974) 9(24) *Economic and Political Weekly* 951

Bagchi, A., Rao, R.K. and Sen, B., *Raising the Tax-Ratio by Reining in the 'Tax Breaks': An Agenda for Action*, National Institute of Public Finance and Policy Working Paper No. 54 (December 2005), available at www.nipfp.org.in/newweb/sites/default/files/wp05_nipfp_tr_038.pdf

– *Tax Breaks for the Small Scale Sector* (May 2006), available at www.nipfp.org.in/working_paper/wp06_nipfp_tr_042.pdf

Balance, Eurodad, Oxfam, Tax Justice Network, 'Mopani Copper Mines is Dodging Taxes in Zambia' (10 February 2011), available at www.ctpd.org.zm/index.php?option=com_content&view=article&id=133:mopani-copper-mines-is-dodging-taxes-in-zambia&catid=66:blogs&Itemid=124

Baldwin, R., *Rules and Government* (Oxford: Oxford University Press, 1995)

Banerjee, A. and Duflo, E., *Poor Economics: A Radical Rethinking of the Way to Fight Global Poverty* (New York: Public Affairs, 2011)

Banerjee, A., Duflo, E., Chattopadhyay, R. and Shapiro, J., *Targeting the Hard-Core Poor: An Impact Assessment*, Preliminary Working Paper (2010), available at http://poverty-action.org/sites/default/files/Shapiro.pdf

Banerjee, A., Duflo, E., Glennerster, R. and Kinnan, C., *The Miracle of Microfinance? Evidence from a Randomized Evaluation* (30 May 2009), available at http://economics.mit.edu/files/4162

Banks, J. and Diamond, P., *The Base for Direct Taxation*, Prepared for the Report of a Commission on Reforming the Tax System for the 21st Century, Chaired by Sir James Mirrlees (Institute for Fiscal Studies, 2008), available at www.ifs.org.uk/mirrleesreview

Barker, W.B., 'An International Tax System for Emerging Economies, Tax Sparing and Development: It is All About Source!' (2007) 29 *U Pa. J Int'l L* 349

Barrows, S., 'Racing to the Top … at Last: The Regulation of Safety in Shipping' in W. Mattli and N. Woods (eds), *The Politics of Global Regulation* (Princeton, NJ: Princeton University Press, 2009) 189

Barthel, F., Busse, M. and Neumayer, E., 'The Impact of Double Taxation Treaties on Foreign Direct Investments: Evidence from Large Dyadic Panel Data' (2010) 28(3) *Contemporary Economic Policy* 366

Becker, J. and Fuest, C., 'The Taxation of Foreign Profits: The Old View, the New View and a Pragmatic View' (2011) 46(2) *Intereconomics* 92

Benshalom, I., 'The New Poor at Our Gates: Global Justice Implications for International Trade and Tax Law' (2010) 85 *NYUL Rev.* 1

Bergsman, J., *Advice on Taxation and Tax Incentives for Foreign Direct Investment* (1999), available at www.ifc.org/ifcext/fias.nsf/AttachmentsByTitle/Advice_on_Taxation_and_Tax_Incentives_for_FDI.pdf/$FILE/Advice%2Bon%2BTaxation%2Band%2BTax%2BIncentives%2Bfor%2BFDI.pdf

Berkowitz, D. *et al.*, 'Economic Development, Legality and the Transplant Effect', available at www.law.columbia.edu/law-economicstudies/papers/wp195.pdf

Bird, R.M., *Tax Policy and Economic Development* (Baltimore, MA: Johns Hopkins Press, 1992)

– 'Administrative Dimension of Tax Reform' (2004) *Asia-Pacific Tax Bulletin* (March) 134, available at http://unpan1.un.org/intradoc/groups/public/documents/UNPAN/UNPAN015761.pdf

– *Tax Challenges Facing Developing Countries*, University of Toronto, Institute for International Business Working Paper Series, IIB Paper No. 12/2006 (2006)

Bird, R.M. and Casanegra de Jantscher, M. (eds), *Improving Tax Administration in Developing Countries* (Washington, DC: International Monetary Fund, 1992)

Bird, R.M. and Oldman, O. (eds), *Readings on Taxation in Developing Countries* (Baltimore: Johns Hopkins Press, 1964)

– *Taxation in Developing Countries* (Baltimore, MA: Johns Hopkins Press, 1990)

Bird, R.M. and Zolt, E.M., 'Tax Policy in Emerging Countries' (2008) 26 *Environment and Planning C: Government and Policy* 73

Bittker, B.I., 'A "Comprehensive Tax Base" as a Goal of Income Tax Reform' (1967) 80(5) *Harvard Law Review* 925

– 'Accounting for Federal "Tax Subsidies" in the National Budget' (1969) 22(2) *National Tax Journal* 244

Bittker, B.I. and Lokken, L., *Federal Taxation of Income, Estates, and Gifts* (2nd/3rd edn, London: Thomson Reuters, 2011)

Bittker, B.I., McMahon, M. and Zelenak, L., *Federal Income Taxation of Individuals* (3rd edn, London: Thomson Reuters, 2011)

Blanchard, O. and Shleifer, A., 'Federalism With and Without Political Centralization: China Versus Russia' (2001) 48 *IMF Staff Papers*, Special Issue 171–9

Blank, J., 'In Defense of Individual Tax Privacy' (2011) 61 *Emory Law Journal*

Boadway, R., 'The Annual Tax Expenditure Reports: A Critique' (2007) 55(1) *Canadian Tax Journal* 106

Bohler-Muller, N., 'South African International Relations and the Emergence of China: Is Development at All Costs the Answer?', African Institute of South Africa (AISA) *AfricaGrowth Agenda* 6 (2011), available at hwww.africagrowth.com/july11_narnia.html

Boskin, M.J. and McLure, C.H., Jr (eds), *World Tax Reform: Case Studies of Developed and Developing Countries* (San Francisco, CA: ICS Press, 1990)

Boss, W.H. and Sharp, W.M., Jr, 'The Swiss–US "Turnover" Ground Rules: A Technical Update', *Tax Notes*, 7 November 2011

Botha, J., 'Towards Africa's Global Integration: Trade, Investment and Development' (2003) 27(2) *Studies in Economics and Econometrics* 53

Bovenberg, A.L. *et al.*, 'Tax Incentives and International Capital Flows: The Case of the United States and Japan' in A. Razin and J. Slemrod (eds), *Taxation in the Global Economy* (Chicago, IL: University of Chicago Press, 1990)

Braithwaite, J., *Regulatory Capitalism: How it Works and Ideas for Making it Work Better* (Cheltenham, UK and Northampton, MA, USA: Edward Elgar, 2008)

Braithwaite, J. and Drahos, P., *Global Business Regulation* (Cambridge: Cambridge University Press, 2000)

Brauner, Y., 'An International Tax Regime in Crystallization' (2003) 56 *Tax Law Review* 259

– 'International Trade and Tax Agreements May Be Coordinated, But Not Reconciled' (2005–2006) 25 *Virginia Tax Review* 251

– 'A Framework for an Informed Study of the Realistic Role of Tax in a Development Agenda' (2010) 42 *University of British Columbia Law Review* 275

Broecker, C., 'Better the Devil You Know: Home State Approaches to Transnational Corporate Accountability' (2008) 41 *New York University Journal of International Law and Politics* 159

Brooks, K., 'Denying Tax Sparing Provisions: Another Way for High-Income Countries to Dictate the Tax Policy of Low-Income Countries?', paper presented at the annual meeting of the Law and Society Association, Berlin, 25 July 2007 (unpublished manuscript) (2008), available at www.allacademic.com/meta/p177927_index.html

– 'Global Distributive Justice: The Potential for a Feminist Analysis of International Tax Revenue Allocation' (2009) 21 *Can. J Women and L* 267

– 'Inter-nation Equity: The Development of an Important but Underappreciated International Tax Policy Objective' in J.G. Head and R. Krever (eds), *Tax Reform in the 21st Century: A Volume in Memory of Richard Musgrave* (Alphen aan den Rijn: Wolters Kluwer Law & Business, 2009)

– 'Tax Sparing: A Needed Incentive for Foreign Investment in Low-Income Countries or an Unnecessary Revenue Sacrifice?' (2009) 34 *Queen's Law Journal* 508

Brown, K.B., 'Transforming the Unilateralist into the Internationalist: New Tax Treaty Policy Towards Developing Countries' in K.B. Brown and M.L. Fallows (eds), *Taxing America* (New York/London: New York University Press, 1996)

– 'Harmful Tax Competition: The OECD View' (1999) 32 *George Washington Journal of International Law and Economics* 311

– 'Missing Africa, Should U.S. International Tax Rules Accommodate Investment in Developing Countries?' (2002) 23 *University Pennsylvania Journal International Economic Law* 45

Browning, L., 'Insight: Microsoft use of low-tax havens drives down tax bill', *Reuters*, 27 July 2011, available at www.reuters.com/article/2011/07/27/us-microsoft-tax-idUSTRE76Q6OB20110727

Buchanan, J., *The Demand and Supply of Public Goods* (Chicago, IL: McNally, 1968)

Burton, M., 'Making the Australian Tax Expenditures Statement an Effective Policy Instrument: From Fiscal Record to Transparent Report' (2005) 8 (1) *Australian Journal of Taxation* 1

– 'Capturing Contemporary "Democracy": The Shortcomings of Australian Tax Expenditure Management and their Ideological Foundations' in L. Philipps, N. Brooks and J. Li (eds), *Tax Expenditures: State of the Art* (Canadian Tax Foundation, 2011)

Burton, M. and Stewart, M., *Promoting Budget Transparency through Tax Expenditure Management: A Report on Country Experience for Civil Society Advocates* (3 June 2011), available at http://papers.ssrn.com/sol3/papers.cfm?abstract_id=1864324

Cai, H. and Treisman, D., 'State Corroding Federalism' (2004) 88 *Journal of Public Economics* 819

Carkovic, M. and Levine, R., 'Does Foreign Direct Investment Accelerate Economic Growth?' in T.H. Moran, E.M. Graham and M. Blomström (eds), *Does Foreign Direct Investment Promote Development?* (Washington, DC: Institute for International Economics, 2005)

Carr, K. and Grow, B., 'Special Report: A Little House of Secrets on the Great Plains', *Reuters*, 28 June 2011, available at www.reuters.com/article/2011/06/28/us-usa-shell-companies-idUSTRE75R20Z20110628

Charnovitz, S., 'The Illegitimacy of Preventing Civil Society Participation' (2011) 36 *Brooklin J Int'l L* 891

Christian Aid, *Accounting for Change: Shifting Sands* (November 2010), available at www.christianaid.org.uk/images/accounting-for-change-shifting-sands.pdf

Christians, A., 'Hard Law, Soft Law, and International Taxation' (2007) 25 *Wisconsin International Law Journal* 325
– *Global Trends and Constraints on Tax Policy in the Least Developed Countries*, University of Wisconsin Legal Studies Research Paper No. 1086 (2009)
– 'Networks, Norms and National Tax Policy' (2010) 9 *Wash. U Global Stud. L Rev.* 1
– 'Taxation in a Time of Crisis: Policy Leadership from the OECD to the G20' (2010) 5 *Northwestern Journal of Law and Social Policy* 19
Clarke, D.C. (ed.), *China's Legal System: New Developments, New Challenges* (Cambridge: Cambridge University Press, 2008)
Clegg, D. and Stretch, R., *Income Tax in South Africa* (Durban: Lexis Nexis, 2010)
Clément, J.A.P. and Peiris, S.A., *Post-Stabilization Economics in Sub-Saharan Africa: Lessons from Mozambique* (Washington, DC: International Monetary Fund, 2008)
Cnossen, S., *Tax Policy in the European Union*, CESifo Working Paper No. 758, Category 1: Public Finance (August 2002), available at http://papers.ssrn.com/sol3/papers.cfm?abstract_id=340905
Cockfield, A.J., 'The Rise of the OECD as Informal "World Tax Organization" through National Responses to E-Commerce Tax Challenges' (2006) 8 *Yale Journal of Law and Technology* 136
– 'Protecting Taxpayer Privacy under Enhanced Cross-border Tax Information Exchange: Toward a Multilateral Taxpayer Bill of Rights' (2010) 42 *University of British Columbia Law Review* 419
Coelho, C., 'Tax Sparing and Brazil's Tax Treaties' (2008) 51(8) *Tax Notes International* 690
Coen, D. and Thatcher, M., 'Network Governance and Multi-level Delegation: European Networks of Regulatory Agencies' (2008) 28 *Journal of Public Policy* 49
Collier, P., *The Bottom Billion: Why the Poorest Countries are Failing and What Can be Done about It* (New York: Oxford University Press, 2007)
Collins, D., Morduch, J., Rutherford, S. and Ruthven, O., *Portfolios of the Poor: How the World's Poor Live on $2 a Day* (Princeton, NJ: Princeton University Press, 2009)
Commission of Enquiry into Certain Aspects of the Tax Structure of South Africa, *Government Gazette* 15924, *Regulation Gazette* 5378 of 1994, available at www.treasury.gov.za
Counter Balance, *The Mopani Copper Mine, Zambia: How European Development Money has Fed a Mining Scandal*, available at www.counterbalance-eib.org/wp-content/uploads/2011/03/Mopani-Report-English-Web.pdf

Crandall, W. and Bodin, J., *Revenue Administration Reform in Middle Eastern Countries, 1994–2004*, IMF Working Paper WP/05/03, available at www.imf.org/external/pubs/cat/longres.aspx?sk=18595
Cui, W., 'Fiscal Federalism in Chinese Taxation' (2011) 3 *World Tax Journal* 455
Dagan, H., *Property, Values and Institutions* (Oxford: Oxford University Press, 2011)
Dagan, T., 'The Tax Treaties Myth' (2000) 32(939) *Journal of International Law and Politics* 47
– 'The Costs of Cooperation in International Taxation' in E. Benvenisti and G. Nolte (eds), *The Welfare State, Globalization and International Law* (Heidelberg: Springer-Verlag Berlin, 2004)
– 'Commuting' (2006) 26 *Virginia Tax Review* 185
– 'Itemizing Personhood' (2009) 29 *Virginia Tax Review* 93
– 'Ordinary People, Necessary Choices: A Comparative Study of Childcare Deductions' (2010) 11(2) *Theoretical Inquiries in Law* 588
Davies, R., 'Tax Treaties and Foreign Direct Investment: Potential versus Performance' (2004) 11(6) *International Tax and Public Finance* 775
Dean, S.A., 'The Incomplete Market for Tax Information' (2008) 49(1) *Boston College Law Review* 1
Desai, M.A. and Hines, J.R., Jr, 'Evaluating International Tax Reform' (2003) 55 *Nat'l Tax J* 487
Deutsch Bank Research, *EU Savings Directive: One Piece in the Puzzle of Cross-Border Tax Policy* (22 June 2009)
Devereaux, M.P., 'The Impact of Taxation on International Business: Evidence from the Ruding Committee Survey' (1992) 2 *EC Tax Review* 105
Dourado, A.P., *Separation of Powers in Tax Law*, EATLP International Tax Law Series 7 (IBFD, 2010)
– 'The Delicate Balance: Revenue Authority Discretions and the Rule of Law: Some Thoughts in a Legal Theory and Comparative Perspective' in C. Evans, J. Freedman and R. Krever (eds), *The Delicate Balance, Tax, Discretion and the Rule of Law* (IBFD, 2011)
Draper, W.H., III, 'Foreword' to UN Development Programme, *Human Development Report 1990* (1990), available at http://hdr.undp.org/en/media/hdr_1990_en_front.pdf
Duflo, E., Gale, W., Liebman, J., Orszag, P. and Saez, E., 'Saving Incentives for Low- and Middle-Income Families: Evidence from a Field Experiment with H&R Block' (2006) 121 *Quarterly Journal of Economics* 1311
Dworkin, R., *Taking Rights Seriously* (Cambridge, MA: Harvard University Press, 1978 (1977))

Easson, A.J., *Tax Incentives for Foreign Direct Investment* (The Hague: Kluwer Law International, 2004)
Easterly, W., *The White Man's Burden: Why the West's Efforts to Aid the Rest Have Done So Much Ill and So Little Good* (Oxford: Oxford University Press, 2006)
– 'Can the West Save Africa?' (2009) 47 *Journal of Economic Literature* 373
Easterly, W. (ed.), *Reinventing Foreign Aid* (Cambridge, MA: Massachusetts Institute of Technology Press, 2008)
Ebrill, L., Stotsky, J. and Gropp, R., *Revenue Implications of Trade Liberalization* (Washington, DC: International Monetary Fund, 1999)
European Commission, *Report*, COM(2008)552 final (2008)
Facchi, A., *I Diritti nell' Europa Multiculturale, Pluralismo Nomativo i Immigrazione* (Rome: Editori Laterza, 2008)
Feigenberg, B., Field, E.M. and Pande, R., *Building Social Capital through Microfinance*, National Bureau of Economic Research Working Paper No. 16018 (2010), available at www.nber.org/papers/w16018
Fenster, M., 'The Transparency Fix: Advocating Legal Rights and their Alternatives in the Pursuit of a Visible State', available at http://ssrn.com/abstract=1918154
Field, E. and Pande, R., 'Repayment Frequency and Default in Microfinance: Evidence from India' (2008) 6 *Journal of the European Economic Association* 501
Field, E., Jayachandran, S. and Pande, R., 'Do Traditional Institutions Constrain Female Entrepreneurship? A Field Experiment on Business Training in India' (2010) 100 *American Economic Review: Papers and Proceedings* 125
Field, E., Pande, R. and Papp, J., *Does Microfinance Repayment Flexibility Affect Entrepreneurial Behavior and Loan Default?*, Centre for Micro Finance Working Paper Series No. 34 (2010), available at www.povertyactionlab.org/sites/default/files/publications/EFieldDoesMicrofinanceRepayment%20.pdf
Firger, D., 'Lifting the Resource Curse: Will Dodd-Frank Do the Trick?', available at http://industry-news.org/2010/09/28/daniel-firger-lifting-the-resource-curse-will-dodd-frank-do-the-trick-2/
Fisher, K., 'Locating Frames in the Discursive Universe' 2 *Social Research Online* 3, available at www.socresonline.org.uk/2/3/4.html
Fleischer, M.P., 'Generous to a Fault? Fair Shares and Charitable Giving' (2008) 93 *Minnesota Law Review* 165
Fleming, J.C., Jr, and Peroni, R.J., 'Reinvigorating Tax Expenditure Analysis and its International Dimension' (2008) 27 *Virginia Tax Review* 437

Forgione, A., 'Clicks and Mortar: Taxing Multinational Business Profits in the Digital Age' (2003) 26 *Seattle U L Rev.* 719

Forsyth, M., 'A Typology of Relationships between State and Non-State Justice Systems' (2007) 56 *Legal Pluralism and Unofficial Law* 67

Fu, H., 'The Understanding and Evaluation of the Framework Rules for Tax Legislative Power' (2004) 12 *Taxation Research* 33

Fuest, C. and Riedel, N., 'Tax Evasion, Tax Avoidance and Tax Expenditures in Developing Countries: A Review of the Literature' *Report Prepared for the UK Department for International Development*, available at http://94.126.106.9/R4D/PDF/Outputs/EcoDev/60670_TaxEvasionReportDFIDFINAL1906.pdf

Fuller, L., 'Positivism and Fidelity to Law: A Reply to Professor Hart' (1958) 71 *Harvard Law Review Forum* 630

– *The Morality of Law* (revised edn, New Haven, CT: Yale University Press, 1969)

Gabbatt, A., 'U2 Glastonbury tax protest: activists condemn "heavy-handed" security', *Guardian*, 25 June 2011, available at www.guardian.co.uk/music/2011/jun/25/u2-bono-tax-protest-glastonbury

Galle, B., 'Keep Charity Charitable' (2010) 88 *Texas Law Review* 1213

Gergen, M.P., 'The Case for a Charitable Contributions Deduction' (1998) 74 *Virginia Law Review* 1393

Ghai, D., 'Introduction' in *The IMF and the South: The Social Impact of Crisis and Adjustment* (London: Zed Books, 1991)

Gillis, M. (ed.), *Tax Reform in Developing Countries* (Durham, NC: Duke University Press, 1989)

Glaeser, E.L. (ed.), *The Economics of Agglomeration*, NBER Conference held 30 November–1 December 2007 (unpublished drafts), available at www.nber.org/books/glae08-1/

Global Governance Reform Project, *Reimagining the Future: Towards Democratic Governance* (Saint Kilda/VIC: Vista Publications, 2000)

Global Witness, 'A Crude Awakening', available at www.globalwitness.org/library/crude-awakening

Godbole, M., 'Task Force Reports on Direct and Indirect Taxes: Some Issues' (2002) 37(49) *Economic and Political Weekly* 4884

Goffman, E., *Frame Analysis: An Essay on the Organization of Experience* (Northeastern University Press, 1974)

Gomes, R., 'Love the iPhone, hate the tax cheat: US Uncut protests Apple, and Apple gets aggressive', *AlterNet*, 8 June 2011, available at www.alternet.org/vision/151252/love_the_iphone,_hate_the_tax_cheat%3A_us_uncut_protests_apple,_and_apple_gets_aggressive_/

Gordon, R. (ed.), *Taxation in Developing Countries: Six Case Studies and Policy Implications* (New York: Columbia University Press, 2010)

Gordon, R.H. and Li, W., 'Provincial and Local Governments in China: Fiscal Institutions and Government Behavior' in J. Fan and R. Morck (eds), *Capitalizing China* (forthcoming, University of Chicago Press)

Graetz, M.J., 'Taxing International Income: Inadequate Principles, Outdated Concepts and Unsatisfactory Policies' (2001) 54 *Tax L Rev.* 261

Graetz, M.J. and Schenk, D.H., *Federal Income Taxation Principles and Policies* (Mineola, NY: Foundation Press, 2002)

Grant, R. and Keohane, R.O., 'Accountability and Abuses of Power in World Politics' (2005) 99(1) *American Political Science Review* 29

Griffiths, J., 'What is Legal Pluralism?' (1986) 24 *Journal of Legal Pluralism and Unofficial Law* 1

Grubert, H. and Mutti, J., 'Do Taxes Influence Where U.S. Corporations Invest?' (2000) 53 *National Tax Journal* 825

Guangxi Ethnic Autonomous Region Bureau of Finance, *Report on Strengthening Unified Tax Administration, Effectively Organizing Tax Reductions and Exemptions*, approved and released by the Guangxi People's Government, Guizhengfa [1981] 80 (9 May 1981)

Günther, K., *The Sense of Appropriateness, Application Discourses in Morality and Law* (New York: State University of New York Press, 1989)

– 'Rechtspluralismus und Universaler Code der Legalität: Globalisierung als Rechtstheoretisches Problem' in J. Habermas, L. Wingert and K. Günther, *Die Öffentlichkeit der Vernunft und der Vernunft der Öffentlichkeit* (Frankfurt: Suhrkamp, 2001)

Gupta, S. and Tareq, S., 'Mobilizing Revenue' (IMF, September 2008), available at www.imf.org/external/pubs/ft/fandd/2008/09/gupta.htm

Gustafson, C.H. *et al.*, *Taxation of International Transactions: Materials, Text and Problems* (West Group, 2011)

Habermas, J., *Faktizität und Geltung, Beiträge zur Diskurstheorie des Rechts und des demokratischen Rechtsstaats* (2nd edn, Frankfurt-am-Main, 1992)

Hamzaoui, R., 'Mauritius: Corporate Taxation', Country Surveys (International Bureau of Fiscal Documentation), available at www.ibfd.org

Hari, J., 'Vision: Everyday Brits are in revolt against wealthy tax cheats: can we do that here?', *AlterNet*, 5 February 2011, available at www.alternet.org/teaparty/149806/vision%3A_everyday_brits_are_in_revolt_against_wealthy_tax_cheats_–_can_we_do_that_here/

Hart, H.L.A., *The Concept of Law* (Oxford: Oxford University Press, 1961; 1994)

Heady, C., 'Tax Expenditures: Definitional and Policy Issues' in L. Philipps, N. Brooks and J. Li (eds), *Tax Expenditure Analysis: State of the Art* (Canadian Tax Foundation, 2011)

Helms, B., *Access for All: Building Inclusive Financial Systems* (World Bank Publications, 2006)
Helpman, E., *The Mystery of Economic Growth* (Cambridge, MA: Harvard University Press, 2004)
Hemels, S.J.C., 'Are We in Need of a European Charity? How to Remove Fiscal Barriers to Cross-Border Charitable Giving in Europe' (2009) 37 *Intertax* 424
Hemmelgarn, T. and Nicodeme, G., *Tax Co-ordination in Europe: Assessing the First Years of the EU-Savings Taxation Directive*, CESIFO Working Paper No. 2675 (June 2009)
Higgott, R., 'Public Goods, Global Governance and Private Actors: Learning from the WTO' in G. Fraser-Moleketi (ed.), *The World We Could Win* (Amsterdam: IOS Press, 2005)
Hill, F.R. and Mancino, D.A., *Taxation of Exempt Organizations* (London: Thomson Reuters, 2010)
Hills, R.M., Jr, 'Poverty, Residency, and Federalism: States' Duty of Impartiality toward Newcomers' (1999) *Supreme Court Review* 277, available at http://papers.ssrn.com/sol3/papers.cfm?abstract_id=182628
Hines, J.R., Jr, 'Will Social Welfare Expenditures Survive Tax Competition?' (2006) 22(3) *Oxford Review of Economic Policy* 330
Hirschman, A.O., *Exit, Voice and Loyalty* (Cambridge, MA: Harvard University Press, 1970)
Holland, D. and Vann, R.J., 'Income Tax Incentives for Investment' in V. Thuronyi, *Tax Law Design and Drafting* (Washington, DC: International Monetary Fund, 1998) vol. 2
Howard, C., 'The Politics of Tax Expenditures in Wealthy Democracies' in L. Philipps, N. Brooks and J. Li (eds), *Tax Expenditure Analysis: State of the Art* (Canadian Tax Foundation, 2011)
Huang, Y., *Capitalism with Chinese Characteristics: Entrepreneurship and the State* (Cambridge: Cambridge University Press, 2008)
Hulme, D., 'The Story of the Grameen Bank: From Subsidized Microcredit to Market Based Microfinance' in D. Hulme and T. Arun (eds), *Microfinance: A Reader* (New York: Routledge, 2009)
Hulme, D. and Arun, T. (eds), *Microfinance: A Reader* (New York: Routledge, 2009)
Hundt, R.E., *In China's Shadow: The Crisis of American Entrepreneurship* (2006), available at www.american.com/archive/2006/december/copy_of_chinas-shadow-looking-east-toward-the-dawn%20w-o-numbers
Huo, J., 'Sixty Years of Evolution of the System of Tax Administration in New China' (2010) 3 *Research on Contemporary Chinese History* 52

Ijeoma, E.O., 'Evaluating Development Projects and Programmes in Africa: The Case of the New Partnership for Africa's Development – NEPAD' (2008) 37(4) *African Insight* 61

ILADT, *Modelo de Convenio para América Latina, Instituto Colombiano de Derecho Tributario* (Cartagena, 2010)

IMF, *Experimental Report on Transparency Practices: Argentina* (15 April 1999)

– *Manual of Fiscal Transparency* (Washington, DC: International Monetary Fund, 2007)

– *Kenya, Uganda, and United Republic of Tanzania: Selected Issues*, IMF Country Report No. 08/353 (October 2008), available at www.imf.org/external/pubs/ft/scr/2008/cr08353.pdf

Infanti, A.C., 'Spontaneous Tax Coordination: On Adopting a Comparative Approach to Reforming the U.S. International Tax Regime' (2002) 35 *Vand. J Transnat'l L* 1105

– 'Tax ~~Equity~~' (2008) 55 *Buff. L Rev.* 1191

Institute for Wisconsin's Future, 'Who Does Not Pay Taxes', available at www.wisconsinsfuture.org/

Internal Revenue Service (US), *Withholding of Tax on Nonresident Aliens and Foreign Entities*, Publication No. 515 (2011)

International Budget Project, *Open Budget Questionnaire, India* (September 2009), available at http://internationalbudget.org/wp-content/uploads/2011/04/India-OBI2010QuestionnaireFinal.pdf

Ioannou, I. and Serafeim, G., *The Impact of Corporate Social Responsibility on Investment Recommendations*, Harvard Business School Working Paper 11-017, available at www.hbs.edu/research/pdf/11-017.pdf

Janssen, R.F., 'Income tax snooping through history', *Wall Street Journal*, 6 May 1970

Jin, H., Qian, Y. and Weingast, B.R., 'Regional Decentralization and Fiscal Incentives: Federalism, Chinese Style' (2005) 89 *Journal of Public Economics* 1719

Jogarajan, S., 'Prelude to the International Tax Treaty Network: 1815–1914 Early Tax Treaties and the Conditions for Action' (2011) 31(4) *Oxford Journal of Legal Studies* 679

Jogarajan, S. and Stewart, M., 'Success or Failure?' (2007) 22 *Australian Tax Forum* 3

Johnston, D.C., 'Wiping out Wisconsin taxes', *Reuters*, 26 August 2011, available at http://blogs.reuters.com/david-cay-johnston/2011/08/26/wiping-out-wisconsin-taxes/

Jun, J., 'Korea's Tax System: A Growth-Oriented Choice' in R.H. Gordon (ed.), *Taxation in Developing Countries* (Columbia University Press, 2010)

Kahler, M. and Lake, D., 'Economic Integration and Global Governance: Why So Little Supranationalism?' in W. Mattli and N. Woods (eds), *The Politics of Global Regulation* (Princeton, NJ: Princeton University Press, 2009)

Kampen, T.A. and Rijke, L.J., 'The Kreditetbank Luxembourg and the Liechtenstein Tax Affairs: Notes on the Balance between the Exchange of Information between States and the Protection of Fundamental Rights' (2009) *EC Tax Review* 2008-5 221

Kapekele, M., 'Government saving face on mine tax issue', *Zambia Post Online*, 15 June 2011, available at www.postzambia.com:3128/post-read_article.php?articleId=21201

Kaplow, L. and Shavell, S., 'Why the Legal System is Less Efficient than the Income Tax in Redistributing Income' (1994) 23 *Journal of Legal Studies* 667

Karlan, D. and Appel, J., *More than Good Intentions: How a New Economics is Helping to Solve Global Poverty* (Dutton: Dutton Adult, 2011)

Karlan, D. and Valdivia, M., *Teaching Entrepreneurship: Impact of Business Training on Microfinance Clients and Institutions* (2010), available at http://karlan.yale.edu/p/TeachingEntrepreneurship_revision_jan2010.pdf

Karlan, D. and Zinman, J., 'Expanding Credit Access: Using Randomized Supply Decisions to Estimate the Impacts' (2010) 23 *Review of Financial Studies* 434

Karzon, A.U., 'Tax Expenditures and Tax Reform' (1985) 38 *Vand. L Rev.* 1397

Kaufman, N.H., 'Fairness and the Taxation of International Income' (1998) 29 *Law and Pol'y Int'l Bus.* 145

– 'Equity Considerations in International Taxation' (2001) 26 *Brook. J Int'l L* 1465

Kaufmann, D., 'Human Rights and Governance: The Empirical Challenge' in P. Alston and M. Robinson, *Human Rights and Development: Towards Mutual Reinforcement* (New York: Oxford University Press, 2005)

Keen, M., 'Taxation and Development – Again', IMF Working Paper WP/12/220 (September 2012)

Keen, M. and Ligthart, J.E., 'Information Sharing and International Taxation: A Primer' (2006) 13 *International Tax and Public Finance* 81

Keen, M. and Simone, A., 'Tax Policy in Developing Countries: Some Lessons from the 1990s and Some Challenges Ahead' in S. Gupta *et al.* (eds), *Helping Countries Develop: The Role of Fiscal Policy* (Washington, DC: International Monetary Fund, 2004)

Kelkar, V.L. *et al.*, *Report of the Task Force on Direct Taxes* (New Delhi, 27 December 2002), available at www.prsindia.org/uploads/media/DTC%20Bill/kelkar%20direct%20taxes.pdf

Kelsen, H., *Teoria Pura do Direito* (4th edn, Arménio Amado (ed.), Coimbra, 1976)

Kickert, W.J.M., Klijn, E.H. and Koppenjan, J.F.M. (eds), *Managing Complex Networks: Strategies for the Public Sector* (London: SAGE Publications, 1997)

Kilkenny, A., 'We're not broke': the movement that helped spark Occupy Wall Street', *The Nation*, 13 January 2012, available at www.thenation.com/blog/165635/were-not-broke-movement-helped-spark-occupy-wall-street

Kleinbard, E.D., 'Tax Expenditure Framework Legislation' (2010) 63 *National Tax Journal* 353

– 'The Congress within the Congress: How Tax Expenditures Distort our Budget and our Political Processes' (2010) 36 *Ohio Northern University Law Review* 1

Kleinhaus, M.M. and Macdonald, R.A., 'What is a Critical Legal Pluralism' (1997) 12 *Canadian Journal of Law and Society* 25

Kocieniewski, D., 'GE's strategies let it avoid taxes altogether', *New York Times*, 24 March 2011, available at www.nytimes.com/2011/03/25/business/economy/25tax.html?_r=1&scp=3&sq=ge&st=cse

Kornhauser, M.E., 'Doing the Full Monty: Will Publicizing Tax Information Increase Compliance?' (2005) 18 *Canadian Journal of Law and Jurisprudence* 1

Krever, R., *Reform of the Mongolian Corporate Income Tax* (Development Alternatives, Inc. (DAI), for the USAID-financed Economic Policy Support Project, 24 September 2003)

– 'Interpreting Income Tax Laws in the Common Law World' in M. Achatz, T. Ehrke-Rabel, J. Heinrich, R. Leitner and O. Taucher (eds), *Steuerrecht, Verfassungsrecht, Europarecht, Festschrift für Hans Georg Ruppe* (Vienna: Facultas wuv, 2007)

Kuczynski, P.P. and Williamson, J. (eds), *After the Washington Consensus* (2003)

Kuhn, R.D., 'United States Tax Policy with Respect to Less Developed Countries' (1963) 32 *George Washington Law Review* 262

Lang, M., Pistone, P., Schuch, J., Staringer, C. and Zagler, M. (eds), *Tax Treaties from a Legal and Economic Perspective* (Amsterdam: IBFD Publications, 2010)

Langa, V., 'Mining companies should divulge earnings', *Newsday Zimbabwe*, 29 August 2011, available at www.newsday.co.zw/article/2011-08-29-mining-companies-should-divulge-earnings

Laurey, D., 'Reexamining U.S. Tax Sparing Policy with Developing Countries: The Merits of Falling in Line with International Norms' (2000) 20 *Virginia Tax Review* 467

Lawsky, S.B., 'Money for Nothing: Charitable Deductions for Microfinance Lenders' (2008) 61 *Southern Methodist University Law Review* 1525

Ledgerwood, J., *Microfinance Handbook: An Institutional and Financial Perspective* (Washington, DC: World Bank Publications, 1999)

Legwaila, T., 'The Tax Treatment of Holding Companies in Mauritius: Lessons for South Africa' (2011) 23 *South African Mercantile Law Journal* 1

Lenaerts, K., 'Constitutionalism and the Many Faces of Federalism' (1992) 38(2) *American Journal of Comparative Law* 205

Lepard, B.D., *Customary International Law: A New Theory with Practical Applications* (New York: Cambridge University Press, 2010)

Levi, M., *Of Rule and Revenue* (Berkeley, CA: University of California Press, 1988)

Levi-Faur, D., *The Global Diffusion of Regulatory Capitalism*, Annals of the American Academy of Political and Social Science (2005)

Levmore, S., 'Taxes as Ballots' (1998) 65 *University of Chicago Law Review* 387

Levy, S. M., *Federal Money Laundering Regulations, Banking, Corporate and Securities Compliance* (Aspen Publishers, 2008)

Li, J., 'The Rise and Fall of Chinese Tax Incentives and Implications for International Tax Debates' (2007) 8 *Fla. Tax Rev.* 669

– 'Improving Inter-nation Equity through Territorial Taxation and Tax Sparing' in A.J. Cockfield (ed.), *Globalization and its Tax Discontents: Tax Policy and International Investments* (Toronto: University of Toronto Press, 2010)

Lienert, I., *Role of the Legislature in Budget Processes* (IMF Fiscal Affairs Department, April 2010), available at http://blog-pfm.imf.org/files/fad-technical-manual-9.pdf

Lipsey, R.E. and Sjöholm. F., 'The Impact of Inward FDI on Host Countries', available at www.iie.com/publications/chapters_preview/3810/02iie3810.pdf

Lodin, S., 'Outline of the Symposium' in *Visions of the Tax Systems of the 21st Century*, International Fiscal Association Jubilee Symposium (IBFD, 1996)

Lou, J. and Wang, S. (eds), *Public Finance in China* (Washington, DC: World Bank, 2008)

Luke, C.D. and Abramovsky, A., 'Managing the Next Deluge: A Tax System Approach to Flood Insurance' (2012) 18 *Connecticut Insurance Law Journal* 1

MacDonald, L.T., 'Why the Carter Commission Had to Be Stopped' in N. Brooks (ed.), *The Quest for Tax Reform* (Carswell Company Ltd, 1988)

MacNamara, W. and Thompson, C., 'Shell chief's warning on Dodd-Frank', *Financial Times*, 2 March 2011, available at www.ft.com/intl/cms/s/0/f5dcb758-450a-11e0-80e7-00144feab49a.html#axzz1a4W6lVt8

– 'EU closer to US-style financial reform', *Financial Times*, 3 March 2011, available at www.ft.com/intl/cms/s/0/32b8327e-45ce-11e0-acd8-00144feab49a.html#ixzz1FcK0UAYW

Madani, D., *A Review of the Role and Impact of Export Processing Zones* (1999), available at http://siteresources.worldbank.org/INTRANETTRADE/Resources/MadaniEPZ.pdf

Maduro, M.P., *We the Court: The European Court of Justice and the European Economic Constitution* (Oxford: Hart Publishing, 1998)

– 'Contrapunctual Law: Europe's Constitutional Pluralism in Action' in N. Walker (ed.), *Sovereignty in Transition* (Oxford: Hart Publishing, 2003)

– *A Constituição Plural, Constitucionalismo e União Europeia* (São João do Estoril, Cascais: Principia, 2006)

Maher, M.T., 'Framing: An Emerging Paradigm or a Phase of Agenda Setting' in S.D. Reese, *Framing Public Life: Perspectives on Media and our Understanding on the Social World* (Mahwah, NJ: Lawrence Erlbaum Associates, 2001)

Maluwa, T., 'The African Union, the Southern African Development Community, and the New Partnership for Africa's Development: Some Observations on South Africa's Contribution to International Law-making and Institution Building in Africa, 1994–2000: Symposium' (2004) 29(5) *South African Yearbook of International Law* 12

Mankiw, N.G., 'The Growth of Nations' (1995) 1 *Brookings Papers on Econ. Activity* 275

Margalioth, Y., 'Tax Competition, Foreign Direct Investment and Growth: Using the Tax System to Promote Developing Countries' (2003) 23 *Virginia Tax Review* 161

Martineau, F., 'Sharp Criticism for Bill C-300: Lawyers Tell Parliamentary Committee Private Member's Bill Threatens Canada's Minerals Industry', available at www.fasken.com/firm-opposes-bill-c-300-in-ottawa/

Martinez-Vazquez, J. and Timofeev, A., *Decentralization Measures Revisited*, Andrew Young School of Policy Studies International Program Working Paper No. 09-13 (2009)

Mason, R., 'Tax Expenditures and Global Labor Mobility' (2009) 84 *NYU L Rev.* 1540

Masterguides, F., *Law's Empire* (Glasgow: Frank Kermode, 1986)

Mazansky, E., 'New Headquarter Company Regime' (2011) 65(3) *Bulletin for International Taxation* 166
Mazz, A. and Pistone, P. (eds), *Reflexiones en torno a un modelo latinoamericano de convenio de doble imposición* (Montevideo: Fundación de cultura universitaria, 2010)
Mazza, S., 'Taxpayer Privacy and Tax Compliance' (2003) 51 *University of Kansas Law Review* 1065
McCaffery, E.J., 'Tax's Empire' (1996) 85 *Georgetown Law Journal* 71
– *Fair not Flat: How to Make the Tax System Better and Simpler* (Chicago, IL: University of Chicago Press, 2002)
McCracken, S.K., 'Going, Going, Gone … Global: A Canadian Perspective on International Tax Administration Issues in the Exchange-of-Information Age' (2002) 50 *Canadian Tax Journal* 1869
McDaniel, P.R., 'The U.S. Tax Treatment of Foreign Source Income Earned in Developing Countries: A Policy Analysis' (2003) 35 *George Washington International Law Review* 265
McIntyre, M.J., 'How to End the Charade of Information Exchange' (2009) 56 *Tax Notes International* 255
McNeill, D., 'Human Development: The Power of the Idea' (2007) 8(5) *J Hum. Dev.* 11
McQuaig, L., *Behind Closed Doors: How the Rich Won Control of Canada's Tax System … and Ended Up Richer* (Canada: Penguin Books Canada Ltd, 1987)
Meirelles, M., 'Tax Sparing Credits in Tax Treaties: The Future and the Effect on EC Law' (2009) *European Taxation* 263
Mel, S. de, McKenzie, D. and Woodruff, C., 'Returns to Capital in Microenterprises: Evidence from a Field Experiment' (2008) 123 *Quarterly Journal of Economics* 1329
Menskim, W., 'Indian Secular Pluralism and its Relevance for Europe' in R.D. Grillo, R. Ballard, A. Ferrari, A.J. Hoekema, M. Maussen and P. Shah (eds), *Legal Practice and Cultural Diversity* (Farnham/Burlington: Ashgate, 2009)
Merry, S.E., 'Legal Pluralism' (1988) 22(5) *Law and Society Review* 870
Ministry of Finance, *Report regarding Tightening Fiscal Management and Preventing Unauthorized Revenue Reductions and Expenditure Increases*, approved and released by the State Council (26 March 1982)
Misol, L., 'Private Companies and the Public Interest: Why Corporations Should Welcome Global Human Rights Rules' in Human Rights Watch, *World Report* (2006)
Moore, M. and Rakner, L., 'The New Politics of Taxation and Accountability' (2002) 33(3) *International Development Studies Bulletin* 1

Moore, S.F., 'Law and Social Change: The Semi-Autonomous Social Field as an Appropriate Subject of Study' (1973) 7 *Law and Society Review* 719

Morgan, B. and Yeung, K., *An Introduction to Law and Regulation* (Cambridge: Cambridge University Press, 2007)

Morris, W., 'Is Country-by-Country Reporting the Answer?', available at www.oecdobserver.org/news/fullstory.php/aid/3229/Taxation_and_development.html

Mortaza, M.G. and Begum, L., *Tax Expenditures in Bangladesh: An Introductory Analysis* (Policy Analysis Unit, Bangladesh Bank, 2006)

Murphy, L. and Nagel, T., *The Myth of Ownership* (Oxford: Oxford University Press, 2002)

Murphy, R., *Reporting Turnover and Tax by Location, Association for Accountancy and Business Affairs Limited* (2003), available at www.richard.murphy.dial.pipex.com/A%20New%20International%20Accounting %20Standard.pdf

– *Country by Country Reporting: Holding Multinational Corporations to Account Wherever They Are* (June 2009), available at www.financialtaskforce.org/wp-content/uploads/2009/06/Final_CbyC_Report_Published.pdf

– 'Why is Country-by-Country Financial Reporting by Multinational Companies so Important?', available at www.taxresearch.org.uk/Documents/CountrybyCountryReporting.pdf

Musgrave, P.B., *United States Taxation of Foreign Investment Income: Issues and Arguments* (Harvard University Law School, 1969)

– 'International Tax Differentials for Multinational Corporations: Equity and Efficiency Considerations' in United Nations Department of Economic and Social Affairs, *The Impact of Multinational Corporations on Development and on International Relations* (United Nations, 1974)

– 'The OECD Model Tax Treaty: Problems and Prospects' (1975) *Colum. J World Bus.* (Summer) 29

– 'Fiscal Coordination and Competition in an International Setting' in L. Eden, *Retrospectives on Public Finance* (Durham, NC: Duke University Press, 1991)

– 'Substituting Consumption-based Direct Taxation for Income Taxes as the International Norm: A Comment' (1992) 45 *Nat'l Tax J* 179

– 'Consumption Tax Proposals in an International Setting' (2000) 54 *Tax L Rev.* 77

– 'Interjurisdiction Equity in Company Taxation: Principles and Applications to the European Union' in S. Cnossen (ed), *Taxing Capital Income in the European Union: Issues and Options for Reform* (Oxford: Oxford University Press, 2000)

– 'Sovereignty, Entitlement and Cooperation in International Taxation' (2001) 26 *Brook. J Int'l L* 1335

– 'Combining Fiscal Sovereignty and Coordination: National Taxation in a Globalizing World' in I. Kaul and P. Conceição (eds), *The New Public Finance: Responding to Global Challenges* (Oxford: Oxford University Press, 2006)

Musgrave, R., 'Criteria for Foreign Tax Credit' in *Taxation and Operations Abroad* (Tax Institute Symposium, 1960)

– 'Ability to Pay' in *The Encyclopedia of Taxation and Tax Policy* (2005)

Musgrave, R.A. and Musgrave, P.B., 'Inter-nation Equity' in *Modern Fiscal Issues: Essays in Honor of Carl S. Shoup* (Toronto: University of Toronto Press, 1972)

Nelken, D., 'Legal Pluralism, Privatization of Law and Multiculturalism: Eugen Ehrlich, Living Law, and Plural Legalities' (2008) 9 *Theoretical Inq. L* 443

Nicodème, G., 'Corporate Tax Competition and Coordination in the European Union: What Do We Know? Where Do We Stand?' in G.N. Gregoriou and C. Read (eds), *International Taxation Handbook* (London: Elsevier, 2007)

Nov, A., 'The "Bidding War" to Attract Foreign Direct Investment: The Need for a Global Solution' (2006) 25 *Virginia Tax Review* 835

OECD, *Tax Expenditures: A Review of Issues and Country Practices* (OECD Publishing, 1984)

– *Taxpayer Rights and Obligations: A Survey of the Legal Situation in OECD Countries* (27 April 1990), available at www.oecd.org/dataoecd/24/52/17851176.pdf

– *Tax Expenditures: Recent Experiences* (Paris: OECD Publishing, 1996)

– *Harmful Tax Competition: An Emerging Global Issue* (1998), available at www.oecd.org/dataoecd/33/1/1904184.pdf

– *Tax Sparing: A Reconsideration* (OECD Publishing, 1998), available at www.oecdbookshop.org/oecd/display.asp?lang=EN&sf1=identifiers&st1=9789264160224

– *Towards Global Tax Co-operation, Report to the 2000 Minister Council Meeting and Recommendations by the Committee on Fiscal Affairs: Progress in Identifying and Eliminating Harmful Tax Practices* (OECD, 2000), available at www.oecd.org/dataoecd/9/61/2090192.pdf

– *Best Practices for Budget Transparency* (15 May 2001), available at www.oecd.org/dataoecd/33/13/1905258.pdf

– *Corporate Tax Incentives for Foreign Direct Investment* (2001), available at http://unctad.org/es/Docs/iteipcmisc3_en.pdf

– *The OECD's Project on Harmful Tax Practices: The 2001 Progress Report* (2001), available at www.oecd.org/dataoecd/60/28/2664438.pdf

– *Checklist for Foreign Direct Investment Incentive Policies* (2003), available at www.oecd.org/dataoecd/45/21/2506900.pdf
– *Tax Policy Assessment and Design in Support of Direct Investment: A Study of Countries in South East Europe* (2003), available at www.oecd.org/dataoecd/46/14/34466352.pdf
– *The OECD's Project on Harmful Tax Practices: The 2004 Progress Report* (2004), available at www.oecd.org/dataoecd/60/33/30901115.pdf
– *Commentary and Manual on the Implementation of Exchange of Information Provisions for Tax Purposes*, approved by the OECD Committee on Fiscal Affairs on 23 January 2006, available at www.oecd.org/taxation
– *The Development Dimension: Integrating Human Rights into Development* (Paris: OECD Publishing, 2006)
– *The OECD's Project on Harmful Tax Practices: The 2006 Progress Report* (2006), available at www.oecd.org/dataoecd/1/17/37446434.pdf
– *Governance, Taxation and Accountability: Issues and Practices*, DAC Guidelines and Reference Series (Paris: OECD, 2008)
– *Tax Expenditures in OECD Countries* (2008), available at www.oecd.org/dataoecd/40/6/39944419.pdf
– *The OECD's Current Tax Agenda 2008* (2008), available at www.oecd.org/dataoecd/38/17/1909369.pdf
– *Progress Report on the Jurisdictions Surveyed by the OECD Global Forum in Implementing the Internationally Agreed Tax Standard* (10 November 2010), available at www.oecd.org/tax/transparency
– *Informal Task Force on Tax and Development, Preparatory Note from the Sub Group on Transparency in Reporting Financial Data by Multinational Corporations* (17 March 2011), available at www.oecd.org/dataoecd/57/4/47521678.pdf
– *Tax: Global Forum Delivers Concrete Results to the Cannes G20 Summit* (26 October 2011), available at www.oecd.org/document/7/0,3746,en_21571361_44315115_48940615_1_1_1_1,00.html
– *International Database of Budget Practices and Procedures* (12 February 2012), available at www.oecd.org/gov/budget/database
– 'Relations with Business and Labor', available at www.oecd.org/document/53/0,3746,en_2649_34495_1910965_1_1_1_1,00.html
– 'Global Relations, Non-Member Participation in Formal OECD Bodies', available at www.oecd.org/pages/0,3417,en_36335986_36339055_1_1_1_1_1,00.html
OECD/EU, 'Revised Explanatory Report for Convention of 1988 and Amending Protocol of 2010', available at www.oecd.org

Oguttu, A.W., 'A Critique on the OECD Campaign Against Tax Havens: Has It Been Successful? A South African Perspective' (2010) 21(1) *Stellenbosch Law Review* 172

Oksenberg, M. and Tong, J., 'The Evolution of Central-Provincial Fiscal Relations in China, 1971–1984: The Formal System' (1991) 125 *China Quarterly* 1

Olivier, L., 'Residence Based Taxation' (2011) 14 *Tydskrif vir the Suid Afrikaanse Reg* 20

Olivier, L., Brincker, E. and Honiball, M., *International Tax: A South African Perspective* (3rd edn, Cape Town: Siberink CC, 2005)

Oner, C., 'A Different Approach to the Agreement on Exchange of Information in Tax Matters (Turkey Has Secretly Approved Model Tax Agreement)' (2009) 37 *Intertax* 483

Oxford Centre for Business Taxation, *Transparency in Reporting Financial Data by Multinational Corporations* (July 2011), available at www.sbs.ox.ac.uk/centres/tax/Documents/reports/Transparency_reporting_multinationals_july2011.pdf

Paolini, D., Pulina, G., Pistone, P. and Zagler, M., *Tax Treaties and the Allocation of Taxing Rights with Developing Countries*, CORE Discussion Papers (Université Catholique de Louvain, Center for Operations Research and Econometrics), available at http://econpapers.repec.org/scripts/redir.pf?u=http%3A%2F%2Fuclouvain.be%2Fcps%2Fucl%2Fdoc%2Fcore%2Fdocuments%2Fcoredp2011_42web.pdf;h=repec:cor:louvco:2011042

Parchomovsky, G. and Siegelman, P., 'Selling Mayberry: Communities and Individuals in Law and Economics' (2004) 92 *California Law Review* 75

Pedraza-Farin, L.G., 'Conceptions of Civil Society in International Law-Making and Implementation: A Theoretical Framework', available at http://ssrn.com/abstract=2017312. www.globalwitness.org/about-us

Peerenboom, R., *China's Long March toward Rule of Law* (Cambridge: Cambridge University Press, 2002)

Peerenboom, R. *et al.* (eds), *Judicial Independence in China: Lessons for Global Rule of Law Promotion* (Cambridge: Cambridge University Press, 2010)

Peroni, R. and Fleming, J.C., Jr, 'Can Tax Expenditure Analysis Be Divorced from a Normative Tax Base?: A Critique of the "New Paradigm" and its Denouement' (2010) 30 *Virginia Tax Review* 135

Peterson, K., 'GE Chief Defends Company's 2010 Tax Bill', *MSN Money*, 1 April 2011, available at http://money.msn.com/top-stocks/post.aspx?post=a0b9a8f0-4c1a-4387-b76f-dc71e05e90d0

Pheeha, M. and Troskie, D., 'An Analysis of the Inclusion of South Africa to BRIC Countries: The Fit for South Africa's Agricultural Sector' (2011) 8(1) *Agriprobe* 28

Philipps, L., 'Taxing the Market Citizen: Fiscal Policy and Inequality in an Age of Privatization' (2000) 63 *Law and Contemporary Problems* 111

Philipps, L. and Condon, M., 'Connecting Economy, Gender, and Citizenship' in Law Commission of Canada (ed.), *Law and Citizenship* (Vancouver: UBC Press, 2006)

Philipps, L. and Stewart, M., 'Fiscal Transparency: Global Norms, Domestic Laws, and the Politics of Budgets (2009) 34(3) *Brooklyn Journal of International Law* 797

Picciotto, S., *International Business Taxation as a Study in the Internationalization of Business Regulation*, Law in Context Series (London: Weidenfeld and Nicolson, 1992)

Pigou, A.C., *The Economics of Welfare* (3rd edn, London: Macmillan, 1929)

Pires, M., *Da dupla tributação jurídica internacional sobre o rendimento* (Lisbon: Centro de Estudos Fiscais, 1984)

Pistone, P., 'Rasgos fundamentales del Proyecto de Modelo de Convenio para América Latina' in A. Mazz and P. Pistone (eds), *Reflexiones en torno a un modelo latinoamericano de convenio de doble imposición* (Montevideo: Fundación de Cultura Universitaria, 2010)

– 'Tax Treaties with Developing Countries: A Plea for New Allocation Rules and a Combined Legal and Economic Approach' in M. Lang, P. Pistone, J. Schuch, C. Staringer and M. Zagler (eds), *Tax Treaties from a Legal and Economic Perspective* (Amsterdam: IBFD Publications 2010)

– 'General Report' in M. Lang, P. Pistone, J. Schuch and C. Staringer, *The Influence of the OECD and UN Model Conventions on Bilateral Tax Treaties* (Cambridge: Cambridge University Press, 2012)

Pistone, P. and Goodspeed, T., 'Rethinking Tax Jurisdictions and Relief from International Double Taxation with regard to Developing Countries: Legal and Economic Perspectives from Europe and North America' in M. Zagler, *International Tax Coordination: Virtues and Pitfalls* (New York: Routledge, 2010)

Plümper, T., Troeger, V.E. and Winner, H., 'Why Is There No Race to the Bottom in Capital Taxation? Tax Competition Among Countries of Unequal Size, Different Levels of Budget Rigidities and Heterogeneous Fairness Norms' (2009) 53(3) *International Studies Quarterly* 761

Poirson, H., *The Tax System in India: Could Reform Spur Growth?*, IMF Working Paper WP/06/93 (2006)

Pomp, R.D., 'The Disclosure of State Corporate Income Tax Data' (1993) 22 *Capital University Law Review* 373

Pospisil, L., *The Anthropology of Law: A Comparative Theory of Law* (New York: Harper and Row, 1971)

Poston, R.J. and Williams, C.M., *Extraction and Compliance: New Reporting Requirements for Issues Involving Oil, Natural Gas or Minerals* (Thomson Reuters Accelus, 3 November 2010), available at www.complinet.com/dodd-frank/news/analysis/article/extraction-and-compliance-new-reporting-requirements-for-issuers-involving-oil-natural-gas-or-minerals.html

Pozen, D.E., 'Hidden Foreign Aid' (2007) 8 *Fla. Tax Rev.* 641

Prichard, W., *Taxation and State Building: Towards a Governance Focused Tax Reform Agenda*, Institute of Development Studies Working Paper 2010/341 (2010)

Prospectors and Developers Association of Canada (PDAC), 'Corporate Social Responsibility in the Mineral Industry, Issues and Advocacy', available at www.pdac.ca/pdac/advocacy/csr/index.html

Publish What You Pay, 'The Cardin-Lugar Amendment (Dodd-Frank 1504)', available at www.publishwhatyoupay.org/about/stock-listings/cardin-lugar-amendment-dodd-frank-1504

Ranis, G. *et al.*, 'Human Development: Beyond the Human Development Index' (2006) 7 *J Hum. Dev.* 323

Rao, M.G. and Rao, R.K., *Trends and Issues in Tax Policy and Reform in India* (October 2005), available at www.ncaer.org/downloads/Journals/ipf0506-paper2.pdf

Ratner, S., *Taxation and Democracy in America* (Charlottesville, VA: University of Virginia, 1967)

Ring, D.M., 'What's at Stake in the Sovereignty Debate? International Tax and the Nation-state' (2008) 49(1) *Virginia Journal of International Law* (Fall) 155

– 'Democracy, Sovereignty and Tax Competition: The Role of Tax Sovereignty in Shaping Tax Cooperation' (2009) 9 *Fla. Tax Rev.* 555

Robinson, M.S., *The Microfinance Revolution: Sustainable Finance for the Poor* (Washington, DC: World Bank Publications, 2001)

Rodden, J., 'Comparative Federalism and Decentralization: On Meaning and Measurement' (2004) 36(4) *Comparative Politics* 481

Rodrik, D., *The New Global Economy and Developing Countries* (Overseas Development Council, 1999)

– *One Economics, Many Recipes: Globalization, Institutions, and Economic Growth* (Princeton, NJ: Princeton University Press, 2008)

Roin, J., 'Competition and Evasion: Another Perspective on International Tax Competition' (2001) 89 *Georgetown Law Journal* 543

Romer, P.M., 'Increasing Returns and Long-Run Growth' (1986) 94 *Journal of Political Economy* 1002

– 'Endogenous Technological Change' (1990) 98 *Journal of Political Economy* 71

– 'Economic Growth' in *Concise Encyclopaedia of Economics*, available at www.econlib.org/library/Enc/EconomicGrowth.html

Roos, J.E., '100,000 Rally against Austerity in Portugal: in Pictures', available at http://roarmag.org/2011/10/100000-rally-against-austerity-in-portugal-in-pictures/

Rosenberg, N. and Birdzell, L.E., *How the West Grew Rich: The Economic Transformation of the Industrial World* (Basic Books, 1986)

Rosenbloom, H.D., 'International Tax Arbitrage and the "International Tax System"' (2000) 53 *Tax Law Review* 137

Rosenbloom H.D. and Hora Do Paço, D., 'Considerações sobre a negociação de um tratado para evitar a dupla tributação da renda com os EUA' (2010) 174 *Revista Dialética de Direito Tributário* 25

Rosenzweig, A.H., 'Harnessing the Costs of International Tax Arbitrage' (2007) 26 *Va. Tax Rev.* 555

Roy, A., *Poverty Capital: Microfinance and the Making of Development* (New York: Routledge, 2010)

Rushe, D. and Taylor, M., 'UK Uncut inspires US groups to attack cuts and tax avoidance', *Guardian*, 25 February 2011, available at www.guardian.co.uk/uk/2011/feb/25/uk-uncut-us-groups-cuts

Rutherford, S. and Arora, S., *The Poor and their Money: Microfinance from a Twenty-first Century Consumer's Perspective* (Practical Action Publishing, 2009)

Sachs, J., *The End of Poverty: How Can We Make It Happen in Our Lifetime?* (New York: Penguin Books, 2006)

Santos, B.S., 'Por uma Concepção Multicultural de Direitos Humanos, Reconhecer para Libertar, Os Caminhos do Cosmopolitismo Multicultural' in B.S. Santos (ed.), *Civilização Brasileira* (Rio de Janeiro, 2003)

Sawyer, A., *Developing a World Tax Organisation: The Way Forward* (Fiscal Publications, 2009)

Schenk-Geers, T., *International Exchange of Information and the Protection of Taxpayers* (Alphen aan den Rijn: Kluwer Law International, 2009)

Schiavo-Campo, S., 'The Budget and its Coverage' in A. Shah (ed.), *Budgeting and Budgetary Institutions* (International Bank for Reconstruction and Development/World Bank, 2007)

Schneiderman, D., 'Commentary, Pluralism, Disagreement, and Globalization: A Comment on Webber's Legal Pluralism and Human Agency' (2006) 44(1) *Osgood Hall Law Journal* 199

Seer, R. and Gabert, I. (eds), *Mutual Assistance and Information Exchange* (Amsterdam: IBFD, 2010)

Sen, A., 'The Impossibility of a Paretian Liberal' (1970) 1 *Journal of Political Economy* 152

– *Inequality Reexamined* (Cambridge, MA: Harvard University Press, 1992)

– 'Capability and Well-Being' in M. Nussbaum and A. Sen (eds), *The Quality of Life* (Oxford: Clarendon Press, 1993)

– 'Development Thinking at the Beginning of the XXI Century' in L. Emmerij, *Economic and Social Development into the XXI Century* (1997)

– *Development as Freedom* (New York: Anchor Books, 1999)

– *Identity and Violence, The Illusion of Destiny* (New York/London: W.W. Norton & Company, 2006)

– 'Introduction' in UN Development Programme, *Human Development Report* (2010)

Shachar, A., *Multicultural Jurisdiction, Cultural Differences and Women's Rights* (Cambridge: Cambridge University Press, 2001)

Shannon, H.A., 'The Tax Expenditure Concept in the United States and Germany: A Comparison' (1986) 33 *Tax Notes* 201

Sharman, J., *Havens in a Storm* (Ithaca, NY: Cornell University Press, 2006)

Shaviro, D.N., 'Rethinking Tax Expenditures and Fiscal Language' (2004) 57 *Tax Law Review* 187

Sheppard, L.A., 'Don't Ask, Don't Tell, Part 4: Ineffectual Information Sharing' (2009) 122 *Tax Notes* 1411

Shih, V., *Factions and Finance in China: Elite Conflict and Inflation* (Cambridge: Cambridge University Press, 2007)

Silverstein, K., 'As oil pours into Gulf, oil industry fights anti-corruption measure', *Harpers*, 11 May 2010, available at http://harpers.org/archive/2010/05/hbc-90007021

Simonian, H. and Fekter, M., 'Iron Lady steeled for "solid programme" to reduce debt', *Financial Times*, 27 September 2011

Simons, H., *Personal Income Taxation: The Definition of Income as a Problem of Fiscal Policy* (Chicago, IL: University of Chicago Press, 1938)

Slaughter, A., 'Global Government Networks, Global Information Agencies and Disaggregated Democracies' (2003) 24 *Michigan Journal of International Law* 1041

– *A New World Order* (Princeton, NJ: Princeton University Press, 2004)

Slemrod, J., 'Tax Principles in an International Economy' in M.J. Boskin and C.E. McLure, Jr (eds), *World Tax Reform: Case Studies of Developed and Developing Countries* (ICS, 1990)

Slemrod, J. and Bakija, J., *Taxing Ourselves: A Citizen's Guide to the Debate Over Taxes* (Massachussets Institute of Technology Press, 1996)

Smith, A., *An Inquiry into the Nature and Causes of the Wealth of Nations* (4th edn, 1925)

Snow, D. and Benford, R., 'Framing Processes and Social Movements: An Overview and Assessment' (2000) 26 *Annual Review of Sociology* 11

Solow, R.M., 'Technical Change and the Aggregate Production Function' (1957) 39 *Review of Economics and Statistics* 312

– 'A Contribution to the Theory of Economic Growth' (1965) 70 *Quarterly Journal of Economics* 65

Staudt, N., 'Taxation Without Representation' (2002) 55 *Tax Law Review*

Stegarescu, D., 'Public Sector Decentralization: Measurement Concepts and Recent International Trends' (2005) 26(3) *Fiscal Studies* 301

Stephan, H. and Hervey, A.F., 'New Regionalism in Southern Africa: Functional Developmentalism and the Southern African Power Pool' (2008) 27(3) *Politeia* 54

Stewart, M., 'Domesticating Tax Reform: The Family in Australian Tax and Transfer Law' (1999) 21 *Sydney Law Review* 453

– 'Global Trajectories of Tax Reform' (2003) 44(1) *Harvard International Law Journal* 139

– 'Tax Policy Transfer to Developing Countries: Politics, Institutions and Experts' in H. Nehring and S. Florian (eds), *Global Debates about Taxation* (Basingtoke: Palgrave Macmillan, 2007)

Stewart, M. and Jogarajan, S., 'The International Monetary Fund and Tax Reform' (2004) 2 *British Tax Review* 146

Stiglitz, J.E., *Globalization and its Discontents* (New York: W.W. Norton & Co., 2002)

Sunley, E., 'Tax Expenditures in the United States: Experience and Practice' in H.P. Brixi, C.M.A. Valenduc and Z.L. Swift (eds), *Tax Expenditures: Shedding Light on Government Spending through the Tax System: Lessons from Developed and Transition Economies* (Washington, DC: International Bank for Reconstruction and Development/World Bank, 2004) 155

Surrey, S.S., 'The Pakistan Tax Treaty and "Tax Sparing"' (1958) 11 *National Tax Journal* 156

– *Pathways to Tax Reform: The Concept of Tax Expenditures* (Cambridge, MA: Harvard University Press, 1973)

Surrey, S.S. and McDaniel, P.R., *Tax Expenditures* (Cambridge, MA: Harvard University Press, 1985)

Swift, Z.L. *Managing the Effects of Tax Expenditures on National Budgets*, World Bank Policy Research Paper 3927 (May 2006), available at www-wds.worldbank.org/servlet/WDSContentServer/WDSP/IB/2006/05/23/000016406_20060523092056/Rendered/PDF/wps3927.pdf

Tanzi, V., *Taxation in an Integrating World* (Washington, DC: Brookings Institution, 1995)

– 'The Impact of Economic Globalization on Taxation' (1998) *International Bureau of Fiscal Documentation Bulletin* 338

– 'Is There a Need for a World Tax Organization?' in A. Razin and E. Sadka (eds), *The Economics of Globalization: Policy Perspectives from Public Economics* (New York: Cambridge University Press, 1999)

– *Policies, Institutions and the Dark Side of Economics* (Cheltenham, UK and Northampton, MA, USA: Edward Elgar, 2000)

Tanzi, V. and Zee, H.H., *Tax Policy for Emerging Markets: Developing Countries*, IMF Working Paper No. 35 (2000), available at www.imf.org/external/pubs/ ft/wp/2000/wp0035.pdf

– 'Can Information Exchange be Effective in Taxing Cross-Border Income Flows?' in K. Andersson, P. Melz and C. Silfverberg (eds), *Modern Issues in the Law of International Taxation* (Stockholm: Kluwer Law International, 2001)

– *Tax Policy for Developing Countries*, Economic Issues No. 27 (IMF, 2001), available at www.imf.org/external/pubs/ft/issues/issues27/

Tax Justice Network, *Country-by-Country Reporting: How To Make Multinational Companies More Transparent* (March 2008), available at www.taxjustice.net/cms/upload/pdf/Country-by-country_reporting_-_080322.pdf

– 'OECD may detract from UN work' (19 May 2011), available at http://taxjustice.blogspot.com/2011/05/oecd-may-detract-from-un-work.html

– 'UN versus OECD: not a football match' (23 June 2011), available at http://taxjustice.blogspot.com/2011/06/un-versus-oecd-not-football-match.html

Thaler, R.H. and Benartzi, S., 'Save More Tomorrow: Using Behavioral Economics to Increase Employee Saving' (2004) 112 *Journal of Political Economy* 164

Thaler, R.H. and Sunstein, C.R., *Nudge: Improving Decisions about Health, Wealth, and Happiness* (New Haven, CT: Yale University Press 2008)

Thirsk, W. (ed.), *Tax Reform in Developing Countries* (Washington, DC: World Bank, 1997)

Thuronyi, V., 'Tax Expenditures: A Reassessment' (1988) 6 *Duke Law Journal* 1155

– *Comparative Tax Law* (London/New York: Kluwer Law International, 2003)
– 'Recent Treaty Practice on Tax Sparing' (2003) 29 *Tax Notes International* 301
Thuronyi, V. (ed.), *Tax Law Design and Drafting* (Washington, DC: International Monetary Fund, 1996)
Tiebout, C.M., 'A Pure Theory of Local Expenditures' (1956) 64 *Journal of Political Economy* 5
Trebilcock, M.J. and Daniels, R.J., *Rule of Law Reform and Development: Charting the Fragile Path of Progress* (Cheltenham, UK and Northampton, MA, USA: Edward Elgar, 2008)
Tshuma, L., 'Hierarchies and Government versus Networks and Governance: Competing Regulatory Paradigms in Global Economic Regulation', *Law, Social Justice and Global Development Issue* 1999-1 (1999)
Tullock, G., 'Problems of Majority Voting' in K.J. Arrow and T. Scitovsky (eds), *Readings in Welfare Economics* (London: George Allen & Unwin, 1969)
Twinning, W., 'Normative and Legal Pluralism: A Global Perspective' (2009–2010) 20 *Duke Journal of Comparative and International Law* 473
UN General Assembly, *Follow-up and Implementation of the Outcome of the 2002 International Conference on Financing for Development and the 2008 Review Conference, Report of the Second Committee* (13 December 2011)
UN Social and Economic Council, *Strengthening of Institutional Arrangements to Promote International Cooperation in Tax Matters, including the Committee of Experts on International Cooperation in Tax Matters: Report of the Secretary General* (United Nations, 2011)
UNCTAD, *Incentives and Foreign Direct Investment: A Global Survey*, ASIT Advisory Studies No. 16 (United Nations, 2000)
– *World Investment Report 2005, Transnational Corporations and the Internationalization of R&D* (United Nations, 2005), available at www.unctad.org/en/docs/wir2005ch3_en.pdf
UNCTAD/DTCI, *Incentives and Foreign Direct Investment*, Current Studies Series A, No. 30 (United Nations, 1996)
United States Treasury, *Annual Report of the Secretary of the Treasury on the State of the Finances for the Fiscal Year ended June 30, 1969* (US Government Printing Office, 1969), available at www.archive.org/details/annualreportofse1969statiunit
Vogel, K., 'The Search for Compatible Tax Systems' in H. Stein (ed.), *Tax Policy in the Twenty-first Century* (Wiley, 1988)

– 'Worldwide vs. Source Taxation of Income: A Review and Re-evaluation of Arguments (Part III)' (1988) 11 *Intertax* 393

– 'World-wide vs. Source Taxation of Income: A Review and Reevaluation of Arguments' in *Influence of Tax Differentials on International Competitiveness* (Amsterdam: Kluwer, 1989)

– 'Tributação da renda mundial' in *Cadernos de Direito Tributário e Finanças Públicas* (São Paulo: Revista dos Tribunais, 1994) vol. 7

Waldron, J., *Law and Disagreement* (Oxford: Oxford University Press, 1999)

– 'Legal Pluralism and the Contrast between Hart's Jurisprudence and Fuller's' in P. Cane (ed.), *The Hart–Fuller Debate in the Twenty-First Century* (Oxford/Portland, OR: Hart Publishing, 2010)

Washlick, J.R., 'Joint Ventures Involving Tax-Exempt Organizations' (2007) 478 *BNA Tax Management Portfolio*

Watson, A., *Legal Transplants: An Approach to Comparative Law* (Athens, GA: University of Georgia Press, 1993)

Webb, M.C., 'Defining the Boundaries of Legitimate State Practices: Norms, Transnational Actors and the OECD's Project on Harmful Tax Competition' (2004) 11(4) *Review of International Political Economy* 787

Weisbach, D.A., 'Line Drawing, Doctrine and Efficiency in the Tax Law' (1999) 84 *Cornell Law Review* 1627

Weiss, L., 'The State-Augmenting Effects of Globalization' (2005) 10(3) *New Political Economy* 345

Wells, L.T., Jr, Allen, N.J., Morisset, J. and Pirnia, N., *Using Tax Incentives to Compete for Foreign Investment: Are They Worth the Costs?* (International Finance Corporation and World Bank, 2001)

Williamson, J., 'What Washington Means by Policy Reform' in J. Williamson (ed.), *Latin American Readjustment: How Much Has Happened* (Washington, DC: Institute for International Economics, 1989)

Wilson, G.P., 'The Role of Taxes in Location and Sourcing Decisions' in A. Giovannini, R.G. Hubbard and J. Slemrod, *Studies in International Taxation* (Chicago, IL: University of Chicago Press, 1996)

Wilson, J.D., 'Theories of Tax Competition' (1999) 52(2) *National Tax Journal* 269

Wilson, J.D. and Wildasin, D.E., 'Capital Tax Competition: Bane or Boon?' (2004) 88(6) *Journal of Public Economics* 1065

Wong, C.P.W., 'Fiscal Reform and Local Industrialization: The Problematic Sequencing of Reform in Post-Mao China' (1992) 18 *Modern China* 200

Woodman, G.R., 'The Challenge of African Customary Laws to English Legal Culture, Legal Practice and Cultural Diversity' (unpublished, 2009)

World Bank, *China: Revenue Mobilization and Tax Policy Issues and Options* (1990), available at www-wds.worldbank.org/external/default/WDSContentServer/WDSP/IB/2000/01/20/000009265_3960927103346/Rendered/INDEX/multi_page.txt

– *Lessons of Tax Reform* (1991), available at http://elibrary.worldbank.org/content/book/9780821319062

– *Export Processing Zones* (1992), available at http://siteresources.worldbank.org/INTRANETTRADE/Resources/239054-1126812419270/1668207-1282573753114/PREMnote11.pdf

– *India: Sustaining Reform, Reducing Poverty* (14 July 2003), available at: http://siteresources.worldbank.org/INDIAEXTN/Resources/Reports-Publications/Sustaining-reform/executive_summary.pdf

– *List of Economies* (2011), available at http://shop.ifrs.org/files/CLASS.pdf

– 'Civil Society Organizations', available at http://web.worldbank.org/WBSITE/EXTERNAL/TOPICS/CSO/0,,contentMDK:20127718~menuPK:288622~pagePK:220503~piPK:220476~theSitePK:228717,00.html

World Bank Group, *Voices of Transparency* (World Bank, 2011), available at http://siteresources.worldbank.org/INTOGMC/Resources/EITI_Final_Brochure.pdf

Wouters, J. and Meuwissen, K., *Global Tax Governance: Work in Progress?*, Leuven Centre for Global Governance Studies Working Paper No. 59 (February 2011)

Ye, S., 'Member of the Political Consultative Conference strongly opposes the Property Tax, asks the Government to "save face" for the Constitution', *21st Century Business Herald*, 27 January 2011

Young, C., 'Momentum for a millionaire's tax', *Boston Review*, 7 December 2011, available at www.bostonreview.net/BR36.6/cristobal_young_occupy_movement_future.php

Yun, C., 'Unifying fiscal and economic work', *People's Daily*, 4 March 1950

Yunus, M., *Banker to the Poor* (New York: Public Affairs, 2007)

Yunus, M. and Weber, K., *Building Social Business: The New Kind of Capitalism that Serves Humanity's Most Pressing Needs* (New York: Public Affairs, 2010)

Zee, H.H., Stotsky, J.G. and Ley, E., 'Tax Incentives for Business Investment: A Primer for Policy Makers in Developing Countries' (2002) 30 *World Development* 1497

Zodrow, G.R., and Mieszkowski, P., 'Pigou, Tiebout, Property Taxation and the Underprovision of Local Public Goods' (1986) 19(3) *Journal of Public Economics* 356

Zolt, E.M. and Bird, R.M., 'Redistribution via Taxation: The Limited Role of the Personal Income Tax in Developing Countries' (2005) 52 *UCLA Law Review*

Index